THE RECONSTRUCTION OF THE NATION

THE RECONSTRUCTION
OF THE NATION

Rembert W. Patrick

NEW YORK

OXFORD UNIVERSITY PRESS

LONDON 1967 TORONTO

To Eleanor

☆

PREFACE

FOLLOWING THE Civil War the central theme of American history was reconstructing the Union. The primary national concern was the creation of loyal governments in the former Confederate states. President Johnson believed that his reconstruction plans would secure the desired loyalty; but congressmen questioned the validity of his work, rejected most of it, and formulated their own plans. White Southerners disliked some of the presidential requirements. They vigorously protested and opposed the entire congressional program. In their opinion, the ante-bellum Union existed, except for secession and slavery, and Southerners needed to do no more than reconstitute their states and send senators and representatives to Washington.

Disagreement was heightened by the Afro-American problem. The permanency of the Union and abolition were well-established purposes of the Civil War. Equality under law for all citizens, regardless of race or color, had received little attention during the conflict; but the demand became significant after victory, and in a sense it became, retroactively, a third war aim. Northerners disagreed as to the method of protecting the freedman, and were even more divided on how many rights he should have. Relatively few postwar Northerners demanded complete equality for Afro-Americans. The overwhelming majority of white Southerners rejected all attempts to give the Negro a voice in government or a high status in society. Their guiding principle was white supremacy. Any idea which challenged it was anathema.

The story of the Reconstruction era is complicated, so complex, in fact, that unified accounts can best be achieved by concentrating on biography, politics, an event, a federal bureau, or a state. Many of these studies lack perspective. Fraud appears as a unique characteristic of southern Republican regimes when, in reality, it was nationwide. Increased state services which necessitated high taxes were moreover not peculiar to the southern states. While political battles raged in Washington, the country made rapid advances, and important developments occurred in the economy and in society.

This attempt to provide an overall, somewhat detailed and interpretative account of the Reconstruction period for readers and students is ambitious. Of necessity emphasis shifts from national to local scene, from Washington to state capitals, from personality to event, and from foreign affairs to domestic concerns. This approach precludes the unity attainable

vii

in a specialized study; it summarizes significant events and oversimplifies involved issues. Although the author believes a chapter on "The People" essential, he realizes that its inclusion detracts from the unity of the theme. By extending the racial phase of the Reconstruction era to 1900, he breaks with traditional coverage. But fixing the caste system in custom and law was the final phase of many endeavors to reconstruct the nation, and belongs to the period.

The author gratefully acknowledges his indebtedness to the universities of Florida and Georgia for encouraging the research and writing of this book. Since most of the work was completed while on the staff of the University of Florida, his graduate students at that institution contributed valuable constructive criticisms of chapters, often having the professional courage to point out factual errors, question interpretations, and suggest improvements in composition. I am proud of and grateful to those students of the 1964–66 seminars on Reconstruction: Gloria A. Boddie, Edward M. Davis, James J. Dwyer, Frederick L. Eckel, Edward K. Eckert, S. Etchells, K. H. Funk, Richard German, Robert A. Hawk, Austin S. Herrington, S. M. Hubbell, Nolene Justice, Stuart Kaufman, Martin M. LaGodna, James W. Mosher, Charles Multop, Philip H. Nochlin, Mary L. Pankowski, Thomas A. Parker, John F. Reiger, Milton A. Russos, Leslie E. Shumway, Jr., Peter S. Smith, William L. Will, and George J. Williams.

My colleague at the University of Florida, William E. Barringer, read the manuscript twice and offered constructive criticisms. Phyllis B. Durell typed the final manuscript from a difficult-to-read copy. Above all others, my wife Eleanor typed, edited, and encouraged.

The friendly services given by staff members of many libraries facilitated research. Among them are kind individuals of the Duke, Florida, Georgia, and North Carolina (Chapel Hill) universities; the Library of Congress and National Archives; and the New York Public Library. To list the name of every person who assisted me would require pages. Especially noteworthy was the help given by Elizabeth Alexander and Linda Sasser of the University of Florida.

Responsibility for the remaining errors is the author's. Neither the University of Florida nor the University of Georgia approves or disapproves of the selected facts or their interpretations.

REMBERT W. PATRICK

Athens, Georgia
September 1966

☆

CONTENTS

MAPS

☆

ILLUSTRATIONS

THE RECONSTRUCTION OF THE NATION

War Results and Plans for the South

HOLDING the hand of his small, tongue-tied son Tad, Abraham Lincoln walked up Richmond's Main Street with long awkward strides. An elderly Negro workman dropped his shovel and said: "Bress de Lord, dere is the Messiah! He's bin in my heart fo' long years an' he's cum to free his children from bondage!" Slaves, free Negroes, and some white people crowded the path of the sun-tanned, tired President. Most white residents remained in their homes, their eyes mirroring hatred, suspicion, or fear as they peered at the visitor through half-closed blinds.

For a week the President had made his headquarters on the *River Queen*, anchored in the James River off City Point, Virginia. With boyish enthusiasm and impatience he had read the dispatches sent by General Grant from his headquarters near Petersburg. On April 3, 1865, the President had gone into that city behind the victorious Army of the Potomac. The next day he shrugged away warnings for his personal danger and, protected by no more than twelve men, entered the capital of the Confederacy which had been occupied the day before by General Godfrey Weitzel's federal forces. Lincoln conferred with the general at "the White House of the Confederacy" at Twelfth and Clay streets, talked with John Archibald Campbell, who had resigned from the Supreme Court in 1861 to serve the South, about bringing Virginia back into the Union, and viewed the burned areas of Richmond. Before nightfall he gratified his friends and protectors by returning to the safety of the *River Queen*.

The Material Cost of War

Lincoln saw twenty blocks of Richmond a smoking ruin of blackened walls and lonely chimneys. Almost $30 million worth of buildings, merchandise, and personal property were lost on April 3 in the fire set by evacuating Confederate soldiers and put out by occupying federal troops. In miniature the city reflected the billions of dollars in property losses suffered by the defeated South. The major campaigns and battles of the war had been on southern soil. The defending armies had foraged the land and destroyed property to prevent its acquisition by federal troops, and invading forces had picked the best that was left and destroyed most of the rest.

Evidences of the war blighted the entire South; Atlanta, Savannah, Columbia, Charleston, and Richmond lay in ruins. Iron rails were wrapped around trees, the ashes of crossties lined many railroad beds; wrecked freight and passenger cars surrounded burned depots; and creeks and rivers were without trestles. Ruts made by military supply wagons and inadquate maintenance left roads impassable. Telegraph wires were tangled around fallen poles; boats, docks, and ferries were under water. The transportation and communication systems of the South were casualties of war.

Desolation marked the wide swath cut by General Sherman in his march from Atlanta to the sea. One Northerner saw no building remaining along the railroad from Macon to Savannah, and another reported Sherman more destructive in South Carolina than in Georgia. The once productive Shenandoah Valley of Virginia would need years to recover from the ravages of Philip H. Sheridan's cavalry. By destroying sources of supply and weakening southern morale, the policy of near total war shortened the conflict and saved human life, but it left a seemingly impossible task of rehabilitation.

The methods of Sherman and Sheridan received most of the publicity, but the crossing and recrossing of southern terrain by other commanders resulted in a destruction almost equaling that of the specialists in total war. Town and countryside—north, east, and south of Richmond—reflected many hard-fought battles. Areas of Tennessee and Mississippi were prostrate; Alabamians claimed their losses amounted to $300 million, and $100 million was the estimated damage to sugarcane plantations in Louisiana. Repeated invasions of coastal Florida and raids into the interior counties of that thinly populated state caused a greater percentage decline in property values than in the battle-scarred commonwealth of Virginia. In frontier Arkansas the percentage decrease in taxable property surpassed that of Florida and topped the Confederate states.

The most spectacular was the despoliation of cities, towns, and villages, where property and ruins were concentrated, but dispersed plantations and farms also received crippling blows. Pillaging troops stripped mansions of silverware, linens, and furniture. Prized books in personal libraries went into haversacks or were trampled under heavy boots. Axes felled stately shade trees for firewood and wagons broke hedges and flowering shrubs. Occasionally ancestral homes of prominent secessionists went up in flame and smoke. Greedy soldiers grabbed the best household furnishings of prosperous farm homes and the cooking utensils of hovels.

Even in the areas untrampled by invading or defending armies, dilapidation was apparent. Fallen fences, sagging barn roofs, and dwellings crying for repair; wooden plows without iron tips on their sweeps, worn-out hoes, handleless axes, and other broken implements of agriculture; and storage bins with insufficient corn and other grains for seed testified to four years of use, neglect, and consumption. More than a quarter of a century would pass before losses in horses, mules, oxen, cattle, milch cows, and hogs could be made up. Except in the frontier states of the South, farm acreage and production would not attain prewar proportions for twenty years.

The end of war brought collapse to the South's monetary and credit system. Confederate bonds and currency, notes and securities of states, local governments, and corporations were worthless. Banks and other financial agencies, which had based their operations on the securities of a revolutionary government, closed their doors. Southern life and fire insurance companies went into bankruptcy.

Many Southerners owned lands and bales of valuable cotton. But treasury agents swarmed over the South to levy and collect the direct tax of 1861 or auctioned off land of owners who could not pay. The ownership of cotton bales was questioned: was cotton stored on plantation and farm the property of individuals, or had it been sold to the Confederate government for bonds during the war and therefore belonged to that defunct government? The answer to this question lined the pockets of grafting treasury agents, or eased the pecuniary problems of Southerners willing to make deals with dishonest civil servants. Later, federal judges ordered millions of dollars paid to owners of illegally seized cotton, but litigation consumed years and gave no aid to the destitute in the months immediately following the war.

Some Southerners possessed silver and gold coin, federal currency, animals, or lands unencumbered by tax liens. Former Confederate secretary of state Robert Toombs, who escaped imprisonment by fleeing to Europe, claimed he "ate an acre of land" a day; that is, he sold land to pay his daily expenses. The generosity of Grant and other federal commanders in allowing captured southern soldiers to claim their horses and mules supplied draft animals on many farms. Silver, china, and jewelry were bartered for the necessities of life. Throughout the war some southern families had retained stock in northern corporations; a few, among them Judah P. Benjamin, held cotton which had been shipped past northern blockading squadrons to Europe. Fortunate, also, were individuals who had invested in cotton mills and other factories rather than in slaves.

The major capital loss of the South was the freeing of four million slaves without compensation to their owners. Estimates of the amount invested in human property ranged from one to four billion dollars depending on whether one uses the original cost or the replacement value. Almost thirty years before the Civil War, Great Britain had liberated all slaves within her dominions with payment to their masters. If, in 1860, Southerners had realized the antipathy of the Western world to slavery, they could have won some payment for freeing their human chattel; but most Southerners preferred war to compensated emancipation, which in their opinion would have pierced the heart of their economy and loosed a semi-barbaric race upon their society. Although prior to the war Lincoln had suggested payment to owners, after the war victory over the "slavocracy" and public opinion combined to reject compensation to slaveholders even in the loyal border states.

The elimination of slavery benefited Negroes and eventually all Southerners, but the immediate effect was economic dislocation below the Potomac. As John Kenneth Galbraith pointed out in *The Liberal Hour*, capital "in slaves was not destroyed. It was transformed from the plantation owner to freedmen, and there was social loss only so far as the labor produced by the latter was less efficient." Undoubtedly, as Galbraith has stated, the South before the war relied on "an obsolescent agrarian economy in which poverty was disguised by slavery and the power, prestige and income of a considerable ruling class on which all attention centered." In this context the repudiation of state and Confederate currency and bonds destroyed nothing more than claims of the privileged few against future public revenue: however, the loss of capital invested in government securities and in slaves wrecked the southern economy. In 1865 the southern credit system and a considerable part of private investments were wiped out, and the southern economy was forced to adapt itself to northern standards.

The rest of the nation did not escape from the war unscathed. Confederate raids into border states and a few major campaigns into northern territory destroyed property; Chambersburg and Gettysburg, for example, received a taste of war. The bonded indebtedness of the nation soared to unbelievable heights for the nineteenth century. It, however, was not repudiated, for Northerner and Southerner later paid its interest and principal. Northern property losses in the conflict were minuscule compared to the South's.

In industrial development the South certainly lost more than the North. The old theory that national industrialization stemmed from the Civil War has been thoroughly repudiated by twentieth-century scholarship. During the 1850's industrial growth in the South had surpassed that of the North on a percentage basis, but the war set the southern region back by almost a generation. Supplying federal armies stimulated many northern industries, but war also disrupted patterns of growth in some industrial enterprises. A carrying trade pushing the English merchant marine for supremacy on the high seas was ruined by the depredations of Confederate cruisers and the consequent high insurance rates. Industries tooled for peacetime were altered to meet war purposes, and shifted again after the war. A sharp reduction of agrarian representation in Congress was conducive to the formation of a climate salubrious to big business—a fact not immediately recognized by capitalists in the Republican party. On the whole, however, the war probably checked rather than stimulated the industrialization and urbanization of America.

The Human Loss

Only in human life did the North suffer greater losses than the South. Exact numbers of men enrolled in the armies and lives lost in service may never be known. Thomas L. Livermore found the comparable totals of northern and southern three-year service terms to be 1,556,678 and 1,082,119 respectively. Union forces lost 110,070 men in battle and 250,152 from all other causes making 360,220 in total deaths. These figures have the validity of careful estimates. Confederate losses are more difficult to determine; the most defensible figures are 94,000 soldiers killed in battle, 164,000 dying from all other causes, for a total of 258,000. Based on these figures more than 23 per cent of northern servicemen lost their lives and almost 24 per cent of southern enrollees died. In total population, not including slaves, the South lost 4 per cent of her citizens and the North 1.5 per cent. According to Charles P. Roland, "If the North during the Civil War had suffered commensurately [to the South] she would have lost more than 1,000,000 men instead of 360,000. The American Colonies in revolt against England would have lost 94,000 instead of 12,000. The United States in World War II would have lost well over 6,000,000 men instead of somewhat more than 300,000."

In addition to the men who died, at least 275,000 federals suffered debilitating wounds of various degree. Lack of records prevents valid comparison for southern forces. Southern medical and nursing services were inferior to those of the Union, and a comparative deficiency in soothing and healing drugs undoubtedly resulted in a larger percentage of deaths in the ranks of Confederate wounded than those of the North. A fair estimate of Southerners incapacitated by war would approximate 150,000.

The potential earning power of almost 620,000 men cut down in youth or the prime of life amounted to billions of dollars. From an entirely materialistic point of view, the 425,000 wounded veterans were more of an economic handicap to their wives or relatives than soldiers killed in action. Federal veterans received some compensation from the national treasury, but southern soldiers waited long for pittances from their states. Federal pensions, however, provided no more than necessities to families who might have enjoyed some of the comforts of life had their breadwinners lived or returned from the war sound in body and in mind. Statistics never reflect the pain and suffering of the wounded or ill or the heartbreak of their families.

Almost every northern and southern household mourned the death of a husband, father, or brother, or cared for a wounded relative. In an age before psychiatry became popular, the veterans with their physical faculties unimpaired but broken mentally by the horrors of war were unidentified. Nevertheless, the mentally ill burdened their families economically and caused anguished, often mystified, relatives to invent explanations for the abnormal behavior of loved ones.

A potential human reservoir of hate and vengeance existed in the kin of the northern killed and wounded. In 1865 the joy of peace submerged base emotions. With effective statesmanship these emotions might never have surfaced, and victorious Northerners, who blamed their losses and the war on arrogant Southerners, might have won the peace as well as the war. Soundly defeated and politically impotent, Southerners contained their feelings in the hope of regaining their former power within the Union.

Political and Constitutional Results

Victory on the battlefield required no law, constitutional amendment, or court decree to establish the obvious. Confederate defeat repudiated secession as a practical or legal device of a disgruntled minority. In blood at the front and anguish behind the lines the Union became a permanent political organization composed of indestructible federal and state governments. The collapse of the Confederacy abolished the institution of slavery. The exigencies of war increased the powers of the President and the central government, and even in attempted independence the southern people experienced more centralization than their leaders had ever feared from the national government.

Ingrained in the American mind, however, was the desire for constitutional or other legal authority, whenever possible, to sanction change. "Neither slavery nor involuntary servitude, except as a punishment for crime whereof the party shall have been duly convicted, shall exist within the United States, or any place subject to their jurisdiction," became the Thirteenth Amendment, but long before its ratification on December 18, 1865, the "peculiar institution" had passed into limbo.

Four years after the war the Supreme Court in *Texas* v. *White* declared the Union indissoluble. The case had its origin in the federal bonds received by Texas for territorial concessions made by Texas in the compromises of 1850. During the existence of the Confederacy, Texas had sold these bonds to buy supplies. The reconstructed state government brought suit for recovery of the securities, arguing that Texas had never left the Union and, therefore, that the acts of a wartime government were illegal. In a four-to-three decision the Supreme Court ruled: "The union between Texas and the other States was as complete, as perpetual, and as indissoluble as the union between the original States. There was no place for reconsideration or revocation except through revolution, or through consent of the States." By refusing in 1861 to recognize their constitutional obligations, the Court stated, the citizens and government of Texas assumed the character of enemies of the United States and the first duty of the nation was to suppress the rebellion. The insurgent government of Texas possessed no legality, the Court concluded, and sale of the bonds was invalid.

Although the case referred only to Texas, the principles enunciated demolished the former southern argument which held that the federal government was the creation of sovereign states. Independence or sovereignty of the state vanished, but the respective powers and rights of states and the central government within a permanent union remained for politicians to debate. Losing this recourse to state sovereignty, minorities could still claim state rights in attempts to defeat proposed laws, force compromises, or limit court interpretations not to their liking.

Wartime extension of federal powers established precedents and formed patterns which would endure and be augmented by conditions of peacetime. Even the southern people, dedicated to sovereign states and a weak central government, found their bid for independence necessitated jurisdiction for the Confederacy unforeseen by ardent secessionists. The prestige of victory and the ignominy of defeat strengthened nationalism and weakened localism. In the post-bellum era the pace of industrialization and expansion of trade, the volume of interstate transportation and speed of communication, and the growth of monopolies and formation of trusts created situations better controlled by a national than a state government. As the sparsely settled, rural country of the Founding Fathers became the thickly populated, urban nation of the latter nineteenth century, old ideas and laws were altered to meet the needs of a new age. The vitality, even the existence of America, depended on federalism yielding to centralism, and reluctant as they were to give up the good old days, the American people demonstrated their adaptability to changed physical and intellectual environments.

The war increased both presidential and congressional power. By exercising his constitutional function as commander-in-chief and by assuming authority in the national crisis, the President overshadowed the legislators. But puissant congressional committees, as illustrated by the Committee on the Conduct of the War, demonstrated legislative strength. The Wade-Davis Bill and the Manifesto which followed Lincoln's pocket veto of the bill detailed the differences between the legislative and executive branches of the government. By 1865 congressmen were not in a submissive mood. With the Union restored the President would lose much of the support formerly given him by legislators. During the Reconstruction era, Congress was to become the dominant branch of the federal government.

In postwar America new party alignments favored the Republicans. Most Union soldiers organized into the Grand Army of the Republic supported the party that had preserved the Union, the party which also appeared to be the best source for general pension legislation. The newly freed and enfranchised Negro voted for candidates of "Father Abraham's" party. Northern agrarians joined with the businessmen of their region to elect Republicans. Skilled workmen believed their interests would be best cared for by Republican officeholders.

During and after the Civil War localism met defeat; centralization in government, business, and culture emerged victorious. From deep sorrow, excruciating pain, and awesome fear, the country entered a new era with her people changed in their philosophy. The United States could never revert to old folkways and mores or be the same again in politics, economics, or culture.

Intangible Results of the War

The people's attitudes are more difficult to assess than the material factors of a revolutionary age. During the war a majority of Southerners had unbounded faith in the righteousness of their cause and the support of their God. Defeat shattered illusions. Relatively few committed suicide or sought haven in Latin American countries. Reluctantly, most white Southerners accepted defeat. They clung, however, to imagined glories of the past—to their lost cause and their military heroes—they romanticized the Old South into an illusion. Completely defeated in war, they nevertheless heard the hoofbeats of cavalry for generations and ardently supported military training in colleges. Southerners never reproved their God for failing them; but, stimulated by "hell-fire and damnation" preachers and tent evangelists, they blamed themselves for not worshipping God sufficiently; they found the cause of defeat in their religious failures, and sought eventual victory over "Godless Yankees" in revival and camp meeting. In the process the South became the "Bible Belt," the puritanical region of the nation.

Despite slogans which proclaim the value of sportsmanship and the joys of competition, win or lose, Americans are elated by victory and depressed

by defeat. In the deadliest contest of all—war—made chivalrous by the dev-
otees of militarism and supposedly regulated by rules but with no referee
to enforce them, success is sweeter and defeat more bitter than in any
other competition. Depressed Southerners had few outlets for their emotions other than idealization of the past. Their life was drab and their future dimmed by uncertainty. "The night may seem long," Jefferson Davis
wrote, "but it is the part of fidelity to watch and wait for morning."
Former Associate Justice Campbell viewed the overthrow of the political
doctrines and social system of the South as a mighty revolution; he expected northern social, political, and economic principles to dominate the
nation and increase in strength in the future; and he hoped Northerners
would be content with triumph and be moderate in their treatment of
Southerners.

Former leaders of the Confederacy admitted that defeat had established
the perpetuity of the federal government. In addition to admitting the
permanency of the Union, these Southerners recognized the abolition of
slavery. Few of them would go further to appease the North. Southerners
expected to control their state and local governments as they had done before the war; they saw no reason for federal troops in the South and rejected Negro participation in politics.

Throughout the war southern Negroes acted in diverse ways. Governor
John Milton of Florida found their faithfulness to master and duty superior to the patriotism and sacrifice of white Confederates. Despite invading, liberating armies and the absence or infrequent appearance of regulating patrols, most slaves remained on plantations working at their accustomed tasks. How much their faithfulness depended on affection for individual whites, on contentment with servile conditions, or an ignorance
which made the slaves fear change remains an unanswered question. Illiterate, superstitious Negroes followed the pattern of other uneducated
humans; they clung to the known and feared the untried.

Desire for freedom conquered the emotion of fear in a surprisingly large
number of slaves. They found haven near protecting federal forces where
they joined thousands of Negroes liberated by occupying armies. Not
knowing how to classify them before emancipation, some northern commanders labeled them "contrabands" and fed the propertyless Negroes
from military stores. Later many freedmen labored on farms under the
supervision of northern agents in conquered areas of the South. Tens of
thousands—motivated by gratitude and patriotism, by the adventure of
military service, by government bounties and payments from Northerners
sending substitutes, or hatred of southern whites—went into the federal
armies.

At the end of the war almost 4 million former slaves hailed freedom joy-ously or accepted it calmly. Some mothers with tears of happiness streaming down their lined faces whispered to uncomprehending infants of what God had wrought. A larger number of Negroes thought freedom meant the absence of work—Saturday afternoons and Sundays of the slave system "come every day." The peculiar institution had not trained its laborers for freedom or responsibility. The rewarded Negro of yesteryear had been the conformist, the one who obeyed without question.

For generations the slave's few comforts in life depended in large part on bending the knee to the master race, on gifts from ruling families, on shirking duties almost to the point of bringing the lash on his back, and on cunning ways and actual theft. By custom and law neither slave husband nor wife had the rights or responsibilities of white partners in marriage. Children witnessed the whipping of parents, families were broken by sales, and the female slave was accessible to Negro and white males. Slavery gave the African Negro a speaking knowledge of the English language, a distorted idea of Christian principles, and a rudimentary understanding of staple-crop agricultural production. Freedom came to the American Negroes, 95 per cent of whom were illiterate, and thrust them into a white man's world without adequate preparation.

Surprising, therefore, was the large percentage of former slaves who remained on plantation and farm or sought work for wages in urban places, and the relatively small percentage of them who ran to city and town hoping to subsist on federal handouts. After the occupation of Richmond a *New York Times* reporter interviewed a dozen Negro men. None looked forward to a life of ease; all wanted to work for wages: "Not for none of dis yer money [Confederate] dat ain't werf nuffin, but de money [federal currency] dat you has."

Children of a closed society and captives of their own propaganda, many Southerners were shocked by the departure of beloved servants who apparently had been content under slavery. One young wife cried herself to sleep after the disappearance of a personal slave with whom she had been raised and with whom she had shared most experiences in life. Like many Southerners she had not realized the longing of Negroes to attain human dignity. On the other hand, northern visitors—captives of abolitionist propaganda —could not understand the affection of some former slaves for onetime masters and mistresses. On occasion gainfully employed Negroes returned to familiar households to give impoverished mistresses a few dollars in greenbacks.

The diversity of emotions and variety of reactions of the freedmen contradicted the stereotype of the happy, simple child of slavedom. Perhaps fears of the unknown kept most Negroes at the former source of food, clothing, and housing. From experience they knew that land and crops produced good food, fine clothes, and comfortable houses for white people. This fact, together with the freedmen's skill in planting, cultivating, and harvesting staple crops, made ownership of land appealing. They held out supplicating hands to victor and vanquished for farms as a means of livelihood. And since ability to read was equated in the freedman's mind with social and economic power, fathers and especially mothers, asked for schools for their children. Thoughtful Negroes sought a better world and hope was stirred in their hearts by vague but wonderful-sounding words— freedom, opportunity, and democracy.

In contrast to a divided South, permeated by the whites' feelings of depression and uncertainty and the freedmen's joy and expectancy, a united North celebrated peace as the harbinger of a better tomorrow. By northern fighting and sacrifice the Union had been saved and a "government of the people, by the people, for the people" would not perish from the earth. The abolition of slavery cleansed the nation of a moral canker, and most Northerners felt righteous. Despite their lowly economic status, working men saw labor dignified by the elimination of human bondage in America. In the past, underpaid, overworked laborers had blamed their plight on the southern slaveowner as much as on the entrepreneur for whom they toiled.

During the war businessmen and investors enjoyed high profits and generous returns for their enterprise. The National Bank Act of 1863, with amendments the following year, guaranteed a sound, uniform currency under federal supervision. The Contract Labor Law of 1864 assured owners of factories and construction companies immigrant laborers who could be cowed, by signed agreements, to repay the costs of transportation to America. The Pacific Railway Act of 1862 provided lavish natural resources to railroads and foreshadowed other grants to mining industries. A high protective tariff gave steel and other manufacturers protection against low-priced import commodities. With these acts aiding industry and contravening laissez-faire principles, the climate of national government indicated support for business. In business aids—but not in supervision—the United States would interfere with supply and demand, marginal utility, and competition. Furthermore, the desire of states and localities for railroads and factories foretold police support from states, counties, and cities for capitalists rather than laborers.

The entrepreneur sensed but did not realize his advantages in 1865. In time he did begin to realize them, and then made himself the important factor in government. His lobbies and his money bought legislators at state and national capitals and selected governors and Presidents. In combination with politicians, the industrialists won support from northern veterans, farmers, skilled laborers, Negroes, worshippers of Lincoln, nationalists, and onetime reformers. Combined they made the Republican party supreme and found opposition only in the Democratic party organizations in northern cities. Southern agrarians, who might combine with northern farmers, posed a threat to future national domination by business, but the defeated South could be handled by adroit maneuver or force.

In April 1865, Northerners foresaw neither the opportunities nor the problems of an industrial, urban society. Exhilaration at winning the war found vent in various activities for the most part expressing thanksgiving. Some citizens gave raucous applause to speakers who demanded the punishment of southern leaders, but most Northerners were content to forgive. The victors' minds were too filled with rejoicing and pride in their country to think of methods by which the South would resume her place in the Union.

Lincoln's Plan and Beginning of Reconstruction

Reconstructing the South had been on President Lincoln's agenda for years. From the firing on Fort Sumter until his assassination his paramount concern was to save the American Union. Lincoln approved of the Crittenden-Johnson resolutions in the House and the Senate which stated that the purpose of the war was to "maintain the supremacy of the Constitution and to preserve the Union, with all the dignity, equality, and rights of the several states unimpaired. . . ." He neither recognized secession nor denied the continued existence of the southern states in the Union. The pragmatic President considered debating the legal status of the states within the Union a waste of time; since the rebellious states were obviously not in their proper or practical relation with the Union, his objective was to restore them to their former relationship as quickly as possible.

In Lincoln's opinion a combination of disloyal citizens, too strong for federal civilian agencies to subdue, had seized southern governments. He never characterized all Southerners as enemies or rebels and consistently sought to win the support and aid of loyal residents of the South. Lincoln believed the restoration of republican state governments in the South was a constitutional duty of the President, whose authority rested on his powers as commander-in-chief of the army and navy.

The exact method of returning the states to their old relationship in the Union was never fixed in Lincoln's mind. At the onset of the war, his major concern was to keep Maryland, Kentucky, and Missouri in the Union. Without the continuation of loyal governments in these states, the demise of the nation, he realized, was almost a certainty. He moved swiftly in Maryland, declaring martial law and using federal troops to prevent action by legislators who favored the South. In Kentucky and Missouri the President acted cautiously. For a time he tacitly recognized the neutrality of these states while biding his time for forceful action. Lincoln's success in the border slave states probably saved the American Union.

Winning these preliminary victories by civil and military action gave Lincoln ideas. He also relied on precedents of the Mexican War, the opinions of a lawyer-heavy cabinet, and ideas of military advisers. Wherever possible, he would appoint military governors and rely on maximum popular support for their regimes. Within a year federal conquests gave him the opportunity to reconstruct segments of three southern states. In 1862 he appointed Andrew Johnson military governor of Tennessee and endowed that loyal American with powers necessary to enable patriotic citizens to reestablish a republican form of government, which would entitle the state to federal protection against invasion and domestic anarchy. Under the direction of presidential governors, loyalists of Arkansas and Louisiana also attempted the political reorganization of their states.

In Virginia-West Virginia the President found a situation peculiar to the South. The mountainous counties of western Virginia seceded from the state and, protected by federal armies, established themselves as the loyal government of Virginia. By receiving permission from this artificial state government, the western counties met the legal technicalities of the Constitution, requested recognition as a state, and on June 19, 1863, became the thirty-fifth state of the United States. The loyal government of Virginia, headed by Francis Pierpont, established itself at Alexandria in the shadow of the national capital. Although Governor Pierpont's territory varied in size with the fortunes of war, President Lincoln recognized the Alexandria government as the legal one of Virginia.

Reunion was the sole purpose of these first presidential attempts at reconstruction, but necessity and congressional action forced the President to consider other problems. In August 1861, the first federal confiscation act authorized seizure of all property, including slaves, being used to aid the rebellion. This mild measure whetted the appetite of the radicals for harsher measures. They approved General Benjamin F. Butler's policy of declaring escaped slaves "contrabands of war" during the first invasions of Virginia and his using them as laborers to help the North. Other federal commanders, however, frequently returned slaves to their masters. In March 1862, a law of Congress ended this practice, and all escaped slaves became confiscated property. In 1861 and 1862, General John C. Frémont in Missouri and General David Hunter in South Carolina went further and declared all slaves free within the areas of their respective commands. President Lincoln annulled these orders and rebuked the commanders for their unwarranted attempts to make civilian policy.

Both President and nation were being driven inexorably toward a new war aim. In July 1862, Congress passed the second confiscation act, one of the most drastic property laws ever enacted by the American government. In addition to providing special punishment for persons convicted of treason in the rebellion and providing for confiscation of property, other than slaves, held by Southerners, it gave freedom to all slaves whose masters were aiding the Confederacy. In practice the condemnation of property was negligible: forfeitures required proceedings in federal courts and the attorney general made few efforts to enforce the act.

Lincoln wrote a veto of the second confiscation bill, and only an explanatory joint resolution of Congress won reluctant presidential approval of the measure. Lincoln eventually came to support one part of the act: in September 1862, he issued the Emancipation Proclamation which gave Southerners until January 1, 1863, to cease their rebellion or suffer economic loss in the freeing of all their slaves.

The Emancipation Proclamation actually freed no slave within Confederate-held territory but it added a second purpose to the war. From secession until his death, Lincoln advocated compensated emancipation. On December 1, 1862, his special message to Congress recommended gradual emancipation, with all slaves freed by 1900, and federal bonds to states that provided constitutional guarantees for freedom. Perhaps this message reflected presidential desires to end the war and restore the Union by assuring slaveholders of the border states of their property rights and offering inducements to Confederate citizens, rather than providing simply for the abolition of slavery. Whatever his motives, the course of military events determined eventual action. After the promulgation of the Emancipation Proclamation, only a Confederate victory or southern independence by means of foreign intervention could retain slavery in North America. Human freedom joined restoration of the Union as a purpose of war and reconstruction.

The freedom issue became an integral part of the President's paramount concern of restoring the Union. Writing to Military Governor Johnson on September 11, 1863, he urged speedy action in Tennessee: "Let the reconstruction be the work of such men only as can be trusted for the Union. Exclude all others, and trust that your government so organized will be recognized here as being the one of republican form to be guaranteed to the State, and to be protected against invasion and domestic violence." Lincoln warned that his tenure as the national executive was limited by elections and the Constitution, and no one knew who would next occupy the White House or what his policies would be. He invoked the blessing of God on Johnson for advocating emancipation in Tennessee and added: "Get emancipation into your new State government—constitution —and there will be no such word as fail for your course."

Almost three months later, on December 8, 1863, the President furthered his plans in his Proclamation of Amnesty and Reconstruction. Essential to restoring the states to their practical proper relation within the Union was the identification of loyal citizens. Lincoln would discover these loyal persons by a general amnesty to almost all Southerners who would on oath promise to "henceforth faithfully support, protect, and defend the Constitution of the United States and the Union of the states thereunder," and recognize all acts of Congress and presidential proclamations relating to slaves. By taking and observing this oath individuals who had participated directly or indirectly in the rebellion would gain a full pardon and the restoration of all property rights except slaves. Ineligible for amnesty and pardon were six general classes of Southerners: (1) civil and diplomatic officers and agents of the Confederacy; (2) those who left judicial positions of the United States to aid the South; (3) all Confederate officers above the rank of colonel in the army and lieutenant in the navy; (4) former United States congressmen who resigned to support the rebellion; (5) officers in the American army or navy who relinquished their commissions and afterwards helped the Confederacy; and (6) all persons who failed to treat federal Negro soldiers, or officers in charge of them, as prisoners of war.

Whenever the number of oath-takers in a state equaled or surpassed 10 per cent of the votes cast in that state in the presidential election of 1860 and these loyal citizens had organized themselves into a republican government, Lincoln promised to recognize it as the true government of the state. Except for modifications made necessary by national laws and executive proclamations, he suggested use of prewar names, boundaries, political subdivisions, constitutions, legal codes, and voting qualifications for the loyal governments. Thus, he emphasized the continued existence of the states and made neither request nor demand for enfranchising Negroes. Indirectly he urged the abolition of slavery and aid to freedmen by promising no executive opposition to any provisions relating to freedmen "which shall recognize and declare their permanent freedom, provide for their education, and which may yet be consistent as a temporary arrangement with their present condition as a laboring, landless, and homeless class. . . ."

The President offered his reconstruction plan as the best one he could devise at the moment. He did not rule out executive changes at a later date to fit new circumstances or claim his ideas superior or more acceptable than other possible ones. This statement left an opening for suggestions from loyal Southerners, but mainly offered appeasement to Radical * congressmen. Lincoln emphasized one fact: compliance with his plan of reconstruction did not guarantee seats to representatives and senators sent

* It is difficult to identify the Radicals. In general they opposed Lincoln during the war and demanded harsher treatment of white Southerners than he did.

to Washington by reformed and loyal state governments. Admission of legislators to Congress, he knew, was granted by the members of the Senate and House of Representatives.

Conscious of opposition to his lenient plans by some congressmen, the President nevertheless felt himself obligated by constitutional and war powers to restore the southern states to their former places in the Union. In no rebel state did the federal military control an entire commonwealth. Early in 1864 Lincoln saw an opportunity to gain such control of one state and reconstruct it as a political unit. He supported an invasion of the least populated state of the Confederacy—Florida—and proposed sending an army west from Jacksonville and another east from Pensacola to conquer it. There were, in addition to the political advantages, valid military reasons for an invasion. It would cut the Confederacy's supply of beef, pork, and fish from peninsular Florida and increase the recruitment of Negro and white soldiers from an area which had already contributed relatively well to Union armies. The federal army was checked at the Battle of Olustee on February 20, 1864, and gave up the attempt to conquer Florida; consequently Lincoln never had the opportunity to reconstruct an entire state.

Throughout the war every effort to restore an occupied part of a southern state came from presidential initiative, but little by little congressional opposition to Lincoln's work gained strength. In 1862 the newly organized loyal Louisiana government sent two representatives to Washington. In April 1864, a convention wrote a constitution which abolished slavery and, by a vote larger than 10 per cent of the number cast in 1860, the loyalists accepted the constitution and elected state officers and federal congressmen. Although enforcing national conscription in occupied Louisiana, Congress refused to seat senators and representatives from the loyal government. Representatives from Tennessee served in the House in 1862–63, but after loyal Tennessee had accepted a constitution in 1864–65 with provisions abolishing slavery and repudiating secession, and elected the ambitious unionist William G. [Parson] Brownlow to the governorship, neither its senators nor its representatives won the approval of Congress. In March 1864, Arkansas loyalists accepted a constitution which ended slavery. Irregularities occurred in the voting and the loyal government never received congressional approval nor recognition of legislators sent to Washington. Congress accepted West Virginia's congressmen and counted the state's electoral vote in 1864. Some acts of loyal Virginia at Alexandria were considered valid: consent for the establishment of West Virginia, apportionment of the debt, and drawing state boundaries. The House of Representatives, however, refused seats in the Thirty-Ninth Congress (1863–65) to loyalists from Virginia, and the Senate only reluctantly accepted one senator from the state.

Opposition to Lincoln's Reconstruction Efforts

Like the executive, the Congress picked its way gingerly to a reconstruction policy. In July 1861, only two representatives and five senators voted against the Crittenden-Johnson resolutions. The Congress, however, soon added purposes other than preservation of the Union to its war aims. Late in 1861 it created the Committee on the Conduct of the War with senators Benjamin Franklin Wade of Ohio and Zachariah Chandler of Michigan and Representative George Washington Julian of Indiana among its seven members. On February 11, 1862, Senator Charles Sumner's resolutions called for the abolition of slavery, claimed the southern states committed suicide by secession, and announced the obligation and right of Congress to reconstruct the South. Many congressmen also looked with disfavor on leniency in pardoning "rebels" and allowing them to vote. Not satisfied with a simple oath of allegiance as a test of loyalty, by an act of July 2, 1862, Congress authorized what was later called the "iron-clad" oath. Originally designed for northern officeseekers, the oath was later required of southern officeholders, requiring them to swear that they had never voluntarily borne arms against the United States or supported hostile state or Confederate governments and had not aided individuals fighting the Union.

Early in 1864, critics of Lincoln accused him of favoring an invasion of Florida and reconstruction of an entire state to secure three electoral votes in the forthcoming presidential election. Six months later the President believed it wise to approve a joint resolution which denied electoral votes to all states of the Confederacy and the loyal governments therein organized under executive direction. He justified his position by declaring that the right to count electoral votes belonged exclusively to the Congress and neither the military nor the executive could make rules and determine results in state presidential elections.

Just before adjourning on July 8, 1864, Congress outlined its plan of reconstruction in "An Act to Guarantee to Certain States whose Government Have Been Usurped or Overthrown a Republican Form of Government." This Wade-Davis Bill demonstrated the divergent stands of the President and Radicals. Its basic philosophy was the right and duty of the Congress to determine reconstruction with the President executing laws rather than making policy. The bill provided for provisional governors, appointed by the President and approved by the Senate, to administer the civil government until loyal governments were organized and recognized by the President and Congress. Specific steps were required for a state to obtain a recognizable government. After a majority of adult, white males of a state took a loyalty oath, the provisional governor would authorize the election of delegates to a constitutional convention to write a document which must abolish slavery and repudiate all Confederate and state war debts. If a majority of the qualified voters approved the constitution, the President with congressional sanction would proclaim a legal government and elections could be held to select senators, representatives, and electors.

Other provisions of the Wade-Davis Bill related to slavery, office-holding, and the eligibility of voters. Not only must freedom be acknowledged, but persons convicted of re-enslaving freedmen were subject to a minimum fine of $1500 and from five to twenty years imprisonment. United States citizenship was taken from all high civil and military officials who continued resistance after passage of the bill, and the same persons and those who voluntarily warred on the United States could neither vote for nor be delegates to the constitutional conventions. The more important civil and military officers of the seceded states and the Confederacy were not eligible to serve as governors or legislators in the reconstructed governments. The fundamental differences between congressional and presidential plans were: direction by laws and approval by Congress rather than by executive fiat, a rigorous rather than a lenient oath to determine loyalty and voting, and a majority of voters rather than a small minority to establish a loyal government.

Fully conscious of powerful opposition to his plans, President Lincoln debated his action and finally pocket-vetoed the bill. Not satisfied with remaining silent and thereby killing the congressional plan, he issued an explanatory proclamation. Many reasons, he explained, prevented his approval of the bill: he was unwilling to commit himself to a single plan of reconstruction, was not inclined to set aside the loyal governments already operating in Arkansas and Louisiana, and was not ready to admit the constitutional right of Congress to abolish slavery. The President, however, expressed his hope for abolition by a constitutional amendment. He admitted the plan of reconstruction in the Wade-Davis Bill was proper; and, if the loyal citizens of any state chose it, he would render them every aid and assistance in restoring their state.

This presidential finesse angered the Radicals who knew no southern state would prefer their rigorous plan to the lenient executive one. The Wade-Davis Manifesto blasted Lincoln: "We have read without surprise, but not without indignation, the Proclamation of the President of the 8th of July, 1864. . . ." This proclamation was neither an approval nor a veto of the Wade-Davis Bill, the Manifesto continued, and, therefore, was a peculiar document in relation to the laws and Constitution of the United States. Wade and Davis accused the President of issuing a manifesto against the friends of his administration, of keeping the electoral votes of the rebel states under his control to further his personal ambition, and fomenting another civil war by encouraging rebels to control the southern states.

They scoffed at the presidential claim that the bill was presented to him an hour before the *sine die* adjournment of Congress: at his request a draft of the proposed law had been sent him during the winter of 1862–63 which gave him ample time to study its provisions. The Manifesto authors claimed that Lincoln was determined to prevent the people from using laws to attain security "from the rebel states against a removal of the rebellion, before restoring their power to govern us." In a spirited expression of congressional authority to legislate, the Manifesto declared "the whole body of the Union men of Congress will not submit to be impeached by him of rash and unconstitutional legislation; and if he wishes our support, he must confine himself to his executive duties—to obey and execute, not make the laws—to suppress by arms armed rebellion, and leave political reorganization to Congress."

Public Reactions to Reconstruction Plans

Perhaps one result of the Wade-Davis Manifesto was the rejection by Maryland voters of Henry Winter Davis in his bid for re-election to the House of Representatives in 1864. Davis was a magnetic public speaker, but his belated support of the Republican party, advocacy of abolition, and anti-secession activities had brought him censure from the Maryland legislature and defeat in 1860. Two years later he returned to Congress where he became a vitriolic critic of Lincoln. After losing his bid for re-election in 1864, as a private citizen he exerted tremendous influence on some representatives.

Based entirely on Davis's defeat and Lincoln's re-election in 1864, one might assume popular approval of presidential reconstruction plans and rejection of the congressional program. This conclusion ignores many political and military influences. In reality methods of restoring the southern states to the Union interested comparatively few voters in 1864. Their paramount concern was victory and peace. The cool reception given the Wade-Davis Bill and the Manifesto made Radicals take stock and bide a more propitious time for aggressive action.

On the other hand, the sharp differences between his own and congressional ideas forced Lincoln to appease and compromise. Never did he claim that his plan of reconstruction was the only possible one. He kept his mind open and considered demands expressed in Radical-inspired legislation and bills. In addition to unconditional surrender, restoration of the Union, and abolition of slavery, he evidently gave deep thought to repudiating rebel war debts, protection of the freedmen, and changes in his announced method of establishing loyal governments in the South.

In his Second Inaugural Address, Lincoln extended one hand in friendship to Southerners and the other in appeasement to Northerners. Well-known and often printed is the last paragraph of the address: "With malice toward none, with charity for all, with firmness in the right as God gives us to see the right, let us strive on to finish the work we are in, to bind up the nation's wounds . . . and cherish a just and lasting peace among ourselves and with all nations." Less known and infrequently quoted is his explanation of the cause of civil war: slavery "was somehow the cause of the war. To strengthen, perpetuate, and extend this interest was the object for which the insurgents would rend the Union even by war. . . ." According to Lincoln, responsibility for the bloody debacle lay on southern shoulders and retribution belonged to the victor. "It may seem strange that any men should dare to ask a just God's assistance in wringing their bread from the sweat of other men's faces," the President declared, and added, "but let us judge not, that we be not judged."

Some weeks after his inauguration the President left Washington for Virginia where he waited impatiently for federal troops to occupy Petersburg and Richmond. His brief stay in the partially burned, federally occupied former Confederate capital was marked by discussions of restoring Virginia to the Union rather than by expressions of joy and demands for vengeance. Returning to Washington on April 11, 1865, he delivered his last public address. Military victory, he told an admiring crowd standing below the White House balcony, made Reconstruction the issue of the day. He admitted that the problem of restoration was complicated by differences among sincere loyal Northerners "as to the mode, manner, and measure of reconstruction." The President reviewed his efforts to establish loyal governments in the South, and emphasized the work in Louisiana.

He had purposely avoided the question of whether the so-called seceded states were in or out of the Union: they were out of their practical relation with the Union and the sole object of the national government was to restore them to that proper practical relation. "Finding themselves safely at home, it would be utterly immaterial whether they had been abroad," he said, and pointed to Louisiana where 12,000 voters had sworn allegiance to the United States, given the benefit of public schools equally to black and white, empowered the legislature to enfranchise freedmen, and ratified the Thirteenth Amendment. If the nation rejected and spurned loyal Louisianans, the President declared, the effect would be to "say to the white men: You are worthless or worse; we will neither help you nor be helped by you. To the blacks we say: This cup of liberty which these, your old masters, held to your lips, we will dash from you, and leave you to the chances of gathering the spilled and scattered contents in some vague and undefined when, where, and how." Lincoln urged his listeners to support no exclusive and inflexible plan of reconstruction, but accept what had been done and on its foundation build a more united and better America.

By April 11, Lincoln favored enfranchising "the very intelligent" Negroes and all those who had served in the Union army. While admitting deficiencies in the political philosophy of loyal Louisiana, he advised accepting advances already made and encouraging additional progress. Three days later he sought cabinet support for getting southern governments into successful operation and the Union re-established before the meeting of Congress in December. Stanton proposed rigid military control of the South until loyal governments could be organized and become functional. Lincoln objected but encouraged his secretary to develop his ideas and present them at the next cabinet meeting.

In truth no cabinet member knew exactly what the President was thinking. Was he preparing to declare the war over and issue a general amnesty? Or was he on the verge of admitting that his reconstruction policies were too lenient and hasty and ready to advocate a more rigorous and deliberate program? Perhaps even he did not know, but Lincoln did realize that reconstruction would be one of the most difficult problems ever faced by the nation.

The North had won the war. Could it also win the peace? Fate prevented the war President from using his tact and influence in resolving the peace. On the evening of April 14, he acceded to his wife's wishes by attending the play at Ford's Theater where he was shot by the half-demented John Wilkes Booth. The following morning the mind and soul left the body of the great American.

REFERENCES

Among contemporary visitors who penned good descriptions of the devastated South were: Sidney Andrews, *The South Since the War* (Boston, 1866); Edward King, *The Great South* (Hartford, 1875); Whitelaw Reid, *After the War: A Southern Tour, May 1, 1865 to May 1, 1866* (New York, 1866); John T. Trowbridge, *The Desolate South, 1865–1866*, edited by Gordon Carroll (Boston, 1956); and Robert Somers, *The Southern States Since the War, 1870–1* (London, 1871). *The Fall of Richmond* (Baton Rouge, 1960) by R. W. Patrick portrays the evacuation and occupation of the Confederate capital, the reaction to victory by Washingtonians, and Lincoln's visit to Richmond. Feminine response to defeat is recorded in Myrta Lockett Avary's sentimental *Dixie After the War* (New York, 1906) and young Emma LeConte's valuable diary, *When the World Ended* (New York, 1957), edited by Earl S. Miers. In *Numbers and Losses in the*

Civil War in America, 1861–65 (New York, 1901) Thomas L. Livermore assesses the human cost of the conflict. Andrew F. Rolle, *The Lost Cause: The Confederate Exodus to Mexico* (New York, 1965), deals more with Maximilian's empire than Confederate migration to Mexico. W. C. Nunn, *Escape from Reconstruction* (Fort Worth, 1956), and Alfred J. and Kathryn A. Hanna, *Confederate Exiles in Venezuela* (Tuscaloosa, 1960), adequately account for the relatively few Southerners who left their homeland. One chapter of *The Lincoln Nobody Knows* (New York, 1958) by Richard N. Current has a quality account of Lincoln's role in reconstructing the South. Charles H. McCart's *Lincoln's Plan of Reconstruction* (New York, 1901) and James G. Randall's *Lincoln and the South* (Baton Rouge, 1946) are useful; also William B. Hesseltine, *Lincoln's Plan of Reconstruction* (Tuscaloosa, 1960). Willie Lee Rose's prize-winning book, *Rehearsal for Reconstruction: The Port Royal Experiment* (Indianapolis, 1964) deals with the transition of Afro-Americans from slavery to freedom. In a scholarly work Charles L. Wagadt, *The Mighty Revolution: Negro Emancipation in Maryland, 1862–1864* (New York, 1964), presents the problems of reconstructing a border state. See also James G. Randall and Richard N. Current, *Lincoln the President: Last Full Measure* (New York, 1955); T. Harry Williams, *Lincoln and the Radicals* (Madison, 1941); G. McWhiney (ed.), *Grant, Lee, Lincoln, and the Radicals* (New York, 1964); W. A. Ross, "The Struggle between President Lincoln and Congress over Disfranchisement of Rebels," *Susquehanna University Studies,* 1947 (pp. 177–205) and 1948 (pp. 221–248); and Benjamin Quarles, *Lincoln and the Negro* (New York, 1962).

Presidential Reconstruction

WHILE President Lincoln inspected Petersburg and Richmond on April 3 and 4, 1865, Washingtonians celebrated victory with wild enthusiasm. Bands played and people sang "John Brown's Body" and "The Year of Jubilee." Horses galloped through the streets, pulling steam fire-engines, their whistles splitting the air and mingling with the boom of cannon. Exuberant Negroes danced on street and sidewalk. "De day of Jubelo am come," a whirling dancer yelled; and another cried: "No more hoeing of corn for dis pore child, and no more lashes from dat cruel overseer." An unseen hand waved clerks and laborers from their jobs into days and nights of revels. At night candles and gas lights illuminated buildings and crowds demanded speeches from political leaders.

In the President's absence, attention centered on Vice President Andrew Johnson. Treason, he told the throng, was the highest crime known in the catalogue of crimes, and "traitors must be punished and impoverished, their social power broken, they must be made to feel the penalty of their crime. . . ." The vice president answered the question of what he would do with traitors by declaring: "I would arrest them; I would try them; I would convict them; and I would hang them." Representative Green Clay Smith of Kentucky supported Johnson's plea for punishment. Stimulated by the crowd, Smith declared: "The city of Richmond, that citadel of treason . . . was taken possession of by a lot of soldiers of African descent, and led by a Dutchman. Now, where is that bragging chivalry of the South, which flattered itself that one of them could whip five Yankees, in the beginning of the war, when now fifty thousand of them run from a thousand Negroes." Charles S. Spencer, president of the Republican Club of New York, saw the most signal instance of divine justice the world had ever seen in the occupation of "haughty, slave-driving Richmond" by Negro soldiers. "The first shot fired at Fort Sumter bore on its felon wings the death of slavery; and today," he stated, "this nation tears from its limbs the black sackcloth of slavery, and robes them in the pure and bridal white of universal emancipation." The crowd applauded these and other speakers, and calls for hanging Southerners received warm response, but most Washingtonians preferred peace to vengeance.

Less than two weeks later Washington and the rest of the nation mourned the passing of President Lincoln. Other officials had been marked for assassination by the plotters. Secretary of State William H. Seward, bedridden from injuries suffered in a carriage accident, survived blows of a would-be assassin. Vice President Johnson, and perhaps others, escaped when intended murderers failed to execute their appointed assignments. Accusations were leveled at Jefferson Davis and his administration and the first reaction of Northerners was to accept these false indictments and demand punishment of Confederate officials.

While the nation mourned, some Northerners gloated in secret over a tragedy which might serve their purposes. The linking of Confederate officials with the assassination of Lincoln, though false and unjust, fixed itself in many northern minds as true and served to increase their suspicion and distrust of Southerners. Animosities created by four years of death on the battlefield could not be overcome by a fortnight of peace celebrations. The assassination of Lincoln dulled the triumph of victory. It removed from national politics a statesman of influence and tact, versed in handling recalcitrant congressmen, and one who could bring out the more sensible and generous qualities of the victors. Lincoln's death elevated Andrew Johnson, a Southerner, to the presidency. Johnson was apparently a vindictive man, impulsive in speech, who lacked the personal following of the martyred President and could not claim the latter's savior-of-the-Union mantle. Mustered-out soldier, freedman, and humanitarian identified military service, freedom, and good works with Lincoln, not Johnson.

Andrew Johnson

The first duties of President Johnson related to war rather than restoration. After leaving Richmond on April 2, the Confederate cabinet fled south through Virginia to Greensboro, North Carolina. On the 9th, Lee surrendered to Grant at Appomattox and General Joseph E. Johnston's feeble Confederate force in North Carolina was pressed by the army of General William T. Sherman. At Greensboro, Johnston pointed out to the southern cabinet the military impotence of the Confederacy. Until this time Jefferson Davis had stoutly maintained that his constitutional duty lay in continued defense of the South. Advised by Johnston and a majority of his cabinet, Davis agreed to terms offered by Sherman. In return for disbanding armies and recognizing the authority of the United States, Davis demanded that existing southern state governments be preserved, all property and political rights of Southerners be respected, and no punishment be inflicted on those who had supported the Confederacy.

Armed with these instructions, General Johnston negotiated with Sherman. Although ruthless in war, Sherman had roots in the South and was more interested in the cessation of hostilities than in the politics of reconstruction. In the Sherman-Johnston Convention he made a magnanimous political armistice. He guaranteed southern property in slaves, recognized the insurgent state governments, and left the repudiation of Confederate and state war debts in limbo.

Sherman's policy-making amazed Stanton who, in the absence of Seward, had the ear of Johnson. The President and his war secretary rejected the military convention and ordered Sherman to resume his campaign. On April 26, Sherman gave and Johnston accepted terms similar to those signed by Lee at Appomattox. Before the end of May the other Confederate armies east and west of the Mississippi River surrendered, the remaining unconquered state capitals were occupied, and resistance ceased in the South.

Many secession leaders and Confederate and state officials, fearing the punishment for treason might be hanging, attempted escape. Secretaries Benjamin and Breckenridge, and hot-tempered Robert Toombs, eluded federal cavalry to find haven in foreign countries. Among the more important Confederate leaders captured or arrested were Jefferson Davis, Stephens, Mallory, Seddon, Memminger, Trenholm, Reagan, and George Davis. These men, along with some former United States congressmen from the South and a few state officials, were imprisoned at the military prisons in Fort Pulaski (Savannah) or Fort Warren (Boston).

The physical punishment meted out by the victor was inconsequential. Major Henry Wirz, a friendless Swiss-American accused of being responsible for the deaths of more than 12,000 Northerners at Andersonville prison in Georgia, was tried by a military commission and hanged on November 10, 1865. Other than Wirz, southern civil and military officers suffered no more than imprisonment for terms ranging from weeks to almost two years. Stanton and Judge Advocate General Joseph Holt investigated the chances of condemning Confederate leaders but brought none of them to trial.

Southern armies disappeared and demands from Union soldiers and their friends brought quick national demobilization. On May 23 and 24, 1865, proud and resplendent troops paraded down Pennsylvania Avenue to the shouts of admiring citizens. Following this tribute to valor and union, men of the federal forces returned to civilian life and eventually to the status of veterans in the Grand Army of the Republic. Within little more than two years after the end of the war less than 60,000 officers and men remained and a year later this number was reduced by 25 per cent.

Meanwhile President Johnson formulated and began to execute his reconstruction policies. A native of Raleigh, North Carolina, who had be-

come a tailor at Greeneville, Tennessee, he was a veteran of politics. Behind him was service as city alderman, mayor, state representative and senator, governor, United States representative and senator, military governor,
and vice president. Yet, when he took the presidential oath on April 15,
1865, few of his political principles were known. No one could legitimately
question his loyalty to the Union. His rash remarks and public demand for
vengeance made moderate men shudder.

Although endowed with abundant native intelligence, Andrew Johnson
was the product of environment. Recollections of youthful poverty, of
learning attained in adulthood with the aid of a patient wife, and of the
contrast between poor farmer and aristocratic plantation owner were
deeply etched in his mind. The rough and tumble campaign debates of
eastern Tennessee were his political schoolhouse. For him politics was
fun—a good show. Frequently he made and the voters accepted his statements as campaign showmanship rather than guiding principles for action
in office.

Despite his exhibitionism on the stump, principle dominated Andrew
Johnson. In addition to his staunch loyalism, he possessed a veneration for
the Constitution of the United States. Nowhere in that document could
he find authority for the central government to take over or destroy a state;
he clung tenaciously to the doctrine of the permanency of federal and state
governments. In many respects he followed Jefferson's strict construction
of the Constitution and held sacred the residual powers of the states. Furthermore, Johnson believed the chief executive should be supreme in his
sphere of the national government. The Tennesseean was a stubborn man
and, when convinced of the rightness and justness of a cause, he would
fight relentlessly for its acceptance.

The Republicans welcomed Johnson without knowing his principles or
understanding the Southerner in the White House. They pledged him
their support, but a few of them feared he would deal too harshly with
former Confederates. Yet despite his rough language and tactless manner,
he was capable neither of studied cruelty nor enjoyment of human suffering. His belief in adherence to constitutional principles was strong enough
to overcome any personal desire for vengeance.

For a month the President hesitated to move on reconstruction. Undoubtedly his desire was to guarantee fulfillment of the twin purposes of
the war: restoration of the Union and abolition of slavery. Military victory
accomplished both objectives, but did not determine the methods to be
used in restoring states or freeing slaves. Nor did it solve the fundamental
difference between the President and the Congress as to control of reconstruction. By the summer of 1865 many Northerners had accepted equality
before the law, particularly in the South, as a third war aim and they fore-

saw the necessity of national legislation to prevent the former planter-aristocrats from denying citizenship rights to freedmen and the mass of southern white people.

The Presidential Plan

Before the end of May the President found his solution to these problems and, thereafter, clung stubbornly to his policies. Like Lincoln, Johnson thought reconstruction an executive rather than a legislative function. Unlike his predecessor, however, he demonstrated no willingness to compromise or to consider restoring the southern states as a joint function of President and Congress. The long congressional recess gave him six months to re-establish loyal governments before the regular session in December and enabled him to present functioning states to Congress.

Since, in Johnson's opinion, secession had always been null and void, the southern states remained in the Union. Thus far he went with his compatriots below the Mason-Dixon Line, but he rejected their simple solution to reunion—namely, the election of state officials and federal senators and representatives who would resume their seats in Congress as though the past four years had never been. The President demanded evidence of southern governments elected by loyal men. The abolition of slavery presented no great difficulty. The peculiar institution of the South had been dealt fatal blows by military conquest and executive proclamation. State constitutional provisions and an amendment to the Constitution legalized its demise. Equality, the third war aim, he rejected except for suggesting the advisability of allowing Negroes, qualified by property holdings or educational attainments, to vote.

Johnson believed his essential duty lay in identifying loyal citizens in the South and directing their creation of state governments. On May 9, in a proclamation relating specifically to Virginia, he declared rebel authority in the southern states null and void and recognized the governments established by Lincoln in Virginia, Arkansas, Louisiana, and Tennessee. Most congressmen considered this action a tribute to the memory of Lincoln. Twenty days later another presidential proclamation clearly identified Johnson with the lenient policies of his martyred predecessor.

In this proclamation of May 29, he accepted almost in toto the amnesty ideas of Lincoln. Johnson offered pardons to all former rebels except those falling into fourteen categories in return for their taking a simple oath of allegiance. The notable addition to Lincoln's exceptions were Southerners who possessed taxable property assessed at $20,000 or more. All persons denied pardons by the proclamation were promised clemency "liberally extended" on special application to the President. Thousands of Southerners gave their oaths to federal military officers, or in many instances to county officials, and requests for pardons filled the presidential mail. Many Southerners requested pardons with mental reservations. Among them was Josiah Gorgas who wrote in his diary: "pardon for having done my duty in the cause I deemed the best on earth! But conquerers have a right to dictate terms and ours have not been magnanimous." Perhaps the erstwhile tailor's apprentice, Johnson, received a personal satisfaction from the appeals of southern aristocrats. Nevertheless, he granted pardons liberally; and on December 25, 1865, he gave amnesty for all offenses of treason during the Civil War and restored all rights, privileges, and immunities under the Constitution and the laws of the United States to ex-Confederates.

In other proclamations, and especially in his December 6, 1865, message to Congress, the President explained his reconstruction policies. Under the supervision of presidentially appointed provisional governors, citizens of southern states were to take an oath of allegiance, register for voting, and elect delegates to constitutional conventions. The important evidence of loyalty was future support of the Union. Johnson said nothing about Lincoln's 10 per cent of the number of voters in 1860, for he assumed that a majority of white males would take the oath of allegiance. In this respect the President bowed to a principle of the Wade-Davis Bill. The constitutional conventions were to declare secession null and void, repudiate state war and currency debts, recognize all laws passed by the United States since 1860, and abolish slavery. Determination of the qualifications of voters and the eligibility of citizens for officeholding was left to the state conventions. After writing a constitution, and its acceptance in a general vote, a state would proceed to elect state officials and federal congressmen in a state-wide election. At its first meeting, a state legislature was to ratify the Thirteenth Amendment. Then, supposedly, state senators and representatives would be seated in Congress and the civic authority would supplant provisional governors and military rule in the South.

Despite the entry by Gorgas in his diary, and similar opinions held by other Southerners, the presidential demands on those who had rebelled against their national government were lenient. Except for recognition of realities brought on by military defeat, Johnson offered Southerners control of their state and local governments. No provision in his reconstruction plans prevented the continuation of a South dominated by white people or demanded real punishment for rebellion.

The Presidential Plan in Action

On May 29, Johnson appointed William H. Holden provisional governor of North Carolina, and within less than two months chose Benjamin

F. Perry for South Carolina, James Johnson for Georgia, William Marvin for Florida, Lewis E. Parsons for Alabama, William L. Sharkey for Mississippi, and Andrew J. Hamilton for Texas. These men were Southerners by birth or long residence and had opposed secession. In making his appointments the President heeded the recommendations of northern financial and mercantile leaders and conservative Southerners. As a result, the governors pleased northern businessmen and generally won the approval of Southerners. The provisional governors urged former Confederates to recognize the results of the war and give the freedmen justice, and told ex-slaves to assume the responsibilities of free men. Southern newspaper editors advocated co-operation with the military forces and the provisional governors to achieve the speedy recovery of their states.

These provisional administrations combined civil and military governments. On appointment of a provisional governor, the old Confederate or rebellion governors, legislators, and other civil officials would cease to function, but the provisional governor immediately continued in office local officials—judges, tax collectors, sheriffs, and county commissioners—who could and would take the oath of allegiance. In addition to the provisional governor, every state had a military governor whose primary duty was to command the army and enforce martial law. Although tremendous authority resided in the military, it was seldom used and martial law affected the lives of few people. While the military governor kept order, the provisional executive was to direct processes designed to establish regular and loyal state units.

Other federal agencies co-operated with the governors to restore national authority and services in the South. Post offices and mail routes were placed in operation by the postmaster general, customhouses and internal revenue offices were opened by the secretary of the treasury, and federal courts were called into session by the attorney general. Johnson directed his secretary of the treasury and postmaster general to give loyal Southerners preference in officeholding and appoint residents of other states only when qualified Southerners could not be found.

After Southerners took the oath of allegiance and registered at precincts, the provisional governors set dates for electing delegates to constitutional conventions. Voting eligibility and election districts followed ante-bellum rules and geographical divisions, and frequently the loyal male citizens selected former leaders of the Old South and erstwhile Confederates to write new state constitutions. For the most part the delegates adhered to presidential directives at the constitutional conventions. Neither the abolition of slavery nor recognition of federal laws passed since 1860 met serious opposition, but a few conventions repealed ordinances of secession rather than declaring them null and void and some delegates attempted to scale down state war debts and currency rather than repudiate them. Insistence by Johnson forced recalcitrant delegates to accept repudiation.

Basically the new constitutions were replicas of prewar documents. Freedmen gained some privileges—freedom of movement, the right to testify in courts whenever they were parties of concern, and guarantees in property transactions and contracts. Constitutions not only failed to enfranchise Negroes with property holdings or educational attainments but a few contained provisions prohibiting "persons of color" from voting.

Some democratic advances were achieved. Property qualifications for officeholding were eliminated, formerly appointive positions became elective, and South Carolina transferred the election of presidential electors from the legislature to the people. The three-fifths compromise of the Constitution in counting the Negro population for representation was retained, but by refusing to count Negroes for state representative apportionments, the predominately white regions of Alabama and South Carolina gained influence at their state capitals.

On completing the constitutions, the conventions submitted their work for voter reaction. In most states the electorate expressed opinion on the new constitution and at the same time elected a governor, senators, and representatives. Political leaders assumed the constitutions would be accepted and the restoration of a commonwealth in the Union would be speeded by electing state officers and representatives to the United States House of Representatives. While the number of white southern registrants and voters was smaller than in 1860, the decrease was attributable more to manpower losses in war than to apathy or the relatively few men denied political rights. Not only were the constitutions approved but also many former leaders of ante-bellum and Confederate years won high positions in the state governments.

Candidates for office ran as conservatives rather than Democrats or Republicans. This white solidarity was planned by Southerners to achieve unity among former Democrats, Whigs, secessionists, and unionists. Often at the head of a state ticket, and running without opposition for the governorship, was an erstwhile Whig or Constitutional Unionist with a record of opposition to secession but service to the Confederacy. Many individuals who had once held office as Democrats ran for cabinet, legislative, and other positions in state governments. Most successful candidates were old Whigs, but generally the election results indicated southern determination to retain a traditional civilization and rely on men with political and military experience.

The constitutions and the number of ex-Confederates elected to office angered northern editors. *Harper's Weekly* and the *New-York Tribune* criticized the constitutional conventions for doing nothing not absolutely required of them by the President. Liberals interpreted some constitutional provisions as blueprints for developing a labor system intermediate between slavery and freedom. The Mississippi constitution directed future legislatures to enact laws for freedmen which would "guard them and the State against any evils that may arise from their sudden emancipation." Other southern states copied these words and Northerners feared passage of laws to limit the personal and economic rights of Negroes. On August 19, 1865, the moderate *New York Times* warned the South that the sentiment of the northern people was "firmly fixed upon this moral necessity for securing complete protection of the freedmen. . . . The Northern congressmen will insist. Unless the South gives it, the result may be continued military government and other painful consequences."

Harper's Weekly demanded an explanation for the South's failure to enfranchise the Negro. At this time eight American states allowed Negro suffrage and four of these (Massachusetts, Rhode Island, New York, and Delaware) severely restricted it by residence, tax, property, or literacy requirements. Many southern editors replied to northern criticism with editorials which counseled home rule and defiance and belittled the consequences of independent legislative action. In contrast, Representative Stevens and Senator Sumner declared the southern elections dishonored the Union soldier and proved the determination of the South to keep the Negro in chains. The federal armies had allowed Southerners to surrender too soon, Sumner thought, and he viewed the election of former Confederates as acts of defiance by a disloyal people.

Notwithstanding bitter words, the southern states quickly complied with presidential directives. Before January 1866, every state except Texas wrote and adopted new constitutions; and legislatures convened at state capitals and ratified the Thirteenth Amendment. Only Mississippi rejected the amendment on the ground that her constitution abolished slavery and ratification would give the federal government excuse for interference in state government. Southern senates chose United States senators, who, with elected representatives, went to Washington. Full delegations from many ex-Confederate states presented their credentials to the Senate and House in December 1865, but were refused seats while Congress investigated Presidential Reconstruction.

Within the states Johnson's provisional governors relinquished their offices to elected executives when the President recognized the loyal governments. Ostensibly, restoration was completed with elected governors in office, legislatures in session, and Southerners pardoned. In reality, the Johnson governments were no more than elaborate facades disguising weak houses. Military commanders could disallow state laws, limit the authority of governors, and interfere with courts; agents of the Freedmen's Bureau supervised the former slave and protected him from discriminatory laws and acts; and Congress recognized neither the states nor their representatives. By waiting until the first months of 1866 to restore the writ of *habeas corpus* and not declaring the end of the war until autumn of the same year, Johnson failed to support completely his own creations. At times he exercised his authority as commander-in-chief to check excessive interference by military commanders and he strove ineptly to influence Congress.

The South in 1865

Both the physical conditions within their region and the psychological attitudes of the southern people influenced the legislation enacted by the Johnson state governments. Slaveholder and small farmer, who had always feared servile insurrection and believed the institution of slavery a necessary agency of control, demanded laws to curb the expected and dreaded licentiousness of freedmen. Poor, illiterate Negroes without training for responsibility pondered the meaning of freedom. Owners of devastated farms lacked money to finance rehabilitation or to feed their families through the long growing season. Human losses of war and the abolition of the controlled labor system made farm laborers a critical need.

Federal and private agencies anticipated the material necessities of the South. On March 3, 1865, the Congress authorized "a Bureau for the Relief of Freedmen and Refugees." Given life for the duration of the war and one year thereafter, the Freedmen's Bureau became the national government's most important agency of relief and rehabilitation. Empowered to call on the war department for provisions, clothing, and fuel to supply immediate and temporary assistance to freedmen and loyal white refugees, the Bureau gave millions of rations to the destitute of both races. In the months following the collapse of the Confederacy, it saved hundreds of thousands from acute hunger and many from starvation. Freedmen and refugees were assigned as many as forty acres of abandoned lands and supplied with farm implements and seed for agricultural production. Bureau agents persuaded or forced ex-slaves to return to or remain on farms and to sign labor contracts. Although the paramount concern was protection of the freedmen, in operation the Bureau often worked to the advantage of landholders in supplying them with low-cost labor. The remarkably large harvests in 1865 were certainly attributable in part to the Freedmen's Bureau.

A second activity of the national government restored railway service in the South. During the war federal commanders seized the roads within conquered areas, and for a few months after cessation of hostilities the United States controlled all southern railroads. Necessity rather than generosity forced the federal government to act. Moving and supplying troops stationed in interior regions depended on the railroads. On essential lines the government rebuilt roadbeds, tracks, and bridges; added freight and passenger cars to rolling equipment; and supplied sidings and stations. By presidential order the railroads were returned to private ownership in August. The federal government paid for military usage and charged for improvements at 7½ per cent interest with payments extended over many years. Most southern railroads paid these obligations, but by delays and appeals to courts some companies won reduced assessments or escaped payment. In 1871 a congressional relief act scaled down the debt and, during the Reconstruction era, railroad stockholders fared better than other industrialists and farmers.

Northern churches and relief associations supplemented federal aid. Residents of New York, Philadelphia, St. Louis, and other cities appealed for grain, money, and clothing to be distributed to impoverished Southerners. The Southern Relief Fair collected more than $100,000 in Baltimore, and distant California contributed $45,000 in assistance. Within two years approximately $3 million was given in the northern and border states. Religious organizations helped to rehabilitate sister churches in the South as many missionaries and schoolteachers left their homes for service at small pay in southern pulpits and schoolhouses. Publishing houses sent thousands of elementary textbooks to alleviate a great need.

Federal aid and private relief, added to state grants and largess of Southerners prevented most acute personal suffering. Landowners and laborers cultivated the soil; vessels plied the waters and stevedores unloaded cargoes; merchants sold and bartered their goods, and factories resumed operations. Demand for cotton, grain, and tobacco put the South in business again.

Remolding ideas required more intelligent action than restoring production: southern Negroes and whites were enigmas to themselves as well as to Northerners. The latter believed that abolition not only released the slave from bondage but also endowed the freedman with virtue and ambition.

In contrast, the Southerner, living beside Negroes and familiar with their habits, thought he could properly evaluate the freedmen. Most Southerners considered the Negro biologically inferior to Caucasians and that this natural limitation made the freedman irresponsible, lazy, thieving, and licentious—a person requiring white supervision to prevent his return to barbarism and needing rigid police control to restrain him from rapine and murder. In reality neither Southerner nor Northerner knew or understood the Negro.

In fact the vast majority of former slaves demonstrated a surprising stability and industry in view of their training and experience. They remained on plantation and farm, willing to work for fair wages and just employers, and anxious to acquire land for economic advancement. Without the obligations imposed by legal marriage, most husbands and wives clung to one another and sought opportunity for their children. Requests for remunerative work on equitable terms, for a chance to own land, and for education came from millions of Negroes.

The nonconformist Negro who wandered to towns and cities became the subject of editorial, diary entry, and letter. Historians have quoted the statement of Stephen Mallory, the former Confederate navy secretary, that all the Negroes in West Florida had left their cabins to run wild in Pensacola, but many failed to read further in the Mallory diary or quote a later entry in which Mallory admits his description applied to less than 10 per cent of the Negro population. An Alabama census of 1866 proved that both freedman and white had moved from rural to urban communities immediately following the war, and that the percentage of Negroes was not significantly larger than that of the white people. The arrival of some freedmen in a small town or city increased tremendously the percentage of Negroes in populated centers. White urban residents and rural visitors thus apparently saw an unusually large number of Negroes loafing on streets or existing in abandoned buildings or shacks.

The precise number or percentage of former slaves who sought ease or fortune in towns will never be known. The wanderers were sufficiently numerous to create problems for police and to anger landowners who needed laborers to cultivate their crops. Moving to town was the ultimate test of freedom for many slaves, for they recalled former years when passes were necessary to exempt them from punishment for going beyond plantation boundaries. Some freedmen gained personal satisfaction from loafing away the days without fear of the overseer's command or the driver's lashes. Vagrant Negroes lacked adequate food, clothing, and shelter, but they proved their freedom. Slavery had taught them that two of the mitigating influences of a hard existence were shirking work and complete freedom from labor.

Other heritages from the slave regime plagued southern white and Negro. Pilfering from the master's abundant store of goods had given undetected culprits minor luxuries, and habits developed in slavery survived in freedom. The ease with which chickens could be moved from barnyard to frying pan made them favorite loot for light-fingered freedmen. Hogs, cattle, horses, and mules also disappeared. During the summer of 1865, owners of watermelon patches, fruit orchards, and vegetable gardens suffered from the raids. The harvest season brought cottonpicking and cornpulling under the cover of darkness and the bartering of these crops for supplies at stores. The connivance of dishonest storekeepers and the desire of impoverished farmers for draft animals at bargain prices abetted thievery, and quick consumption of edible produce made proof of theft difficult.

Rumors of free land bolstered the former slave's belief in his rights to plantation property. The use of up to forty acres per person of abandoned or confiscated lands, reports of general confiscation and distribution of land, and loose talk by army personnel and agents of the Freedmen's Bureau helped create the fiction that every Negro would have "forty acres and a mule." Unscrupulous men capitalized on the Negro's desire for land by selling him colored stakes to mark the corners of his future grant. Many illiterates clung hopefully to an official-looking paper, believing it to be a deed when in reality its words described how four dollars had been lifted from the victim. Even prospects of a cabin, forty acres, and a mule were not sufficient inducement for many of the laborers to work for wages; instead they chose a bare existence while waiting for their property, satisfied that land would provide a good life.

Idleness removed many Negroes from the South's labor force. Abolition, one southern matron wrote a friend, had deprived her of cooks and maids and destroyed her religious faith. The actual percentage of non-working Negroes was small but their number appeared large to landowners looking for laborers. Pessimistic southern white men made three predictions: the Negro would not work unless compelled, another crop would never be planted in the South by Negro labor, and the Negro race would disappear in the United States. The editor of the *Natchez Democrat* told his readers "that child is already born who will behold the last Negro in Mississippi"; without control by the superior white man, the editor prophesied that the Negro race was sure to become extinct. George Fitzhugh, whose antebellum writings furnished ammunition for abolitionists, declared that the "majority of them [Negroes] are about as well qualified to hire themselves out as Hottentots." Southerners believed what tradition had taught them and what they wanted to believe. Though accepting the fact of abolition, few admitted that slavery had been an evil, and many refused to offer ex-slaves fair wages.

The sincerity of their belief was attested by efforts to entice European laborers into the South to replace the former slaves. Famous Confederate naval hero Raphael Semmes advocated importation of Chinese coolies under the federal contract labor law. State laws encouraged forming companies to pay the fares of Europeans, and five corporations were chartered in Virginia for this purpose. The expected influx of foreign white labor was never realized. The experience of John Townsend of Edisto, South Carolina, typified the disillusionment of planters. He persuaded Germans from the North to accept his offer and reported: "They cost me $35 each to bring them from New York to Charleston. I fed them better than ever I thought of feeding my hands, even gave them coffee and sourkrout [sic] when what should they do but demand butter for their bread and milk for their coffee, and the next thing the whole crowd left me." By November 1866, Fitzhugh admitted that Southerners could not depend on European laborers and must rely entirely on Negro farm hands.

Planters faced difficulties in restoring agricultural production. Limited capital forced them into sharecropping contracts, and disagreements arose over division of the crop between landowner and sharecropper. Even when dealing with honest landlords, many a Negro refused to believe the fruits of his labor could amount to so little. Again and again the landowner complained of stealing by freedmen, of the ex-slave's demand for "his rightful share of the plantation," the independence and insolence of laborers, and the wanderings of Negroes. David Golightly Harris pitied the freedmen more than he blamed them. "They are like birds out of a cage," he reported, "and no [sic] not what to do. Ask who you may 'what are you going to do,' and their universal answer is 'I don't know.'"

In their efforts to drive the freedmen back to farms, police demolished shacks in some towns and cities. Fear of uprisings during the 1865 Christmas season led to brutal repression by public officials. With little regard for individual rights, police searched Negroes for knives, guns, and other weapons. White Southerners organized bands to regulate the freedmen, punish them for crimes, or force them to labor. Independent Negroes responded in kind and the violence practiced by both races increased the South's homicidal rate. At the end of 1865, however, most areas of the South enjoyed quiet, and the feared racial uprising never materialized.

The migration of Negroes to city and town was a temporary phenomenon and certainly not as large as contemporary accounts indicated. After first encouraging Negroes to expect free land, Freedmen's Bureau agents used their personal influence and official power to persuade and force freedmen to sign labor contracts. Army personnel laid heavy hands on vagrants to drive them from urban to rural areas. Because the supply of free food and clothing was being exhausted, wanderers settled down and sought employment. Before the agricultural season of 1866 had advanced into summer, a surprisingly large percentage of land was under cultivation and harvests promised a prosperity unknown during the last years of the war. The number of new bales of cotton on freight platforms and shipping wharves testified to the productivity of free labor. Notwithstanding the disappearance of a labor supply controlled by the lash, the South was producing, and despite wandering, thievery, and independence of the freedmen, southern agriculture was being restored.

This relative prosperity made white men revise their opinions of the free

Negro as a workman. A Galveston editor wrote: "There are men who truly complain that they cannot get hands. But they are men of known brutality or financial weakness. Sambo will not work for the man who was a cruel master, nor the one who did not pay him last year." In Mississippi, Samuel A. Agnew's "Negro Yard" was empty on January 1, 1866, because his reputation made freedmen shun him. In 1865 his offer of food and housing in return for labor had been rejected by freedmen; and, forced to pay wages, he had attempted to recoup expenses by demanding extra work. In December 1865, he was unable to sign a single field hand or domestic servant to a contract. In contrast, the David L. Yulee plantation at Archer, Florida, was surfeited with applicants who had heard of the fair treatment and regular payment received there. Evidently the freedmen quickly acquired one characteristic of free Americans. They willingly signed labor contracts whenever an employer's reputation promised fair wages, good working conditions, and opportunity for economic betterment.

Anticipating congressional investigation of southern loyalty and the treatment of freedmen, President Johnson sent prominent Northerners into the South. Beginning in the fall of 1865, Carl Schurz, Benjamin C. Truman, Chief Justice Chase, and General Grant spent periods on tour ranging from a few weeks to eight months. Denied the presidential nomination in 1864 but still hoping for it in 1868, Chase concentrated on political fence-building and favored the enfranchisement of the Negro. German-born Schurz found Southerners unrepentant, worshipping their Confederate heroes, and determined to fix the Negro's status at some intermediate point between slavery and freedom. In his opinion no civilized region of the world contained "such an accumulation of anarchial elements" as the South, and his plan for the section was a directed social and political revolution. The first step in this upheaval, and one essential for protecting the freedman, was Negro suffrage. Angered because the observer expressed his views to newspapermen before reporting to him, the President requested no report but Schurz wrote one which was later used effectively by Johnson's congressional enemies.

The other presidential representatives were pleased by the progress of the South. Truman reported Southerners pacified, loyal, and eager to resume their place in the Union. A presidential secretary and former newspaperman, Truman spent eight months in the South and was a perceptive observer. Despite his brief tour which extended only to Atlanta, General Grant's reputation gave his views national importance. "I am satisfied," he wrote, "that the mass of thinking men of the South accept the present situation of affairs in good faith." In the general's opinion, Southerners regarded slavery and secession as settled on the battlefield and believed the settlement good for all Americans. He found "universal acquiescence in the authority of the general government" throughout the areas visited, but recommended the continuance of federal troops in localities where freedmen were numerous and thought the use of white troops preferable to Negro soldiers.

An accurate report on the South would have combined the views of Schurz and Grant. Southerners accepted abolition and permanent union as the results of military victory. They did worship their Confederate military heroes and in daydreams frequently heard the thundering hoofs of victorious cavalry winning independence. Repentant they were not; but realistically they accepted the requirements of President Johnson, complained of his harshness and were oblivious to his leniency. The white Southerner completely rejected the idea of the freedmen attaining or being allowed social, economic, and political equality. He never questioned the Caucasian's biological superiority over other races and this conviction made him determined to establish southern governments by, for, and of white people. Although violence and extra-legal means of controlling the ex-slave were disliked by the best southern families, their primary concern for white solidarity overcame their pacific inclinations and desire for justice under law. At the end of 1865 the South remained troubled, but she was well on her way to tranquility and economic recovery under the liberal terms of Presidential Reconstruction.

The Black Codes

The first legislative sessions of the Johnson state governments shattered all promise for swift sectional harmony. From the southern point of view, a legal code for the freedmen was absolutely necessary. Emancipation multiplied the number of "free persons of color" sixteenfold, from roughly 250,000 to 4 million people. Freedom, however, neither conferred citizenship on the ex-slave nor defined his rights in a free society. Traditionally the determination of rights and obligation of citizens, marriage and divorce laws, duties of parents and care of children, crime and punishment, and trials and court procedures rested with state government. In southern opinion the free Negro needed tutelage and the white must be protected from the freedman by strict enforcement of a legal code.

Most of Western Christendom believed in the biological superiority of the Caucasian over all other races and this conviction alone warranted continuation of white domination in the South. Furthermore, a comparison of the white man's education, economic status, and political experience with similar attainments of the Negro left no doubt, in the opinion of whites, as to the rightful rulers of southern society. In addition the apparent propensity of some freedmen for idleness and criminal activities necessitated laws to prevent vagrancy and police authority to curb theft, rapine, and murder. The white Southerner never pointed to the lack of training or education as possible sources of the Negro's actions; he held ignorance, loafing, and criminality characteristic of the race and sought means to correct or suppress them. Southern economic survival depended on agricultural laborers, and the white man "knew" the Negro would not work unless compelled. The old built-in racial controls of the slave regime disappeared with abolition and protection had to be provided for women and property. The widespread fear of an uprising of freedmen during the 1865 holiday season demanded legislation to nip an insurrection in the bud.

Models for codes existed in history and practice. Historically the free Negro of the Old South, and of the ante-bellum North, had been a second-class citizen existing under restrictive laws laid down by the dominant white. Continuation of a former system and its application to a tremendously increased number of free persons of color seemed logical. Legal codes of northern states had set precedents for handling vagrants and apprentices. Both Freedmen's Bureau agents and army officers approved of rules to compel Negroes to sign labor contracts and fulfill the agreements. Corporal punishment in lieu of costly imprisonment was not unknown in America. Obviously the moral and sexual standards of the white man should be imposed upon the Negro and the legal intermixture of the races prohibited. Compilation of a code for freedmen entailed more borrowing than innovation.

In their opinions about freedmen, Northerners were even more unrealistic than Southerners. Most Northerners believed temporary aid, educational opportunity, and political rights sufficient to uplift the freedmen. Some Northerners advocated wholesale confiscation of southern-owned land, or other action to give the Negro an economic start; but the businessman's respect for rights in property, except the ownership of human beings, doomed all such plans for economic aid. Northern anger, however, could be fired to white heat by reports of physical violence to the Negro or the enactment of discriminatory laws applicable by intent only to the freedmen.

The rural Mississippi legislators who passed the first "Black Code" of the Reconstruction era gave no consideration to northern public opinion. Their purpose was the continuance of white supremacy in a state containing more Negroes than white people. The idea of Negro control was too absurd to deserve thought by Mississippi legislators who assumed the state would forever be the province of white citizens. Other than necessary recognition of abolition, the problem was protecting the white minority from the "innate bestiality" of the Negro race.

Neither Mississippi nor any other former Confederate state labeled its black code or codified its enactments relating to the free Negro. These laws appeared in statutory records as a series of acts under the headings of civil rights of freedmen, the penal code, vagrancy, or apprenticeship. While some legislation named the Negro or the freedman, most laws apparently applied to both races of the South. The range of penalties for crimes gave the police and judges wide interpretative powers which could result in severe racial discrimination.

The Mississippi code gave freedmen certain rights and recognized existing marital relationship. Negroes could sue and be sued in courts of law and equity and acquire personal property. They could testify in all civil and criminal cases where they were parties of concern. All freedmen living together as man and wife became legally married, their children legitimate, and the parents obligated for care and support of offspring. For both participants the penalty for racial intermarriage was life imprisonment in the state penitentiary.

The need for agricultural workers was reflected in labor contract and vagrancy laws. Contracts made with "freedmen, free Negroes, and mulattoes" for one month or longer were to be in writing and read to the laborer by a governmental official or two disinterested white persons. If the employee left the service of his employer without cause before the termination date of the contract, his wages would be forfeited. In addition private citizens and public officials could arrest any fugitive from a contract and receive payments of five dollars per day and ten cents per mile for transportation. Although this reward was to be paid by the employer, he could assess the cost against the laborer's wages. The Mississippi vagrancy law declared that:

> All rogues and vagabonds, idle and dissipated persons, beggars, jugglers, or persons practicing unlawful games or plays, runaways, common drunkards, common night-walkers, pilferers, lewd, wanton, or lascivious persons in speech or behavior, common railers and brawlers, persons who neglect their calling or employment, misspend what they earn, or do not provide for the support of themselves or their families, or dependents, and all other idle and disorderly persons, including all who neglect all lawful business, habitually misspend their time by frequenting houses of ill-fame, gaming-houses, or tippling shops, shall be deemed and considered vagrants . . . and upon conviction thereof shall be fined not exceeding one hundred dollars, with all accruing costs, and be imprisoned at the discretion of the court, not exceeding ten days.

This legislation was supplemented by a provision classifying as vagrants all freedmen, eighteen years of age and older, without employment on the second Monday of January 1866, and annually thereafter, subject to maximum fines of $50 and ten days' imprisonment. The penalties for a white man, vagrant or employed, mixing in Negro society or living with a freed woman were set at $200 and six months' imprisonment. Any freedman, free Negro, or mulatto refusing to pay the fine levied under the vagrancy laws was to be hired out at enforced labor until he earned a sufficient wage to pay the fine and court costs.

The apprentice law applied to all Negroes under eighteen years who were orphans or whose parents could not or would not provide support. Based on semi-annual reports of sheriffs and justices of the peace, county probate clerks were to apprentice minors to suitable persons on terms determined by the court. Preference was to be given to former masters in the assignment of apprentices, but the interest of the latter was to be "a particular care" of the court. Safeguards protected the apprentice: bonds, payable to the state, were required of masters to guarantee food, clothing, humane treatment, medical care, and elementary education; and corporal punishment was restricted to that allowed by law to parents and guardians in disciplining their children and wards. The law contained no provision for court inspection or supervision of the master-apprentice relationship. By running away, the apprentice could obtain a court hearing and release from an unjust master or be returned to the service of a just one.

Authority for enforcing these laws and restraining the Negro came from a comprehensive penal code. Unless licensed by the police, no civilian freedman could own or carry guns of any kind, ammunition, dirk, or bowie knife. "Any freedman, free Negro, or mulatto committing riots, routs, affrays, trespasses, malicious mischief, cruel treatment to animals, seditious speeches, insulting gestures, language, or acts, or assaults on any person, disturbance of the peace, exercising the function of a minister of the Gospel without a license from some regularly organized church, vending spirituous or intoxicating liquors, or committing any other misdemeanor, the punishment of which is not specifically provided for by law" could be fined ten to one hundred dollars and a maximum of thirty days' imprisonment. Any convicted freedman who failed or refused to pay his fine and court costs could be hired out to "any white person who will pay said fine and all costs, and take said convict for the shortest time."

Until a storm of protest swept down from the North, Mississippi editors hailed the black code as a magnificent achievement of statesmen. Critics ignored beneficial provisions of the laws and concentrated on vagrancy, apprenticeship to former masters, and auctioning convicted freedmen to the highest white bidder. Northern politicians and newspapermen declared that Mississippi was determined to re-enslave the Negro. General Oliver O. Howard instructed his Freedmen's Bureau agents to disregard the law which prohibited Negroes from renting or leasing agricultural land. In January 1866, the army commander negated all racial discriminatory provisions of the laws. Only then did some Mississippi editors condemn the code as the enactment of foolish, if not stupid men.

Shortly after passage of the Mississippi code, the South Carolina legislature completed a more detailed, more comprehensive, and in some respects a more discriminatory one. Under one of its provisions, no freedman could work as an artisan or mechanic without serving a long apprenticeship, and a $100 license was required of a Negro shopkeeper or peddler. The South Carolina code was drawn up by two of the state's eminent justices, who saw no objection to hiring out or whipping Negroes but declared these punishments too degrading for white people.

Before Louisiana acted, her legislators evidently heeded northern criticism of the Mississippi and South Carolina codes. Though severe in many respects, the Louisiana code was relatively mild on vagrancy, trespass, and apprenticeship. Some towns, especially Opelousas and Franklin, more than counteracted the lenient aspects of the state laws by excessively harsh city codes. In Alabama, vetoes by the governor as well as the commendable deportment of the freedmen during the Christmas holidays discouraged enactment of drastic laws.

The codes of 1865, enacted when Southerners needed laborers and still feared an insurrection by freedmen, were by and large harsh, discriminatory, and indiscreet. In addition to the braking force of northern criticism and official countermanding of codes, the movement of Negroes from towns and cities to farms early in 1866 indicated the willingness of former wanderers to accept work. Quiet, rather than the predicted holiday uprising of Negroes, convinced many legislators that the restrictive laws once considered essential were unnecessary. These influences affected consideration or passage of black codes in all but one of the other seven states.

The exception was Florida. After the war the movement of Negroes into this least populous of the former Confederate states made their number almost equal to that of the white people. In some counties of middle Florida, the politically dominant section, freedmen outnumbered whites. These facts account in part for a voluminous report, ridiculous in its pompous bigotry, written by a three-man committee authorized by the 1865 Constitutional Convention to prepare legislation for the freedmen. The report described slavery as a benign institution and the happiest and best system ever devised for a laboring class. Its only evil was the inadequately regulated sex life of slaves, and as many of the good features of slavery as possible should be preserved in the new order.

The committee report was received by legislators contemptuous of the freedman, and in their subsequent action they ignored both the warnings of Governor Marvin and northern reaction to the black codes of Mississippi and South Carolina. The Florida laws made death the penalty for burglary, insurrection, attempted poisoning, and rape, or accessory thereto, of a white female. Especially rigorous was the definition and punishment for vagrancy. Rather than fines and imprisonment for many misdemeanors, thirty-nine lashes and one hour in the pillory could be imposed on convicted freedmen. All Negroes living together as man and wife were given nine months to choose legal marriage or permanent separation; but, whatever their decision, responsibility for children remained with the parents. Schools were authorized for freedmen and then negated by a stipulation that they should be of no expense to the state.

The other former Confederate states passed relatively mild black codes or skipped them. Virginia was as conservative and discreet as Florida was radical and rash. In the Georgia legislature the vindictive and bigoted men were outnumberd by conciliatory and humane legislators. Extreme bills died in committee or met defeat on the floor of house or senate. Punishment for many crimes was reduced, but penalties were increased for offenses expected to be typical of freedmen, and whipping and hiring out were authorized. North Carolina enacted no black code. While certain of its laws could be interpreted to discriminate against Negroes, their phraseology indicated the same treatment for freedmen and white citizens. Texas spelled out more specific guarantees and protections for Negroes than any other southern state. Only in labor contract legislation and in the wide latitude of punishment for crimes were Texas laws inequitable. The Arkansas legislature met once between January 3, 1865, and November 5, 1866, for a twenty-day session to ratify the Thirteenth Amendment. The state's antebellum laws were reaffirmed and all freedmen living together as man and wife were legally married. In 1867 the legislature prohibited racial intermarriage, Negro voting and jury service, and interracial schools.

In Tennessee the radicals * and their Governor Brownlow were enigmatic in speech and action. In the governor's opinion "good Southern men who through raping, arson, perjury and butchery, have filled the land with mourning" were entitled neither to mercy nor forbearance. But he also declared, "if there is anything a loyal Tennessean hates more than a rebel, it is a nigger." For Brownlow, abolition was a punishment for rebels rather than a gain for Negroes. Late in 1865 a rigorous black code passed the Tennessee House of Representatives by a 38-to-18 vote, with fourteen of the eighteen men opposing technicalities in the laws instead of principles. Northern protests and pressure on senators delayed action until 1866 when a mild code was enacted.

Southern apologists gloss over the black codes with various explanations.

* The northern Radical and the southern one were not the same. To distinguish them, the southern will be referred to as radical, the northern as Radical.

A minority of the eleven former Confederate states passed particularly discriminatory laws, and the Negro population of these states was larger than or almost equal to that of the white people. The lawmakers of these states believed that the freedman's lack of preparation for the responsibilities of a free society necessitated laws to prevent idleness and vagrancy, curb or punish crimes, and provide legal codes for 4 million people formerly classified as property. The codes stemmed from experience with free Negroes and slaves, the rules and regulations of the United States War Department, Russia's treatment of her serfs, Great Britain's laws applying to West Indian Negroes, and apprenticeship and vagrancy legislation of northern states.

No explanation can hide the harshness, the intent, and the political stupidity of some southern legislators in enacting the codes. By reputation Southerners were master strategists in political warfare. Their discriminatory racial laws, added to their earlier mistakes, relegated them to the status of novice among amateurs. Consideration and passage of the Mississippi and South Carolina codes occurred at the most inopportune time for the defeated South. On November 14, 1865, a banner headline of the *New-York Tribune* accused South Carolina of re-establishing slavery. A correspondent of the moderate *New York Times* declared the state's legislation "might not inappropriately be styled a bloody code." Representative Burton C. Cook of Illinois asked, "Can we now place the freedmen in the uncontrolled power of their former masters? The Negro codes enacted by the reconstruction Legislatures of Mississippi and South Carolina are our sufficient answer. . . ."

Northern newspapers printed excerpts of the laws along with critical comments and repeatedly used "odious," "vicious," and "terrible" in describing the codes. Few editors gave space to laws other than those of Mississippi and South Carolina and almost none reported the protective provisions or good features of the later codes. Newspapermen and federal officials distorted the laws or their meaning and, by intent or error, accused states of passing acts never placed on their statutory records. These black codes gave Radicals a golden opportunity for propaganda and they effectively used the gift presented by Southerners.

The purposes of the codes were to force freedmen to support themselves and at the same time supply landowners with labor, protect the property and persons of white people, and establish a body of law for millions of ex-slaves. In totality the codes softened the ante-bellum legal controls over the free Negro, made them applicable to the freedmen, and provided certain protections for Negroes while safeguarding white supremacy. Southerners definitely planned second-class citizenship for the freedmen, for in neither the prewar North nor South had free Negroes enjoyed equality with white people.

National and sectional experience and the postwar acts of federal authorities indicated the continuation of established inequalities. At first Commissioner Howard approved the severe contract labor law of Mississippi's Black Code. At the moment of disallowing all the state's laws not applicable equally to both races, General Sickles ordered his lieutenants to formulate suitable regulations for hiring out vagrants. The *New York Times* berated the North Carolina legislature for adjourning in December 1865, without passing laws "for the government or protection of the freedmen . . . the great question of the day."

The black codes were not a conspiracy by Southerners to restore slavery, but some of them were unnecessarily harsh and foolish acts by a conquered people seeking restoration of their states to the Union. The codes were products of anachronistic and emotional attitudes, the baneful heritage of a slave system which deeply rooted in southern minds false conceptions of the Negro—his biological inferiority, his innate criminality, and his refusal to work except under compulsion. The old fear of insurrection, too, survived emancipation to motivate restrictive laws.

Despite the severity of their codes, a reasonable defense can be made for the action of Mississippi and South Carolina legislators. They acted in accord with past experience and current practice. Praiseworthy was the reaction by southern politicians, except those of Florida, to northern criticism and the mild codes drawn after they realized the extent of northern opposition. The Mississippi legislators who authored the Black Code of 1865 repealed its objectionable features the following year. Only Floridians remained bigoted, vindictive, and shortsighted. Although the state's attorney general reported unconstitutional a law prohibiting possession of firearms by freedmen and Governor David S. Walker requested its repeal, the legislature retained it in an act of defiance directed at the "fanatical theorists" of the North.

The black codes never served the purposes intended by their sponsors, but they did influence American history. Counter-orders by army and Bureau officials and repeal by state legislatures nullified the codes except for a short time and in isolated southern localities. A later generation of Southerners, however, revived and used some principles of the codes to relegate Negroes to second-class American citizenship. While the black codes did not father Congressional Reconstruction, they became a powerful weapon in the arsenal of congressmen desiring to discredit Presidential Reconstruction and win national support for congressional policies.

REFERENCES

Good sources for this chapter and for chapters III, IV, and V are the biographies and political studies cited in the General Historiography and Bibliography: Winston, Stryker, and Lomask on Johnson; Brodie, *Thaddeus Stevens;* Jellison, *Fessenden;* Thomas and Hyman, *Stanton;* Trefouse, *Wade;* Krug, *Trumbull,* and West, *Butler;* and McKitrick, *Johnson and Reconstruction;* John and LaWanda Cox, *Politics, Principle, and Prejudice;* and Brock, *American Crisis.*

The Washington *Chronicle,* April 3–16, 1865, carried many reports of activities in the capital, in other northern cities, and in Richmond.

The standard works on pardons and oaths are Jonathan T. Dorris, *Pardon and Amnesty under Lincoln and Johnson* (Chapel Hill, 1953), and Harold M. Hyman, *Era of the Oath* (Philadelphia, 1954). William A. Dunning, "More Light on Andrew Johnson," *American Historical Review,* XI (1906), pp. 574–94, shows that George Bancroft wrote Johnson's first message to Congress and that the President relied on non-cabinet members for advice. Willard Hays, "Andrew Johnson's Reputation," *The East Tennessee Historical Society's Publications,* XXXI (1959), pp. 1–31, reviews historians' interpretations of Johnson. George R. Bentley, *A History of the Freedmen's Bureau* (Philadelphia, 1955), is the best complete study of the federal agency. John and LaWanda Cox, "General O. O. Howard and the Misrepresented Bureau," *Journal of Southern History,* XIX (1953), pp. 427–56, give a more sympathetic treatment. Theodore B. Wilson, *The Black Codes of the South* (Tuscaloosa, 1966), analyzes the controversial codes.

The Politics of Indecision

DURING almost two years of Presidential Reconstruction, northern public opinion and Republican congressmen responded in various ways to political stimuli. Despite periodic change, citizen and legislator moved gradually from supporting lenient policies to advocating rigorous programs in reconstructing the former Confederate states. After the assassination of Lincoln many Northerners questioned the advisability of accepting the martyred President's magnanimous program for restoration of the conquered states. These dubious Americans followed closely the course of Presidential Reconstruction in the South. The actual and reported mistreatment of freedmen, the reluctance of former rebels to accept some of the moderate policies of Johnson, certain provisions of southern state constitutions, the election of former secessionists and Confederates to office, and the black codes alienated northern men of good will.

As time passed, these Northerners demanded more than submissive words and oaths of allegiance from Southerners. The victors knew the South had been conquered but they wanted a national security greater than that embodied in military defeat. They asked for repentance, admission that secession was wrong, and the elimination of the old type of Southerner from political life. They craved positive action—the elevation of southern Unionists and the downgrading of former secessionists, in addition to the repudiation of slavery, guarantees of the freedmen's personal and legal rights, and welcome to Northerners who visited or took up residence in the South. Their military power had conquered the body of the South. Northerners also wanted the mind of the vanquished region. On the other hand, past experience had not taught Southerners how to submit to authority, for Americans had never been conquered in war. In the years following the Civil War the people of the North and South were feeling each other out and understanding was hampered by a lack of communication on both sides.

The long legislative hiatus between the collapse of the Confederacy and the opening session of the Thirty-Ninth Congress in December 1865, prevented congressional approval or disapproval of the President's policies.

Had Johnson called Congress into special session, the legislators would have accomplished little. Notwithstanding the overwhelming majorities they enjoyed in the Senate and House of Representatives, the Republicans were not united and had no definite reconstruction program for the South.

Parties and Political Factions

For sixty years before the Civil War the Democrats and their ideological predecessors, the Jeffersonian Republicans, had suffered few political defeats. But secession and war reduced the formerly powerful Democrats to an impotent minority in Congress. In 1865 the party held less than one-third of the seats in Congress and New Jersey was the only northern state with a Democratic governor. In preparation for fall elections in eight states which had gubernatorial contests in 1865, the Democratic conventions vigorously supported President Johnson. Their platforms declared all ordinances of secession null and void, claimed the southern states still members of the Union, demanded speed in restoring those states to their former status, opposed Negro suffrage, and called for magnanimity in dealing with the southern people. In all eight states of the North, including New Jersey, the Democrats lost as their party plummeted to the lowest depths of its history.

The future of the Democratic party depended on restoring the southern states to full participation in the Union as quickly as possible. Party leaders talked of state rights, of white supremacy in North and South, and of forgiveness. They urged the President to return to his old party; they supported and praised him at every opportunity. In a period of uncertainty, the Democrats took pride in pointing to Johnson's action and in contrasting it with the inaction of the Republicans. In effect, the minority party claimed Johnson and asserted that Presidential Reconstruction was the policy of the Democratic party. Quick restoration of the southern states and the admission of their representatives and senators to Congress would bolster the Democratic party. While the Civil War had been a Republican war and victory, the Democrats could win the peace and regain their former strength by a political reunion of the South and West.

The Republican party, however, had appeal for voters and powerful weapons to use against its opponents. For decades the fighting boys in blue, the martyred Lincoln, the restored Union, and the flag were to be symbols of the Grand Old Party. The vacant chair around the dining table and the empty bed were personal reminders of the sacrifices made by husbands or sons to save the Union. All were personalized as the principles of the Republican party, rooting these principles in emotion and making them easily understood. Republican leaders also personalized the principles of the Democrats, picturing them as the autocratic slaveowner with the bloodstained lash, the unrepentant rebel, and the traitorous Copperhead. The memorials and shrines to valor erected in town and city and the members of the Grand Army of the Republic were to keep alive the virtues of Republicanism.

These assets were mainly potential ones in 1865 as the Republicans questioned the course of Presidential Reconstruction. The President still belonged to them, not the Democrats, and his policies could become those of the Republican party. Some Republicans supported Johnson on the rationale that the southern states had never been out of the Union and that the rights of states remained unimpaired. They found justification for their stand in the principles enunciated in the Constitution and believed the states remained supreme in many political areas including the control of the suffrage. Other Republican representatives favored immediate and unconditional restoration of the southern states to the Union. They praised the Democrats for their stand on reconstructing the former Confederate states and were ready to cast their votes in support of President Johnson's policies. Within the cabinet, Seward, Gideon Welles, and Hugh McCulloch were partisan followers of the President. Outside the cabinet, the able Charles Francis Adams, who had won accolades as wartime minister in Great Britain, and General Sherman favored immediate readmission of the southern states.

These men, however, were not spokesmen for the Republican party in 1865 and their influence was negligible within party councils. They were overshadowed by the moderate Republicans who composed the majority faction of the party. These moderates sought a conservative solution to the problem of reconstruction, favored quick readmission of the southern states but demanded some controls to protect the nation against a reoccurrence of treason. They advocated no enforced social revolution in the South but were unwilling to allow former secessionists and Confederates to resume regional or national political leadership. For them the leading rebels should be branded with infamy, rejected and despised for a generation. Prominent in the moderate ranks were senators William Pitt Fessenden of Maine, Lyman Trumbull of Illinois, James W. Grimes of Iowa, Edwin Morgan of New York, William Stewart of Nevada, and John Sherman of Ohio; and representatives James G. Blaine of Maine, Henry L. Dawes of Massachusetts, Elihu Washburne of Illinois, and James A. Garfield, John Bingham, and Rutherford B. Hayes of Ohio. Governors Oliver Perry Morton of Indiana and John A. Andrew of Massachusetts stood on moderate principles similar to those of Attorney General James Speed, Postmaster General William Dennison, and Secretary of the Interior James Harlan. Non-officeholders within the moderate Republican councils were Henry Ward Beecher, minister; and editors William Curtis of *Harper's Weekly,* Edwin L. Godkin of *The Nation,* and George R. Sterns of the *Boston Advertiser.*

These leaders were not unified in their ideas or course of action. Some joined with Senator Trumbull in believing that the Republican party should prevent the freedmen from being tyrannized, abused, and virtually re-enslaved by their former masters. Henry Ward Beecher looked with suspicion on Southerners whose ideas of honor had embraced slavery. These moderates feared that the tricky Southerners would try every means to win the fruits of victory from the nation and considered it their right to impose terms upon and demand guarantees from the vanquished. Their nearest approach to unity appeared in their demands for preservation of the fruits of victory and guarantees for the future loyalty of Southerners. If assured that President Johnson's policies would establish loyal southern governments headed by patriots rather than unrepentant rebels, the moderate Republicans would restore the states to their former places in the Union and admit their senators and representatives to Congress.

The head of the moderates was Senator Fessenden, a native of New Hampshire, who had been an organizer of the Republican party in Maine. Except for less than a year as Lincoln's secretary of the treasury, he had served his adopted state in the Senate since 1854. Almost sixty years of age, the senator was slim of body and short of temper but a good debater and an excellent negotiator. He was a solid statesman, a balance wheel for his party. Behind him was fifty-three-year-old Senator Trumbull, a native of Connecticut, who had represented Illinois for ten years. In the 1830's Trumbull had taught school for three years in Georgia where he was admitted to the bar. In addition, his experience encompassed five years on the Supreme Court of Illinois. Ten years younger than Trumbull was John Sherman, the brother of William T. Sherman and experienced both as a member of the House and the Senate. Fifty-year-old James Grimes had been governor of his state before entering the Senate in 1859. Oliver P. Morton and John Andrew of the politically important states, Indiana and Massachusetts, were anxious to find equitable solutions to the pressing problems of reconstructing the Union. The Republican party was composed of leaders from many states. No one man or combination of men possessed the power to control the party.

Many individuals belonging to the moderate Republican faction in 1865 slipped away in 1866 or 1867 to join the Radicals. No comprehensive definition of the Radicals is possible. The principles and membership of this segment of the Republican party changed from time to time. No unified organization by radicals ever existed, and the extremists had no program for reconstructing the southern states in 1865. The policies they eventually developed lacked unity, were reached with aggravating slowness, and required supplementary acts to make them workable. Identified mainly by their opposition to Lincoln and by their Wade-Davis Bill and Manifesto during the war, although neither they nor Lincoln met head on, the Radicals were a minority within the Republican party in 1865. Although defeated in his bid for re-election to the House in 1864, Henry Winter Davis remained their leader, but his death in 1865 removed him at a critical period. For a few months the Radicals believed President Johnson to be their bedfellow, an error which left them with little influence in executive councils.

The unorganized Radicals mixed principle and expediency. They desired some form of suffrage for Negroes, but sincere men—Chief Justice Chase, Charles Sumner and Benjamin Gratz Brown, George W. Julian, Carl Schurz, Horace Greeley, and Wendell Phillips—had no meeting of minds. Some wanted the suffrage for all freedmen, others favored limiting the franchise to the particularly qualified Negro; they talked not of universal but of equal or impartial suffrage and a few of them desired voting privileges for Negroes in the South but not in the North. Neither Sumner nor Thaddeus Stevens advocated universal suffrage. Benjamin F. Wade, Henry Wilson, and Jacob Merritt Howard and Stevens and George Sewall Boutwell anticipated policies which would win party ascendancy in the South for the Republicans.

The most perceptive leaders realized the Radicals controlled an insufficient number of votes in Congress to pass legislation involving harsh reconstruction measures. During the summer and fall of 1865 few Radicals talked about the right of Congress to control reconstruction. They were content to watch and wait, hoping Johnson would make mistakes or Southerners would arouse the indignation of Northerners. Many Radicals were willing to work out a joint executive-congressional program of reconstructing the southern states. With as yet undisclosed motives, they saw that their success depended upon winning moderates to their side and appealing to the emotions of northern voters.

In 1865 Stevens and Sumner became the spokesmen and leaders of the Radicals. A native of Vermont and a graduate of Dartmouth College, Stevens's experience included school teaching, legal practice, and industrial management. For him the United States was a wonderful country where he, a poor boy, was able to secure an education and rise to economic affluence and political prominence. In his adopted state of Pennsylvania, he ardently supported public schools, sided with downtrodden minorities, and gave money to philanthropic endeavors. During the war he chaired the powerful Ways and Means Committee of the House and secured ample appropriations for the Union armies. Throughout the war he demanded more from the conflict than the stated purpose of Congress—the preservation of the Union. His dislike of southern civilization was based on principle, not on the destruction of his ironworks near Chambersburg by the forces of General Lee in 1863.

In 1865 Stevens was an old man of seventy-three. His earlier successes were now overshadowed by failures: much of his accumulated wealth had been lost, his attempt as President-maker in Pennsylvania had borne thorns, he had failed to board the Lincoln bandwagon in 1860, and had opposed the nomination of Johnson for the vice presidency four years later. His destructive criticism won him no laurels until after the war. His rapid rise to prominence in Congress has blinded many historians, among them the usually reliable ones who make Stevens chairman of the Joint Committee on Reconstruction.

Stevens impressed freshmen congressmen from the hinterlands of America. They heard rumors that his mullato housekeeper, Lydia Smith, was more to him than a domestic servant, but they saw him exhibit ability as a parliamentarian. His reputation as a considerate employer and a bachelor who aided his aspiring nephews won him praise. Although cynical men laughed at the club-footed representative, they feared and respected his craft and vindictiveness. He sought means to enthrone the Republican party in the defeated South, but he also was concerned for the welfare of the freedmen and poor whites.

Stevens was sincere in his attitudes toward the Negro, but Senator Sumner evidenced more love for theory than personal contact with the freedmen. He could plead for civil rights in well-chosen words and, at the same time, resent the presence of Negroes at social functions in Washington. He contrasted in many ways with his counterpart in the House of Representatives: his height, noble appearance, and intellectual countenance attracted an admiring public. His voice was deep with rich and varied tones. Although obviously vain, his gentlemanly manners impressed the public. Ever since his caning by Preston Brooks in 1856, his political future had been assured by a sympathetic Massachusetts senate. Sumner, though verbose, wasted no time on small talk or amusing anecdotes, seldom made mistakes and was grave and courteous. He was almost childlike in his devotion to principle, and his spotless idealism had found haven in his crusade against slavery. He was sincere and disinterested; and with his knowledge of the classics he should have been a college professor doling out truths unlimited to students.

Against these antagonists, President Johnson—the lone wolf, maverick, and a man of great ability—was unwavering in his determination and support of basic principles as he conceived them. Unlike Lincoln, he was fastidious in dress and insisted on an orderly administration in the executive office. Always in earnest and with none of Lincoln's sense of humor, Johnson conferred with party leaders but was not a party man. He preferred going to the people rather than being loyal to an organization. For strict construction of the Constitution, preservation of the Union, state rights, and local self-rule, he was willing to face personal danger and bear insults; but he would not yield or compromise on principles. He had a remarkable face, not imaginative in appearance, but strong and stubborn—the face of a man who could not be turned from his purpose or trifled with, a man who would have to be killed to be eliminated. He enjoyed the prestige of the presidency, his control of the patronage gave him powers which his enemies feared.

Among the men with diverse points of view in 1865 Andrew Johnson had a head start on his opponents. He not only had a definite program for constructing the South but also was putting the program into operation with the support of the Democrats and conservative Republicans. While not overjoyed by the course of events, Southerners were fairly contented and looked forward to the admission of their senators and representatives to the Thirty-Ninth Congress in December. Many northern businessmen welcomed the prospect of having sectional harmony quickly restored for its beneficial effect on inter-regional trade. Though seriously concerned about the actual loyalty of Southerners, moderate Republicans were willing to give President Johnson time to demonstrate the validity of his program. Only the radical minority of the Republican party was convinced that Presidential Reconstruction was based on fallacy. The Radicals began their campaign of opposition with tremendous odds against them.

Constitutional Theories

To some extent all men measured their ideas, and every party faction considered its stand, against the background of the Constitution. Before the war Southerners complained not of the Constitution but of the northern interpretations of that respected document, interpretations which they considered at variance with the intent of the Founding Fathers. Northerners, however, contended that the Constitution was written by farsighted statesmen who included in its articles and sections provisions to meet unforeseen changes in a country just beginning its existence as a representative democracy in a world dominated by autocratic governments.

Southerners responded to the collapse of the Confederacy by claiming the inherent protections embodied in the Constitution. The attempt to claim state sovereignty had been tried but denied by a war that proved the Union indissoluble and indestructible. Since the United States had defined the rebellion as one of individuals and not states, the southern states existed with all their powers and rights within the Union. Admittedly these states had withdrawn from their accustomed and constitutional place in the Union, but this departure was the work of individuals and the states remained component parts of a permanent federal system. The duty of the national government was to re-establish its agencies in the South—postal service, customs offices, federal courts, treasury offices, and all other constitutional services and agencies of the central government. The duty of Southerners was to create loyal governments and elect officials who would take oaths of allegiance to the United States and promise to support the Constitution. These loyal political units had the right to send congressmen to Washington. Congress was obligated under the Constitution to seat these congressmen and admit that the southern states were completely restored to the Union. The federal government could continue to exercise its delegated powers in the interest of all Americans, but reserved powers and all other powers not specifically given the central government, remained the province of the indestructible states.

According to this southern theory, no individual was to be molested or restricted because of his participation in the late war, if that individual took the oath of allegiance, lived in peace, and obeyed the national laws. After all, sovereignty rested not in states or federal governments, but with the American people, and the latter had determined the permanence of states and the central government. General amnesty to individuals, recognition of all property rights (except ownership of slaves), and readmission of the southern states to equal status with all other states of the Union were the end results of the war. Admittedly Southerners once held a different theory, one involving the sovereignty of states, but that theory had been effectively refuted by Northerners.

Strict constructionist though he was, President Johnson could not accept the southern theory in its entirety. For him the Confederate states had never been out of the Union, but Southerners had elected state officers who attempted to exercise the non-existent right of secession. These treasonable acts had placed the state governments in a deep sleep but had not destroyed their existence. They remained in suspended animation and the President could awaken them by certain constitutional acts—the pardoning power of the executive and his right to recognize loyal governments established by patriotic individuals. By awakening the states he could restore all their rights under the Constitution. But the President was sufficiently realistic to know that he could not give the governments of the southern states unrestricted powers, thus giving up his presidential control. He extended his powers and stretched his theory of strict construction of the Constitution by demanding specified acts of the southern state governments to prove their loyalty. During the Civil War necessity had forced the United States to regard the conflict as an insurrection with sovereignty resting in the federal government and at the same time recognizing the international aspects of the war. But peace restored the Constitution, and the President had both the task and the obligation of reawakening the southern states and leading them to their legal place in the Union. Reconstruction was, therefore, an executive duty, not a duty of Congress.

In contrast to the southern and presidential theories, Stevens had enunciated a radical interpretation as early as 1861. He developed his idea more completely by 1863, and his presentation of it at Lancaster, Pennsylvania, two years later was reported in scores of northern newspapers. According to him, secession and rebellion removed the southern states from the protection of the Constitution. The Confederacy had waged war, had been granted the safeguards of a foreign power engaged in international conflict, and, in reality, had been a foreign power. Its defeat made it a conquered province of the United States, dependent entirely on the mercy and humanitarianism of the victor. Since the acts of Southerners encompassed more than rebellion, the provisions of the Constitution which provided trials for treason did not apply. The use of them would free all southern traitors; for, under constitutional guarantees, they would be tried at the place of their treason and it would be impossible to eliminate traitors from service on trial juries. The southern states became a conquered province; their social and economic systems could be remolded and the property of rebels confiscated and distributed to loyal citizens. Congress possessed unlimited power to reconstruct the South, with no obligation to respect the territorial lines of states.

Steven's conquered-province theory won relatively little support in the North; nevertheless, it did have some logical ideas. For four years the Confederacy was a *de facto* state, a political organization that won the rights of a belligerent and fought a war which closely resembled an international conflict. After the war, the southern region faced difficult problems in restoring its economy and adjusting to almost 4 million freedmen. Years of military control and national wardship might have eased the transition from a controlled to a free democracy.

Senator Sumner's state-suicide theory anticipated parts of both Stevens's conquered-province theory and Johnson's ideas. The senator first proposed his theory in a series of senate resolutions on February 11, 1862. In his opinion, it was impossible under the Constitution to remove territory from the control of the United States. By attempting the inoperative and void act of secession, the southern states committed an act of treason and disrupted the normal constitutional relations between central and state governments. The states, therefore, committed suicide, but the United States retained jurisdiction over the territory of the former states just as she possessed power over territories to establish a republican form of government. Although state territorial lines remained unchanged, neither natural right nor provisions of the Constitution demanded the continuation of slavery; Congress could abolish it and enfranchise the freedmen.

Sumner's state-suicide theory and his clear delineation of powers came close to reconciling actual conditions with provisions of the Constitution, but the suicide connotation made the theory unpopular. Furthermore, Sumner was associated with a too ardent support of civil rights and Negro suffrage. He was unable to win approval of his ideas by firing the imagination of the people.

All four theories were developed before the end of the war. Under the first, the initiative in restoring the states to full participation in the Union rested with the southern states whose existence and rights had continued throughout the war. The presidential theory obligated the national executive to initiate and direct reconstruction, but the conquered province and state suicide theories vested initiative and power in the Congress. These ideas contributed to an eventual compromise theory that became the basis for Congressional Reconstruction.

On January 8, 1866, Representative Samuel Shellabarger of Ohio outlined a "forfeited rights" or compromise theory. He borrowed freely from Sumner: secession was null and void; by implication the states retained their boundaries, for territorial lines could not be altered. By attempting rebellion, the states changed their historic relationship with the Union and forfeited their rights and powers within it. The federal government was obligated by the Constitution to guarantee to each state a republican form of government, the power to determine the existence of a republican government belonged to Congress, and the legislative branch of the federal government should provide legislation which would guarantee a republican form of government in the states that had attempted the illegal act of secession.

Shellabarger's forfeited-rights theory omitted the unappealing word suicide and made no mention of property confiscation. It took control of reconstruction from the President and vested it in the Congress. With the sole exception of retaining state boundaries, the power of the Congress was unlimited until a majority of its members were convinced that republican forms of government had been established in the former states of the Confederacy. By not spelling out legislation, the forfeited-rights theory would enable the Congress to enact laws to meet current conditions. If, in the opinion of congressmen, the formation of a republican form of government required military occupation, the enfranchisement of Negroes, civil rights legislation, or disfranchisement of former Confederates, the Congress could demand any or all of these requirements. Depending on need, reconstruction of the southern states could be lenient or harsh. If satisfied that the Johnson governments were republican in form, congressmen could recognize them, or the legislators could work out a compromise with the executive, or they could find Johnson's work unacceptable and initiate a new program.

The forfeited-rights theory was a shrewd political idea by which the Congress found sanction in the Constitution for any action and was not compelled to act immediately. The Johnson governments in the southern states could be investigated to determine their validity, and during the investigation the Congress would not be required to detail any plan for reconstruction. It supplemented the already agreed upon policy, as will be described later, of holding in abeyance the admission to Congress of senators and representatives from eleven southern states. This course satisfied many moderate Republicans with sincere concerns about the loyalty of Southerners and disturbing questions about the validity of Presidential Reconstruction.

Watchful Waiting

For almost a year there was no real organization of congressmen against President Johnson. Even the Radicals tentatively accepted the presidential proclamations, waiting to see what would happen in the South and willing to discover the spirit in which Johnson would exercise his control over the states. One by one the Radicals arrived at a policy of anti-Johnsonism. Moderate Republicans were more reluctant than their Radical colleagues to oppose the President. While many congressmen were suspicious of his Reconstruction policies, their willingness to give them a chance was evident.

A few Radicals opposed the President almost from the date of his reconstruction proclamation on May 29, 1865. Henry Davis did, and in his recollections George Julian declared that he immediately realized the necessity for Congress to take charge. According to him, he spent most of the afternoon of the day of Lincoln's death in political caucus, discussing changes in the cabinet and the need for a more rigorous policy toward the South than the one initiated by Lincoln. The members of the caucus viewed Johnson's accession to the presidency as a godsend to the country, Julian recalled, but after the new President followed in the footsteps of the old, the Radical representative described Johnson as a "genius in depravity," "devil-bent" on ruining the United States. Although Wendell Phillips and Carl Schurz heartily disliked Johnson's proclamation on North Carolina, they continued to advocate co-operation with the executive. Men who later became rabid Radicals—George Boutwell, Jacob Howard, and Henry

Wilson—expressed their faith in the President. It was not until June and July that James M. Ashley, Benjamin F. Butler, and Benjamin Wade lost confidence in Johnson. Zachariah Chandler supported the President until early in 1866 and Stanton worked for harmony between his chief and the Radicals for almost a year.

The harshness and vindictiveness of Thaddeus Stevens mounted to peaks of intensity in 1867 and 1868, but during the summer of 1865 he was willing to co-operate with Johnson. Stevens believed Presidential Reconstruction was not restoring truly loyal governments in the southern states or making certain that rebellious individuals would never again resort to secession. In his opinion nothing was being done to make rebels pay the cost of the war or to humble the southern aristocrats who brought on the rebellion. More and more he approached the conviction that co-operation with the President was impossible and wrote Sumner that Johnson would be crowned king before Congress met unless a sufficient number of bold men banded together, took control of the ship of state, and steered it from the rocks ahead. Sumner also expressed his fears for the rights of freedmen under the white governments of the South.

By their actions southern leaders unwittingly gave the Radicals ammunition and increased the suspicions of moderate Northerners. The Mississippi Constitutional Convention met on August 14, followed in 1865 by conventions in most other former states of the Confederacy. Members of these conventions and of subsequent legislative sessions acceded reluctantly to many of President Johnson's conditions. South Carolinians repealed their ordinance of secession rather than declaring it null and void, and noted that slavery had been abolished by the United States. A number of conventions repudiated their state's war debt only after the President demanded this action and a few failed to repudiate the Confederate debt. No convention seriously considered enfranchising a limited number of Negroes on the basis of educational attainment or property holding. The South Carolina legislature objected to ratifying the Thirteenth Amendment and the Mississippi legislators rejected it on the ground that it was unnecessary, since slavery was abolished in Mississippi. Then southern legislatures proceeded to enact their black codes to regulate and control the freedmen.

Perhaps more influential than the conventions or codes in turning northern opinion against Southerners was the latter's election of former Confederate civil and military leaders to political office. Sent to the United States Congress were nine Confederate officers—four generals and five colonels—many Confederate congressmen and wartime state legislators, and the Georgia legislature selected Alexander H. Stephens as one of the state's United States senators. Three-fourths of the Alabama legislature were former officers or privates in the Confederate army; James Lawrence Orr, governor of South Carolina, was a former Confederate senator; and

Mississippians elected Benjamin G. Humphreys, an unpardoned Confederate brigadier-general, to the governorship.

If Johnson were troubled by the election of so many former Confederates, his actions further incensed the already aroused and indignant Northerners. Humphreys was elected governor of Mississippi on October 2, and two weeks later at his inaugural he proclaimed a government of white men for his state and asked the legislature for laws to force Negroes to honor their labor contracts. On October 26, Johnson pardoned Humphreys, thus giving him the legal right to occupy the governorship. As early as May 29, some critics thought the President too liberal in extending pardons to Southerners. During the fall of 1865 Johnson's pardons became numerous; often they went to individuals who were politically active in the South.

The course of Presidential Reconstruction—constitutional conventions, black codes, legislatures, and election of former Confederates all coupled with Johnson's liberal and often unwise use of his pardoning power—brought swift and bitter reactions from Northerners. "We tell the white men of Mississippi," the editor of the *Chicago Tribune* wrote on December 1, "that the men of the North will convert the State of Mississippi into a frog pond before they will allow such laws [the black codes] to disgrace one foot of soil in which the bones of our soldiers sleep and over which the flag of freedom waves." Sumner declared that the South had been allowed to surrender too soon, and Stevens talked of confiscating the property of aristocrats and distributing it to freedmen and poor whites. Wendell Phillips thought the nation's crucial hour was at hand. "The rebellion has not ceased," he stated, "it has only changed its weapons. Once it fought; now it intrigues; once it followed Lee in arms, now it follows President Johnson in guile and chicanery."

Southerners had followed the President. Their submission was to military might, not to right and truth as they defined right and truth. By the fall of 1865 many who had welcomed peace were having second thoughts. Submit they would to northern power but they would retain their ideas of a South governed for and by white men. Although willing to admit the demise of slavery and the permanency of the Union, they would go no further. Already the "Lost Cause" was becoming ennobled and its heroes enshrined. Southern leaders wanted to know how far they must go in appeasing the victorious North. And President Johnson told them—not far. He repeatedly told delegations from the South of the permanence of the states, of the rights of states within an everlasting Union of the American people. Southerners wanted to know what to do—how to convince the victor of their loyalty and still keep the South a white man's land. The President, in effect, told them to follow the Constitution and he would interpret that document for them.

Southerners erred in blindly following Johnson's lead. They almost ignored their status as conquered men, and then quibbled in conventions over points which had no real meaning. They failed to appease Northerners by enfranchising a small number of Negroes; elected too many former secessionists and Confederates to office; and enacted strict laws to regulate and control the freedmen, the darlings of the moment to many sincere Northerners. The impression Southerners made on the North was disastrous. The region believed the sacrifices of its men had accomplished no more than defeat of Southerners whose aristocratic leaders remained in power, able to continue their domination over struggling white people of the South and determined to re-enslave the freedmen by invidious laws.

At first Southerners were astonished by the northern reaction to their stand and then their astonishment turned to anger. The Yankees "left me one inestimable privilege," a South Carolinian told visiting author John T. Trowbridge of Massachusetts, "to hate 'em. I git up at half past four in the morning and sit up till twelve at night, to hate 'em." A mediocre Virginia poet, Innes Randolph, not only disliked "The lyin' thievin' Yankees" but hated them "wuss and wuss" as time went by. In addition he hated the "Yankee nation," the Declaration of Independence, and the "glorious Union." His elation over the South's killing "three hundred thousand" Yankees was tempered only by his regret that the number had not been three million.

Southern newspaper editors removed the flag, a symbol of the Union, from their editorial columns and described the Northerners in bitter words. They scoffed at the idea of suffrage for Negroes, attacked the Freedmen's Bureau and its agents, and reported every criminal act of freedmen. Believing that the North supported President Johnson, these unrealistic editors compared the "low buffoonery" and the "little story" antics of Lincoln to the valid reason and sound argument of Johnson. Herschel V. Johnson of Georgia urged the President to issue a proclamation declaring that senators and representatives from the South were entitled to seats in the forthcoming session of Congress. In the opinion of the Georgian, the proclamation would delight Southerners and be a masterly stroke of policy. Other Southerners suggested the use of the army to overawe and, if need be, to control the Radicals in Congress.

First Months of the Thirty-Ninth Congress

Southern diatribes stiffened the backbone of northern moderates who had never questioned the readmission of southern states. Admission was to come, but its timing and its conditions were the questions of concern. The moderate *New York Times* declared the admission of southern congressmen to the Thirty-Ninth Congress would signify the end of reconstruction and advised northern congressmen to delay, wait, investigate, and determine whether the southern state governments were actually loyal. Many Republicans questioned the stand of Johnson. What were his ideas on rights for the freedmen in the South? Why did he not do something about the black codes, even if no more than denounce their principles in a speech? Was he turning his back on the Republican Party and returning to the Democratic fold? In mass meetings Negroes called on the President and the Congress for protection against the whites and demanded the end of "invidious political or legal distinctions" based merely on the color of an individual's skin.

Most Radicals had made up their minds—co-operation with the President was not possible. Stevens stated that the future of the conquered southern states depended on the conqueror. Congress and not the President, he said, should create states and determine when their senators and representatives were entitled to seats in the national legislature. On arriving in Washington, Speaker Schuyler Colfax of Indiana praised the President. Later he pointed to the opposition in some southern legislatures to ratification of the Thirteenth Amendment, their reluctance to repudiate wartime debts, and their repeal rather than repudiation of secession, the proscription of southern Unionists by former Confederates, and the latter's failure to protect the freedmen. He proclaimed the exclusive right of Congress to judge the qualifications and elections of its members.

President Johnson never questioned the right of Congress to pass on the qualifications of its members; but in the peculiar circumstances following civil war, he held the authority of Congress limited to determining the personal qualifications of an individual to a seat in the Senate or House. By exercising his constitutional rights the President believed that he was reconstructing the southern states and the senators and representatives from those states had his approval in every respect except their personal qualifications. He thought any questioning of the legality of the recently established loyal governments of the southern states not within the constitutional powers of Congress.

But Radical and moderate Republicans did question the assumptions of the President. Even the sensitive, moderate James W. Grimes feared the immediate admission of southern congressmen might quickly enable the Democrats to regain control of the federal government, result in payment of the rebel debt, restoration of slavery in a modified form, and return of the leaders of rebellion to power. In October Edward McPherson, clerk of the House of Representatives, announced his intention to omit calling the names of representatives from the former Confederate states at the opening session of the Thirty-Ninth Congress.

McPherson followed this policy and the same tactic was used in the

Senate when Congress convened on December 4, 1865, its first meeting in almost nine months. Stevens moved for the appointment of a joint committee, composed of nine members from the House and six from the Senate, to inquire into conditions of the states formerly known as the Confederate States of America and to report whether those states were entitled to representation in Congress. Until the investigation had been made and the committee report received, Stevens asked that no representative or senator from the states in question be seated. Attempts to delay a vote until the President's message had been heard were beaten down and the House adopted the motion by a 136-to-36 vote. After some debate and some qualification, the Senate, presided over by President Pro Tempore Ben Wade of Ohio, accepted the idea. Most moderate Republicans considered the investigation and delay to be for the national good. Like the Shellabarger forfeited-rights theory of a later date, the Joint Committee on Reconstruction advanced the Radical cause. While the committee investigated, Radicals had time to formulate their plan of reconstructing the southern states and appeal to northern voters for support. The Radicals knew that they had a powerful adversary in the President.

Johnson's message was heard by Congress on December 5, and it was statesmanlike in its moderation and idealism. As a result of the rephrasing of historian George Bancroft, the President's message was of remarkable literary merit. In it Johnson praised Lincoln and requested congressional support for the executive in his attempt to restore national harmony. The Founding Fathers and their Constitution were lauded and the indissoluble Union hailed in glowing words. He detailed his steps in reconstructing the southern states, expressed dislike of indefinite periods of military control, and emphasized the beneficial results from ratification of the Thirteenth Amendment. Its acceptance healed wounds, removed the institution of slavery which for decades had perplexed and divided the people, renewed and strengthened the mutual affection of Americans, and reunited them "beyond all power of disruption." The adoption of the amendment, Johnson declared, left only the admission of congressmen from the southern states to complete the work of restoration and allow those states their rightful status and powers in the Union. He urged Congress to judge only the elections and qualifications of the men sent to Washington by the South.

Some congressmen and editors of magazines and newspapers—*Harper's Weekly, The Nation, New-York Tribune,* and *New York Times*—praised the presidential message. On December 18, however, Stevens made a vicious attack on Johnson and his ideas. Democratic congressmen rose to defend the President. William E. Finch of Ohio spoke at length in support of immediate admission of southern representatives and castigated

Stevens for obstructionism. Henry Jarvis Raymond, member of the House and editor of the *New York Times*, replied to Stevens in a logical, well-written article.

Meanwhile, the Joint Committee on Reconstruction was appointed. This committee was conceived by the Radicals but the child of both moderates and Radicals who approved it in a caucus by a 125-to-35 vote. In the opinion of Fessenden, the readmission of the southern states was of infinite importance to the nation, requiring calm and serious consideration, and the two branches of Congress were duty-bound to select with care men to serve on an investigating committee. Senator Fessenden won the chairmanship of the Joint Committee to which were added three other moderate Republicans, three Democrats, and eight Radicals.* Despite their majority, the Radicals did not control the committee. As chairman, Fessenden was strong and adroit and directed the investigation. Even after the Radicals increased their influence, he wrote the final report. Chairman Stevens of the House section of the committee utilized the hearings to expound his vindictive ideas and to introduce drastic proposals. Newspaper correspondents found him newsworthy and their reports left the impression that his influence was greater than it actually was. More often than not his resolutions failed to win approval. Although Sumner wanted a place on the investigating body and the opportunity to present his views on civil rights and suffrage for Negroes, the Senate refused to appoint him.

While the Joint Committee was not the first investigating committee in American history to employ bias in its hearings, it was the most famous progenitor of congressional committees in the nineteenth and twentieth centuries which used questionable means to influence public opinion. Among the witnesses called were 77 Northerners living in the South, 57 Southerners, and 8 Negroes; many of the northern-born witnesses were federal army officers and officials of the Freedmen's Bureau, but there were also newspaper reporters, southern loyalists, former Confederates Robert E. Lee and Alexander H. Stephens, and then General Grant. Undoubtedly, a majority of the committee members were biased. Their questions held witnesses who were unfavorable to the South for hours of testimony and their silence quickly dismissed those who were pro-southern.

Recognition of this bias, however, could not bury the findings of the investigation. White Southerners were mistreating the freedmen by relegat-

---

* The fifteen members were: (Senate) Fessenden of Maine (Chairman of the committee and chairman of the Senate section), J. W. Grimes of Iowa, Ira Harris of New York, J. M. Howard of Michigan, Reverdy Johnson of Maryland, and G. H. Williams of Oregon; (House) Stevens of Pennsylvania (Chairman of the House section), John A. Bingham of Ohio, Henry T. Blow of Missouri, George S. Boutwell of Massachusetts, Roscoe Conkling of New York, Henry Grider of Kentucky, Justin S. Morrill of Vermont, Andrew J. Rogers of New Jersey, and Elihu B. Washburne of Illinois.

ing them to a servile economic and political status, proscribing members of the white race who had been Unionists during the war, and continuing in power state governments dedicated to white supremacy and controlled by former secessionists and Confederates. Testimony also disclosed that both the army and the Freedmen's Bureau were needed to secure justice for freedmen and equitable treatment for loyalists.

Witness after witness declared the enfranchisement of Negroes the only hope for political reform in the South and the development of a Republican organization in that region. This testimony appealed to committee members who knew the South would pick up twelve seats in the House with the elimination of the three-fifths compromise of the Constitution. Unless Negroes were enfranchised, southern whites would gain an increase in their proportionate representation in the House. Undoubtedly the Radicals were mainly motivated by partisan political desires for the Republican party, but many moderate party members actually feared a resurgent Democratic party would endanger, if not destroy, contemplated social and economic changes.

The hearings of the Joint Committee bore weight. Before long northern newspapers carried columns of testimony. Not content with reporting the numerous authentic instances of personal and legal mistreatment of freedmen and Unionists in the South, correspondents filed fictitious accounts of outrages. By reading their newspapers Northerners concluded that Southerners remained essentially rebellious and anti-American while voicing sentiments of loyalty, that freedmen were being virtually re-enslaved by law and practice. Within months the committee hearings profoundly influenced public opinion in the North and persuaded an increasing number of Northerners to support a more rigorous policy. To a remarkable degree the committee determined the eventual congressional reconstruction of the South.

While all proposed legislation relating to reconstruction policies was referred to the Joint Committee, some bills did not originate in the committee room. By January 1866, the Congress and the President were deadlocked, with the latter insisting on the validity of his southern governments and the former refusing to recognize their legality. Moderate Rupublicans sought means to safeguard the rights of freedmen without antagonizing the President, and believed new life for the Freedmen's Bureau and a civil rights bill would accomplish their purposes. On January 11 both measures were introduced by Senator Trumbull.

A new Freedmen's Bureau Bill appeared to be the best hope for compromise. The original Freedmen's Bureau stemmed from the act of March 3, 1865, which created an agency, operated by the War Department, to provide relief for former slaves and other colored refugees and give aid to needy southern whites. For almost a year the bureau engaged in many activities: rations for the destitute regardless of race, relocation of freedmen and transportation to their new homes, labor contracts with wages and terms of employment, and supervision of labor contracts for the protection of employee and employer. In addition, it established schools and hospitals. Undoubtedly, the bureau accomplished excellent work through its relief, educational, and medical service. Its head, General Howard, was an honest administrator who conscientiously tried to make his sprawling organization effective.

From the first, however, white Southerners considered the bureau a foreign agency supported by an army of occupation. They resented its existence, "regardless of what it might do, for it had power over them and it was beyond their control." White Southerners found justification for their dislike in the bureau's preventing discrimination against the freedman, upholding his civil rights, and abrogating some of the black codes. Justifiable criticisms included the dishonesty of some agents, their high-handedness, and their over-extension of authorized power. Nevertheless, most bureau officials were honest, and the testimony given at the Joint Committee hearings convinced an overwhelming majority of congressmen that some agency to protect freedmen from conniving individuals and lawless bands was imperative.

The first bureau act limited the agency's life to one year after the end of the war. Trumbull's bill gave the bureau existence until terminated by law, extended its sphere to cover freedmen and refugees in the entire nation, and broadened its powers. The bureau was given jurisdiction over all cases involving discrimination against persons on account of race, color, or previous servitude whether this discrimination was based on state or local laws, custom, or prejudice. Military courts of the bureau were authorized to try accused persons and on conviction sentence them up to a year's imprisonment, a $1000 fine, or both.

Fessenden and other senators believed President Johnson willing to accept the amended bureau bill. They had called on him several days prior to its introduction to urge him to do nothing further relative to reconstructing the South unless required to do so by some imperative need and called for harmonious relations between the executive and Congress. Moderate Republicans in Congress believed Johnson ready to support their stand on the need for protecting the rights of freedmen. The bill was passed by overwhelming majorities with moderate and Radical Republicans voting for it in the Senate and House.

But the moderates failed to understand the President—almost every Radical had already decided that co-operation with him was hopeless. Johnson wavered for a time. He estimated the cost of the new Freedmen's

Bureau would amount to $20 million, and told cabinet members that the Joint Committee was an intrigue of Radicals against him, a cabal to dictate to the presidential office. On the afternoon of February 19 he released his veto message. There was no immediate need, he wrote, for the new Freedmen's Bureau Bill because the former act had not expired. Although he shared with Congress "the strongest desire to secure to the freedmen the full enjoyment of their freedom and property and their entire independence and equality in making contracts for their labor," certain provisions of the bill were clearly unconstitutional. It unreasonably extended military power and unnecessarily invaded civil judicial functions. Trials in the bureau courts, he stated, would be without juries or fixed rules of law and evidence. He could not reconcile the proposed system of jurisdiction with provisions of the Constitution which stated that "No person shall be held to answer for a capital or otherwise infamous crime unless on a presentment or indictment of a grand jury. . . ." In his opinion, the "power that would be thus placed in the hands of the President is such as in time of peace certainly ought never be intrusted to one man."

Turning to the status of the southern states, the President declared that the United States "has returned, or is returning, to a state of peace and industry, and the rebellion is in fact at an end." The authority of the central government was disputed in no part of the country, he said, and asked for no unnecessary disturbance of "the commerce and credit and industry of the country by declaring to the American people and to the world that the United States are still in a condition of civil war." Furthermore, at the time the bill was passed there was no senator or representative from the eleven southern states which would be mainly affected by its provisions, and the President viewed this exclusion of congressmen as a clear violation of the Constitution. Johnson disclaimed any intention of interfering with the unquestionable rights of the Senate or House to judge election returns and the qualifications of its members, but these rights could not be used in time of peace to deny any state the representation it was entitled to by the Constitution.

If the southern states were not fully restored to the Union, he urged Congress to work with him "to secure that desirable end at the earliest possible moment." In his opinion, however, the southern states "so far, at least, as depends upon their own action, have already been fully restored, and are to be deemed as entitled to enjoy their constitutional rights as members of the Union." Reasoning based on the Constitution and the actual situation of the country entitled and bound the executive to assume that the jurisdiction of the federal courts were restored in the South; whenever resistance to laws occurred, the courts with the aid of the military would protect and uphold the rights and interests of all classes of people. If they could not, the President had sufficient power to act under the existing Freedmen's Bureau Act, and he would hereafter, as he had done before, employ the armed forces "of the country to suppress insurrection or to overcome obstructions to the laws."

The veto message was reasonable and well-buttressed. It relied heavily on the Constitution, appealed to citizens who disliked the costs of a burgeoning federal bureaucracy, and sought support from businessmen who envisioned profits from the restoration of trade in a reunited country. While the President was emphatic in declaring the Union restored, if the Congress believed the southern states still out of their normal relationship to the federal government, he urged co-operation between the legislative and executive branches of the government to secure quickly a desirable goal. Although Trumbull's Freedmen's Bureau Bill had passed the Senate by a 37-to-10 vote, its proponents could not muster the necessary two-thirds majority to overcome the presidential veto.

The tactlessness of Johnson, however, lost him the temporary advantage of an able veto message. On the evening of February 22, 1866, the anniversary of Washington's birthday, approximately 6000 people serenaded the President at the White House and called for a speech. Johnson responded with an hour-and-ten-minute discourse. He reminded his audience of Washington's and Jackson's devotion to the Union and of the persecution of Christ; he told his listeners that the disunionist designs of certain northern men were just as treasonable as the acts of Davis, Toombs, and other Confederates.

In contrast to these northern men whom the President coupled with traitors, he recounted his battle against traitors and treason in the South and declared himself still on the battlefield to fight those who stood opposed to the restoration of the Union. He denounced the Joint Committee on Reconstruction as "an irresponsible central directory" which arrogated to itself "all the powers of Congress." This committee, the President continued, had denied the purpose of the war, namely the illegality of secession and the permanency of the Union, by assuming the southern states had seceded. Citing the English revolution and the beheading of King Charles I, Johnson implied that Stevens was intent on inciting the assassination of the President.

Without question the Southerner in the White House had been goaded by the rash statements of the Radicals, but his reply in kind aided rather than weakened their standing with northern voters. His speech demonstrated both his realization of the purpose of the Radicals and his tactlessness in dealing with them. From February 22 on, the Radicals were united against the President and Johnson's indiscretion caused many moderates to enter the Radical camp.

REFERENCES

The traditional and recent interpretations of this period deserve study. Beale, *The Critical Year*; Josephson, *The Politicos*; and Hacker, *Triumph of American Capitalism*, should be compared with Sharkey, *Money, Class, and Party*, and Unger, *Greenback Era*, all cited in the General Historiography and Bibliography. Howard K. Beale, "The Tariff and Reconstruction," *American Historical Review*, XXXV (1930), pp. 276–94, and Stanley Coben, "Northern Business and Radical Reconstruction," *Mississippi Valley Historical Review*, XLVI (1959), pp. 67–90, present different points of view. Other valuable articles are: Lawrence H. Gipson, "The Statesmanship of President Johnson: A Study of the Presidential Reconstruction Policy," *Mississippi Valley Historical Review*, II (1915), pp. 363–83; Albert V. House, "Northern Congressional Democrats as Defenders of the South During Reconstruction," *Journal of Southern History*, VI (1940), pp. 46–71; Charles O. Lerche, "Congressional Interpretations of the Guarantee of a Republican Form of Government," *ibid.*, XV (1949), pp. 192–211; Jack B. Scroggs, "Southern Reconstruction: A Radical View," *ibid.*, XXIV (1958), pp. 407–29; John G. Sproat, "Blueprint for Radical Reconstruction," *ibid.*, XVI (1950), pp. 457–71. David Donald, *The Politics of Reconstruction, 1863–1867* (Baton Rouge, 1965), opens a new approach for investigating politics. Among useful diaries and reminiscences are: Beale (ed.), *Diary of Gideon Welles* (New York, 1960); James G. Blaine, *Twenty Years in Congress* (Norwich, 1884); Benjamin F. Butler, *Autobiography* (Boston, 1892); Samuel S. Cox, *Union-Disunion-Reunion* (Providence, 1885); Hugh McCulloch, *Men and Measures of a Half Century* (New York, 1888); Edward L. Pierce (ed.), *Memoir and Letters of Charles Sumner*, Vol. IV (Boston, 1893); Carl Schurz, *Reminiscences* (New York, 1909), and John Sherman, *Recollections*, Vol. I (Chicago, 1895). Claude M. Fuess, *Carl Schurz: Reformer, 1829–1906* (New York, 1963), is critical of Schurz and sympathetic to Johnson. Charles E. Chadsey, *The Struggle Between President Johnson and Congress Over Reconstruction* (New York, 1896), is still useful. Malcolm Moos, *The Republicans: A History of Their Party* (New York, 1956), is the standard history of the party. *Report of the Joint Committee on Reconstruction* (Washington, 1866), and Kendrick (ed.), *Journal of the Committee* (cited in General Historiography and Bibliography), are valuable primary materials. All the sources cited are pertinent to Chapter IV.

The Year of Decision

THE SUSTAINED veto of the Freedmen's Bureau Bill was the President's last legislative victory. Thereafter, the Radicals attempted to destroy his reputation and tear the mantle of presidential respectability from his shoulders. Stevens labeled him "an alien enemy of a foreign state" and Sumner called him "an insolent, drunken brute" who by comparison made the infamous horse of Caligula respectable. Northern editors sympathetic to the Radicals attacked Johnson, and reporters presented him unfavorably. One by one, magazines and newspapers, formerly friendly, turned against him until he was left with virtually no support other than that from staunch Democratic publications. The man of great ability who seldom imbibed alcoholic drinks appeared in the news as a drunken moron. His loyalty to the Union was questioned, his southern-Democratic background and his former ownership of slaves were emphasized, and his elevation to the presidency by the assassination of the great Lincoln was told again and again. No satisfactory explanation of Johnson's political mistakes, ones which aided his enemies, has been presented by historians. For tactlessness, his theories of government, and his background fail to account for his actions.

The Radicals, however, won no sudden or dramatic victory over the President. For a year the moderate Republicans moved with caution, many still hoping and working for a satisfactory compromise between the legislative and executive branch. They did join the Radicals in voting for specific bills whose provisions, they believed, were necessary to protect the rights of freedmen and to insure loyal governments in the South. But, having joined the Radicals in support of a particular bill, the moderates drew back, unwilling to move completely into the Radical camp or undo entirely the work of the President. From March 1866 until the same month of the following year, the moderate Republicans wavered, alternating between support of the Radicals and working for a compromise. For a year a congressional program of reconstruction was in the making.

Presidential elasticity and southern co-operation might have kept enough moderate Republicans from joining the Radicals to defeat many of the latter's plans. The President, however, would not compromise. At times he was mulish, responding to Radical attacks with stubborn dogmatism; at other times he arrived at decisions after much soul-searching, making his decisions on constitutional grounds and his duty as executive. The result was always the same—the southern states were reconstructed and loyal, the President right, and Congress wrong. This presidential stand encouraged independence in the South. White Southerners acted more the part of victors than that of the conquered. They criticized and threatened, they denounced congressional acts and passed laws objectionable to the North; and, in speech and newspaper, they demonstrated a vitriolic hatred of all Northerners who disagreed with Johnson. Thus, in 1866, the year of decision, the President and white Southerners were essentially responsible for giving victory to the Radicals and bringing on Congressional Reconstruction.

The Civil Rights Act of 1866

The first victory for Congress was on civil rights. Along with his Freedmen's Bureau Bill, Senator Lyman Trumbull introduced on January 11 a civil rights bill to guarantee national protection for the Negro as well as to counteract the southern black codes. Trumbull's measure offered the first national legislative definition of American citizenship: "All persons born in the United States and not subject to any foreign power, excluding Indians not taxed, are hereby declared citizens of the United States. . . ." Citizens of every race and color, without regard for previous condition of slavery or involuntary servitude were entitled to equal rights in every state and territory of the country—the right "to make and enforce contracts, to sue, to be parties, and give evidence, to inherit, purchase, lease, sell, hold, and convey real and personal property, and to full and equal benefit of all laws . . . as is enjoyed by white citizens . . . any law, statute, ordinance, regulation, or custom, to the contrary notwithstanding."

To enforce the proposed law, all individuals who deprived any citizen of his rights were subject to trials in federal district courts. Officers associated with these courts and officials of the Freedmen's Bureau were charged and required to institute suits against individuals who violated the rights of a citizen and to prosecute the cases at the expense of the central government. Upon conviction, the accused individual could be sentenced to a year's imprisonment, a $1000 fine, or both. To enforce the act, the President was authorized to give special orders to the courts and to employ the armed forces and militia of the country.

Senators spent comparatively little time debating the bill. The overwhelming majority favored it and passed it on February 2 by a 32-to-12 vote. Only three Republicans voted against the measure. In the House the vote was delayed until March 13. During this delay the Joint Committee on Reconstruction attempted to lay down rules for the admission of Tennessee: the state must repudiate all rebel debts, never repudiate the federal war debt, never again attempt secession, and disfranchise active rebels for five years. These suggestions were debated but not adopted by the committee, but it did agree on February 20 to Stevens's resolution that no senator or representative should be admitted to the national legislature until Congress declared a state entitled to representation. On March 13 the House passed the Civil Rights Bill by an overwhelming 111-to-38 vote.

Moderates in and out of Congress urged the President to sign the bill. With the exception of Secretary Welles, every member of the cabinet advised Johnson to accept it. Governor Oliver P. Morton pleaded for presidential acceptance but the President told the Indiana governor, who at this date was a moderate working for a compromise, that he could not. Newspaper editors emphasized the reasons for the legislation. Northern Democrats, and especially the well-known Fernando Wood, former mayor of New York City, and Southerners gave reasons for a presidential veto.

Johnson faced a difficult decision and he arrived at one on the basis of his considered judgment as an executive bound to uphold the Constitution. On March 27 he sent his veto message to Congress. The power to confer state citizenship, he wrote, rested as exclusively with the several states as the power to give federal citizenship belonged solely to Congress. If necessary to declare Negroes citizens, it was not sound policy to do so with eleven states unrepresented in Congress. Furthermore, citizenship was not essential to enjoyment of rights; all persons domiciled in the United States enjoyed the rights enumerated in the bill, and conferring citizenship on 4 million freedmen, without requiring a period of probation, discriminated against worthy, patriotic, and intelligent foreigners who must wait five years for the privilege of citizenship. It was unconstitutional and unnecessary, he thought, it struck at the power of state judges by making them agents of the central government and binding them to decide cases as directed by Congress, and it would force the President to maintain a large army to secure compliance. In addition to destroying the reserved rights of the states, the bill favored the Negro over the white race.

However valid the President's interpretation of the Constitution, he was entirely out of touch with northern sentiment. At least for a time a majority of Northerners thought it necessary to make freedmen the wards of the nation to protect them from their former masters. These Northerners demanded special favors for the Negro, believing these grants essential to cover the transition from slavery to freedom. Northern newspapers condemned the President for his veto. Many moderate Republicans moved closer to their radical colleagues. Governor Morton coupled the veto to the

Democratic party. That party, he said, "may be described as a common sewer and loathesome receptacle, into which is emptied every element of treason North and South, every element of inhumanity and barbarism which has dishonored the age." Unable to destroy the Constitution by war and checked in their attempts to restore rebels to power, he declared, the Democrats were seeking to negate the great document by presidential interpretation.

On the same day that it received Johnson's veto, the Senate unseated John P. Stockton, a Democrat from New Jersey. There were irregularities in the election of Stockton, but in normal times the Senate would have accepted him. Forewarned of the presidential veto, Republican senators rejected the New Jersey man and thereby gave their party two-thirds of the members of the Senate. On April 6, the senators overrode the veto by a one-vote margin. The pressure brought to bear on moderate Republicans was intense. Senator James H. Lane of Kansas, former antislavery leader, Civil War general, and strong supporter of Lincoln, resisted pressure and voted to uphold Johnson's veto. Criticism of his action unhinged the senator's mind: he returned to his home state a broken man and on July 11 shot himself. This personal tragedy reflected the emotional mood in Congress and the country. On April 9 the Civil Rights Bill became law when the House overrode the presidential veto.

The Fourteenth Amendment

By overriding Johnson's veto, Congress gave itself an imperative task. Neither house ever officially disavowed Presidential Reconstruction, but in effect the Civil Rights Bill was both a congressional declaration of war with Johnson and a repudiation of his major policies in reconstructing the southern states. If the governments established by the President were not satisfactory ones, congressmen must provide some alternative program for creating loyal states in the South. By April 9 the Thirty-Ninth Congress had been in session for more than four months and its accomplishments were mainly negative or delaying measures; the northern public demanded concrete evidence of southern repentance and loyalty but it also wanted the Union to be restored quickly. Unless the Congress acted, the tide of public opinion might turn against the dilatory legislators and the important congressional elections of November 1866 were little more than half a year away.

The problems confronting Congress were manifold. No senator or representative possessed sufficient personal magnetism or advocated a reconstruction program capable of corraling a majority. The President's action and the South's obdurate stand had given Stevens considerable power, but the old Pennsylvania representative who seemed to be dedicating his remaining years to the punishment of rebels was a year away from his peak of influence. Many senators recoiled from the ardent civil rights champion and intellectually cold Senator Sumner. No Republican faction, moderate or radical, commanded a following sufficient to force pet programs through Congress. The relatively few conservative Republicans and the hopelessly outnumbered Democrats were sidelined by the intractable President Johnson and the recalcitrant white Southerners. A congressional program for reconstruction hinged on victory by either the moderate or radical factions within the Republican party or a compromise acceptable to a majority of both factions.

In planning a reconstruction program, the moderate and radical factions could agree on few essentials. One problem was Negro suffrage which Sumner demanded but which politicians from the Middle Atlantic and Middle Western states feared. The idea of enfranchising freedmen in the South was popular, but could they be given the suffrage without extending it to all Negroes? The politically astute Stevens, concerned for the continued supremacy of his party, was aware of the danger of universal male suffrage. Nearly all Republican congressmen were in agreement on the necessity of protecting the rights of the Negro. But the legislators differed on the means to achieve the desired end. Was a law sufficient or was an amendment needed? Some congressmen feared that the Supreme Court would declare the Civil Rights Act unconstitutional. The third area of disagreement was the disfranchisement and disqualification for officeholding of erstwhile rebels. Stevens advocated wholesale and almost permanent proscription of all secessionists and Confederates, but the majority of his colleagues were unwilling to disqualify more than the ranking civil and military officers of the Confederacy for a limited period. Finally there was disagreement over the provisional or permanent nature of a congressional program. Should the Congress enact legislation and on compliance by the southern states admit their senators and representatives to seats in their respective houses? Stevens and Sumner advocated specific requirements from Southerners without promises.

On one concern the moderate and radical factions agreed. Without adequate safeguards, the rebellious states should not be allowed representation in Congress. By throwing out the three-fifths compromise the South would gain twelve seats. If Negroes were eliminated from population returns for purposes of representation in the House, the southern states would lose eighteen seats. This loss would be a serious detriment to re-establishing an agrarian supremacy based on a combination of southern and western representatives. On the other hand, the freedmen needed political rights for their self-protection and to bind them and the poorer whites of the South to the Republican party would make the South a political pocket borough for the Republican party.

All these problems and questions entered into the planning and discussion of what became the Fourteenth Amendment. As early as December 5, 1865, Stevens proposed that representation in the House be based on the number of qualified voters in a state instead of its population. His resolution, and another of January 20, which called for direct taxes and representation on a population basis with proportionate reduction in representation based on the number of persons excluded from voting because of their race or color, received considerable support without mustering majorities in Congress. Senator Jacob Howard of Michigan proposed that the franchise be granted to all Negroes over twenty-one years of age who had served in the United States Army, could read or write, or possessed property worth $250 or more. Senator William M. Stewart urged Congress to provide both amnesty and universal suffrage by statute. His idea was to offer amnesty to all Southerners and guarantee their states representation in Congress after their state governments repudiated the rebel debt, renounced any claim for emancipation of slaves, and promised to disregard color in suffrage and civil rights.

On April 21 Stevens proposed an amendment. Its sections had been outlined by reformer Robert Dale Owen and presented to Oliver P. Morton and Stevens. The main provisions of the amendment called for (1) adequate protection for all citizens in civil rights, (2) no payment of the rebel debt or compensation for slaves, (3) and no suffrage discrimination against either Negroes or former Confederates after July 4, 1876; but, before that date, any state would lose representation in Congress in proportion to the number of its citizens denied the franchise. Coupled with the amendment was a proposed enabling act which provided for seating of southern congressmen following national adoption of the amendment.

Some Republican members of the Joint Committee feared the suffrage provision would be detrimental to their party in the forthcoming elections. In addition to questioning the advisability of universal suffrage, Stevens thought amnesty to Southerners and immediate readmission of the southern states too high a price to pay for enfranchising the freedmen. In April the committee reported a five-section amendment for congressional consideration. The proposal was accepted by the House on May 10 but ran into spirited opposition in the Senate. After a party caucus the Senate added a definition of citizenship, proscribed officeholding for certain classes of former Confederates and provided for removal of the proscriptions by two-thirds vote of Congress, and inserted a guarantee of the payment of the federal war debt. The proposed amendment passed the Senate on June 8, and five days later the House accepted the Senate's version.

The Fourteenth Amendment proved to be the most important addition to the Constitution. All persons born or naturalized in the United States and subject to her jurisdiction were declared citizens of the United States and the state of their residence. The second sentence of section one prohibited a state from passing or enforcing laws which abridged the privileges and immunities of citizens, deprived them of "life, liberty, or property, without due process of law, or denied them equal protection of laws." These clauses certainly gave citizenship to Negroes and applied the Bill of Rights to the states. Before ratification of the amendment, only state constitutional provisions or laws prevented a state from establishing a church, denying citizens freedoms, or other rights; after ratification, the federal government was charged with protecting citizens from any abridgement of these liberties by state action.

Unquestionably the framers of the amendment were primarily and sincerely seeking means of protecting the Negro, but in process of compromise and phrasemaking, they produced two sentences which could be interpreted in many ways. This ambiguity satisfied both the moderates and the Radicals. In the forthcoming elections the moderates could deny that citizenship conferred social equality on Negroes or gave them rights to vote, hold office, serve on juries, or attend schools with white people. The Radicals, however, saw tremendous possibilities for broad interpretations of rights of Negroes in the "due process" and "equal protection of the laws" that harked back to the decades of abolitionism. Furthermore, by accepting less than they desired, the Radicals won many moderates to their side and soundly defeated President Johnson.

In time various interpretations of section one of the Fourteenth Amendment profoundly changed American constitutional history. It and enactments that enlarged habeas corpus jurisdiction increased the power of the federal government and sped the process of centralization, but by interpreting federal responsibility to policing state laws, the courts allowed discrimination of individual against individual to continue. States were also allowed to legislate for classes of their citizens. As long as the privileges and immunities of all within a class were equal and no member of a specified class was denied due process of law or equal protection of law, state governments could enact and enforce special legislation applicable to these classes of persons. Thus a state was allowed to pass laws applying only to railroad workers, to women, to children, to Negroes, or to white people. Eventually this interpretation made it possible for southern and northern communities to develop a caste system, and the protection for Negroes planned by framers of the Fourteenth Amendment lost much of its force.

The "due process of law" phrase gave lawyers a bonanza, for "due process" eluded definition. An individual might be denied due process by the enforcement of an unconstitutional state law or local ordinance, or by almost any number of procedures during a trial. Appeals based on content and procedure multiplied and were brought into federal circuit courts of appeal and to the Supreme Court. What was a fair trial under due process or equal protection of the laws? In the twentieth century the Supreme Court would render many decisions in the attempt to answer that question.

The interpretations which brought about "The Revolution in Law" engendered heated controversy. During the latter part of the nineteenth century the Supreme Court ruled that corporations were legal persons within the meaning of the Fourteenth Amendment and these artificial persons should enjoy the same rights and immunities of natural persons. In describing the rise of big business in post-Civil War America, Charles and Mary Beard accused the framers of the Fourteenth Amendment of a conspiracy to protect corporations and property while proclaiming their interest in safeguarding the Negro. In his memoirs, Roscoe Conkling, a member of the Joint Committee, declared some of his colleagues were thinking of protecting business as well as the Negro when they phrased the amendment.

No reliable contemporary records, however, support the conspiracy theory. Notwithstanding the decisions of judges during the Jacksonian period, which counteracted many of the protections given property by the opinions of a court dominated until 1835 by Chief Justice John Marshall, corporations after the Civil War needed no special protection. In interpreting the Fourteenth Amendment, Supreme Court justices followed their own conservative leanings instead of relying on the intent of its writers. Many court decisions created a "twilight zone" in which corporations could operate without danger from federal or state regulation. This interpretation was to continue until well into the twentieth century and be changed only when a majority of the Supreme Court justices believed human rights to be more important than property rights.

The other sections of the amendment were relatively unimportant in history. Section two eliminated the three-fifths compromise in counting slaves for population representation in the House. But any state that denied the suffrage to any of its adult male citizens, "except for participation in rebellion, or other crime," would have its representation reduced in direct proportion to the number of disfranchised to the whole population of the state. This provision was a compromise between extreme Radicals who demanded suffrage for Negroes and moderates who held that suffrage belong to the states. Many moderates thought the southern states would be forced to enfranchise the freedman to increase their representation in Congress and uphold their interest. This solution would prevent embarrassment of northern politicians representing the states whose people disliked universal suffrage and still give the southern Negro political rights. The Radicals found solace in two possible expectations: the enfranchisement of freedmen or a sharp reduction in the number of southern representatives in the House. Neither hope materialized. Southerners rejected the proffered inducement, and Congress never punished the southern states by decreasing their number of representatives.

Section three of the amendment did prevent thousands of Southerners from holding political office for many years. According to this provision, all congressmen, presidential electors, other civil and military officers of the United States or of the states who had taken the oath of allegiance to support the Constitution and later engaged in rebellion or gave aid and comfort to the enemies of the United States were prohibited from serving in Congress, being a presidential elector, or holding any civil or military office of the Union or a state until their disability was removed by a two-thirds vote of Congress. This enactment was also a compromise between the Radicals' demand for the disfranchisement of former Confederates and moderates' preference for no political penalties for secessionists. It kept many former southern leaders from holding office but allowed them the privilege of voting.

The fourth section of the amendment was unnecessary, though it may have calmed the fears of many northern Civil War veterans or heirs of deceased soldiers. All debts of the United States, including those incurred for payment of bounties or anticipated for pensions, to compensate individuals for personal service in suppressing the rebellion, were declared valid obligations of the country. Both the federal and state governments were prohibited from paying any debt arising from rebellion or claims by former owners for compensation for their slaves. The large federal debt came mainly from the war and its payment was not seriously questioned by responsible Northerners or Southerners, but pensions were a different matter. The United States had never enticed soldiers or officers into any military service by promises of pensions or retirement benefits. Not until after the Civil War did the nation provide retirement for servicemen. The provision in the amendment promised veterans of the Grand Army of the Republic no impediment to pensions for their sacrifices. While it also implied national rejection of pensions for Confederate veterans, it did not prohibit grants from southern states to their veterans.

The Fourteenth Amendment was a compromise measure adopted with misgivings by moderate and Radical Republicans. On June 22, the President informed Congress that the secretary of state would submit the proposed amendment to the states. He refused to recommend its ratification, for he doubted the legality of any amendment initiated while congressmen from eleven states were denied seats in Congress.

Two days before this presidential message, the Joint Committee made its report. In a detailed analysis of the situation in the South, accompanied by a voluminous body of testimony collected by subcommittees but published separately, the entire committee rejected the presidential claim that loyal governments had been established in the former states of the Confederacy. The committee deemed it neither necessary nor proper to discuss the profitless abstraction as to whether "the late Confederate States are still states of the Union, or can ever be otherwise." Sufficient were the facts: the rebellious states were disorganized communities without valid civil governments and constitutions. The former relations between the states and the federal government had been broken by attempted disunion, and those states which had voluntarily deprived themselves of representation in Congress "for the criminal purpose of destroying the Union" had no right to protest the temporary exclusion of their representatives from seats in the national legislature. Since the rebellious states had been conquered by the people "acting through all the co-ordinate branches of the government, and not by the executive department alone," the President could not "fix and regulate the terms of settlement and confer congressional representation on conquered rebels and traitors." The "authority to restore rebels to political power in the federal Government" belonged to and could be exercised only with the concurrence of all departments of the national government.

Although it did not deny the President the exercise of his executive function, the committee agreed that Congress should formulate reconstruction policy by legislative enactment. The committee continued by hitting at a weakness in the presidential plan. Johnson contended, perhaps even believed, that the southern state governments were creatures of the people and that these governments acted on a voluntary basis in accepting his conditions. "All the so-called legislation of state conventions and legislatures," the committee reported, "has been had under military dictation." In the South the President qualified persons to appoint congressmen or empowered others to elect them, and in the opinion of the Joint Committee, these acts gave him virtual control of the legislative department, contravened the Constitution, and practically vested all legislative power in the executive.

Testimony had made apparent the still existing hostility of white Southerners toward the government and people of the United States; this fact forced the committee to conclude that it was necessary to provide "adequate safeguards for the future, before restoring the insurrectionary states to a participation in the direction of public affairs. . . ." Therefore, it concluded "that the so-called Confederate States are not, at present, entitled to representation in the Congress of the United States. . . ."

Many debatable questions arose from the proposed Fourteenth Amendment and the Joint Committee report. Were they traps laid by Congress, or more specifically the Radicals, to ensnare the President and his southern governments? Congressional leaders implied that acceptance of the Fourteenth Amendment by the southern states would be a sufficient demonstration of their loyalty to justify the seating of their representatives and senators. But a proposed act to guarantee readmission of the former Confederate states on ratification of the amendment was not enacted. Although Tennessee was readmitted after her legislature ratified, Congress never offered the Fourteenth Amendment as its plan of reconstruction or promised the southern states admission of their congressmen as a reward for ratification.

A more tactful executive than Johnson, one less dogmatic and more willing to share reconstruction planning with legislators, might have worked out a compromise with Congress. In June 1866, the moderates were the power block in the Republican party and the President was still an influential person. The moderates knew that Northerners demanded concrete evidence of southern loyalty and fair treatment of freedmen but also wanted speedy readmission of the southern states. Certainly the combination of the presidential office, Democrats, conservative and moderate Republicans could have pushed a definite program through Congress. By coupling recognition of his southern governments with their acceptance of the amendment, Johnson would have forged a powerful political weapon. A rejection of this compromise by Congress would have enabled the President to appeal to northern voters by asserting the southern governments had demonstrated their loyalty by ratification of the Fourteenth Amendment and the safeguards demanded by Congress had been provided.

Presidential and Southern Reaction

Northern response to the proposed Fourteenth Amendment was little more than lukewarm. Newspaper editors recognized it as a moderate document, a compromise with excellent voter appeal in the forthcoming elections. Even the pro-Johnson papers considered it reasonable.

But the President rejected it. For him the southern governments were operating, loyal, and solved the basic reconstruction problems. His policies were just and constitutional, the Southern reaction to them fairly satisfactory, and Congress should recognize his accomplishments. He reiterated these themes in speech and document to congressional leaders and to visitors from the South. Southerners believed their compliance with presidential directives entitled their state governments to representation in

Congress and to the exercise of all the powers reserved to the states by the Constitution.

Of the former Confederate states only Tennessee ratified the Fourteenth Amendment in 1866. Conditions in that southern state were unique in the South. William Gannaway Brownlow, who had been a pro-slavery man opposed to secession, was elected governor of Tennessee on the Republican ticket in 1865. Formerly divided between their attachment to the Confederacy and the Union, Tennesseeans had seen their state occupied, invaded, and reinvaded by northern and southern forces. In 1865 peace at any price was welcomed. The state's ratification of the Fourteenth Amendment was accomplished by voting rules which favored election of Republican legislators and the abduction and holding of two assemblymen to obtain a quorum. Brownlow forwarded the ratification to the secretary of the United States Senate with a sarcastic greeting "to the dead dog of the White House."

Nevertheless, Congress quickly seated representatives and senators from Tennessee. In a preamble to the joint resolution, senators and representatives attempted to embarrass the President by proclaiming the right of Congress to reconstruct the southern states. Johnson's desire for the readmission of his state forced his assent, but he hit back at the Radicals by treating the preamble as a statement instead of legislation and rejected the congressional contention that Tennessee had ratified the Fourteenth Amendment. In addition, he recounted his work and expressed his concern for sectional reconciliation and national unity, and lectured Congress for its delaying tactics and failure to advance a program for restoring the southern states to the Union. He signed the resolution, however, and Tennessee was restored to full participation in the Union in July 1866.

In a period extending from October 1866 to February 1867, the other southern states rejected the amendment. The legislators of Florida, Mississippi, and Louisiana were unanimous in their opposition; only one house member in South Carolina and one in Virginia favored the amendment; and in total, 4 senators and 29 representatives in the 10 states voted for ratification. Although section three of the Fourteenth Amendment contained no disfranchisement clause, the exclusion of many former Confederates from federal and state offices was particularly resented by southern legislators. Undoubtedly the strong opposition of Johnson to the amendment encouraged Southerners to present an almost solid phalanx against ratification.

More disastrous to the southern image in 1866 than rejection of the Fourteenth Amendment were the acts and expressions of Southerners. In Memphis, Tennessee, the white people, especially the poorer ones, were disturbed by what they considered the arrogance of federal Negro troops.

On April 30, 1866, a conflict between the soldiers and the city police attracted a mob. Whites joined forces with policemen in raiding the Negro section of Memphis and in killing its residents. After three days of burning, looting, and killing, General George Stoneman restored order; but 47 Negro men, women, and children were dead, more than 80 injured, and 4 Negro churches and 12 Negro schools lay in ashes. According to Stoneman, only one white man was injured, and after the first day of the riot, Negroes had done nothing to foment further violence. The *Memphis Avalanche*, however, gloated over the killings and predicted: "Soon we shall have no more black troops among us. Thank heaven the white race are once more rulers of Memphis."

Tennessee and federal agencies acted. Governor Brownlow persuaded the state legislature to place the Memphis police under a commissioner, Stoneman appointed a military board to investigate, and officials of the Freedmen's Bureau also looked for the causes of the riot. These investigations supplied stories for northern newspapers, but the most damaging propaganda came from the testimony of witnesses who appeared before the three-member House of Representatives committee from Washington. Chairman Elihu B. Washburne heard one pregnant Negro woman tell of white hoodlums robbing her house while one raped her, and another Negro woman described the murder of her husband; altogether 170 whites and Negroes testified. The committee was biased, but its conclusion that the white mob was motivated by a deadly hatred of Negroes was given wide publicity in the North.

Two weeks later a mob struck again, this time in New Orleans. In strife-torn Louisiana politics, the Republicans were divided into moderate and radical factions. Because of his policies of currying favor with former Confederates and supporting the President, Govenor J. Madison Wells was re-elected in November of 1865; but Democrat Albert Voorhees won the lieutenant governorship and the legislature was Democratic. The conservative legislature angered the radical Republicans by passing a severe black code. Local election results foretold the political extinction of the Unionists who had written Louisiana's constitution in 1864 and started reconstruction of the state. By direct order of the President, Governor Wells allowed a mayoralty election in New Orleans which was won by John T. Monroe, an unpardoned Confederate. Johnson immediately pardoned him.

The Unionists or radical Republicans planned to reconvene the constitutional convention of 1864 to regain their power by disfranchising ex-Confederates and, perhaps, enfranchising Negroes. The convention's president, Judge H. Durell, who saw no legal reason for reconvening the assembly, was deposed. Since less than half of the original delegates would appear again, the radicals persuaded Governor Wells to call for the election of additional delegates. But, disgusted by the governor's refusal to do more and by his fixing the election date for September 3, the radicals decided to hold a meeting on July 30. Mayor Monroe informed federal military commander Absalom Baird that he would arrest the delegates unless the military planned to protect them. General Baird dispatched a telegram to Stanton requesting direction, but the secretary of war neither replied nor informed the President of the telegram. Under the circumstances Baird refused to allow the arrest of the delegates. The mayor's order arming the New Orleans police force frightened Lieutenant Governor Voorhees, who appealed to Baird for troops. The general responded but moved the troops so slowly that they played no part in the ensuing riot. Hundreds of Negroes planned to participate in a demonstration and some of them were armed to guard the convention.

On July 30 a procession of Negroes marched toward the Mechanics Institute, the meeting place of the convention. On reaching the building, they stopped to cheer the delegates. Meanwhile, the mayor called every available policeman into service and hundreds of white men stood back of the officers. Brickbats were thrown by Negroes and whites. Most marchers entered the convention hall, but one of the six or eight who remained outside became involved in a row with a policeman. Which side fired first has remained unknown, but the shot was followed by others. By concentrating their fire at the windows of the Institute, the officers forced white flags of surrender. Thereupon they rushed into the building and emptied their revolvers at the delegates and observers. They retired to reload and then forced doors that had been barricaded and repeated their performance. By this time whites and Negroes within the building sought escape but were met by another round of fire by policemen and, behind the latter, the guns of white rioters.

The exact number of killed and wounded was never established. Perhaps as many as 37 Negroes and 3 of their white friends died, and 200 or more of the radicals were wounded. Certainly one assailant lost his life, possibly as many as four, and ten were wounded. All witnesses, however, agreed that the Negro losses were extremely heavy in comparison to those of the policemen and white civilians. General Philip Sheridan declared the riot "an absolute massacre by the police" and estimated that nine-tenths of the dead were the result of "stabbing and smashing in the heads" of the wounded. In his official opinion, the riot was wholesale murder perpetrated by the mayor and his policemen "without the shadow of necessity."

Almost 100 years afterwards it is impossible for an American to comprehend the revulsion in the North to the New Orleans and Memphis riots. Newspapers attracted the attention of the public with block-letter headlines. Editors penned accusations, speakers dramatized the killings, ministers moved their congregations to tears, and Radical congressmen padded official records with reports. "The hands of rebels are again red with loyal blood," the *New-York Tribune* proclaimed. Among reports of the atrocity was the pathetic story of a fifteen-year-old boy who participated in the slaughter because Negroes were trying to take away his right to vote. Although the riots received the widest publicity, accounts of other murders and lesser mistreatment of Negroes and Unionists in the South were fed readers by the newspapers.

By midsummer a majority of Northerners was disgusted with the President and former Confederates. Few Northerners paused to admit that many white Southerners disapproved both of the riots and the mistreatment of freedmen. Northern opinion was swayed by the riots, the killing of Negroes, and the reported hatred of Negroes by white people. Influenced by these events and attitudes, most northern voters viewed Presidential Reconstruction as a complete failure.

The 1866 Elections

The conventions and the campaigns of 1866 were conducted in an atmosphere charged with emotion. Ordinarily non-presidential contests witnessed no political conventions, but 1866 was a peculiar year in American political history. In 1864 Lincoln and Johnson had been the successful candidates of the National Union Party, and in 1866 Johnson technically remained at the head of a party which had resumed the Republican label. The Republicans, however, had virtually repudiated the President and whatever support he could engender depended on Democrats, some conservative Republicans, and a scattering of independents. Under these circumstances Johnson's supporters considered a national convention the best means of rallying support for Presidential Reconstruction.

In February, editor James Gordon Bennett called for the organization of a conservative national party to counteract the Radicals and unify the supporters of Johnson. Following the President's veto of the Civil Rights Bill, a National Union Executive Committee arranged for a soldiers' and sailors' serenade, and on April 18, Johnson described his wartime work to the servicemen and called for immediate admission of southern congressmen. Later the committee incorporated its principles into a political platform: praise for soldiers and sailors, no compromise with traitors, the illegality of secession, payment of the national debt, the right of each state to control its local institutions and to determine suffrage, and objection to excluding a state from the Union or attempting to govern it as a territory. The President endorsed the platform.

From June 11 to 26 pro-Johnson congressmen and other leaders worked out the details for a convention. Senator James R. Doolittle exerted considerable leadership; he and his Republican colleagues, Edgar Cowan and Nathan F. Dixon, joined Democrats in signing the call for a National Union Convention at Philadelphia in August. Secretary Welles failed in an attempt to have the Fourteenth Amendment condemned. Convention leaders wanted a Unionist theme for the convention—an appeal for voter support based on the continuation of Lincoln's wartime party and the restoration of the Union. Despite this plan, most regular Republicans shied away from bolting their party organization and many Democrats feared their support for the convention would weaken their party's chances in state elections. Since the major support for the meeting came from Democrats, they became increasingly influential in preparatory councils for the convention.

Necessity and reality forced the pro-Johnson forces to campaign on the issue of Presidential Reconstruction. In 1866 the tariff, currency, or monopolies were not at issue. These became fundamental concerns in later years but as yet they aroused the political interests of relatively few businessmen or farmers. The campaign of 1866 revolved around the reconstruction of the southern states: had Johnson established loyal governments in the South? Were Southerners treating freedmen and loyalists fairly? Had rebels paid a sufficient penalty for their crime? Should Congress impose additional conditions on the South? National acceptance of Presidential Reconstruction would have terminated the process of reunion; rejection of it would give Congress a virtually unlimited directive to begin anew in restoring republican forms of government in the South. The voter was offered two alternatives, the acceptance of Johnson's policies or giving Congress sanction to proceed on some undefined plan, for neither moderate congressman nor the Radicals offered the voter definite proposals.

Delegates to the National Union Convention assembled on August 14 in a large, damp, half-completed hall at Philadelphia. They suffered from heat and humidity, grumbled about waiting for transportation from hotels located some three miles from the meeting place, but convened in an orderly fashion. Postmaster General Alexander Randall peered down the center aisle. "Gentlemen of the Convention," he shouted, "I have to announce to you the approach of the delegates from Massachusetts and South Carolina, arm-in-arm." Sure enough, there was the large figure of James Lawrence Orr, governor of South Carolina, and the diminutive Darius N. Couch of Massachusetts, former Union general and unsuccessful candidate for the governor of his adopted state, marching down the aisle. The audience then rose and the rafters rang with repeated cheers for the Union as the delegates paired off and paraded arm-in-arm. As a result, the National Union assembly was known as the "Arm-in-Arm Convention."

Temporary chairman and former Union general John A. Dix announced the purposes of the convention were to vindicate and restore the Constitution. When the President declared the war over, Dix said, the states were restored to the Union, but the congressmen of ten states were still denied admission by the Radicals. On the second day, Senator Doolittle's elevation to the permanent chairmanship emphasized the convention's demands for harmony and union. The following day Henry Raymond of the *New York Times* delivered the principal address. Prior to this time his speech had been edited by Southerners who objected to many statements in it. The editor asserted that the war had settled the questions of secession and slavery, the purpose of the Civil War was to maintain the Union and not to enhance the power of the federal government; the war was over and now the paramount concern of the nation was reunion. In his message to the convention Johnson referred to Congress as representing some of the states of the Union. The delegates adopted resolutions which strongly endorsed Presidential Reconstruction.

Less than two weeks after adjournment of the convention President Johnson fathered the political "Swing Around the Circle." His official reason was the dedication of the Stephen A. Douglas monument at Chicago. Some friends who disapproved of his stump-speaking methods in Tennessee advised him to remain in the White House, but the "swing" left Washington with Senator Doolittle, generals Grant and Custer, Admiral Farragut, Postmaster General Randall, and other dignitaries in attendance. The President's reception in Pennsylvania, New Jersey, and New York cities was good and his audiences responsive. He began his talks by saying that he was not there to make a speech, and continued with an account of his political career and services during the war. He compared his policies of amnesty and forgiveness with the principles of Christ and denounced the Radicals who were attempting to make a Judas out of him. He pleaded with voters to protect the Constitution and the Union. Johnson was back on the hustings in Tennessee giving his opponents their due. He failed to realize the change of place and the change of times. Reporters detailed his speeches, and before long his audience knew exactly what he was going to say. Even the sympathetic Secretary Welles admitted that Johnson gave only one often-repeated speech.

As the President proceeded around the circle, local politicians became more and more reluctant to greet him and the number of hecklers in his audience increased. Johnson responded to the latter, but in doing so, lowered the dignity of his office. In answer to one question he suggested hanging Thad Stevens. At St. Louis the President referred to the New Orleans riot, but rather than expressing regret for the killings, he condemned the radical faction in Louisiana and continued with a denunciation of the Radicals in Congress. Friends shuddered as the President responded to calls for speeches at unscheduled stops. Before the end of the swing his audiences were silently unfriendly or vocally antagonistic. What had begun as a hopeful venture terminated on September 15 as a complete fiasco.

Meanwhile the Radicals organized their campaign against the President and his reconstruction policies with skill and expert management. They sarcastically referred to Johnson's "My Policies," and their speakers followed his route to accuse him of having a "personal government," or the transfer of "the entire government from the control of loyal men to Copperheads and rebels." On September 12, the Radicals answered the National Union Convention with the Northern and Southern Loyalists Convention at Philadelphia, which condemned Presidential Reconstruction and demanded an end to rule in the southern states by former Confederates. Albion W. Tourgée, formerly of Ohio but settled in North Carolina, spoke for Negro suffrage, but the convention endorsed neither suffrage or equality programs for the Negro. In reality the presence of famous Negro leader Frederick Douglass, a delegate from Rochester, caused some embarrassment. The Democrats promptly dubbed the meeting the "Black and Tan Convention" or a congregation of "Nigger Worshippers."

Two other conventions met in September. The Soldier and Sailors Convention assembled in Cleveland on the seventeenth to endorse Johnson's policies. One week later another with the same name met in Pittsburg to condemn the President. Speakers in various states contrasted the interest of Congress in the welfare of the veteran with fictitious accounts of Johnson's plans to shortchange the soldier and sailor. Veterans were stirred to hold the first convention of the Grand Army of the Republic at Indianapolis in November. Although the G. A. R. proclaimed itself a nonpartisan organization, it eventually became almost an adjunct of the Republican party. As antagonism to the President mounted, some men feared veterans might march on Washington to remove Johnson from office by force.

In a campaign of vituperation both sides were guilty of lies and imprudent remarks. Johnson was called a drunken brute, a traitor, and the assassin of Lincoln. In an age when newspapers had little fear of libel suits, newsmen spread their accusations on front pages and editors wrote caustic editorials. Most northern papers supported the Radicals, but Bennett's *New-York Herald*, with the largest circulation in the nation, labeled the

Northern and Southern Loyalists Convention a meeting of black and whites, free lovers, spiritualists, and miscegenationists. Another headline in the *Herald* promised readers an account of the drunken orgies of the Radicals at convention hotels in Philadelphia. But the overwhelming victory of Republicans in Maine's early election quieted Bennett. The unpopularity of moderate support for Johnson's policies forced Raymond of the *New York Times* to desert the President to save his newspaper from losses that were endangering its solvency.

On election day the people rejected Johnson's claim that reconstruction was finished and voted to have Congress proceed along whatever line it chose to establish loyal governments in ten southern states. Every governorship in the northern states went to the Republicans and they also won more than a two-thirds majority in both houses of Congress. Only in the border states of Delaware, Maryland, and Kentucky did the Democrats score victories. Overjoyed by their success, Radical congressmen anticipated a dominant role for themselves within the Republican party and a drastic change from the presidential plan of restoring the southern states.

Decision at Last

Under ordinary circumstances the newly elected congressmen would not assemble for the first session of the Fortieth Congress until December 1867. Even the most optimistic Radical feared the power of the presidential office. Notwithstanding Johnson's unpopularity with voters, many moderate Republican congressmen remained willing to compromise for the sake of harmony. If the President and his southern supporters heeded the election returns, they might still defeat Radical plans by co-operation to appease Northerners. Before the elections Texas had refused to ratify the Fourteenth Amendment and Georgia soon rejected it; Florida, Alabama, North Carolina, Arkansas, and South Carolina turned it down in December; and Virginia, Mississippi, and Louisiana did so in January and February. The fact that Delaware and Kentucky also voted against the amendment was not important, for the opposition of ten former Confederate states was sufficient to prevent adoption.

The President was no more willing than were Southerners to yield a little in the hope of winning something. Always a fighter, Johnson refused to be turned from what he considered right by the defeat of his supporters. On December 3, 1866, he delivered to the "Lame Duck" session of the Thirty-Ninth Congress a stinging message on reconstruction. He reviewed the work done in restoring the southern states and described how Southerners had responded by establishing loyal governments until their efforts and those of the President were checked by Congress. "Ten States," Johnson declared, or more than one-fourth of the Union, "remain without representation; the seats of fifty members in the House of Representatives and of twenty members in the Senate are yet vacant, not by their own consent, not by failure of election, but by a refusal of Congress to accept their credentials." Their admission, he continued, would be in accord with the great principles of the Declaration of Independence and the provisions of the Constitution.

At the beginning of the war each house of the Congress had declared with remarkable unanimity the purpose of the conflict, and Johnson quoted from the legislative resolution. The United States was not waging a war "in any spirit of oppression, nor for any purpose of conquest or subjugation, nor purpose of overthrowing or interfering with the rights or established institutions of those States, but to defend and maintain the supremacy of the Constitution . . . , and to preserve the Union, with all the dignity, equality, and rights of the several States unimpaired. . . ." In all of his work, the President affirmed that he had followed this directive of Congress. The war was over, he stated, and with its termination all excuse for the exercise of powers of doubtful constitutionality ceased. All men, he concluded, should unite to reconcile laws with the Constitution, "bring legislation within the boundaries prescribed by the Constitution and to return to the ancient landmarks established by our fathers. . . ."

Response to the presidential message received support or opposition according to individual congressmen. Senator Sumner stated his intention to offer a resolution declaring the existing southern governments illegal, excluding their representatives from Congress, and barring the states from voting on constitutional amendments. The latter part of this resolution would have insured acceptance of the Fourteenth Amendment but would also have repudiated an already established principle of Congress in the adoption of the Thirteenth Amendment of counting all the states, even if some of them were not officially reconstructed.

Other senators and representatives thought acceptance of the Fourteenth Amendment should still be the test of southern loyalty. Radical Ben Wade and moderate John Sherman indicated they favored this idea, and John Bingham definitely did. Representative James G. Blaine of Maine wanted assurance of Negro suffrage in the South, but his colleague, John M. Broomall of Pennsylvania, introduced a resolution on December 10 which promised readmission of the southern states upon their ratification of the proposed amendment. His resolution was referred to and buried by the Joint Committee.

After the election of 1866 many Radicals had scores to settle with Johnson. Stevens recalled the President's advice to hang Stevens. The Pennsylvania congressman, however, had goaded the President to indiscreet utterances. Back in May 1866, the sarcastic representative referred "to the late lamented Johnson of blessed memory." By 1867 the vindictive Stevens was determined to devote his remaining months of life to the punishment of traitors. He opposed amnesty for "rebels" and announced his intention of demanding that a part of the national debt be paid from the proceeds of property confiscated in the South. More clearly than any other legislator, he saw the impossibility of breaking the political power of southern aristocrats as long as they retained their economic power. To him, confiscation of large estates and distribution of them to former slaves was more important than enfranchising Negroes. Without a means of economic independence, he thought the vote would gain the Negro no more than temporary respite from exploitation by white Southerners.

In 1867 Stevens's open avowal of party purposes shocked many independent-minded Americans. For him, the safety of the nation depended upon the continued supremacy of the Republican party. Unless freedmen were enfranchised, he prophesied that every southern state would "send a solid rebel representative delegation to Congress, and cast a solid rebel electoral vote." On the other hand, a combination of the lower income class in the South, poor whites and Negroes, would send almost solid Republican delegations to Washington and cast electoral votes for Republican candidates.

Stevens reached his political peak in 1867. His tongue lashed out with bitter words and his colleagues smiled when he sarcastically referred to former Confederates as "chivalric gentlemen." But Stevens also had deep societal concerns for lower-income Americans. In his youth he had been one of them and he believed the United States should always be a land where a child with motivation and ability could move forward. Actually Stevens was almost race-blind, his interest in the welfare of Negroes being frequently aroused by their economic plight; Negroes' identity with Americans of little property rather than the color of their skin interested him. Even in 1867 Stevens was unable to dictate congressional policies for reconstructing the southern states. In the subsequent decades historians made him the symbol of vindictiveness contrasted to the Lincoln-Johnson image of magnanimity. In the process Stevens emerged with greater power and more influence than he actually held in 1867. Again and again he witnessed the deletion of his provisions from bills; his ideas of confiscation and redistribution of property were rejected; practically nothing was done to better the economic situation of southern whites and Negroes.

Stevens was in the midst of the decision-making, and decisions were repeatedly made in the Lame Duck session of the Thirty-Ninth Congress. Sumner, who proclaimed the philosophy that "anything for human rights is constitutional," introduced a bill to enfranchise Negro residents of the District of Columbia. It was passed by both houses, vetoed by the President, and made law by overriding his veto.

A series of acts enhanced the power of Congress and limited that of the

President. By the Act of January 22, 1867, the first session of the Fortieth Congress, and of Congresses in the future, was to begin on March 4, following elections of the preceding year. This act advanced the session by nine months and eliminated a long period in which the executive department could operate with no check from the legislative branch.

March 2, 1867, was truly legislative day. The Tenure of Office Act attempted to limit the President's authority to dismiss cabinet members. The Army Appropriations Act fixed the general of the army's headquarters in Washington and gave legal sanction only to those orders of the President and secretary of war which were issued by the general of the army, who could not be removed from office or assigned to duty outside of Washington without the consent of the Senate. In addition, the militia in the former Confederate states, a militia which in the opinion of Congress supported rebels and harmed freedmen and Unionists, was disbanded.

During this period of decision-making, President Johnson remained unmoved. His major support consisted of Democrats in Congress. The only chance of the minority party lay in preventing the President from getting together with moderate Republicans and forging a reconstruction policy which would move ahead. To northern Democrats the 1866 elections were not a national acceptance of the Fourteenth Amendment. Southern refusal to ratify it would bring the Radicals to an impasse. They had done their worst; they would not dare impose military rule or territorial status on the southern states, for either would be declared unconstitutional by the Supreme Court. The only recourse of the Radicals would be Negro suffrage and its advocacy would shift northern voters into the Democratic fold.

Southerners eagerly accepted these pleasant ideas of northern Democratic leaders. Southern editors quoted freely from the *New York World*, now the mainstay of northern democracy. According to the *World*, the Fourteenth Amendment was a fraud and a swindle, proposed to humiliate the South; it offered no guarantees that ratification would result in the seating of southern congressmen; and was suggested as a devious means to entice Southerners to barter their honor for representation, thereby making possible Negro domination of the Southland. The South could still rely on the President and the Supreme Court, and delay would bring northern public opinion to bear on the Radicals, forcing them to settle for an honorable restoration of the southern states to the Union.

Southern leaders not only succumbed to this propaganda but their countrymen defied northern public opinion. Reports reaching the North told of southern ostracism, "that terrible inquisition of Southern society," of Unionists and Republicans. Often they were derisively greeted on the street with "I smell a Radical and he stinks like a nigger," or "There's a Republican—he's no better than a dog." In Ocala, Florida, James Denton was tried for the murder of a freedman. He was convicted, fined $225, and sentenced to one minute in jail. Southern wags said, "The price of niggers has gone down since freedom." In January formerly friendly North Carolina newspapers turned on the administration of Governor Jonathan Worth, forcing him to complain of the gross negligence of officials in bringing malefactors to justice. Democracy was failing in the South because usually responsible citizens created a public opinion that warped the senses of local police and local courts. The public made heroes of individuals who insulted, assaulted, or even murdered politically active Unionists and Negroes.

Too late, sincere Southerners realized their Southland was traveling a dead-end road. Neither Johnson nor northern Democrats correctly assessed northern opinion. Instead of latent objection to the plans of Radicals, most Northerners supported their design to repudiate most of what the President had done and to attempt by congressional action a remolding of the South. On March 2, 1867, the Congress took charge of reconstruction by overriding the President's veto of the first reconstruction act.

REFERENCES

Joseph B. James, *The Framing of the Fourteenth Amendment* (Urbana, 1956), has supplanted Horace E. Flack, *The Adoption of the Fourteenth Amendment* (Baltimore, 1908). Louis B. Boudin, "Truth and Fiction about the Fourteenth Amendment," *New York University Law Review*, XVI (1938), pp. 19–82, refutes the economic interpretation of the amendment. Conspiracy theories are examined by Howard J. Graham, "The 'Conspiracy Theory' of the Fourteenth Amendment," *Yale Law Review*, XLVII (1938), pp. 371–403 and by James F. S. Russell, "The Railroads in the 'Conspiracy Theory' of the Fourteenth Amendment," *Mississippi Valley Historical Review*, XLI (1955), pp. 601–22. The roles and ideals of abolitionists are the themes of books and biographies: James M. McPherson, *The Struggle for Equality: Abolitionists and the Negro in the Civil War and Reconstruction* (Princeton, 1965); Walter M. Merrill, *Against Wind and Tide: A Biography of Wm. Lloyd Garrison* (New York, 1963); Irving H. Bartlett, *Wendell Phillips: Brahmin Radical* (New York, 1961); and Jacobus ten Brock, *The AntiSlavery Origins of the Fourteenth Amendment* (Berkeley, 1951). Milton R. Konvitz, *A Century of Civil Rights*, with a *Study of State Law Against Discrimination* by Theodore Leskes (New York, 1961), applauds abolitionists and Radicals; and Robert J. Harris, *The Quest for Equality* (Baton Rouge, 1960), traces the history of equality under law for all citizens. Ira V. Brown, "Pennsylvania and the Rights of the Negro, 1865–1887," *Pennsylvania History*, XXVIII (1961), pp. 45–57, and David Montgomery, "Radical Republicanism in Pennsylvania, 1866–1876," *Pennsylvania Magazine of History and Biography*, LXXXV (1961), pp. 439–57, investigate Radical idealism. John R. Flicker, *History of Reconstruction in Lou-

isiana (Baltimore, 1910), describes the new Orleans riot; and Jack D. Holmes, "The Underlying Causes of the Memphis Race Riot of 1866," *Tennessee Historical Quarterly*, XVII (1958), pp. 195–221, discusses the Memphis affair. In a series of articles, Gregg Phifer follows President Johnson in 1866: "Andrew Johnson Takes a Trip," "Andrew Johnson Argues a Case," "Johnson Delivers His Argument," and "Andrew Johnson Loses His Battle," *Tennessee Historical Quarterly*, II (1952), pp. 3–22, 148–170, 212–234, 291–328. The studies of southern states, to be cited at the end of Chapter VII, portray the action and thought of Southerners.

Congressional Reconstruction

THE CONGRESSIONAL plan of reconstruction was an amazing political accomplishment. The odds against the Radical faction of the Republican party in the spring of 1865 appeared insurmountable. For almost nine months President Johnson enjoyed the advantage of operating without the interference of Congress. In December 1865, he presented the national legislature with accomplished facts—most of the southern states possessed operating governments, their senators and representatives were waiting to be seated in Congress, and reconstruction was practically completed.

As the Thirty-Ninth Congress convened in December 1866, the Radicals possessed no more than slender support. Perhaps the act of February 8, 1865, which excluded the former Confederate states from participating in the 1868 presidential election and the Freedmen's Bureau offered some possibilities to the Radicals. Their strongest staff was the number of dissatisfied moderate Republicans, men who conscientiously questioned the loyalty of the Southerners who dominated the "loyal" governments established by presidential directive. Still in embryo was a potentially powerful idea that equality should be added to union and abolition of slavery as purposes of the war. Yet the only act the moderate and Radical Republicans could agree on was negative—refusal to seat congressmen from the South pending an investigation of Johnson's reconstructed southern states.

In 1867 the Radicals fell heir to two unexpected boons: the intransigence of Johnson and the resistance of the Southerner. Of the two attitudes, that of the President is historically less defensible. At almost any time during a period of more than a year, he certainly could have won congressional support by agreeing to some modification of and additions to his policies. Rather than compromising, he clung to his ideas and his steadfast opposition to congressional demands encouraged Southerners to defy northern opinion.

The elections of 1866 were the turning point in the argument between the executive and the legislators, but they did not give the Radicals carte blanche to proceed. Moderate Republicans retained sufficient power to have controlled reconstruction with co-operation from the President, northern

Democrats, and Southerners. In December 1866, T. C. Weatherly of the South Carolina legislature conferred with moderates who told him that southern acceptance of the Fourteenth Amendment would mean readmission. According to Weatherly, the President advised him and other Southerners to stand firm in their resistance. Though Johnson denied Weatherly's statement, southern newspapers spread the idea, attributed to the President, through the South. In Alabama the governor advised the legislature to reconsider its vote on the amendment to prevent Congress from imposing territorial status on the southern states. In January 1867, he informed Johnson by telegram of efforts being made to secure ratification and of reports reaching the South that acceptance of the amendment would win seats for southern congressmen. In reply the President urged no faltering, saw no advantage in reconsidering, and believed Americans would stand behind the Constitution and reject any congressional plan to subvert it.

The position of Southerners in 1866 and 1867 is understandable. They were the heirs to some seldom questioned beliefs: the Negro race was biologically inferior, its inherent tendency toward criminality had to be controlled, its members required direction and supervision, and Negroes were incapable of voting intelligently or performing the duties of public office. Few Southerners considered Negro suffrage justified. Furthermore, they believed they had met the presidential requirements for reconstructing their states and demonstrated their willingness to be loyal citizens of a permanent Union which banned slavery. Southerners of judgment and responsibility correctly interpreted the elections of 1866, but for them the pleasant ideas of the President and the northern Democratic press were an opiate in contrast to the painful adjustments and superhuman efforts required to face reality. They chose the paved road to the rocky path and walked themselves straight into Congressional Reconstruction.

Beginning with no definite plan of reconstruction, Congress first altered and then repudiated the presidential plan. Civil rights for Negroes, a more powerful Freedmen's Bureau, and the Fourteenth Amendment drastically changed Presidential Reconstruction. Congress never put its plan for reconstructing the South in one neat package. Its reconstruction acts were a hodgepodge of ineptly phrased laws which had to be amended and interpreted by additional legislation.

In 1867 Congress declared that no legal governments existed in ten southern states. Implied in this statement was a disavowal of all acts of those governments; but, with an unexplained inconsistency, Congress recognized work done by those governments. Their repudiation of wartime debts, recognition of laws passed by the United States during the war, denial of secession, and ratification of the Thirteenth Amendment were accepted as legal acts. Though repudiating Presidential Reconstruction,

Congress validated much of the work done by Johnson's "illegal" southern governments.

The Congressional Plan

Congressional laws on reconstruction were the result of compromises between moderate and radical factions of the Republican party. No one man wrote the laws or was responsible for their enactment. At times during the process of debate and vote, Democrats joined Radicals to defeat moderate measures. Almost invariably this Democratic tactic resulted in more rigid requirements being imposed on the southern states than would have been the case had northern Democrats supported moderate Republicans. Extreme Radicals demanded unrestricted military rule over the South, and the most generous moderates wanted the existing southern states to reconstruct themselves along lines laid down by Congress. Since most Republicans believed some military rule essential, compromise was possible.

After the Christmas holidays of 1866 the reassembled House members heard Stevens advocate the passage of his reconstruction bill. It stated that ten former Confederate states had forfeited all their rights, that their present governments were illegal, ex-Confederate civil and military leaders must be shorn of their citizenship for at least five years, new southern state constitutions with provisions for Negro suffrage were essential, and for a time, the only safe recourse of the nation was military control of the South. Stevens described the desperate conditions under which loyalists existed in the South: they needed to be protected "from the barbarians . . . who are murdering loyal whites daily and daily putting into secret graves not only hundreds but thousands of colored people. . . ." Rufus P. Spalding of Ohio wanted Southerners to be given until March 4 to ratify the Fourteenth Amendment. On January 16, John A. Bingham, who would later move into the Radical camp, attacked the Stevens bill with bitter words; he thought the amendment the best way of bringing the southern states back into the Union. When the House wavered between Stevens's call for speed and Bingham's desire for delay, George Julian of Indiana offered a simple bill to extend military rule throughout the South. By a vote of 88 to 65 the Stevens bill was sent to the Joint Committee for consideration, but the committee refused to accept it. Then Stevens agreed to have Senator George H. Williams introduce the Julian bill in the Senate. The Joint Committee received and amended it, and asked Stevens to report the altered bill to the House.

Debate proceeded in the House with the Democrats shifting from moderate to the Radical side. After Democrats and Radicals had joined to defeat a moderate compromise, the Democrats were shocked by House passage of Julian's military control bill. Moderates who disliked military control preferred it to continual stalemate. In the Senate, Williams, who took charge of the bill, accepted and then rejected an amendment whereby adoption of the Fourteenth Amendment and enfranchising Negroes would guarantee readmission of the southern states. From a party caucus of February 16 came a committee, headed by John Sherman, charged with amending the bill to make it acceptable to the Senate. Thus the final revisions of the First Reconstruction Act were mainly the work of Sherman. The patched bill was accepted by both houses.

On March 2, 1867, President Johnson vetoed it. He objected to placing the people of ten states "under the absolute domination of military rulers." He declared the existing southern states were as legal as any northern state and following every principle of northern states in provisions for the "preservation of order, the suppression of crime, and the redress of private injury." Again he referred to the congressional resolution of July 1861, which stated the purpose of the war was not subjection but enforcement of the Constitution and national laws. It was accepted by northern and southern Unionists as "expressing honestly and truly the objects of the war"; lives were sacrificed for this principle, and to repudiate it would be a breach of honor to which Johnson would not assent. The war was over, he asserted, the laws and courts of federal and state governments were in undisturbed and harmonious operation and there was no legal excuse for placing ten states under military rule. "I submit to Congress," he said, "whether this measure is not in its whole character, scope, and object without precedent and without authority, in palpable conflict with the plainest provisions of the Constitution. . . ." Congress brushed aside these arguments by overriding his veto on March 2 by a vote of 138-to-48 in the House and 38-to-10 in the Senate.

According to the preamble of the law no legal governments existed in the ten southern states. To provide for the adequate protection of life and property in the "rebel States" and to enforce peace and good order until loyal and republican state governments were established, Congress divided them into five military districts. To command each of the districts, the President was to appoint an officer holding the rank of brigadier general or higher, and supply him with a federal force sufficient to enforce his orders. The duties of these commanding officers were: protection of all persons in their individual and property rights; suppression of all insurrection, disorder, and violence; and punishment of all disturbers of the public peace and other troublemakers. At their discretion these military officers could continue civil officials in office or establish military courts to try disturbers of the peace. If forced to exercise the latter authority, their power transcended that of state and local officers. The commander was instructed to see that any accused person be tried without undue delay and that penal-

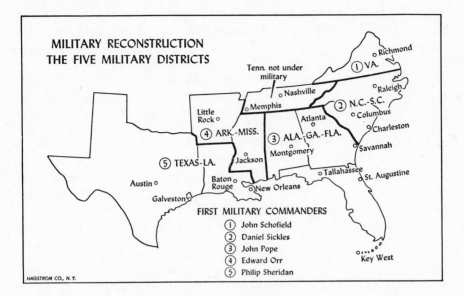

MILITARY RECONSTRUCTION
THE FIVE MILITARY DISTRICTS

Tenn. not under military

① VA.   o Richmond

o Nashville   ° Raleigh

o Memphis   ② N.C.-S.C.   o Columbus

Little Rock o   Atlanta o   ⊙ Charleston

④ ARK.-MISS.   ③ ALA.-GA.-FLA.   ⊙ Savannah

o Montgomery

⑤ TEXAS-LA.   Jackson

Austin o   Baton o Rouge   o Tallahassee   St. Augustine

Galveston ⊙   ⊙ New Orleans

FIRST MILITARY COMMANDERS
① John Schofield
② Daniel Sickles
③ John Pope
④ Edward Orr
⑤ Philip Sheridan

Key West

HAGSTROM CO., N.Y.

ties be just. All death sentences were subject to review by the President.

The duration of military control depended on co-operation of citizens of a particular state. After they had elected delegates to a constitutional convention by a vote of all adult male residents, regardless of race except those persons disqualified by participation in rebellion, the delegates framed a constitution which enfranchised all male citizens who had the qualifications to serve as members of the convention, and the constitution was accepted by a majority of the registered voters, elections could be held for a governor and legislators. When the legislature ratified the Fourteenth Amendment and it became a part of the Constitution, the duly elected representatives and senators of the co-operating state would be entitled to seats in Congress. Until these provisions were met, any government in the ten states was provisional subject to the paramount authority of the United States.

The act almost relegated the conquered states to the status of territories. Although two or more states were combined into a military district, boundary lines remained intact. The extent of military control would depend on the discretion of a commander and the co-operation of citizens residing within his district. The constitutions to be written were to contain sections enfranchising Negro males, but the law required no disfranchisement of white Southerners in the new southern state governments. Many Radicals considered this failure to proscribe former Confederates a weakness of the act.

The First Reconstruction Act was followed by a second, also overriding a presidential veto, on March 23, 1867. The first act planned Congressional Reconstruction and the second provided the means of putting the plan into operation. The second act ordered the commanding generals to register the qualified voters before September 1, called for the election of delegates to constitutional conventions, and set dates for the elections and the conventions. Except in Virginia from which West Virginia had been carved, the number of delegates was to be the same as that of the most numerous branch of a state's 1860 legislature. The military commander was authorized to apportion the geographic areas within a state to determine representation in the convention. If a majority of the registered citizens in a state voted for a convention in an election in which more than half of the registrants participated, the commanding general must call for a convention within sixty days at the place of his choice.

After being written the new constitution was to be submitted to those who had voted for a convention and its delegates. If a majority of those voting and more than half the total registrants accepted the constitution, the president of the convention was to transmit a copy of the constitution to the President. He was to forward it to Congress. If, after examining it, congressmen were satisfied "that the election was one at which all the registered and qualified voters in the State had an opportunity to vote freely and without restraint, fear or the influence of fraud . . . ," the state representatives and senators would be eligible for seats in Congress.

The crucial item in this supplementary act was the method of identifying individuals who were excluded from voting to authorize a constitutional convention, elect delegates to serve in it, and ratify the constitution produced. To register one had to be a male, twenty-one years of age or older, a resident of the state, and a loyal citizen of the United States. Furthermore, he was required to swear or affirm that he had not been disfranchised for participating in rebellion or civil war, or had ever held state or federal office and later engaged in insurrection, or given aid and comfort to the enemies of the United States.

Any registrar or other federal officeholder had to take the iron-clad oath.

> I, _____, do solemnly swear (or affirm) that I have never voluntarily borne arms against the United States since I have been a citizen thereof; that I have voluntarily given no aid, countenance, counsel or encouragement to Persons engaged in armed hostility thereto; that I have neither sought nor accepted nor attempted to exercise the functions of any office whatever, under any authority or pretended authority in hostility to the United States; that I have not yielded a voluntary support to any pretended government, authority, power or constitution within the United States, hostile or inimical thereto. And I do further swear (or affirm) that, to the best of my knowledge and authority and ability, I will sup-

port and defend the Constitution of the United States, against all enemies, foreign and domestic; that I will bear true faith and allegiance to the same; that I take this obligation freely, without any mental reservation or purpose of evasion, and that I will well and truthfully discharge the duties of the office on which I am about to enter, so help me God.

Despite the demands of Radicals, no applicant for registration was ever legally required to take the iron-clad oath. Generals in charge of registration found even the oath required for officeholding subject to various interpretations. The status of Confederate soldiers, state officeholders, and local officials was in question. Attorney General Stanbery ruled that municipal officers, state militia, and Confederate conscripts were not eliminated by the oath. In addition he ordered registrars to accept any Southerner's oath as evidence of past loyalty and leave trials for perjury to the courts. Radical spokesmen declared that no rebel could be trusted and that leaving perjury to the courts would tie up dockets for a generation.

To clarify the ambiguities of the first two acts, the Third Reconstruction Act became law on July 19, 1867. Military commanders were given virtually unlimited power, subject to approval of the general of the army and review by Congress, to remove civil or military officials in the ten southern states. The most important provisions of the act, however, clarified the authority of each district commander and his agents in registering citizens for the forthcoming elections of delegates to constitutional conventions. Members of boards of registration were not only empowered but also advised of their duty to ascertain whether or not an applicant was entitled to register.

This provision allowed registrars to investigate the loyalty of a white applicant who took the oath. Rigid enforcement of this directive would have eliminated thousands of southern white males. But in an effort to encourage the enrollment of Negroes, precinct registrars were paid on a fee basis, usually 25 cents for every person registered. This financial inducement made registrars lax in their investigations. They allowed former Confederates to register or failed to question the right of white Southerners to be enrolled. In reality it was not refusal of registrars but decision by whites not to participate that kept down the white registration. Because of a lack of qualified registrars, some ex-Confederate officeholders served as registrars.

Although he had lost his power to check Congress, President Johnson continued his appeal to the public by veto messages. The Second Reconstruction Act, he declared, placed an unreasonable obligation upon applicants for officeholding; they were forced to decide, under peril of punishment by military courts, whether their acts during the Civil War did or did not constitute aid or comfort to rebellion. The President also objected to the minimum qualifications set for registrars. The qualifications were too indefinite, for the only real requirement to serve was proof of loyalty to the

United States; the registrars could be members of the armed services, residents of a particular state, or sojourners in it.

The ten states, Johnson asserted, had constitutions, but these were branded as neither loyal nor constitutional by Congress. What was necessary, he asked, to make the constitution of a state loyal and republican?

> It is universal Negro suffrage—a question which the Federal Constitution leaves exclusively to the States themselves. All this legislative machinery of martial, military coercion, and political disfranchisement is avowedly for that purpose and none other. The existing constitutions of the ten States conform to the acknowledged standards of loyalty and republicanism. Indeed, if there are degrees in republican forms of government, their constitutions are more republican now than when these States, four of which were members of the original thirteen, first became members of the Union.

Congress, he continued, demanded not a single provision of existing constitutions be changed except the one limiting the suffrage to adult white males. According to Congress the sole test of a republican form of government was a constitutional clause enfranchising "the male citizens of said State 21 years old and upward, of whatever race, color, or previous condition, who have been resident in said State for one year previous to the day of" an election. Since without this provision no constitution framed by the ten states would be of any avail with Congress, the test of loyalty and republican form of government must be suffrage for Negroes.

> Measured by such a standard, how few of the States comprising the Union have republican constitutions! If in the exercise of the constitutional guaranty that Congress shall secure to every State a republican form of government universal suffrage for blacks as well as whites is a *sine qua non*, the work of reconstruction may as well begin in Ohio as in Virginia, in Pennsylvania as in North Carolina. . . .

Characteristics of Johnson which angered Radicals were his ability and his tenacity. A man as repeatedly beaten as he should not bring up embarrassing questions. Not only did most northern states not allow Negro suffrage, but not many of their legislatures had ratified the Fourteenth Amendment. As if to make amends for the difference between the requirement of Negro suffrage in the South and not in the North, more and more northern states ratified the Fourteenth Amendment.

Beginning of Congressional Reconstruction

Although he believed the reconstruction acts unconstitutional, Johnson knew his duty lay in complying with them until the Supreme Court declared them invalid. With the advice of General Grant, the President appointed John M. Schofield commander of the first district (Virginia), Daniel E. Sickles for the second (North Carolina and South Carolina), George H. Thomas for the third (Georgia, Alabama, and Florida), Edward O. C. Ord for the fourth (Mississippi and Arkansas), and Philip H. Sheridan for the fifth (Louisiana and Texas). These men were major generals with creditable military records. Perhaps best known in the South was Thomas, the Virginian who had remained faithful to the Union, but before Thomas took office, he was transferred and John Pope replaced him.

This initial change in commanders was the forerunner of many to come. Sheridan's rigid rule in Louisiana compared, Southerners maintained, to his devastation of the Shenandoah Valley during the war. After six months of duty, Johnson replaced him with Winfield S. Hancock, whose administration was welcomed by Louisianians and Texans. Pope was generally disliked by Southerners of the third district, who found his replacement, George G. Meade, more acceptable. One-legged Sickles, the incredible little bantam who gained notoriety before the war by killing his wife's lover, was hated, as was Edward Richard S. Canby, a Kentuckian who was one of the men who followed Schofield in Virginia.

These men, called "military satraps" by white Southerners, were the key officials in initiating Congressional Reconstruction. They left most civilian authorities untouched, but did remove the governors of Georgia, Mississippi, Texas, and Virginia, and replaced lesser officials whenever they believed it necessary. Frequently civil court functions were taken over by military tribunals and at times Negroes were allowed to serve on juries. To replace ousted officials the military commanders turned mainly to army officers and Freedmen's Bureau agents. Few Negroes were appointed to office. Most often the military sided with white Southerners, and the latter seldom voiced complaints against northern white officers but they did denounce Negro officials. With less than 20,000 men stationed in the ten southern states, and most soldiers quartered at camps distant from population centers, military occupation was more token than reality.

Many conservative Southerners preferred military governments to the questionable civilian establishments to be created under the terms imposed by Congress. They believed northern and southern veterans of the war could agree to support a white-dominated society in the South; they feared a remodeling of southern economic, political, and social patterns if governments were controlled by white radicals placed in office by Negro voters. Some Southerners were convinced that their white colleagues in the five military districts were happier than their counterparts in restored Tennessee. Delay in instituting congressional plans might have either of two beneficial results: perhaps the Supreme Court would declare the entire fabric of reconstruction unconstitutional, or a shift from anti- to pro-southern point of view in the northern states would bring changes in the reconstruction acts.

The military commanders, however, proceeded by exercising the initiative demanded of them by Congress. State registrars were appointed, and with their advice, district officers selected three-member boards for precincts. In the attempt to secure loyal Americans, the commanders and their agents relied on soldiers and Freedmen's Bureau agents. Some educated and some uneducated Negro residents were appointed to local boards.

The remuneration of the registrars varied from state to state. In Florida registrars received 15 to 40 cents for enrolling an individual. The variation in fee was determined by the distance traveled to secure the enrollee. In addition, travel pay was fixed at five cents per mile on railroads and steamboats and ten cents for country terrain in which no regular transportation facilities existed. This system encouraged registrars to list as many people as possible: underage Negroes, the same person under different names, and whites who could not honestly take the prescribed oath.

Whatever the frauds committed, the results were not far out of line with the racial composition of the population. In the registrations which proceeded through the summer, 627,000 whites and 703,000 Negroes were enrolled. White Southerners estimated the number of their race eliminated at from 300,000 to 500,000 but a modern historian has lowered the number to 150,000. In addition to the loyalty oath, two other factors held down registration by whites: the losses of manpower during the war and the refusal of many to participate in the Congressional Reconstruction. On the other hand efficient Republican organizations did a remarkable job in stimulating Negro males to register.

In Alabama, Florida, Louisiana, Mississippi, and South Carolina Negro registrants outnumbered whites. A majority of the people of Mississippi and South Carolina was Negro and more than 40 per cent of the residents of the other three states was colored. In every state with more Negro than white registrants there were overwhelmingly white and overwhelmingly Negro counties, but the majority of the counties were white. This concentration of potential Negro voters in a minority of the counties worried some southern radicals. One solution advocated by them was gerrymandering to combine Negro-dominated counties with white ones into election districts so as to give Negro voters control. Sub-commander John Sprague not only did this in Florida but also assigned more delegates to Negro-dominated districts.

In accordance with the laws of Congress, the military commanders set the dates for elections in their respective districts. By congressional enactment the process of reconstruction could be speeded by voting on an issue and selecting delegates in one general election. Thus the qualified voters could vote yes or no on calling a convention, assume it would be authorized, and choose delegates to it. If the convention were called and a constitution framed, the voters went to the polls to approve or disapprove it and at the same time elect governor, state legislators, and congressmen. Before the end of 1867 every state but Texas had held elections, authorized the calling of conventions, and elected delegates to serve in them. The process of Congressional Reconstruction was well on its way.

The Action in the South

The congressional acts shocked and then embittered white Southerners. Though at times acting with reluctance, they had complied with presidential demands. They believed the worst was over. While they rejected the Fourteenth Amendment, in doing so they had followed the President, northern Democrats, and pro-administration newspapers. Many Southerners were confused by the debates and action in Congress. They wondered whether ratification of the Fourteenth Amendment would give their congressmen seats in the Senate and House, and terminate a reconstruction imposed from Washington. Their letters of inquiry never received satisfactory answers.

Despite assurances of the President and Northerners friendly to the South, Congress almost wiped the slate of Presidential Reconstruction and then covered it with ambiguous laws. Southerners protested these laws as unfair, the nation's faith broken by their passage, the Constitution shattered. Some militant individuals advocated fighting, but cooler heads prevailed and asked what would be used for weapons. Intelligent men knew that they must submit to the overpowering force of the nation.

As long as the federal government refrained from treating Southerners as a conquered foreign people, the South possessed actual and potential weapons. While considering the enfranchisement of Negroes the idiotic idea of moon-struck reformers, onetime slave owners recalled the close association of some masters and their domestic slaves and believed whites would win their political support. If the Negroes could be directed, enfranchisement might be counteracted and the propertied class find a potent ally at the polls.

The South's final hope had many facets which could be utilized or employed one after another to take the best advantage of conditions. The first facet was a continual barrage of criticism in speech, newspaper, pamphlet, and book. Its purposes were to unify southern whites, divide southern Republicans, and eventually win Northerners to the southern point of view.

If the central government allowed freedom of speech, press, religion, and assembly in the South, and complete denial of these rights was inconceivable, the chances of success were good. Also, assuming some squeamishness on the part of the federal government and a reluctance to impose military control with extreme harshness, threat of force or force itself were means to control the Negro. To resort to this extreme involved immediate and unknown dangers. The federal government could answer force with force and extend its period of control beyond that which Northerners would sanction under peaceful conditions. Denial of individual rights to a minority, encouragement of lawbreakers, and stimulation of racial hatreds could bequeath a baneful heritage to generations of Southerners. But the white conservative Southerner of the post-Civil War era saw immediate problems and, if he had doubts about leaving his sons a heritage of hate and lawlessness, they were sublimated by his paramount concern for giving his descendants a land where Caucasions ruled supreme.

A final major facet of the South's hope for winning the peace was the economic power of white Southerners. If left in control of their property, they could regulate both the freedmen and the almost property-less poor whites. Jobs and pay, land and houses, food and clothing, medical and other services belonged to the conservative whites and could be used for political advantage.

In 1867 Southerners were not sufficiently foresighted to recognize all these possibilities or plan for their realization. They worked on a hit-or-miss basis, suffering repeated reverses and moving from defeats to untried schemes. Only in retrospect does a plan emerge, but notwithstanding the absence of blueprints for the desired structure, it gradually took shape. Quickly and almost simultaneously the Supreme Court and the southern appeal to Negro voters became forlorn hopes. The many-faceted third hope was realized after what seemed interminable years to conservative Southerners.

The overwhelming majority of white Southerners would have applauded complete political disinterest by freedmen. Even before the initiation of Congressional Reconstruction, Negroes had participated in some local elections. Their interest in politics was whetted by informal organizations of Republicans or by agents of Radicals. Friends of Chief Justice Chase, for instance, busied themselves in attempting to win Negroes to support the presidential aspirations of the former secretary of the treasury. Astute Republicans realized that molding the freedmen into politically articulate organizations was a Herculean task. Mostly illiterate, with little understanding of democratic processes, the Negroes might forego politics unless their interest was aroused and their welfare identified with voting and office-holding.

During the registration period of 1867 and the first elections under the congressional plan, rival political organizations emerged in the South. The most readily defined of these was the Conservative-Democrats, composed mainly of whites—former Confederates, Democrats, Whigs, and Constitutional Unionists. Although they gathered in some Negroes, the fundamental policy of the conservatives was white supremacy. Therefore they opposed the congressional Radicals and all plans for reconstruction under the aegis of Congress. But there was division within the conservative ranks. A faction advocated planned inaction, no participation in registration and voting. The larger faction sought to unify the white people, attract Negroes, and win control of reconstructed state governments. After failing to corral the freedmen, most members of this faction decided to vote against the constitutions written by Republican-dominated conventions by staying away from the polls. Then both conservative factions united in active politics to destroy the Republican government. Until that desired goal was achieved, many conservatives worked with Republican governments to feather their nests by sharing in the legitimate endeavors and fraudulent schemes.

The Republican party in the South was a composite of Northerners, Southerners, and Negroes, divided into conservative, moderate, and radical factions. The Radical Republican of the South was considerably left of the northern Radical, the moderate southern Republican corresponded most nearly to the Radical of the North, and southern conservative Republican corresponded to the moderate northern faction. These comparisons come close to delineating differences within the southern Republicans, but in a political organization composed of men with many opinions, no exact identification is possible. The unifying factor of white Republican leaders was their desire to establish Republican state governments controlled by white men who would be assured of election and re-election by Negro votes. Some of these leaders sought political office for personal power or economic gain; others were dedicated public servants.

The simple customary method of identifying southern Republicans was by their sectional origin and race: Carpetbagger, Scalawag, and Negro. Names applied to citizens of northern birth varied. In sections of North Carolina they were Squatters; some Georgians called them Showhegan Skunks; southern-born Unionists referred to them as Newcomers, but Carpetbagger won over these and other names. Southern conservatives seldom distinguished between the self-seeking and the dedicated Northerner in politics—the derogatory name of Carpetbagger was applied indiscriminately to all. The name indicated a Northerner who packed his meager possessions into a cheap carpetbag and headed South with the expectation of filling his bag with loot. Horace Greeley described Carpetbaggers as individuals bent on "stealing and plundering, many of them with both arms around Negroes, and their hands in their rear pockets, seeing if they cannot pick a paltry dollar out of them." Migrants from north of the Mason and Dixon Line who entered the South to establish farms, engage in business, or render professional service were usually welcomed by southern-born whites.

Unlike the Carpetbagger, the Scalawag was a native Southerner who entered the Republican fold. The Conservative-Democrat considered him a local leper, itching for political office, "a mangy dog, slinking through the alleys—defiling with tobacco juice the steps of the Capitol, stretching his lazy carcass in the sun on the Square. . . ." The place of its origin or the original meaning of the word "scalawag" is undetermined, but Conservatives enjoyed any one of a number of possible meanings: filthy sheep; scaly pig; venomous, shabby, scabby, scrubby, scurvy cattle; or mangy dog. Many Conservative-Democrats claimed the Scalawags were white renegades motivated entirely by desire for power or pelf. Historians who find a class conflict or who present a Marxian interpretation of Reconstruction claim that Scalawags came from the poor whites of the ante-bellum South who had been held in economic bondage by the planter-politician and who saw the possibility of establishing democracy in the post-bellum South by joining Negroes in a common endeavor.

In reality the existence of Scalawags indicated little more than an attempt to re-establish the southern ante-bellum two-party system, a more vital one than had existed in the Old South. Most of them came from old line Whigs who had found themselves stranded in the 1850's without a national party. In background they were planters, merchants, or industrialists; ardent or reluctant secessionists and former Confederates. Many of them could not stomach the Democrats while others believed that co-operation with the Republicans was the speediest way to bring a tranquility conducive to profitable farming and business enterprise. The mountainous areas of the South, especially those of North Carolina and Tennessee, and in other smaller geographic districts, where the people had historically opposed the dominant party, also contributed many individuals to the southern Republicans. At first these Scalawags enjoyed political advantage in the party, but they soon lost their initial advantage by their reluctance or refusal to mingle with freedmen at social-political rallies.

The third and by far the largest component of the Republican party was the Negro. Relatively few Negroes had requested enfranchisement. This fact made their white leaders fear political apathy or even complacent acceptance of the advice given by former masters. These fears were probably major reasons for the feverish activities of Carpetbagger and Scalawag, and their success in arousing the political interest of the Negro and getting him to the polls was a nineteenth-century miracle.

Their method was the secret society with an awe-inspiring initiation ritual and solemn oaths binding the initiate to certain performances on pain of supernatural punishment for failure. The whites borrowed rituals from Masonic or similar organizations and plans from the Union League. The latter was brought southward by soldiers and Freedmen's Bureau agents. In an impressive ceremony, beginning in a darkness illuminated at crucial intervals by flashes of light, the initiates were given glimpses of the Bible, the Declaration of Independence, and the American flag. Interspersed with these materials which denoted ideas were the concrete signs of action; the sword, anvil, sickle, and ballot box. After the ritual, speakers told of how the combined work of Lincoln, northern armies, and Republicans had freed the slaves from bondage and how the allegiance of freedmen to the party of liberation and voting for its candidates would prevent former masters from again enslaving them. Lincoln, liberty, loyalty, and league were the combination of passwords used to identify true members of the Union League. The initiation fee and small monthly dues served the double purpose of furnishing the Republicans with some income and stimulating members to vote where their money was spent. Auxiliaries were organized to add feminine influence and supply companions at social gatherings. In Florida the Lincoln Brotherhood and in North Carolina the Heroes of America operated in a fashion similar to the Union League.

To attribute the freedmen's political interest entirely to the activities of these secret societies is unrealistic. At its height of membership the Union League and similar organizations enrolled a minimum of one-fourth and a maximum of less than one-half of the registered Negroes. There were educated colored people who realized that one hope of their race lay in voting. More numerous were the unlettered freedmen who also thought their desires could best be achieved by political action.

To counteract Republican efforts and to win the Negro vote for themselves Conservative-Democrats made overtures to the freedmen. Fishfries and barbecues were arranged. The whites praised Negro cooks for their culinary accomplishments and patted colored table-setters on the back, but when the time for eating arrived, white men sat down after telling the Negroes that there was plenty of food for the second tables. The Conservative-Democrats hired "good" Negroes to tell their brethren of the white man's former care of colored people, their love of freedmen, and the necessity of following whites into the unknown paths of politics. The Conservative-Democrats failed miserably in their appeal for Negro support. Again and again, even in white-sponsored meetings, the freedmen sensed insincerity. They responded with resolutions which disclaimed any animosity toward their former masters, praised the martyred Lincoln, and resolved to support the Republican party which had freed them from an inhuman bondage.

Shocked and incensed by the reaction of once docile Negroes, the Conservative-Democrats turned to condemning the entire philosophy of the Congressional Reconstruction Acts. Many of these white people recalled their friendly relationship with domestic slaves and never realized that the ante-bellum propaganda which pictured the majority of all slaves as happy individuals was anything but the truth. Spurned by the ignorant, politically inexperienced former slave, the Conservative-Democrat turned against them and their northern sponsors.

White Southerners castigated the Negro and the Northerner. The Gainesville, Florida, *New Era* declared it would continue to propound the right of white men to govern themselves and resist the aspirations of "mulattoes, Radicals, or any other class of idiots—General Pope, or any other Negro-loving Judas Iscariot to the contrary notwithstanding." A Tallahassee newspaper described the politically active Freedmen's Bureau agents as "an army of malignant Southern haters, Negro fanatics, and needy adventurers." Another southern writer stated: "Formerly the Negro question was called the Slavery question, which was political and social at the same time. Today the question is purely a social one. The discussion is no longer whether the Negro is to be free or enslaved, but whether he has the right to exist." Editors quoted and frequently took sentences out of context from the writings of Harvard professor Louis Agassiz, to prove the fundamental difference between the white and Negro races, relying particularly upon Agassiz's pseudo-scientific analysis of skeletal structures and blood chemistry. Southerners also welcomed the idea of New England-born John William Draper, president of the Medical School of the City of New York, who claimed the Negro had fulfilled his labor mission in America and should be banished to his true home in Africa.

When possible, Southerners bolstered their resistance by relying on Northerners. The 1867 elections in many northern states encouraged Democrats all over the nation. Former President Franklin Pierce told his audience at Concord, New Hampshire, that Democratic victories assured the continued rule of white men in America. "A revolutionary Congress," he stated, "has undertaken to demolish our government and . . . establish a Negro despotism enforcing its will at the point of a bayonet, but the courts of the United States will save us from this terrible doom. . . ." Writings of Union officers and Freedmen's Bureau agents were quoted by newspapers. Former federal commander W. Howell Robinson characterized Negroes as wholly ignorant except in manual labor. Although he blamed slavery for coarsening them and lowering their capacities, he maintained they had descended to a state of unlimited license. D. M. Hammond, the Bureau agent at Fernandina and member of the Jacksonville Republican party, considered the enfranchisement of Negroes a great evil because the race was "dishonest, untruthful, and ungrateful."

Conservative-Democrats, however, found relatively few agents sympathetic with the southern point of view. Again and again these agents defended the Negro. Although admitting numerous robberies and thefts in his district and the insolence, laziness, and unfaithfulness of many freedmen, one agent attributed their crimes and indolence to the dishonesty of white planters who stole from the Negro laborer by refusing to pay promised wages or by sharp bookkeeping practices. Another agent praised the peacefulness of freedmen in the face of calculated attempts by men of property to incite them to violence, hoping that lawlessness and riots by Negroes would turn other Americans against the freedman.

Tremendously influential in molding white public opinion were twenty articles entitled "Notes on the Situation" published in the *Augusta Chronicle & Sentinel*, reprinted by many other newspapers in the South, and eventually brought out as a pamphlet. The author was Benjamin Harvey Hill, a well-educated Georgian, a former Whig and Know Nothing party member who, after opposing secession, became a strong supporter of Jefferson Davis in the Confederate senate. He argued the unconstitutionality of Congressional Reconstruction laws, urged the President not to enforce them, and told Southerners to ignore them. Hill's choice derogatory words were aimed at Scalawags, but he saved some biting ones for Carpetbaggers and Northerners. Yet his writings were mild in comparison with those of other Southerners. A Mississippi editor requested that Southerners be remembered as people

> What hates the Cotton Mather
> And Roger Williams' stock
> That dirty pile of Hell's manure
> First dumped on Plymouth Rock.

Never in history had so many critical words and so much bitter invective been publicly directed at the conqueror by the conquered.

This foolish criticism, however, gained no immediate advantage. Freedmen flocked to the polls to cast ballots for constitutional conventions and to elect white and Negro delegates. Utterly defeated in their attempt to control the Negro and faced with Republican control of the election machinery, many registered conservatives refused to vote. Their vain hope was the selection of ignorant and incompetent delegates who would frame such legal monstrosities that the Radicals in Congress would refuse them. The more politically astute conservatives advocated participation by whites in the election, advising them to vote for calling conventions and for the most intelligent delegates available. Every state except Texas, which delayed elections until 1868, authorized conventions in 1867 and sent representatives to assemblies in state capitols.

The Republicans won resounding victories, but the number of Negro delegates elected was considerably smaller than their proportionate vote in the election. Nine Negroes were sent to the Texas convention and 76 to South Carolina's, the only state with a majority of Negro delegates. In all the states the combined forces of conservative, moderate, and radical Republicans composed an overwhelming majority of the constituent assemblies. Generally, however, the conservative and moderate Republicans controlled the process of constitution-making in the South.

Infractions of parliamentary rules and legislative enactments by inexperienced men were jeered by the Conservative-Democratic press. Editors informed their readers of the illiterate Negroes and the fugitives from justice of both races in convention halls but seldom mentioned the educated Negroes or the dedicated delegates. Parliamentarians winced at the boisterousness of some individuals and their disregard of established forms of procedure. Delegates were determined to secure adequate personal compensation: the Florida Convention declared itself in session retroactively almost a month before the delegates assembled, paid its members from the fictitious date, and gave false travel allowances. The constitutional conventions assumed legislative powers to pass laws staying debt collections and changing names of counties. Legislative enactments of the constituent conventions and delays caused by disorderly methods extended the length and increased the cost of many conventions.

To race-intolerant white Southerners the most unfortunate acts of the "mongrelized" conventions were the constitutions produced. These constitutions were not just good, they were better than any previous frameworks of government written by Southerners for their states. Negro delegates evidenced little vindictiveness and generally opposed the imposition of political disabilities on their former masters. Only Louisiana disfranchised some former Confederates, and this limitation, as well as mild prohibitions in Alabama and Arkansas, was either not enforced or unenforceable. Attempts by the Mississippi and Virginia conventions to prevent former Confederates from holding office were defeated by special elections in those states. As a result only the nationally imposed limitations on office-holding by the Fourteenth Amendment applied in the South.

The constitutions written under the directive from Congress gave the southern states more democratic frameworks of government than the ones they supplanted. Universal manhood suffrage with no requirements of property-holding for voting or officeholding was established. While local governments were strengthened by democratic procedures, the powers of governors were enlarged, especially their authority to appoint state executive officers and officials of local governments. Frequently extensive appointive powers were purposely given governors by moderate Republicans to assure white control of counties with overwhelming Negro populations. On a state-wide vote the whites believed they could win the governorship of every southern state and the right of a governor to appoint local officials would assure white domination in predominantly Negro counties. No conservative or moderate Republican, and relatively few white radical ones desired southern state or local governments directed by Negro officials. The white Republicans agreed with Conservative-Democrats on white supremacy; the only basic difference between them was the Republican's success and the Conservative-Democrat's failure in winning the Negro voters. No southern constitution provided the means to turn southern society upside down, placing the Negro on top politically, economically, or socially.

In addition to a wider democracy, the constitutions provided for increasing state services. The right of every child to opportunity for education and the obligation of the people to supply educational facilities were integral parts of the constitutions. Delegates debated the question of integrated schools. Negroes generally favored one public school system for both races, fearing separation would bring unequal schools. The South Carolina constitution declared public schools and colleges were to be open to all without regard to race; Louisiana's prohibited the establishment of any public school exclusively for a particular race, but the other state constitutions contained no sections or clauses on educational segregation.

Many constitutions obligated the state to care for individuals unable to provide for themselves, the insane, the orphan, the deaf and dumb, and the poverty-stricken. Imprisonment for debt was eliminated but confiscation of the property of former Confederates and distribution of land to freedmen was not authorized. On the other hand, general rules made it easier to form corporations and other constitutional provisions encouraged industrialization and immigration.

Following acceptance of the constitutions by the delegates in convention the documents were submitted to voters. Military commanders were authorized by law to have voters elect state and national officers concurrently with approving or rejecting the new frameworks of government. Most Conservative-Democrats sought to defeat the constitutions by taking advantage of a flaw in the congressional plan whereby acceptance of them required a majority of the registered voters to participate in the election. Under this condition, staying away from the poll was more effective than casting a ballot; all opponents of the constitutions voted against its acceptance by staying home, and all proponents who failed to vote, whether because of inertia, sickness, death, or change of residence, counted in the opposition column. Despite advantage to the opposition, constitutions of six states were accepted by the electorate.

Two states, however, defeated proposed constitutions. Mississippians marshalled sufficient opposition to reject the document, and while those who cast ballots in Alabama favored the constitution, less than 50 per cent of the registered voters went to the polls. Now anxious to see its reconstruction program move forward, the Congress quickly enacted a fourth reconstruction act which validated any constitution accepted by a majority of the votes cast in an election. This law legalized the Alabama document, and changes in requirements which allowed Mississipians to reject political discriminations against former Confederates resulted in the acceptance of that state's constitution. By delaying the call for a convention, Texas continued under the military rule and Virginia achieved a similar result by hesitating to submit its constitution to the voters. In the other eight states, governments were oganized, the Fourteenth Amendment ratified, and congressmen seated during the summer of 1868.

Conservative-Democrats damned these initial steps by calling names rather than criticizing the work of conventions and legislatures. They denounced the North Carolina convention with its 15 Negro, 14 northern-born, and 75 southern-born delegates as an "Ethiopian [and] Ham radicalism in its glory" dominated by "baboons, monkeys, mules . . . and other jackasses." Although South Carolina's constitution was not the butt of attack, its writers became so: "Sixty-odd Negroes, many of them ignorant and depraved, together with fifty white men, outcasts of Northern society, and Southern renegades, betrayers of their race and country." Critics called the Louisiana convention the lowest and most corrupt body of men ever assembled in the South. An honest Floridian really gave the conservative white man's true objection. "Its manhood Negro suffrage," he stated, "is a curse which should sink this infamous document beneath the detestation of every white man of our State. . . . A thousand benighted Africans with no more conception of the origins, the principles, the practice of free government than have the mules they drive, may balance the votes of a thousand of our most enlightened and capable citizens. . . . A more base prostitution of the ballot has never been witnessed upon earth." Another Floridian attacked the concept of political equality of the two races in America. Under its practice, he declared, there could be Negro jurors, constables, sheriffs, clerks, legislators, judges, governors, congressmen, and even Negro administrators of the estates of white men—Negro guardians of impressionable young white males and sweet, pure white girls.

The constitutions of the southern states were written by delegates with limited or no political experience. An unlettered former slave in South Carolina, Beverly Nash, admitted "We are not prepared for this suffrage. But," he added, "we can learn. Give a man tools and let him commence to use them, and in time he will learn a trade. So it is with voting. We may not understand it at the start, but in time we shall learn to do our duty." Most white Southerners, however, were unwilling to give the Negro time to learn. They disregarded any worthwhile result simply because Negroes contributed to it. The southern constitutions of 1868 and the governments established under them were written and organized in an atmosphere of incredible hostility. In part the outstanding result came from copying good constitutions of northern states, but the lack of vindictiveness of a people oppressed by past bondage must be given some credit for supporting democratic principles.

The Supreme Court

From the first beginnings of congressional opposition to Johnson, conservative Southerners expected the Supreme Court to be a bulwark against the Radicals. The President encouraged these hopes by repeated reference to the unconstitutionality of bills enacted over his veto. Historically the Court had supported southern philosophies. The Dred Scott decision was considered a great legal victory for the South. During the war, the Court in *Miller* v. *U.S.* ruled that the Federal government was both a sovereign and a belligerent in its relationship to the South. In the Prize cases of 1863 the Court split five to four in deciding that Lincoln had the right to declare a blockade of southern coasts before the Congress recognized the existence of war. Even in the Civil War a strong minority of justices was apparently determined to keep the Court independent of the executive and legislative branches.

Southern hopes were bolstered and radical fears increased in 1866 by the Court's ruling in *Ex parte Milligan*. The case arose from the act of March 3, 1863, which authorized the President to suspend the writ of *habeas corpus*, and came to the Supreme Court from the Circuit Court of the District of Indiana. On October 4, 1864, L. P. Milligan and a number of his associates were arrested, charged with conspiracy to release Confederate prisoners, and sentenced to be hanged by a military commission. Appeal for a writ of *habeas corpus* stayed execution and early in 1867, the Supreme Court rendered its decision. The opinion written by Justice David Davis condemned the use of military tribunals in areas where civil courts were functioning. "Martial law cannot arise from *threatened* invasion," he stated; that law became legal only in cases of foreign invasion or civil war which closed civil courts, and immediately after the danger had passed, civil functions must be restored, otherwise "a gross usurpation of power" would be sanctioned. Martial law "can never exist where the courts are open, and in proper and unobstructed exercise of their jurisdiction." Four judges dissented from the majority on some points but concurred with the majority in the judgment.

Radical orators and editors denounced the Court and some of them advocated its abolition. By implication from Ex parte Milligan, the trial, sentencing, and execution in 1865 of Henry Wirz, the Swiss-born Catholic commander of Andersonville Prison, were a miscarriage of justice. More important to current events, the Milligan decision would endanger the congressional acts for reconstructing the southern states. These acts swept aside civil courts and denied habeas corpus in establishing a miltary regime after the Civil War was declared over by the President. Representative Stevens suggested that the appellate jurisdiction be denied the Court in any case arising from the reconstruction acts. Other Republicans urged various curtailment of the judicial branch: packing the Court, reducing its membership, limiting its procedures, and requiring a two-thirds majority to declare a law unconstitutional. On March 27, 1868, the Congress overrode a presidential veto to take appellate jurisdiction from the Court in all cases involving habeas corpus.

The hidden intention of this act was to prevent a decision appeal in the McCardle case. William H. McCardle was arrested for a bitter attack on military authority in Mississippi, printed in his Vicksburg Times. After his appeal on a writ of habeas corpus had reached the Supreme Court and it was preparing to render a decision, the Congressional Act of March 27, 1868, took jurisdiction away from the Court. The justices were relieved of another potentially troublesome decision by army officers. E. M. Yerger, editor of the Jackson News (Mississippi), succeeded in getting his accusation for murder into appellate jurisdiction, but the army avoided a constitutional decision by allowing his case to be handled by the civil authorities.

Both the Radical fears and the Conservative-Southerner's hopes were unfounded. In 1867 the Court in Ex parte Garland declared a lawyer, admitted to practice before the Supreme Court in 1860, and who subsequently served in the Confederate army and was pardoned by the President, could not be excluded from practicing before the Supreme Court. But this decision did not foretell condemnation of the reconstruction acts. In Mississippi v. Johnson the Court refused to act on a political question or to interfere with the President in the performance of his official duty. In Georgia v. Stanton the Court again refused to hobble the agent of the executive in political function. The Court reaffirmed the results of the war in Texas v. White (1869): the Union was complete, perpetual, and indissoluble; ordinances of secession were absolutely void. In reviewing the course of reconstruction, the Court laid a base for expressing its opinion on

The ruins of burned and occupied Richmond, view from the Arsenal.
Photograph by Mathew Brady.

PLATE 1

Harper's Weekly, May 12, 1866

Celebration of the abolition of slavery in Washington, D.C. by the Colored People.

PLATE 2

Rebel soldiers taking the oath of allegiance in the Senate chamber at Richmond.

PLATE 3

Office of the Freedmen's Bureau, Memphis, Tennessee.

PLATE 4

The Trial of President Johnson, showing the Republican senator Edmund Ross (standing left) casting his vote for acquittal, the defense attorneys, the House managers, and Chief Justice Chase. From *Leslie's Illustrated Newspaper*.

PLATE 5

Harper's Weekly, May 13, 1865

Harper's Weekly, April 7, 1866

PRESIDENT ANDREW JOHNSON

THADDEUS STEVENS

Harper's Weekly, May 26, 1866

Harper's Weekly, July 22, 1865

EDWIN M. STANTON

OLIVER O. HOWARD,
head of the Freedmen's Bureau.

PLATE 6

ULYSSES S. GRANT

HAMILTON FISH

CHARLES SUMNER

WILLIAM H. SEWARD

PLATE 7

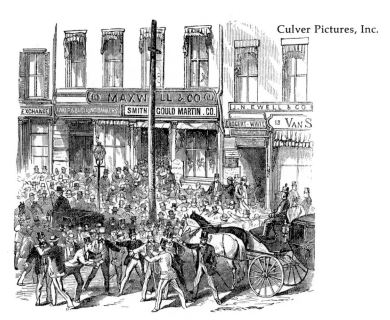

Confusion on Wall Street, September 24, 1869, as depicted by Thomas Nast.

Thomas Nast's caricature of Grant. The President appointed Zachariah Chandler, defeated for re-election to the Senate in 1874, Secretary of the Interior.

PLATE 8

the acts of Congress but refused to render judgment on them. Friends of Johnson and southern sympathizers accused the justices of cowardice in bowing to Congress. Undoubtedly the justices were influenced by public opinion and the election returns, but the Court's power increased during the Reconstruction era.

In addition to the congressional acts already cited, other legislation during the Civil War and Reconstruction periods changed the number of justices on the Supreme Court. On March 3, 1863, the President was authorized to appoint an additional justice. An act of July 23, 1866, prevented the President from filling any vacancy until the Court was reduced to a chief and six associate justices; but the purpose of the act was a more efficient judiciary system and not to curb the President or the justices. On April 10, 1869, Congress re-established a nine-member Court by permitting Grant to appoint additional justices.

The federal judiciary dealt with the case of Jefferson Davis. The ex-president of the Confederacy was arrested in May 1865, and for a time wore shackles in a cell at Fortress Monroe, Virginia. During most of his two-year imprisonment, however, he occupied good quarters and was allowed considerable freedom. After a period of virtual solitary confinement, he was allowed visits by his wife, doctor, and legal counsel. But for two years, access to civil courts along with bail and a speedy trial were denied him. The hardships of imprisonment won popularity for Davis in the South and personified him as the "Lost Cause."

The imprisoned man became an embarrassment to the federal government. In May 1867, Davis was released from military prison and freed under surety of a $100,000 bond signed by Horace Greeley, Gerrit Smith, and other prominent Northerners. A new indictment charged Davis with treason under the Act of April 13, 1790, which carried the penalty of death. The former Confederate president would be tried at Montgomery or Richmond, the locale of his treason, but the possibility of getting a twelve-man jury to declare him guilty was slim. Furthermore, questions arose as to the legality of the indictment under provisions of the proposed Fourteenth Amendment. On circuit duty in Richmond, Chief Justice Chase favored quashing the indictment. Proceedings dragged until President Johnson issued his final proclamation of amnesty on December 25, 1868. Shortly thereafter Davis was freed when the government dropped court proceedings.

References

The limited number of citations listed below does not indicate relatively unimportant subjects. The studies already cited, particularly the biographies,

Hyman, *Era of the Oath,* and other studies listed at the end of Chapter VII cover the material. The *U. S. Statutes at Large* (Boston, 1866 and 1868) give the texts of the Reconstruction acts. William A. Russ, Jr., has published many articles on disfranchisement in state and national journals; all of them are based on his dissertation, "Congressional Disfranchisement, 1866–98" (University of Chicago, 1933), an excellent study. Charles Warren's classic account of the Supreme Court has been successfully challenged by recent papers delivered at historical meetings and a few articles, but Warren's coverage of the Milligan case by northern newspapers is still useful. Louis B. Boudin, *Government by Judiciary* (New York, 1932), Vol. II, criticizes the Court for considering reconstruction questions. Stanley I. Kutler, "Reconstruction and the Supreme Court: The Numbers Game Reconsidered," *Journal of Southern History,* XXXII (1966), pp. 42–58, erases errors on packing the Court. Roy F. Nichols, "United States vs. Jefferson Davis, 1865–1869," *American Historical Review,* XXXI (1926), pp. 266–84, and R. H. Dana, "Reasons for Not Prosecuting Jefferson Davis," Massachusetts Historical Society, *Proceedings,* LXIV (1932), pp. 201 ff., give reasons why the Confederate president was not tried.

Impeachment and the Election of 1868

AMID the turbulent Reconstruction era a president was impeached for the first and only time in United States history. The unique act has baffled Americans who frequently misunderstand the impeachment and trial processes of the Constitution. The President was impeached by the House of Representatives, an action in reference to an officeholder which is similar to the indictment of a private citizen by a grand jury, and then tried by the Senate. At an impeachment trial the chief justice presides, prosecutors from the House of Representatives present the case against the accused, counsel defends him, and to convict, at least two-thirds of the senators present must vote him guilty of the charges. Conviction carries no penalty other than "removal from Office, and disqualification to hold and enjoy any Office of Honor, Trust or Profit under the United States. . . ." Any additional proceedings against an official declared guilty by the Senate are the responsibility of government attorneys in an indictment and trial in regular courts.

Explanations of impeachment and trial procedures are simple in comparison with the reasons for action against President Johnson. Apparently Congress had made the executive a powerless functionary by the reconstruction acts. But in reality the President retained extensive powers and many Radicals and army officers considered his interpretations of and actions in relation to the congressional reconstruction acts a series of provocations. Stanton and some generals believed the Union endangered. Most advocates of impeachment were convinced that a trial in the Senate would be brief and conviction certain. Was impeachment a Radical plot to remove the last possible obstacle to complete Republican domination in the nation and full control of the South? Or was the removal of Johnson an attempt to weaken the executive branch of the government, enhance the power of Congress, and move toward the British system of ministerial responsibility? Or was impeachment no more than a political maneuver to strengthen the Republican party?

Perhaps the most logical explanation of impeachment is a simple one of human frailty. It was a towering act of vindictiveness against a President who by infuriating his opponents had made them abandon reason to strike back at him. The year 1868 was an age of madness with men imitating the knavery and selfish political ambition of B. F. Wade and B. F. Butler. Audiences applauded rigged hearings in congressional committee rooms, army officers avoided promotions tendered by the President, the secretary of war barricaded himself in his office to defy another claimant to his position, and popular General Grant reneged on his word and wavered between the political inducements of Democrats and Republicans. In this atmosphere some knavish politicos envisioned personal advantage in completing the rout of the President and other vindictive ones desired the personal satisfaction of humiliating him.

More occurred in 1868 than the impeachment and trial of Johnson. The Fourteenth Amendment was added to the Constitution by unusual procedures and the Fifteenth was started on the route to ratification. It was a year of achievement as well as madness.

Impeachment

After repeated attempts to impeach the President, the House voted charges against him in 1868 with haste and little debate. On December 17, 1866, Radical Representative James M. Ashley of Ohio moved to appoint a committee to inquire into the actions of Johnson, but his colleagues refused to vote on it. On January 7 of the following year, he again offered a resolution: "I do impeach Andrew Johnson, Vice President and acting President . . . of high crimes and misdemeanors." This time the House supported Ashley. The supposedly secret hearings of the Judiciary Committee, to which the resolution was referred, were daily reported to Johnson by Allan Pinkerton, head of a detective agency.

For months the Judiciary Committee heard testimony and winnowed fact from fiction. Ashley was convinced that Johnson had a hand in planning the assassination of Lincoln. Pressed for substantiation of his charges, he hid behind feeling and intuition. George S. Boutwell and Butler supported the "testimony" of Ashley. Butler claimed that pages had been torn from the diary of John Wilkes Booth, pages which told of Johnson's part in the plot. "Who spoliated the book?" he asked with a dramatic flourish of his hands.

The release of Jefferson Davis from military prison in May 1867 brought new accusations against Johnson. Unreliable witnesses testified that the President refused to bring the former Confederate executive to trial, because he feared oath-bound witnesses would connect him with Davis in the plot to kill Lincoln. Other untrustworthy witnesses testified that the President had been drunk most of the time on his Swing Around the Circle in 1866 and was using federal funds to corrupt government employees. These accusers of the President presented no facts to support their contentions. But of all high officials in Washington, Johnson stood foremost in his desire to try Davis. He was not intoxicated during the campaign of 1866, and he had not used federal funds illegally. On June 3, 1867, the Judiciary Committee, chaired by Henry Wilson (no friend of the President or of the South), reported that no evidence of high crimes and misdemeanors had been found to justify charges against the President.

Relieved for the time, Johnson issued instructions for the execution of the Congressional Reconstruction acts which infuriated many Radicals. The registrars appointed by military commanders in the South, the President advised, had no power to challenge an applicant's oath, the only recourse was in court action. In addition, Johnson severely restricted a district commander's power to remove civilians from office or to issue decrees having the force of laws. Congress responded by passing the Third Reconstruction Act on July 13, and six days later promptly overrode the President's veto of it. Not content with giving district commanders authority to remove civilian officials and registrars the right to challenge claimants for registration, the Congress added: "That all provisions of this act and of acts to which this is supplementary shall be construed liberally, to the end that all the intents thereof may be fully and perfectly carried out."

Meanwhile, the Judiciary Committee was instructed on June 11, 1867, to continue its investigation of the President and report to the next session of the House. Ben Butler headed a special committee, the "Assassination Committee," charged with unearthing all facts relating to the murder of Lincoln. The hearings became such a farce that Butler's committee never reported to the House.

During the summer, fall, and early part of winter Johnson continued to exercise his power. Against the advice of General Grant, he removed a number of district commanders, among them Sheridan, Sickles, and Pope, and some Freedmen's Bureau officials. After discovering the part played by Stanton in writing the Third Reconstruction Act, the President requested the secretary's resignation on August 5. He refused to resign and Johnson urged Grant to take over the war office. Grant, fearing the Tenure of Office Act protected Stanton, was reluctant to become involved but accepted the *ad interim* appointment after the President suspended Stanton on August 12, 1867.

Though Radicals firmly believed the Tenure Act a congressional bulwark against the executive, nothing could be done until Congress convened in December. From its passage on March 2, 1867, many able minds considered the Tenure of Office Act unconstitutional. The entire cabinet disapproved of it, and Stanton helped Seward write the President's veto of it.

Furthermore, it hardly protected Stanton, a holdover from Lincoln's cabinet. While the act authorized Senate concurrence in the dismissal of any person whose appointment had required confirmation, cabinet officers were to hold their positions "for enduring the term of the President by whom they may have been appointed and for one month thereafter, subject to removal by and with the advice and consent of the Senate." Stanton, Seward, Hugh McCulloch, and Gideon Welles were Lincoln's appointees; Attorney General Henry Stanbery, Postmaster General Alexander W. Randall, and Secretary of the Interior Orville H. Browning were Johnson's.

With the exception of Stanton, the cabinet members worked harmoniously with the President. The war secretary's opposition to Johnson and his complete alignment with congressional Radicals were gradual developments. Undoubtedly Stanton was an able individual. The nation owed him much for his administration of the war department, but he was not a lovable person. Many of the best northern military officers hated the cold, unattractive, devious man in charge of the war office. As reconstruction passed from the hands of Johnson into those of Congress, Stanton, moved into the Radical camp. With all personal sincerity he believed the country needed his services to save it from the machinations of Johnson, northern Democrats, and "still rebellious" Southerners. Defenders of Stanton can point to his efforts to achieve a compromise between Radicals and the President. Certainly the adamantine stand of the latter affected Stanton, contributed to his joining the Radicals, and helped convince him that the national good required his continuation in the cabinet.

The suspension of Stanton had little apparent effect on the Judiciary Committee. On December 2, 1867, its five-to-four majority report recommended impeachment because of Johnson's "usurpation of power" in pardoning rebels, vetoes, and restoration of property to former Confederates. According to the majority report, the most damaging offense of the President was his reconstructing the "rebel states by his will, in the interests of the criminals who carried them into rebellion." Henry Wilson, chairman of the committee, presented a minority report which urged censure rather than impeachment of the President. Democratic members of the committee declared that the investigation had disclosed "not a particle of evidence" against Johnson "which would be received by any court of the land." No articles of impeachment accompanied the committee resolution and the attempt to impeach him was defeated on December 7 by a 108-to-57 vote.

Congressmen in their determination to rid the country of Johnson now concentrated on the tenure of Stanton. Their hand was bolstered by the President's stated determination in his third annual message to Congress to maintain his executive rights, and his request for a congressional vote of thanks to Democratic General Winfield S. Hancock, who had virtually ignored the Third Reconstruction Act in commanding the Louisiana-Texas district of the South. The President also gave the Senate his reasons for removing Stanton. After considering Johnson's reasons, the Senate Committee on Military Affairs reported a vindication of Stanton, and on January 13, 1868, the Senate refused to concur in the suspension of the secretary of war.

Public attention now focused on General Grant. The greatest northern hero of the Civil War had basked in the glory given him by an admiring public. But he was also besieged by friends of Johnson and by Radicals, by Democrats and Republicans, who all desired the asset of his popularity in the forthcoming presidential election. The wealthy showered gifts on him, audiences applauded his after-dinner speeches at sumptuous banquets, and crowds cheered him when he appeared on city streets. Apparently he was loyal to Johnson; he accompanied the President on the Swing Around the Circle in 1866, and then posed as a non-partisan general; but Grant was sufficiently shrewd to realize that his future lay with the Republican party, and by the summer of 1867 he was co-operating with Stanton and other Radicals.

Certainly the President believed Grant had accepted the *ad interim* appointment with promises either to hold the office until the courts could rule on the Tenure of Office Act or resign before the Senate acted, thereby allowing Johnson to appoint another man who would remain in office until the constitutionality of the act was tested. But after the Senate refused to sanction the suspension of Stanton, Grant sent a note to Johnson in which he claimed the Senate's action made it mandatory for him to relinquish his office. On being pressed by the President for reasons, Grant first stated that the Senate had acted more quickly than he expected, and then claimed that he had not promised to hold the secretaryship. Actually the President had caught Grant in a lie, but the general was willing to make amends by allowing Johnson to issue orders through him, thus effectively bypassing Stanton.

The President, however, chose to defend himself and expose the perfidy of Grant. To support his accusation Johnson secured from the cabinet members statements which accused the popular hero of lying. The President and general exchanged letters, a correspondence which also substantiated the presidential charge. Both Grant and the Radicals were caught by the determined President. The Radicals later abruptly terminated an investigation before disclosures would have exposed the hero's unreliability; any denunciation of the President would have hurt Grant, the man they were promoting for the presidency in the forthcoming election. On

January 13, 1868, the Joint Committee on Reconstruction laid its consideration of impeachment on the table, and Stevens declared in disgust that he would "never bring up this question of impeachment again."

The President's friends urged him to forget Stanton, but Johnson was determined to force the secretary from the war office. One man after another refused appointment as *ad interim* secretary; General Sheridan said no and then left Washington; General George A. Thomas rejected the offer; elderly, respected Thomas Ewing declined the office; John Potts, chief clerk of the war department, wanted no promotion. Finally Johnson found a man in the semi-retired General Lorenzo Thomas. Somewhat of a buffoon, a dandy in social circles whose chief claim to fame was his organization of Negro troops during the war, Thomas accepted the appointment on February 21.

The same day he visited Stanton, now barricaded and living in his offices, and demanded that the secretary vacate. Stanton shunted him aside with a promise to think about it. That night Thomas amused himself at a party by telling listeners of his plan to oust Stanton by force the next day. In the morning a federal marshal served an arrest warrant, sworn out by Stanton, on Thomas, who arranged bail and proceeded to the White House. There he was advised to show his courage by taking the office from Stanton.

The Radicals quickly convinced Stanton to drop charges against Thomas. Prosecution of the general would get the controversy into the courts, and play into the hands of Johnson whose desire was to test the constitutionality of the Tenure of Office Act.

The Thomas fiasco triggered passage on February 24, 1868, of a resolution offered by Representative John Covode of Pennsylvania "That Andrew Johnson, President of the United States, be impeached of high crimes and misdemeanors in office." There was no real debate on the resolution, but Radicals used it to denounce and slander the President. They repeated the unfounded charges against him—drunkenness, complicity in the assassination of Lincoln, and other equally absurd accusations. The dismissal of Stanton and flouting of the Tenure of Office Act were the accepted reasons for impeachment, but realistic Radicals admitted that these actions by the President were not the fundamental causes for their votes against him. Representative Ashley declared that congressmen would not have voted to impeach if they had been concerned only about the attempted removal of Stanton. William Lawrence of Ohio believed the President was impeached because he violated the Constitution by his wicked attempt to create governments in the rebel states and make those states full partners in the Union. The Covode Resolution presented no specific charges against the President, but by a vote of 126 to 47, the House members passed the resolution.

The articles of impeachment were not agreed upon by the House until March 2 and 3. There were eleven articles with numbers one through nine stating variations of the charge that Johnson on February 21, 1868, "unmindful of the high duties of his office, of his oath and of the requirement of the Constitution that he should faithfully execute laws, did unlawfully and in violation of the Constitution and laws of the United States issue an order in writing for the removal of Edwin M. Stanton from the office of Secretary for the Department of War. . . ." These articles contained copies of Johnson's letters to Stanton and Thomas.

The tenth article accused the President of attempting "to bring into disgrace, ridicule, hatred, contempt, and reproach the Congress . . . by making on August 18, 1866, and other days in a loud voice certain intemperate, inflammatory, and scandalous harangues, and did therein utter loud threats and bitter menaces . . . amidst the cries, jeers, and laughter of the multitudes then assembled. . . ." This article was supported by three specifications with details of the President's speeches at Washington on August 18, 1866, at Cleveland on September 3, and at St. Louis on September 8. Quotations from all were included in the specifications, but the longest quotation was taken from the St. Louis speech. In it the President had traced the source of the New Orleans riots to the Radicals in Congress and accused every man who participated in the illegal Louisiana convention of being a traitor to the United States and the originator of "another rebellion" originating in the Radical Congress. The President had admitted that his opponents had called him a Judas, but "If I have played the Judas, who has been my Christ . . . was it Thad Stevens . . . was it Wendell Phillips . . . was it Charles Sumner? These are the men that stop and compare themselves with the Savior, and everybody that differs with them in opinion, and tries to stay and arrest their diabolical and nefarious policy, is to be denounced as a Judas. . . ."

Article eleven summarized the charges against the President in language which differed little from the preceding ten. This "omnibus article" accused Johnson of characterizing the Thirty-Ninth Congress as representative of a part of the states "thereby denying and intending to deny that legislation of the said Congress was valid or obligatory upon him," and repeated the charge of his flouting the Tenure of Office Act "by unlawfully devising and contriving, and attempting to devise and contrive means by which he should prevent Edwin M. Stanton from forthwith resuming the functions of the office of Secretary for the Department of War, notwithstanding the refusal of the Senate to concur in the suspension. . . ." In addition, the eleventh article declared that the President had devised and continued means to prevent the execution of the army appropriation and the reconstruction acts of March 2, 1867, and by his action of February 21, 1868, did "commit and was guilty of a high misdemeanor in office."

The earlier attempt to impeach the President was based on a preliminary resolution which had been referred to committee for hearings, and, after concluding its investigations, the committee reported to the House. In 1868 there were no specified charges, no investigation or hearing of testimony by a committee, but only the Covode Resolution of condemnation with articles and specifications to be formulated at a later date. After the House voted the impeachment, Stevens's motion for the appointment of a committee of two to prepare charges against the President was passed under House agreement to suspend rules temporarily. The House gave seven of its members the responsibility of preparing the impeachment charges. George S. Boutwell of Massachusetts who presented the charges drawn up by the committee praised their "artistic structure" and predicted that House managers of the impeachment could "safely go to the Senate and the country for the judgment of guilty against the person accused." Radicals were confident, for Senate conviction of the President appeared certain.

The Trial

Few officials had been impeached by the House, fewer convicted by the Senate. No President had ever been so humiliated and there were no precedents to follow in trial. Johnson rejected the House call for his presence and continued to act as President despite Radical claims that an honorable man would relinquish the office after being condemned by an overwhelming number of representatives. Constitutional provisions on impeachment and trial were minimal. The House of Representatives had the "sole Power of Impeachment." Senators had the "sole Power to try all Impeachments. When sitting for that Purpose, they shall be on Oath or Affirmation. When the President of the United States is tried, the Chief Justice shall preside: And no Person shall be convicted without the Concurrence of two thirds of the Members present." Were senators in a role similar to that of jurors, bound by their oaths to weigh evidence and base their verdict on it, or in the trial of a President could they disregard evidence to vote entirely on political considerations?

A majority of senators considered themselves politicians. In a legislative process begun before the impeachment, the Congress added to the Union one state whose senators were almost certain to favor conviction of the President but rejected another whose senators would have undoubtedly supported Radical desires. In May 1866, Johnson vetoed the bill to admit Colorado to statehood by pointing to the territory's population, probably less than the 40,000 estimated by optimists, when the ratio for representation in Congress was 127,000. His veto was sustained. In 1867 renewed efforts were made to admit Colorado and Nebraska, and the presidential veto was overridden to make Nebraska the thirty-seventh state. Senators from that state later voted to convict the President. The Colorado case was too palpable a fraud for two-thirds of the senators to override the presidential veto.

The Radicals never admitted that the Senate was a court. In Charles Sumner's opinion the trial was a political one with a political object—the removal of the last obstacle in the last great battle against slavery. This idea was reiterated in administering the oath to Ben Wade. As president *pro tempore* of the Senate he would become President of the United States on conviction of Johnson. No fair-minded senator considered Wade a disinterested juror, but the Senate allowed him to take the oath. He had already selected some members of his cabinet, including his equal in rascality, Ben Butler, as secretary of state.

The House selected seven managers to present its case: Stevens, George S. Boutwell, John A. Bingham, Benjamin F. Butler, John A. Logan, Thomas Williams, and James F. Wilson. Except for Butler and Williams, these were the men who had drawn the articles of impeachment against the President. Butler and Boutwell bore the burden of the prosecution, for death hovered over the elderly Stevens. The House managers possessed a powerful weapon in the eleventh article of impeachment which had been written with an eye to capturing the votes of senators who believed Johnson had reluctantly administered Congressional Reconstruction acts and resented his criticism of congressmen. In addition, the senators who sat in judgment with their minds already set on conviction gave the Radicals a comfortable majority; the House managers needed to convince only one or two senators to secure a two-thirds majority.

In contrast to these advantages were attempts to make rules which tended to give the trial a similarity to regular court procedure. Chief Justice Chase was determined to use his power as presiding officer with judicial impartiality. Furthermore, the President was represented by able legal counsel: brilliant and witty William M. Evarts of New York assumed the burden of the defense. Evarts, who became Johnson's attorney general in July 1868, was ably assisted by outstanding lawyers Benjamin Curtis, William S. Grosebeck, Henry Stanbery, and Thomas Nelson.

After senators took the oath,* the trial opened on March 7, 1868. Many days of deliberations on procedure passed before the opening argument for the House managers was presented by Butler on March 30. He claimed the Senate in no way resembled a court; its duty lay in determining whether

---

* I solemnly swear (or affirm) that in all things appertaining to the trial of the impeached . . . now pending, I will do impartial justice according to the Constitution and laws: so help me God.

the acting President had the political right to continue in his office. Johnson, who had attained his executive position by a "most foul" murder and who had called the Congress an assembly of "factious and domineering" men and accused it of fomenting another rebellion, had been condemned by the House. Members of that body had done their duty, Butler stated, by bringing the criminal to the bar of the Senate and demanding senatorial judgment for his great crimes. The prosecutor never charged the President with dishonesty or corruption; he concentrated on denouncing Johnson's speeches and attempted to convince senators that any action subversive to a "fundamental or essential principle of government or highly prejudicial to the public interest" was sufficient cause for conviction.

Stevens did little at the trial, his body was too weak, his voice too feeble. He sat in a cushioned chair, lacing and unlacing his long boney fingers, leaning his head forward, appearing lost in deep thought, his eyes closed. Friends drew close to catch words which seemed little more than the rattle of a dying man. When he opened his eyes they appeared lusterless. Seated at the House manager's table, he listened while his brief speech was delivered by Butler.

Stevens accused the President of no criminal act. In the congressman's opinion, criminal intent or criminal act were not a part of the impeachment, but Johnson's violation of the intent of congressional laws on reconstructing the southern states justified the Senate's condemnation. If Stevens had possessed his former fire, he would have pointed a long finger at the senators and warned each of them that a vote of acquittal would forever doom the misguided legislator to self-torture "on the gibbet of everlasting obloquy." But as he shifted his aching body in his chair, no flicker of his former fire emerged as Butler delivered the thrust.

Three other House managers delivered opinions which reiterated the ideas of Butler and Stevens. Representative Logan was content to file a brief, and the prosecution rested. In its opinion the senatorial vote should be a political one and on this assumption no verdict other than guilty was imaginable.

The burden of the defense was carried by William M. Evarts. The Boston-born fifty-year-old lawyer was an exceedingly capable man who had served his country on diplomatic missions to England in 1863 and 1864. His first defensive victory was the Senate's refusal to demand the appearance of Johnson at the trial. Evarts began his speech by asking what high crimes and misdemeanors had been done by the President. Had he sold public favors for private gain, had he betrayed the people's trust by giving away a fleet, or surrendering a fortress to the enemy? The only accusation against Johnson was his removal of Stanton. But this charge was invalid, for Stanton was still in office. The President had done no more than test the constitutionality of the Tenure of Office Act.

Evarts reviewed the Tenure Act and quoted from statements made by some senators who had voted for it. Neither senators Sherman nor Doolittle believed it limited the President's power to remove cabinet members inherited from Lincoln's administration. The act did no more than give tenure to cabinet members for "the term of the President by whom they may have been appointed and for one month thereafter" unless their removal was agreed to by the Senate. Senator Sherman had admitted that it gave no protection to Stanton, and, furthermore, the senator had affirmed his willingness to support the President, if any holdover from Lincoln's cabinet "was so wanting in manhood . . . as to hold his place after the politest intimation by the President . . . that his services were no longer needed. . . ."

Evarts also brought into focus the constitutional questions involved and the impassioned state of public opinion. In the era of the Articles of Confederation, he declared, the legislature was a combination of executive and lawmaking powers. But Americans had rejected this philosophy of government to embrace separation of powers. If successful, the action to remove Johnson would re-establish the discredited system of concentration of power in the legislature. Furthermore, the evidence throughout the country indicated pressure on senators to act from an emotional rather than a reasoned basis. Fundamental decisions made on this basis, he warned, were not harbingers of a virile country.

Other presidential lawyers ably supported Evarts. Henry Stanbery, who had resigned as attorney general to participate in the defense of Andrew Johnson, was quick to take advantage of slips made by the House managers. When Butler inadvertently referred to the Senate as a court, Stanbery jumped to his feet to congratulate the prosecutor on his admission that senators were jurors bound by oath to render a verdict on the basis of evidence. Butler attempted to gloss over his error, but the defense reiterated its contention that the Senate was a court.

The press followed the trial with absorbed interest. Southern and northern Democratic newspapers colored their reports to present the case for the President. Actually the Democratic press found itself in an enviable position. Even some staunch Republican editors refused to lecture their readers with editorials and news slanted to favor the Radicals. Other Republican newspapers, among them Greeley's *Tribune*, followed the Radical line, and perhaps a majority of Northerners wanted a verdict which would remove the Southerner from the White House.

Tremendous pressure was brought on Republican senators who evidenced pro-Johnson sentiments before the first vote on May 16. There was no question about the ten Democratic senators favoring acquittal, and Daniel S. Norton of Minnesota, a Union Conservative, and Peter S. Van Winkle of West Virginia, a Unionist, were opposed to conviction. Many

Republicans must have been disturbed by the sight of Ben Wade and Ben Butler and by the thought that a "yea" would elevate them to positions as President and secretary of state. In alphabetic order the senators voted: Dixon of Connecticut and Doolittle of Wisconsin answered "Not guilty," and Fessenden agreed with them. Fowler, Grimes, Ross, and Trumbull followed and Chief Justice Chase announced to the Senate that "Andrew Johnson, President of the United States, stood acquitted of the charges contained in the eleventh article of impeachment" by a vote of 35 to 19.

To give themselves time to work on the recalcitrant senators, the Radicals recessed the Senate. For ten days every conceivable pressure was brought to bear on the seven Republicans to change their vote. The general conference of the Methodist Church gave an hour of prayer to ask God to save the senators from error and give their decisions the aura of "truth and righteousness." Kansans pressured Senator Ross and, believing him more susceptible to change than the other six Republicans, the Radicals badgered him unmercifully.

The Senate reconvened on May 26 and the first vote was taken on the second article of impeachment. Dramatic interest mounted as the roll call proceeded with senators repeating their vote of May 16. When the call reached the R's, all eyes were on Ross who hesitated before giving his "Not guilty" reply. As a last resort a vote was taken on article three, but the result was the same—35 for conviction and 19 for acquittal. On motion "the Senate sitting for the trial of the President upon the articles of impeachment" adjourned *sine die*.

Both praise and abuse were the rewards of the seven Republicans. In years to come they were practically read out of their party, but for a time they were feted by their admirers. Fessenden died in 1869; Grimes, who had been stricken with apoplexy during the trial and had to be carried into the Senate, lingered until 1872; and Trumbull continued in the Senate until 1873, became a liberal Republican and eventually returned to the Democratic party.

Some of the leading Radicals passed from the political scene while others became powers in the Grant administration. Ben Wade who missed being President by one vote was not even renominated to the Senate by Ohio Republicans. Stevens, who suggested assassination as the only method of removing Johnson, died in 1868. According to his wishes, his body was buried in a racially unsegregated cemetery at Lancaster, Pennsylvania. On his tombstone was placed an epitaph written by Stevens: "I repose in this quiet and secluded spot, not from any natural preference for solitude, but finding other cemeteries limited by charter rules as to race, I have chosen this that I might illustrate in the death the principles which I

advocated through a long life, Equality of man before his Creator."
Sumner remained in the Senate but ran afoul of Grant. Logan represented
Illinois in the senate from 1871 to 1877 and again from 1881 until his
death five years later. The unprincipled but talented Butler became an in-
fluential adviser to Grant. George Boutwell did neither himself nor the
Grant administration honor by serving as secretary of the treasury.

By the narrowest possible margin the Senate declined to convict a president on political grounds. Had Johnson been removed from office and later
presidents had suffered similar fates at the hands of politically motivated
congressmen, the American concept of an independent executive department might have shifted to the British idea of ministerial responsibility to
the legislature.

The Supreme Court never completely clarified the President's right to
remove his appointees from office. In 1926 the Court ruled in the Myer's
case that the executive power of removal was not subject to Senate approval. Yet in 1935 the Court declared in *Rathbun* v. *U. S.* that Congress
had the constitutional power to limit a President's power to remove appointed officials who were not members of the cabinet. Despite general
agreement on its unconstitutionality, the Tenure of Office Act has never
been legally declared invalid by a specific decision of the Supreme Court.

Since the President was acquitted in 1868, a study of the reasons for the
vote of individual senators is more academic than real. Each senator was
given the right to file a written statement to justify his vote. Many who
voted for acquittal believed the Senate a court and found the evidence insufficient for conviction. Other senators held Johnson had the right to remove Stanton and political expediency on the part of the dominant party
was not cause for removal. Some proponents of conviction were determined to rid the country of Johnson whatever the evidence. Among these
were Senator Sumner, who persuaded himself that the President was guilty
of all the charges presented "and infinitely more." John Sherman, friend of
Johnson and basically a moderate man, used devious reasoning for his sid-
ing with the majority. Was his vote cast against the President or against the
apparently continued rebellion of Southerners and the uncompromising attitude of Johnson? Was his "guilty" the result of pressure by Radicals and
selfish fears for his future? Would he and some other moderately inclined
Republicans have changed their votes, if any of the seven Republican senators had deserted Johnson? Was the President as near conviction as the 35-
to-19 vote indicated? These and other questions about the only impeachment and trial of a President offer intriguing questions for debate.

The fact of acquittal remains. Stanton gave up his office without further
contest, and Johnson passed over the dandy, Thomas, to appoint John M.
Schofield as secretary of war. The attempt to remove him from office did

not prevent the President from continuing his policy amnesty for former Confederates. Prior to his trial, proclamations of May 29, 1865, and September 7, 1867, had left approximately 300 Southerners under the edict of rebellion. On July 4, 1868, Johnson gave amnesty and pardon to all except a number of top Confederate officials, and at Christmas 1868, he pardoned the rest. Prior to the later date he sent his last annual message to Congress. He advocated legislation to reduce the foreign-held debt, estimated at $850 million, and a consequent reduction in the flow of interest payments to foreigners. The nation was justifiably proud of freeing 4 million slaves, he stated, but it should not countenance a large permanent debt, thereby enslaving the American taxpayer. By equating interest payments in gold on purchases made with deflated currency, he estimated investors were receiving a return of 17 per cent on their original investment. Johnson suggested refinancing outstanding bonds at lower interest rates.

Amendments

Among the notable achievements of the 1787 convention was a workable method of amending the Constitution. The Founding Fathers discarded the unanimity required by the Articles of Confederation, a provision which in practice made amendment impossible, but hedged the written Constitution with safeguards to prevent it from being amended with ease. The states, not the people, possessed the final say on an amendment, and ratification by three-fourths of them was necessary. Proposing and voting on amendments remained a cumbersome process. If the Bill of Rights or first ten articles are considered essentially parts of the original Constitution, only two amendments were ratified in more than three-quarters of a century. And these two—the Eleventh in 1798 and the Twelfth in 1804—were obviously necessary to protect states from myriads of suits and correct a deficiency in electing presidents and vice presidents.

For sixty years the agrarian rulers of the United States had agreed on no amendment, but Civil War and Reconstruction brought three within five years, each in part ratified by means of conditions imposed upon the South by President or Congress. Least controversial was the Thirteenth, for military defeat of the Confederacy killed slavery and the Thirteenth Amendment was no more than constitutional sanction of fact. Southern governments of white men accepted the abolition of slavery and northern legislatures reflected the altruism of their citizens in ratification of an amendment which removed a social canker from the nation.

The Fourteenth and Fifteenth amendments, however, presented problems. The third purpose of the Civil War—equality regardless of race—was an afterthought of conflict and support, for it developed at a slow pace. Not only white Southerners but also white Northerners actively opposed or seriously questioned acceptance of the Fourteenth Amendment. When first proposed in 1866, unanimity of the northern and border states could not have forced ratification. Its rejection by some of these states and by ten of the former Confederate states apparently doomed it. But congressional laws for reconstructing the South resuscitated the amendment. By making its acceptance a requisite to participation in the Union, Congress secured ratification from those southern states whose delegates quickly wrote new constitutions and whose legislators ratified the amendment. Meanwhile northern state legislatures approved it. During the time-consuming process, the New Jersey and Ohio legislatures ratified and then later resolved to withdraw approval. One question arose immediately: was initial acceptance binding on a state, or could its legislature change its stand?

On the surface the process of amending the Constitution was clearly defined. After congressional proposal of a change, acceptance would become effective on ratification by three-fourths of the state legislatures. Congressional Radicals inconsistently protested that the southern states were not coequals in the Union, while at the same time maintaining they had the right to contribute their part in legalizing an amendment. In addition, the congressional plan of reconstruction assumed ratification of the Fourteenth Amendment before it was approved.

Secretary Seward was in a dilemma. Although not empowered by the act of April 20, 1818, to decide the authenticity of actions by state legislatures, or the right of a state to withdraw its ratification, he relied on that law to proclaim the Fourteenth Amendment. He stated on July 20, 1868, that the amendment had been accepted by 23 northern states and by 6 assemblies claiming themselves the legislatures of southern states, but the Ohio and New Jersey legislatures had subsequently passed resolutions recinding their action. Assuming the original ratification by these two states legal, he certified the amendment in force.

Unsatisfied by this statement, a concurrent congressional resolution declared the Fourteenth Amendment part of the Constitution and directed the secretary of state to promulgate it. Congressmen passed it with a minimum of consideration. A total of 127 representatives voted for it and senators accepted it without recording their votes. The resolution listed the 27 ratifying states and declared them three-fourths and more of the states composing the Union. By Seward's count the United States was composed of 37 states in 1868 and 27 was a mere fraction under the 75 per cent. The Congress, however, considered only the fully reconstructed southern states members of the Union and by this interpretation, 27 ratifications met constitutional requirements. The secretary of state complied with the resolution on July 28 by issuing another certification, and this date became the accepted one for the amendment. Seward named the states which had ratified and also those which had withdrawn their consent (eventually Ohio, Oregon, and New Jersey). Modern judicial interpretation dates the existence of an amendment from the day of its ratification by that state which completes the three-fourths requirement. But court decisions have not settled the question of the irregularity involved in the acceptance of the Fourteenth Amendment. Despite the controversy associated with its ratification, the amendment has been completely validated by practice and judicial decree.

The Fourteenth Amendment failed to satisfy individuals who demanded universal manhood suffrage. Possible reduction of representation in the House did not guarantee suffrage to Negroes. Most Radicals considered this backhanded slap at dominant southern whites insufficient political protection for freedmen, and many other people wanted the base of democracy widened by constitutional amendment. The prospects of enfranchising millions of Negroes in the South and binding them to the Republicans were pleasant to members of the party. Since their political organization was a relatively new one, forged in perilous times from a number of factions, Republican leaders believed the Negro vote necessary to the perpetual enthronement of the "party of the Union." Despite their desire to enfranchise freedmen in 1866, Radicals feared ratification of an amendment unattainable.

Negro suffrage involved many other questions. Certainly the small number of northern states allowing manhood suffrage was an embarrassment to Radicals who wished to enfranchise the freedmen of the South. The unavoidable and most critical objection to a suffrage amendment was the illiteracy of Negroes. Opponents of the measure warned the public repeatedly of potential danger in enfranchising millions of citizens, over 90 per cent of whom could neither read nor write. They pointed to the incongruity of literate white women who could not vote and illiterate Negro men who would be enfranchised by the amendment. Politically, however, race was more important than sex during the Reconstruction era.

No reiteration of certain facts could bury other equally significant ones. Widespread illiteracy among Negroes reflected their previous condition of servitude instead of their native ability. Notwithstanding past votes cast by millions of illiterate white men, the United States had rapidly advanced in strength and power. Inability to read or write was not necessarily an indication of unintelligent action at polling places, even though most Americans believed an educated electorate a concomitant of representative democracy Furthermore, the heritage of slavery was responsible for the Negro's lack of interest in the suffrage; his horizon was limited by ignorance. The right to vote would create political awareness and undoubtedly stimulate desire for education. Finally, proponents of Negro suffrage viewed it as completing the processes of emancipation. Without rights at the polls Negroes in the South would be the political wards of white men, and legislatures of states reconstructed by Johnson were proving the white man's unfairness as warden.

Step by step Congress moved toward a national amendment providing manhood suffrage. The first move was in the District of Columbia whose residents were allowed no congressman. In 1865 the people of the District overwhelmingly rejected Negro suffrage in a special election but on January 8, 1867, Congress enfranchised Negro males living in the District of Columbia by overriding a presidential veto. Johnson hit at Senator Sumner by contrasting the density of the Negro population in the District to its sparsity in Massachusetts. In addition, he held the suffrage unnecessary to the protection of Negro rights and disliked imposing it upon those who had not asked for it.

The second and third steps were in legislation for territories and the southern states. On January 31, 1867, manhood suffrage became obligatory in all territories. Then in the various reconstruction acts Republicans concentrated their efforts on enfranchisement in the South, thereby avoiding the politically dangerous question in the North, and by southern state action obtained suffrage for a majority of Negroes. Other than the Fourteenth Amendment with one section pertaining to enfranchisement, Republicans left the northern states alone until 1869. Then the Fifteenth Amendment was proposed by Congress and submitted to the states for ratification. According to the amendment, "The right of citizens of the United States to vote shall not be denied or abridged by the United States or by any State on account of race, color, or previous condition of servitude." By using the Fourteenth Amendment's definition of citizenship, women could argue that the Fifteenth enfranchised them, but this was neither the intent of Congress nor the ratifying states and women waited half a century for the suffrage. In a sense the amendment was a fifth reconstruction act, for three southern states (Mississippi, Texas, and Virginia) were required to accept it. On March 30, 1870, the Fifteenth Amendment was promulgated by Secretary of State Hamilton Fish.

The three amendments of the Reconstruction period were forced respectively on 11, 10, and 3 southern states. Enforcement of their provisions within the South was mainly the work of southern state governments under the monitorship of the federal Congress. Voting and officeholding rights of Negroes were in practice the gifts of Republican southern governments supported by federal military power. After withdrawal of the occupation forces from the South, white Southerners negated all three amendments to some extent, the Thirteenth by peonage and the others by various acts of individuals and governmental units.

The Election of 1868

Negro suffrage was not an issue in the campaign of 1868. Wary Republicans stated in their platform that suffrage belonged to the states. In the North speakers evaded the issue or soft-pedaled it. Radicals were satisfied with the progress being made in the South to enfranchise the Negro and create in him an interest in political affairs. They saw no reason to weaken their appeal in some northern states by advocating manhood suffrage for the entire Union.

In 1868 overconfidence was not rampant in Republican ranks. The year before Democrats had won in some important northern state elections and they demonstrated evidence of once more becoming a national party. Since the public was a fickle political master, thoughtful Republicans pondered its reaction to impeachment and Congressional Reconstruction. No Republican senator, representative, or governor was in a commanding position to carry the banner of his party in a campaign.

The most available congressman was Schuyler Colfax, speaker of the House since 1863. The forty-five-year-old Indianian, a native of New York City, possessed an impressive political record: service in the Whig party, organization of the Republican party in Indiana, and continuous membership in the House since 1855. Colfax enjoyed the confidence of Radicals and his pleasing personality endeared him to moderate Republicans.

The man anxious for the nomination was Chief Justice Chase. During the war, his treasury agents worked to build a Chase organization in conquered areas of the South and at one time Chase believed the 1864 nomination might fall to him. His advocacy of Negro suffrage made him the darling of the Radicals. As Chief Justice of the Supreme Court his political activity was severely limited and his moderation prevented him from going all the way with the Radicals. They practically read him out of the Republican party, denouncing him without mercy, after he refused to preside as a political partisan at the trial of Andrew Johnson. Before the Republican convention assembled Chase had abandoned his party and began to think of the Democratic nomination.

In contrast to Chase, the impeachment and trial of Johnson enhanced Grant's political career. The young war hero was not a politician (his only presidential vote was cast in 1856 for Buchanan), and the Democrats had hopes of winning him for their party. His break with the President over the Stanton affair threw Grant into the arms of the Radicals. The Republicans drafted him in an impressive demonstration of unity in their convention which opened at Chicago on May 20. With no man presented for the presidential nomination other than Grant, the delegates nominated him unanimously on the first ballot. On the sixth ballot Colfax won the vice-presidential nomination.

The Radicals wrote a shrewdly worded platform which intermingled accusations of Johnson with praise of congressional enactments and promises of good things to come. Whenever the platform touched on controversial subjects its wording was sufficiently vague to allow different interpretations. The martyred and safely buried Lincoln was lauded and Johnson castigated. According to their platform the President had been "properly pronounced guilty" by 35 patriotic Republican senators and 7 renegades had voted against truth. Congratulations were extended to the American people for the success of their congressmen's plan to assure loyal governments in the South. Although it explained that Congress must guarantee Negro suffrage in southern states, voting requirements in the loyal northern states were the exclusive rights of their governments.

The Johnson administration was accused of political corruption and Americans were assured of reform and honesty under Grant. Promises were directed at several groups: veterans and the widows and children of Union soldiers were promised pensions and preferential treatment of their applications for federal jobs; sympathy was expressed for oppressed people "struggling for their rights" (an appeal to Americans of Irish extraction and the Fenians in their struggle for Irish independence from Great Britain); and the validity of the public debt was affirmed in language which bondholders could interpret as guaranteeing payment in specie and inflationists could translate differently. Delegates from every state except Texas, evidencing the national base of the Republican party for the first time, approved of the platform with apparent unity.

The Democrats delayed until July 4 for their convention in New York City. Their problems were threefold: a plethora of candidates, reconstruction issues, and the public debt. Many delegates favored Chase. But his association with the Republican party and the failure of the Ohio delegation to support him were adverse factors. His only hope lay in a deadlock which could be broken by a stampede to him. Southern state delegations strongly supported Johnson and his reconstruction policies appealed to men from other states. Famous war heroes—McClellan, Hancock, Farragut, and Sherman—had supporters, but the latter refused to enter the political arena. The favorite, however, was George H. Pendleton of Ohio, author of the "Ohio Idea" to pay bondholders in greenbacks whenever the national debentures did not specify payment in specie. On the first ballot he received 105 votes, almost one-third of the total number cast. On the fourth ballot scattered votes appeared for Horatio Seymour, president of the convention, but he insisted that honor forced him to withdraw. On the twenty-second count, Ohio shifted from Pendleton to Seymour and the New Yorker was nominated by shouting, enthusiastic delegates. For vice president the convention selected Francis P. Blair, Jr. of Missouri, former congressman, supporter of and adviser to Lincoln, and Union general.

As expected, the Democratic platform denounced Congressional Reconstruction as "unconstitutional, revolutionary, and void." Instead of restoring the Union, the Radicals placed ten southern states under military rule and Negro domination, thereby indefinitely delaying actual reunion. The platform also advocated termination of the Freedmen's Bureau, subordination of military to civil authority, and an end to congressional usurpation and military despotism. Secession and slavery, the Democrats asserted, were decided; the current issues were reuniting Americans, amnesty for past offenses, restoration of the rights of the states, and recognition of their authority on suffrage. While promising to pay the national debt, they endorsed Pendleton's Ohio Idea.

In the ensuing campaign Grant and Seymour remained in the background, but leaders of both parties "slugged it out" in abusive language. Republicans attacked the war record of Seymour, who had served as governor of New York from 1853 to 1855 and from 1863 to 1865. Although he had used his power to quell the New York City draft riots of July 1863, his opponents accused him of expressing sympathy for the rioters and of opposition to the war. His defenders pointed to the large number of men sent by New York into Union armies and his record as a state executive. Republicans pictured their party as deserving the support of patriotic Americans for saving the Union, emancipation, and protection of freedmen. Republican speakers presented the Democrats as dominated by Copperheads, southern rebels, and other traitors and defenders of slavery.

Democratic speakers denounced the military despotism of congressional acts. Their efforts to project an image of loyalty, conciliation, and reunion of Americans in heart were often dimmed by the biting, sarcastic cartoons of Thomas Nast in *Harper's Weekly*. When violence flared in the South, Republicans used it for political advantage in the North. The Republican platform avoided the tariff or aid to business, but most businessmen considered the Republican party more friendly than the Democratic and consequently contributed heavily to the former. In the North well-organized political machines in most of the larger cities gave the Democrats a vote-producing asset.

Fearing a close election, Republicans had provided for counting the electoral vote in the reconstructed states. All the southern states except Mississippi, Texas, and Virginia were eligible to participate in the election and Grant won in North Carolina, South Carolina, Florida, Alabama,

Tennessee, and Arkansas. These states were not needed, for his electoral vote was 214 and Seymour's was 80. The Democratic candidate won two former Confederate states (Georgia and Louisiana), three border states (Delaware, Maryland, Kentucky), and three northern ones (New York, New Jersey, and Oregon). The popular vote was a more valid indicator of Democratic strength than the electoral one. Seymour gained 2,706,829 to 3,013,421 for Grant, an authority on the election estimates 450,000 Negroes voted for Grant and 50,000 for Seymour. Without the Negro vote, Grant's total may have been 100,000 less than that of his opponent, but the Republican candidate would have won the presidency in the Electoral College without a single Negro ballot. The more than two-thirds majority held by Republicans in the Fortieth Congress was continued in the Forty-First; they increased their majority in the Senate by a large percentage while the Democrats gained a slightly better ratio in the House.

REFERENCES

Johnson's biographers, the recollections of congressmen and biographies of them, and McKitrick, Thomas and Hyman, and Brock, already cited, cover the impeachment and trial of the President. Still a standard is David M. DeWitt, *The Impeachment and Trial of Andrew Johnson* (New York, 1903). Useful articles are: Harold M. Hyman, "Johnson, Stanton, and Grant: A Reconsideration of the Army's Role in the Events Leading to Impeachment," *American Historical Review*, LXVI (1960), pp. 85–100; David Donald, "Why They Impeached Andrew Johnson," *American Heritage*, VIII (1956), pp. 21–25; Ralph J. Roske, "The Seven Martyrs?" *American Historical Review*, LXIV (1959), pp. 323–30. Milton Lomask, "When Congress Tried To Rule," *American Heritage*, XI (1959), pp. 66 ff., raises questions about what would have happened had Johnson been convicted. Ralph J. Roske, "Republican Newspaper Support for the Acquittal of President Johnson," *Tennessee Historical Quarterly*, XI (1952), pp. 263 ff., identifies Republican editorial approval of the seven dissenters. Charles H. Coleman, *The Election of 1868* (New York, 1933), gives a meticulous, detailed account of the campaign and result. Louis T. Merrill, "General Benjamin F. Butler and the Campaign of 1868" (Ph.D. dissertation, University of Chicago, 1938), depicts Butler as a scheming but forceful individual. Some northern periodicals are invaluable for comprehension of the impeachment, trial, and other occurrences, among them: the Republican organs, *Independent*, 1866–68; *Nation*, 1867–68; New York *Sun*, 1866–68; *Chicago Tribune*, 1867–68; the Democratic New York *World*; and mostly independent, *New-York Herald* and *Times*, 1865–68. Although the Dunning School has been discredited by modern scholarship, William A. Dunning's short article, "The Impeachment of President Johnson," American Historical Association, *Papers*, IV (1890), article 2, part 4, gives useful information on political affairs associated with pre-impeachment events and the trial.

The South During Congressional Reconstruction

"BLACK Reconstruction" has become a synonym for a decade of southern history. The term's only validity rests on a Negro vote which placed white men in political control of southern governments.

Congressional Reconstruction was in reality a period in which a large Negro vote and smaller Carpetbag and Scalawag votes combined to elect mainly white officeholders. In no southern state was the "Bottom Rail" placed on top, politically, economically, or socially. With a few notable exceptions, in most states Negroes were relegated to minor offices. Throughout the Republican era 14 Negroes served in Congress, 6 held lieutenant governorships, 8 attained cabinet positions, and 3 were house speakers. From 1868 to 1874 Negroes outnumbered whites in the South Carolina house, but the whites controlled the senate, governor's office, and supreme court. In Mississippi, where the Negro population was greater than the white, the first Republican legislature was composed of 40 Negroes and 75 white lawmakers. Florida, more than 45 per cent Negro, sent 19 of them to her 76-man legislature.

In no state was there a serious attempt to remake the southern economy or society to benefit the Negro. Southern governments rejected confiscation of white-owned property to aid Negroes, and the feeble attempts in two states to help the almost propertyless freedmen produced no worthwhile results. Economic power remained in white hands. White and Negro patronized common transportation facilities, at times ate in the same dining room, and used other public facilities; but this intermingling of the races was a social change only because the freed Negro was no longer on a servant-master relationship. Probably less contact between Negro and white took place during Congressional Reconstruction than in the ante-bellum South. The maddening fact to most white Southerners, however, was the association with Negroes who considered themselves the equals of the white race.

Economically, reconstruction tried the patience of cotton farmers and property owners. The federal tax on cotton—two and one-half cents per pound in 1865 and three cents the following year—was repealed by February 1868. Property owners soon found this Republican gift the only one. Enlargement of state services, increased salaries for governmental officials and employees, and graft doubled and tripled the cost of operating state and local government and multiplied the tax on real property. Land-poor men lost many acres at tax sales and were infuriated by evidence of corruption, fraud, and graft. Negroes shared in petty pilfering, but Carpetbagger, Scalawag, and Conservative-Democrat divided the major spoils among themselves.

Neither taxes nor graft were fundamental reasons for the opposition of Conservative-Democrats to Congressional Reconstruction and Republican rule. Neither did white Southerners fear that control of the South would pass to the Negro. Unless Congress enacted legislation for wholesale confiscation of property and general disfranchisement of former Confederates, these Southerners knew their economic and social control would endure and eventually their political power become dominant. The basic objections of white Southerners to Congressional Reconstruction were Negro voting and officeholding. They never granted that the Negro was entitled to any degree of political, economic, or social equality with white men. They condemned Congressional Reconstruction for imposing "alien" governments on the South. Initially the Congress had set up rules for reestablishing the southern states, but once in operation the governments rested on the will of the majority. Never before in southern history had governments been based as much on majority rule as those of the Reconstruction era. White supremacy was the essential reason for opposition to Congressional Reconstruction.

The Restored Southern States

The first state to meet congressional demands was Arkansas, tenth ranking in population of the 11 former Confederate states. In June 1868, Congress declared that Arkansas was entitled to readmission, and its senators and representatives were admitted to Congress. President Johnson vetoed the act. In his opinion the oath required of citizens by the Arkansas constitution—civil and political equality for all men and civil rights or immunities without regard to race or color—if applied in the northern states would result in a boycott of the polls. Congress overrode the veto on June 22 and the Arkansas delegation was seated on the 23rd and 24th.

The Arkansas enactment set the pattern for six other states. On June 25 Congress declared that North Carolina, South Carolina, Georgia, Florida, Alabama, and Louisiana were entitled to congressional representation whenever their respective legislatures ratified the amendment and guaranteed perpetual enfranchisement of Negroes. Except for Georgia, the states promptly met the congressional stipulations and their delegations were seated.

In Georgia, some Republicans combined with Conservative-Democrats to deny 27 Negro members seats in the legislature. Justification for this action lay in the contention that officeholding was not a concomitant of enfranchisement. In addition, the legislature ignored provisions of Congressional Reconstruction acts and the Fourteenth Amendment in seating some former Confederates. Congress immediately prohibited Georgia from excluding a legislator because of color and authorized the military commander to remove all unqualified men. General Meade seated the Negroes and purged the legislature of the proscribed whites. The recalcitrant editor of the Georgia legislative manual refused to print biographies of the Negro legislators, explaining that no more could be listed about them than their former occupations as waiters, bootblacks, and field hands. This attitude, shared by many whites, did not prevent Congress from requiring additional evidence of co-operation. After the Georgia legislature had ratified the Fifteenth Amendment on July 15, 1870, the state's representatives were seated in the House, but its senators did not enter the upper house until February 24 of the following year.

Mississippi, Texas, and Virginia were also admitted in 1870. The delay in Mississippi was caused by constitutional provisions which denied the franchise to former Confederates and excluded from office all who had promoted secession or aided the Confederacy. Enough non-vindictive Negroes joined conservative whites to reject the constitution by a majority

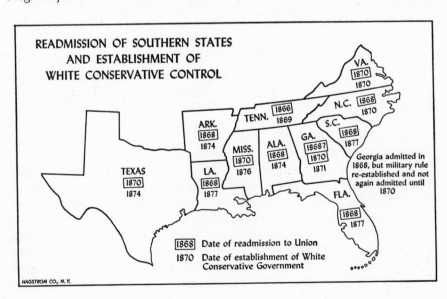

READMISSION OF SOUTHERN STATES
AND ESTABLISHMENT OF
WHITE CONSERVATIVE CONTROL

VA. 1870 / 1870

N.C. 1868 / 1870

TENN. 1866 / 1869

ARK. 1868 / 1874

S.C. 1868 / 1877

GA. 1868? / 1877

MISS. 1870 / 1876

ALA. 1868 / 1874

TEXAS 1870 / 1874

LA. 1868 / 1877

GA. 1870 / 1871

Georgia admitted in 1868, but military rule re-established and not again admitted until 1870

FLA. 1868 / 1877

1868 Date of readmission to Union
1870 Date of establishment of White Conservative Government

HAGSTROM CO., N.Y.

of more than 7600 votes. The admission of Texas was also delayed because of the unpopular constitutional provisions disqualifying former Confederates. In Virginia, conservative leaders maneuvered to prevent a vote on a constitution which contained severe disqualification clauses. After his inauguration, Grant encouraged legislation which allowed a choice between disqualification of former Confederates and manhood suffrage. The voters favored the latter, and after ratifying the Fifteenth Amendment, Virginia, Mississippi, and Texas were restored respectively in January, February, and March of 1870.

The Republican Regimes

In every state except Virginia, Republicans won control. By delaying tactics which enabled Conservative-Democrats to win the state, Virginia escaped the Republicanism of other southern states. In ten states Republican domination lasted from one to nine years. Tennessee, the first to accept the Fourteenth Amendment, thereby winning seats in Congress for her senators and representatives in 1866, was taken over by the Conservative-Democrats in 1869. The Republican regimes lasted a year in Georgia, two in North Carolina, four in Texas, six in Alabama, Arkansas, and Mississippi, and nine in Florida, Louisiana, and South Carolina.

Fair evaluation of the Republican governments was beyond the capabilities of nineteenth-century Americans. In an atmosphere charged with emotion, the observer and the contemporary historian could not escape personal, racial, and regional prejudice. Northern men as well as southern, Negro and white, condemned the product of Congressional Reconstruction. Later, the so-called scientific historians' interpretations were warped by preconceived ideas. Many writers were blatantly partisan in their defense of South or North, condemnation or praise of the Negro, evaluation of Republican and Conservative-Democrats. Even those who attempted impartial appraisal fell victim to bias.

Most famous of the contemporaries was the militant journalist James S. Pike who lampooned the South Carolina legislature in The Prostrate State. Negroes enjoyed a comfortable majority for almost six years in the lower house of the original secessionist state. In 1873, 94 of the 124 representatives were Negro. Pike detailed the antics of inexperienced legislators: their peanut-eating, their plugs of chewing tobacco, their interminable jabbering, their repeated raising of points of order and personal privilege without knowing the meaning of either, their speaking again and again on the same subject. He reported the petty graft: voting $1000 to recompense the speaker of the house for his loss at the race track, large expenditures for cuspidors and other furnishings, excessive payments for travel, appropriations to enable members to buy lingerie for wives or girl friends, and the casual cashing of bonds to pay for meals. What Pike did not report was constructive acts amid the confusion and petty graft.

A modern scholar, Robert F. Durden, discovered that Pike was more interested in discrediting the Grant administration and voicing his antipathy for the Negro than in accurate reporting. A similar indictment is justified against the work of John Wallace, a Negro who served in the Florida legislature. His condemnation of Republican rule was mainly the product of imagination and subservience to white overlords. In reality he gave little more than his name to *Carpet-Bag Rule in Florida*, written by Conservative-Democrat William D. Bloxham, governor of the state from 1881 to 1885, as a campaign document to discredit the Republicans in the state election of 1888. These facts limit the value of Wallace's account as a source and take the sting from his most caustic remarks.

The unreliability of Wallace and Pike does not whitewash the Republican regimes. County tax collectors obtained offices by sharing their take with political bosses. Legal provision for a year's delay in paying collected taxes into state treasuries allowed collectors free use of sizeable sums of money. Some could not resist the temptation of money; they stuffed it in bags and fled. The more astute grafter utilized the leeway of law to feather his nest. He required tax payment in federal currency but made his returns to state treasuries in script, and retained half of his collections because of the difference in value. County tax collectors were forced to share with local bosses who in turn gave to those higher in the political order. Contracts for printing legislative journals went to favored and liberal-spending printers. In Louisiana the Republican printing bill was almost ten times higher than in pre-Congressional Reconstruction years, and in Florida it amounted to more than the former cost of an entire legislative session. Salaries for legislators, governors, and appointed officeholders skyrocketed.

These costs were minuscule compared to more imaginative corruption. Under the guise of securing land for resale to freedmen, South Carolina paid $700,000 for farming acres worth no more than $100,000. To provide temporary capitols, an opera house in Atlanta and a hotel in Baton Rouge were bought at prices many times their current market value. South Carolina authorized a $1,500,000 bond issue to redeem a half million dollars in bank notes. In 1870 the trustees of the Internal Improvement Fund of Florida sold 1,100,000 acres of state land to the New York and Florida Lumber Company for ten cents an acre, paid in state script, worth about 50 per cent of par value. The trustees also conveyed title to 1,300,000 acres to the Southern Island and Navigation Company for payment of one dollar, but a Republican controlled court voided the sale and placed the

Internal Improvement Fund into receivership to protect the land assets of the state. Louisiana "invested" $100,000 in stock of the Mississippi Valley Navigation Company, a venture which never became a reality.

White men—Carpetbagger, Scalawag, and Conservative-Democrat—reaped the major harvest from these fraudulent schemes. A Negro contractor in Arkansas received $9000 for repairing a bridge which originally cost $500. Participants in the three Mississippi embezzlements were a Negro who took books from the library he directed, the white Republican treasurer of a Natchez hospital who stole $7251, and a white Conservative-Democrat state treasurer who absconded with $61,952.

Comparatively few Negroes participated in the largess of promoters buying or developing railroads, the most lucrative of all schemes devised by dishonest citizens and governmental officials. Convinced of their military prowess, Southerners found the cause of defeat in their region's comparative lack of industry. Since transportation was essential to industrialization, improvement of railroads and construction of new ones appealed to all political factions. The popularity of railroads and other internal improvements enabled grafters to reap a harvest by bribing legislators and governors to sell state-owned rail lines at a fraction of their value, to obtain franchises, and to secure state guarantees of bond issues for internal improvements.

Notorious in two southern states were the Carpetbagger Milton S. Littlefield of Maine and the Scalawag George W. Swepson of North Carolina. They and their associates first operated in North Carolina by taking advantage of an established southern system whereby a state aided a privately owned railroad company by purchasing its stock, guaranteeing the principal and interest of its bonds, or granting money or land for every mile of track laid, bridges constructed, stations erected, and rolling-stock acquired. In return the state took mortgages on the railroads, and bankruptcy during and after the Civil War resulted in state ownership. In some states, governments constructed and owned rail lines. Whatever its origin, state ownership enabled promoters to bribe legislators and officials into remunerative leases or sales at a low price. In North Carolina Littlefield and Swepson milked the state-owned railroad, and shared with other schemers more than $17,500,000 of issued bonds.

Indicted, Littlefield and Swepson fled to Florida where they organized a company, a majority of whose members were Conservative-Democrats, and bought up lines acquired by the state in bankruptcy proceedings. By purchasing depreciated railroad bonds and using them in payment, giving some cash, and a worthless check, they obtained title to roads valued at $1,500,000 for little more than $300,000. Then they bribed legislators, and perhaps Governor Harrison Reed, to secure state backing for a $4 million bond issue. These 8 per cent bonds were sold to speculators in northern and European cities for about 70 cents on the dollar. Tens of thousands of dollars were claimed by the promotors for expenses in marketing the bonds; other thousands went for bribes, payment of Swepson's and Littlefield's obligations in North Carolina, and into the pockets of the avaricious schemers. Little more than $300,000 was used in constructing new road-beds and adding equipment to the railroads.

Men like Littlefield and Swepson operated in every southern state except Mississippi where, contrary to the demands of Conservative-Democrats, the Republicans rejected a constitutional provision for state aid to corporations. Poorly kept records make an accurate listing of bond issues for internal improvements an impossibility. Estimated issues in Alabama range from $17 million to $30 million; Arkansas gave 20 promoters almost $9 million in bonds for railroads and levees, and schemers in Georgia obtained almost $6 million. Instances of similar activities could be listed, and many counties and cities gave land and favorable tax rates to entice railroads.

Bonded indebtedness incurred for internal improvements was never a serious burden on the southern people. Almost without exception, the states eventually repudiated their guarantees to pay interest and principal. The southern economy was bolstered by some miles of track, improved roadbeds and equipment, and by the cash pocketed by promoters. Obviously the speculators lost; but the interest rates, often more than 11 per cent on par value and as much as 15 per cent to maturity, indicated the speculative nature of the bonds. Widespread repudiation after 1877 made legitimate investors suspicious of any bonds issued by southern governments. A major cause of this distrust, however, lay in repudiation or scaling down of debts incurred before the Republicans took over the South.

While fraud, graft, and waste characterized southern Republican governments, reasons for increased public expenditures should be examined and the Republican regimes compared with other governments. In the Old South political office was the responsibility of the upper class who did not serve for pay but from a sense of duty. Salaries paid to officials from governors to local officeholders were so low that neither politician nor statesman could exist on them. State services were minimized: notwithstanding some free schools, education was primarily the responsibility of parents; the care of the mentally or physically deficient was basically a private concern; and in the main, recalcitrant slaves were the charge of their owners.

During the Reconstruction era, legislators, governors, and other office-holders needed salaries sufficient to pay their living costs, approximately 4 million former slaves became citizens, public schools replaced private academies, and society assumed responsibility for more and more of its exceptional members. Adequate salaries and increased governmental services required more expenditures and taxes than the agrarian, planter-dominated South had considered necessary. As the tax rate went up and services multiplied, the conservative white spoke of the good old days of individualism and low taxes. Rural, conservative whites never realized that the former philosophy of "what's good for the planter is good for the South" was being changed to a new concept of the most good for the most people, white and colored. Expenditures for public schools, courts, prisons, asylums, and hospitals increased state and local budgets.

Fraud and graft were not a monopoly of the southern Republicans. The take of the Democratic Tweed Ring in New York City dwarfed that of any Republican-dominated southern state, and probably equaled that of all the southern states combined. Less notorious Democratic organizations in other northern cities milked their communities, and similar Republican gangs, particularly the one in Philadelphia, kept pace with their Democratic brothers in graft. Nationally the Grant regime allowed grafters to feather their nests at public expense. In the South, Conservative-Democrats joined white Republicans in fraudulent schemes, and frequently surpassed the latter in the amount of their take.

Shortly after restoration of a "white supremacy government" in Mississippi the Democratic state treasurer stole $315,612, a sum greater than the total taken by light-fingered Republicans during six years of their rule. The Democratic administration of Governor Robert Lindsay in Alabama, sandwiched between Republican governments, equaled the latters' record in fraud and graft. Vernon Wharton has found little difference in Republican- and Democratic-controlled counties of Mississippi in expenditures and tax rates during the Reconstruction Era. In the post-Civil War period graft and larger government expenditures were national, regional, and local: they were not a unique experience of the South.

Finally, charges of tremendous indebtedness have been demolished by the scholars' critical examination of records. A claimed Republican debt of $20 million in Mississippi dwindled to less than half a million. During their last years of control in Florida, Republicans paid off a considerable portion of the bonded indebtedness. Horace M. Bond found the increase added to the Alabama debt by the Republicans to be $2,500,000 instead of the $30 million claimed by Democratic critics.

The Republican regimes added much to the credit side of the ledger. As already stated, the state constitutions were better than those they supplanted. These constitutions remained long after Conservative-Democrats regained power, and new constitutions which replaced them came less from need than from emotional desire to erase the reconstruction document and to eliminate the Negro from politics. The principle of representative democracy was broadened to include all adult males. Generally Negro members of conventions and legislatures favored enfranchisement and officeholding for all their white brothers regardless of past association with secession or the Confederacy. Repeatedly Negro legislators joined other petitioners in requesting the national government to remove the prohibition against officeholding by former Confederates.

The Republicans stimulated public education by constitutional provisions which asserted the right of every child to educational facilities and the obligation of every citizen to provide schools at public expense. They gave meaning to their constitutional directives by state and local appropriations for schools. Other state services—asylums, hospitals, prisons, libraries, and internal improvements—were characteristic of the Republican governments. New laws offered physical and economic protection to women, children, and laborers. In the Old South the sweet, demure, clinging-vine woman had protected herself by her wits and her sex; legislation in many states during the Reconstruction era gave her legal protection from grasping husbands, recognized the rights of mothers to have their children in case of divorce, and protected the children from unscrupulous or sadistic parents. In some states the welfare of the laboring man was advanced by giving him first claim to the assets of bankrupt companies. State agencies were established to promote immigration into southern states and encourage industrialization. Finally, the Republican governments directed the physical restoration of a ravaged region and attempted an orderly transition from controlled to free labor. In this process they strove to establish a workable arrangement between the white and colored races.

On the debit side Republicans were responsible for resurrecting a gambling evil. In 1868 they chartered the Louisiana Lottery, a notorious organization owned and operated by white Southerners who used Confederate military heroes, Pierre G. T. Beauregard and Jubal A. Early, to preside at periodic drawings and lend respectability to the scheme. Lotteries, however, were not the creatures of the Republican party. Although once used extensively in the United States, they had been outlawed before the Civil War. On returning to power, Conservative-Democrats chartered lotteries for many purposes—educational institutions, monuments, to promote immigration, to aid Jefferson Davis, and other purposes. Most lotteries enriched their promoters and the Louisiana Lottery became such a national scandal that congressional action abolished it.

A number of Negroes served with distinction in political office. To the senatorial seat formerly held by Jefferson Davis, Mississippians sent Hiram R. Revels, a South Carolina native who had attended Knox College and was an ordained minister and former school teacher. The other Negro senator from Mississippi, Blanche K. Bruce, came into the world as a slave in Virginia, escaped from servitude, became a teacher, and moved to

Mississippi in 1869. Perhaps the desire of Negroes for education was reflected by the number of their race who served as superintendents of education: Thomas W. Cardoza in Mississippi, W. G. Brown in Louisiana, J. C. Corbin in Arkansas, and Jonathan C. Gibbs in Florida. Corbin was a graduate of Oberlin College and Gibbs, the father of public education in Florida, and an alumnus of Dartmouth and Union Theological Seminary. Florida sent Josiah T. Walls to the House of Representatives. Five Negroes from South Carolina, two from Alabama, and one each from Georgia, Louisiana, Mississippi, and North Carolina gave the South twelve Negro members in the House.

Two Negroes became speakers of the South Carolina house, Mississippi had one, and Jonathan J. Wright was on the South Carolina supreme court for seven years. That state also elected two Negro lieutenant governors; Mississippians selected one, and Louisianians chose three. Most famous or notorious was Pinckney B. S. Pinchback, the son of a white planter and a slave, who served as acting governor of Louisiana for 43 days in 1872. That year he was elected to the House and the following year to the Senate but neither house seated him. In Mississippi, Lieutenant Governor Alexander K. Davis acted as governor during the absence of white Governor Adelbert Ames. There were six Negro secretaries of state and one treasurer.

Conservative-Democrats Fight Back

From the inception of Congressional Reconstruction white conservatives denounced the southern governments as alien institutions forced on a defeated and impotent region. Their failure to win the Negro voter made them lash more vigorously at governments imposed by the conqueror. White Southerners never admitted that the Republican regimes were more representative of all citizens than the former governments of the Old South. Often more vigorous in their denunciations than former planters were the economically less fortunate who had lost status by the abolition of slavery and feared the economic competition of millions of freedmen. Even in poverty the poor had one consolation: they were "better than Negroes." But white opposition to Congressional Reconstruction was no monopoly of the poor. The wealthy and educated, the poor white trash and illiterates united in demanding and working for the restoration of the "home rule." Their objective was white supremacy maintained by controlling or eliminating Negro political activity and by relegating the Negro to an inferior economic and social position. In short, their desire was to substitute a rigid caste system for slavery, enabling whites to exploit the Negro and give members of the higher caste the psychological uplift of belonging to the brotherhood of the superior race. If not openly avowed, white supremacy was implied in every effort to defeat the Republican state governments and restore home rule.

Legal and extra-legal acts were used by white Southerners to discredit Republican governments. Avenues of attack were many: divide the unco-hesive Republican forces; support Negro politicians in their arguments against Carpetbag and Scalawag leaders; protest against increased taxes, larger state expenditures, fraud and graft; point to the good old days when Negroes lived in happiness under benevolent masters; and destroy existing governments by anarchy, if necessary, to establish white supremacy. Vio-lence had been characteristic of the South—violence on troubled frontiers, violence in managing slaves and hunting down those who sought freedom by escape, and violence in duels. It had always existed in contrast to an-other pattern of gentility, respect for womanhood, refinement of manners, an easy and gentle philosophy of life. Violence had never been limited to white versus Negro; it had been employed by both races and for a multi-plicity of purposes.

But conservative whites denounced the use of force by the federal gov-ernment in the South. Repeatedly the presence of army detachments was deplored and the number of troops exaggerated. Actually the federal troops stationed in southern states from 1867 to 1877 were insufficient to patrol the extensive area and powerless to maintain order except at localities of their concentration. For example, in November 1869, there were 1112 sol-diers in Virginia and 716 in Mississippi. Most of the troops in these and other southern states were stationed at military posts. In the vast territorial area of Texas more than three-fourths of the army's 4612 men were guard-ing the frontier from Indian forays. Furthermore, federal commanders fre-quently used their troops to support the conservative whites. This usage was characteristic in South Carolina, and the commander at Jacksonville, Florida, ambushed a large body of almost unarmed Negroes. Invariably the Republican officials called for additional federal troops when actual or fic-titious reports of racial clashes and anarchy were forwarded to Washing-ton, but gradually the occupational forces were reduced until by 1876 they were quartered at regular posts except in Florida, Louisiana, and South Carolina.

Unable to obtain sufficient army regulars to maintain order, Republican governors organized militia forces. In March 1869, Congress repealed its prohibition of state militia for Alabama, Arkansas, Florida, Louisiana, North Carolina, and South Carolina; the following year state forces were authorized for Georgia, Mississippi, Texas, and Virginia. Actually some state organizations came into being as early as June 1868, without opposi-tion from congressional Radicals, who were satisfied that these troops would bolster the authority of southern Republican governments. Neither Georgia nor Virginia created militia forces, and state troops were used mainly in Louisiana, Mississippi, North Carolina, South Carolina, and Texas. Containing a considerable number of Negroes, these militiamen were referred to contemptuously by conservative whites as "black and tan soldiers" and hated with an almost hysterical emotion. Armed, uniformed Negroes on the streets, on horseback, or white and Negro troops stationed together were visual challenges to white supremacy. Beginning before the War of 1812, southern newspaper editors had deleted all references to Negro militia in Spanish Florida, and white citizens maintained that the Negro was incapable of being a soldier. Fear of slave uprisings explained white reaction and philosophy. Although Negro troops were numbered among the northern invading armies during the Civil War and occupation forces during the Reconstruction era, these soldiers were less resented than their brothers in the state militia.

The militiamen were used for various purposes: to counteract the Ku Klux Klan and similar illegal organizations; to keep order and protect Republican voters at elections; and to overawe Conservative-Democrats reportedly planning to overthrow state or local governments. Because of division within Republican ranks, governors sometimes refused to send troops into troubled areas. Governor Reed of Florida hit at his Republican opponents in Jackson County, where anarchy reigned in 1869, by denying them the support of the militia. Opposition both from Republicans and Conservative-Democrats limited the number of militiamen enrolled and deprived them of sufficient military equipment. Furthermore, raiding parties of white men sometimes captured arms and supplies destined for the state troops.

Use of the militia often brought quick retaliation from angry whites. A modern scholar has found the state militia relatively inefficient in maintaining or restoring order but better behaved and more law-abiding than the lawless element of white people. Some Negro soldiers ran amuck, others were overzealous in searching homes for guns or using their authority in other ways. It was the Negro militiamen and not the exceptional acts which aroused the ire of white people. The uniformed Negro soldier, gun in hand, was in their opinion a brute with power, an ever-present danger and a constant challenge to white supremacy.

The Republican governments needed more than regular peace officers —policemen, sheriffs, and federal marshals—to maintain order in many cities and counties. Although the Ku Klux Klan became the symbolic organization of violent southern resistance, the Knights of the White Camellia may have had a larger membership than the Klan. Other organizations—The Sons of Midnight, Pale Faces, White Brotherhood,

Constitutional Union Guards, Order of the White Rose, and Young Men's Democratic Club of Leon County, Florida—operated in various states and localities. All of these sub-rosa societies proclaimed lofty aims but had the one common purpose of white supremacy. Regardless of their stated idealism, they eventually became havens for unscrupulous individuals. They mistreated not only Negroes but also white men and women, members of any race, sex, or religion whose sanity blocked the sway of blind prejudice or whose economic assets were desired and believed obtainable by cowardly men. Their nefarious acts were encouraged by their large numbers and their cowardice was hidden in the anonymity of their sheet-covered bodies. Records of these mobsters who assumed the mantle of southern patriotism were seldom kept and usually destroyed if set down.

The Ku Klux Klan began modestly in 1865 as an organization of unemployed Confederate veterans at Pulaski, Tennessee. Their objective was apparently social. In time they found nocturnal adventure in frightening people—rising suddenly amid gravestones in lonely graveyards and pointing at passersby, sitting white-robed on stumps near pathways. From these beginnings the Klan and similar organizations attracted thousands of members after the initiation of Congressional Reconstruction.

Origin and meaning of the Klan name are shrouded in mystery. Did it come from China, or was it imported from Mexico by American soldiers after the Mexican War? Was the "click, cluck, clack" sounds of a gun being cocked translated into the words "Ku Klux Klan," or was it an adaptation from the Greek word *Kyklos*, meaning circle? Members of the Klan, sworn to secrecy, never explained and probably encouraged speculations to heighten the mystery. The awe-inspiring initiation ritual, high principle stated in grandiloquent phrases, the mystery, the humorous reports of past activity, the elaborate oath of secrecy, and above all the implied violence against Negroes and other Republicans in contradistinction to lofty purposes attracted men of limited means who lived in a drab world. Their only hope for distinction lay in being superior to the large number of Negroes who lived in the South.

In its initial stages Klan-type organizations appealed to many formerly wealthy planters, men who had used force to cow their laborers into submission, who still retained large land holdings in the defeated South. Probably the organizer of the Young Men's Democratic Club of Leon County, Florida, was one of the wealthiest men of that locality who encouraged his followers by recounting the means used to control Negroes in the good old days of slavery. The Klan itself benefited from the organizational ability of Nathan Bedford Forrest, onetime slave trader, plantation owner, and famous Confederate cavalry officer. Under his direction the Klan mushroomed into an important interstate society. At its head the grand wizard presided over an Invisible Empire divided into realms, dominions, provinces, and dens, directed by grand dragons, grand titans, grand giants, and grand cyclops. The lowly members of a den were ghouls, and officers were genii, hydras, furies, night hawks, magis, monks, scribes, sentinels, and turks. There was no official costume for members, but flowing white robes made of bedsheets or more costly material and high hats were characteristic attire.

The instruments of the Klan were written warnings with dire predictions of personal danger and appearances in ghostly attire to frighten the superstitious. The warnings were sprinkled with the words dismal, dark, furious, fearful, awful, and death. Sudden departure from the world and immediate entrance into a Dante-like Hell were predicted for Republican leaders—Carpetbagger, Scalawag, and Negro. "Dead, dead, under the roses," "X marks the spot," and other warnings were secretly attached to the doors of prominent politicians. Trees and buildings were plastered with notices of forthcoming Klan meetings and predictions of fearful consequences to individuals who supported the Republican party. Messages were sent to Congressional Radicals; one forwarded to Thaddeus Stevens predicted "Thy end is nigh." Many of these warnings were illustrated with crude drawings of coffins, graveyards, skulls, and skeletons.

In personal confrontations the major objective was to frighten Negroes. With a clatter of their horses' hoofs, robed horsemen reined in at a Negro's cabin to demand water, drink bucketsful, and declare it the best tasted since being shot at Shiloh or some other well-known battle of the late war. Then they rode away to a rendezvous where they chortled about terrified Negroes handing them buckets of water. What the merrymakers did not know was that the ignorant, superstitious Negro was more frightened by the outline of rifles under sheets than by the juvenile antics of grown men. Every possible means was used to augment the number of robed figures participating in a nightly gallop through a moonlit town. But as the number of Klansmen increased it was possible for as many as 1500 of them to parade at Huntsville, Alabama.

Editors aided the organization by publishing notices of meetings and printing warnings directed at Republican politicians. The editors disclaimed any connection with the Klan, informing readers that notices or warnings had been found tacked to or slipped under doors of newspaper offices. "The Ku Klux Klan are kalled upon to kustigate or kill any kullered kusses who may approve the konstitution being konkokted by the Kontemptible Karpetbaggers at the Kapitol," wrote a Georgia klansman. The popularity of the Klan was capitalized by enterprising tobacco, paint, and hardware companies whose products bore the Klan name. One verse-maker described the imaginary activities of clansmen in doggerel:

We're born of the night but we vanish by day.
No rations have we, but the flesh of man—
And love niggers best—the Ku Klux Klan;
We catch 'em alive and roast 'em whole,
Then hand 'em around with a sharpened pole.
Whole Leagues have been eaten, not leaving a man,
And went away hungry—the Ku Klux Klan;
Born of the night, and vanish by day;
Leaguers and niggers, get out of the way; . . .

But the Klan was a failure in its attempt to counteract the work of the Loyal League. Freedmen joined the League, voted for constitutions, and placed Republicans in office in every state except Virginia, where the Klan was not active. One lucky or well-aimed shot proved the mortality of a sheeted, ghostly horseman trespassing on private property. The radical Klansmen demanded that violence be used in the struggle for white supremacy. As the advocates of whip and dagger supplanted the upholders of fright and intimidation, the more respectable leaders saw the danger of their creation. In 1869 Forrest and other leaders officially disbanded the Invisible Empire.

The beheaded organization remained dormant for a time and then grew a multiplicity of heads. Local dens abandoned the ineffectual ghostly antics. As E. Merton Coulter stated: "They shot, hanged, burned, and drowned Negroes, Carpetbaggers, and Scalawags," Now "in the hands of cut-throats and riffraff," the Klan entered into its second phase of activity in 1870, its original purpose of white supremacy remained, but members also whipped, maimed, and killed for private gain and personal vengeance. White men and women were stripped and beaten from head to foot with leather thongs. Law-abiding citizens were harried from land, frequently acquired by an avaricious Klansman. Robed members stormed the Greenville, South Carolina, jail to release hoodlum associates and lynch six enemies. Murder and dire warnings drove some Carpetbaggers from the South, frightened numbers of Scalawags into becoming "respectable Democrats," and kept many Negroes from casting ballots at election time. A Jewish merchant, long a respected resident of Marianna, Florida, was killed for questioning the right of every white man to superiority over every Negro. The Klansmen respected neither white nor colored womanhood, girl or pregnant woman, but the majority of their victims were Negroes, local politicians, or industrious farmers with desirable land or other coveted property. Hundreds of men who never enrolled in dens used the Klan symbols and methods to achieve pelf. The Klan was so bad that pro-Southern Professor Coulter concluded: "It left a heritage which was to bedevil and disgrace the South thereafter, as mobs took the law into their own hands and engaged in barbarous lynchings—unjustified under any code of civilized rule."

Strange are the warping of facts by time. To children and grandchildren old men spoke with pride of their membership in the Klan. Men who had lived where no Klan existed told wide-eyed youngsters of their hooded exploits. In retrospect the Klan became an organization with noble purposes with its acts forced on it by action of unscrupulous Carpetbagger, Scalawag, or Negro. These raconteurs conveniently forgot or never knew that in 1869 and 1870 respectable Southerners condemned the Klan and all its work.

Even today it remains impossible to assess some effects of the Klan. Certainly it failed in 1868 to prevent the establishment of Republican governments. The reiterated claim that it destroyed the Loyal League has no foundation in fact. The League accomplished its avowed mission in making the Negro politically conscious and then shifted its activities to other fields. In reality the Negro had nothing to sustain him as a voter and office-holder. He neither possessed the property nor had the education to give him competitive status in the political arena. Without support from Northerners he was doomed to second-class citizenship.

Southerners believed that the Ku Klux Klan speeded the restoration of home rule in some southern states, but this opinion is open to question. The obvious criminality of the Klan incensed many Northerners who were growing tired of the "Southern Problem" and showing a willingness to "Let the South govern the South." President Grant had no real concern for the Negro and his call for peace, for letting the South alone, was applauded by millions of northern voters. But the outrages perpetrated by the Klan aroused southern and northern Republicans to enact restrictive legislation. On the whole, instead of speeding the defeat of Republicans in the South, the Klan lengthened the period of Congressional Reconstruction.

Southern politicians realized the danger to their regimes and acted to stem anarchy. Legislatures outlawed the Klan, made wearing of masks a criminal offense, and provided severe penalties against persons in disguise who were guilty of violence. Alabama levied a fine of $5000 against a county in which any person was killed by a mob or by an individual in disguise. Governors declared martial law in the most troublesome areas and utilized the militia to maintain order.

The severest blows against Klansmen and their illegal activities were dealt by the federal government. Congress created a joint committee to investigate and report on the Klan and similar secret organizations. During the summer of 1871 the committee heard hundreds of witnesses, and its thirteen-volume report was published in 1872 under the short title of *Ku Klux Conspiracy*. The so-called Force Bills or Ku Klux Klan Acts were passed before testimony disclosed the extent of lawlessness.

On May 31, 1870, Congress prohibited states and individuals from abridging the right to vote of any person because of race or previous servitude as granted by the Fifteenth Amendment or the equal protection of law as guaranteed by the Fourteenth Amendment. The new and central provision of the act subjected individuals or people associated in Klan-type organizations to heavy penalties for interfering with the civil or political rights of any person. Federal courts were given jurisdiction over all offenses under the law with federal marshals and the regular military forces placed at the disposal of the courts to enforce the act. On February 28, 1871, a second law placed national elections, North and South, under federal control; federal judges were empowered to appoint election supervisors, and marshals were allowed sufficient deputies to maintain order at polling places. Since state and federal officeholders were selected at the same time, the act gave the national authority surveillance over state and local elections.

More comprehensive than the first two was the third Klan Act of April 20, 1871. It enumerated a list of high crimes characteristic of Klan-type societies and enacted penalties, fines of $500 to $5000 and/or imprisonment, with or without hard labor, from six months to six years "as the court may determine." Before serving as a grand or petit juror in any hearing or trial arising under the act, an individual was required to state under oath that he had "never directly or indirectly, counselled, advised, or voluntarily aided" any combination or conspiracy to deny American citizens their political and civil rights. Whenever unlawful combinations became so numerous and powerful as to defy state or federal authority, or whenever the constituted authorities of a state participated in or connived to aid such combinations, and when conviction of the lawless was impracticable, the combinations were deemed rebellion and the President was authorized to suspend "the *writ* of habeas corpus, to the end that such rebellion may be overthrown."

Grant designated nine counties of upper South Carolina as the locale of rebellious combinations and declared martial law. Federal troops were moved to other troublesome areas to nip lawlessness in the bud and prevent anarchy. Marshals and their deputies watched at election precincts, ready to arrest any individual who attempted to intimidate a voter.

Even more effective in destroying the Klan was prosecution of persons accused of interfering with the political and civil rights of citizens. In 1871 and 1872 hundreds of indictments were returned in the South Carolina federal district court and 82 persons, most of whom threw themselves on the mercy of the court, were fined and imprisoned. Almost 500 people were charged in Mississippi, more than 350 in North Carolina, and a smaller number in other states. Approximately 10 per cent of those arrested were indicted and about half the latter were convicted.

This record makes two interpretations possible. Arrests were made more to intimidate Conservative-Democrats and support Republicans than to punish the guilty; second, even with selected juries, it was difficult to place 12 men in the jury box who would render a verdict on the evidence presented. The evidences of violence and the attitude of white citizens, as disclosed by the *Ku Klux Conspiracy*, gives more weight to the latter conclusion. Trials held at Raleigh, Columbia, Charleston, Jacksonville, and Oxford attracted particular interest in the North and South, and many of the convicted Southerners served their relatively short terms in prison at Albany, New York.

Federal power broke the back of the Klan, but Conservative-Democrats possessed more puissant weapons than lawlessness in their fight against the Republican regimes. One of them was a divide-and-rule policy whereby Conservative whites encouraged dissident factions within the dominant party. Illustrative of this strategy was the Conservative-Democratic support of every successful and unsuccessful attempt to impeach Governor Reed of Florida. In reality they held him in higher esteem than most of the other Republican leaders but voted against him to create confusion within the ranks of their political opponents.

In Florida and other southern states, Conservative-Democrats saw the Negro voter and officeholder as the weakest link in the Republican political chain. Again and again they urged Negroes to demand offices commensurate with their power at the polls; they supported a Negro if he was the less able of two Republican candidates; and they attempted in every possible way to create a gulf between the Negro electorate and the Carpetbag-Scalawag leadership. By upgrading the freedman and downgrading the white politician, Conservative-Democrats confused Negro voters and hamstrung many of their capable leaders. The success of this strategy was illustrated in the 1872 Florida Republican convention. Negro delegates hooted down Carpetbagger Marcellus L. Stearns and forced him to relinquish the gubernatorial nomination to Scalawag Ossian Hart, whom the colored delegates believed more friendly to their interests. Stearns accepted second place on the Republican ticket.

Concurrent with this activity was the weaning of voters from the Republican to the Democratic fold. Negroes were told that the former planter knew his needs better, was more interested in him, and would give him more than the alien Carpetbagger and the renegade Scalawag. Taking advantage of the uneducated Negro and an election system which allowed the use of almost any type of ballot, whites prepared ballots marked for Democratic candidates or substituted their party's marked ballots for Republican ones. They told the illiterate Negro that his Republican ballot was actually a Democratic one, convinced him to discard it, and accept theirs. Unless Republican workers reached the Negro, he cast his vote for the Conservative-Democratic candidates, thinking he was voting for Republicans.

Conservative-Democrats appealed to Carpetbaggers and Scalawags, promising forgiveness if they would vote for the party of white supremacy. White Republicans who had experienced social ostracism found homes open to them when they moved from the Republican to the Democratic fold. The popular Carpetbag and Scalawag leaders were given opportunity for political activity within the Democratic party. Every white man, regardless of his former party affiliation or his economic status, was urged to join the crusade. The call for white supremacy was seldom in speeches or party platforms, but it was the unvoiced and unwritten central theme of all Conservative-Democratic programs. The Negro, however, was not disfranchised by word or act. If he was amenable to white leadership, he was welcome to vote and allowed to hold minor political offices.

A particularly effective means of controlling the Negro voter was the use of white economic power. Since white men owned the land, the Negro tenant, laborer, or sharecropper was at their mercy. Voting the Republican ticket or leadership in that party brought retaliation in leasing and hiring. Threats to evict Negro families from white-owned shacks forced many a colored male into voting for Democratic candidates or staying away from the polls. Southern industries were owned by white men, who were not reticent in telling their colored laborers how to vote and threatening them with loss of jobs. Merchants charged higher prices to politically active Negroes than their other customers, lawyers and doctors added 25 per cent to charges for their services to Republican Negroes, and bosses paid more for piece work to Democratic Negroes than to Republican ones. Housewives worked on their domestic help; cooks and maids whose husbands did not vote Democratic or stay away from the polls were threatened with loss of jobs or denied "totin rights," the taking home of leftovers from kitchens. When the Negro found himself deserted by federal officials, he had the choice of submitting to his southern employers or remaining faithful to the Republican party and suffering the economic consequences. Many a hungry Negro protected himself and family by bending his knees to his white overlord.

White landowners were urged to join the crusade for home rule. Republicans, said the Conservative-Democrats, were lining their pockets by graft and pushing the cost of government to unreasonable heights. Every sale of land to satisfy tax liens was used by conservatives to indict the congressional governments. In the Old South, the landowner and slaveowner had contributed relatively little to the costs of government. Ante-bellum South Carolina agrarians enjoyed a total tax assessment of little more than $10 million whereas their city cousins in Charleston had their property listed at approximately $22 million. The Republicans increased the levies on agricultural lands, but even then the tax rate on property assessed at a fraction of its value averaged 15 mills in the 11 former Confederate states in 1870. In contrast, the rate was 45 mills in Illinois. New York State netted more than $48 million at an almost 25-mill levy while the total in 11 southern states was little more than $32 million. Planter and small farmer needed capital to operate their agricultural enterprise; for most of them any tax was a serious burden. Although the higher salaries paid officeholders by Republican governments, increased appropriations for schools, and grants for other community services were justified, hard pressed southern agrarians simply could not afford to pay. Therefore, any instance of graft, waste, and larger governmental budget became an issue at the polls. It was a powerful one for the Conservative-Democrats who used it to establish white solidarity.

Essential to the restoration of home rule was political control of Negro voters and elimination of white Republican leaders. The failure of violence forced white conservatives to experiment with other methods which would not anger Northerners but still be effective in controlling the Negro. They found their answer in the "Mississippi Plan" of intimidation by threat and show of force which usually stopped short of maiming and killing. The latter almost never occurred unless Negroes resorted to arms and inevitably the white forces lost few men and the Negroes many.

Under the Mississippi Plan public display was made of white power and arms. There were no secret societies, no hooded night riders; there were rifle clubs of well-armed and well-trained men or red-shirted companies who drilled openly on vacant lots and marched down main streets. There were shooting contests using a target made to represent a Negro and the bullet-riddled dummy was carried through streets afterwards to demonstrate marksmanship and frighten Negro citizens. Torchlight processions of horsemen rode through town and country. Some politically active Negroes were whipped, others were taken from their homes and forced by threats to forswear further activity, and then made to swear that the oath had been given freely and without intimidation. White men talked of bagging bucks in language which let the Negro know that this buck was no member of the deer family. Stories were circulated of "dead niggers piled as high as the court house" in a distant county with intimations that the pile would be higher at the local county seat if many Negroes attempted to vote.

Continual harassment made life unendurable for Carpetbagger and Scalawag. Two or more armed men would silently keep pace behind a Republican whenever he appeared in public, the silence broken periodically as a gun "accidentally" banged behind him. At any hour of the night the Republican politico and his family might be awakened by gunfire or other noisy demonstrations. Political rallies held in the open were disrupted by the thundering hoofs of charging horsemen and meetings held indoors were disturbed by the vibrations of nearby cannon blasts. One by one, Carpetbagger and Scalawag renounced political activity, joined the Conservative-Democrats, or left for a more peaceful region.

The Restoration of White Supremacy

Years before the Mississippi Plan became effective, Conservative-Democrats won control of several southern states. Tennessee, the first to accept Republican control, was the first to discard it. In 1869 Governor Brownlow resigned to enter the Senate. In the ensuing special election the conservatives supported and elected DeWitt C. Senter, the more conservative of two Republican candidates for the governorship. On his assuming office, the power of the Republicans was broken although they remained influential and a potential danger to the Democratic organization. In 1870 Virginia finally met the requirements of Congress and placed the Conservative-Democrats in power. North Carolina was restored the same year after a hectic period under Governor William W. Holden. In his attempt to destroy the Ku Klux Klan, Holden gave Colonel George W. Kirk extensive powers to arrest men suspected of violence. Kirk's ruthless use of power and the excesses of his soldiers brought on the so-called Kirk-Holden war. Eventually the federal courts intervened to check Kirk and the Democrats won the legislature in 1870. It promptly impeached and removed Holden, thereby elevating Lieutenant Governor Todd R. Caldwell to the governorship. Although Caldwell was elected governor in 1872, the Republican organization remained powerful in North Carolina until wartime Governor Zebulon B. Vance won the governorship in 1876.

Southern Democrats had high hopes in 1872 for a national victory which would speed the restoration of white rule in the South. Division within the Republican party, especially the Liberal Republican movement, encouraged Southerners to anticipate national success and less northern support for measures to protect freedmen. Although Democratic support for presidential candidate Horace Greeley did not defeat Grant, the political tide was turning. As long as southern conservatives made no violent discrimination against Negroes, an increasing number of northern voters were ready to leave the South alone.

An important contributing factor to the restoration of white supremacy was division in southern Republican ranks. In 1873 it enabled the Democratic gubernatorial candidate, Richard Coke, to defeat his Republican opponent and brought "redemption" to Texas in the following year. Alabama conservatives had placed their man in the governor's office in 1870, but the excesses of his regime and aid of federal forces returned the state to the Republican fold in 1872. Unable to keep their political house in order, the Republicans were voted out of office in 1874. Republicans of Arkansas also weakened their party by internal dissension, but the Democrats too were torn by party strife. The latter supported the more conservative of two Republican candidates in 1872 rather than offering voters a Democratic ticket. For two years the proponents of Joseph Brooks and Elisha Baxter made a mockery of representative government as they supported their respective favorites in what amounted to virtual war in the Brooks-Baxter controversy. In 1874 the Democrats abandoned their policy of "the lesser evil within the Republican Party" and nominated their own candidate, Augustus H. Garland, whose victory redeemed the state.

Ever since the readmission of her congressmen in 1870, Mississippi was a battleground of two powerful Republican organizations. In every following election the Conservative-Democrats supported the conservative candidates of the Republicans, only to see the radical ones win office. They gave their approval to Lewis Dent, brother-in-law of Grant, against James L. Alcorn. When the victorious Alcorn veered in the direction of conservatism, the party of white supremacy backed him, but lost the election to Carpetbagger Adelbert Ames. The Mississippi Plan of harassment and intimidation bore fruit in 1875 when the Conservative-Democrats won the legislature. As soon as the newly elected legislators assembled in 1876, they brought fictitious charges against Governor Ames. Rather than face a stacked political vote, he resigned and the Democrats completed their takeover of the state.

As the 1876 national election approached, only Florida, Louisiana, and South Carolina remained in Republican hands; and Florida was apparently moving into the Democratic ranks. The year before, a Democrat, Charles W. Jones, was sent to the United States Senate by the deciding vote of the state senate's presiding officer. The favorite of Negro voters, Governor Ossian B. Hart, had died in office, promoting Marcellus Stearns to the governorship. Stearns had been taught a lesson by Negro delegates and did much to unify Florida Republicans. In 1876 he won the nomination for the governorship. Similar to the two other still-Republican states, Florida Republicans held a potent advantage in controlling the canvassing boards which counted the ballots cast. A few forthright Republicans admitted that the way people voted was not as important as the official tally of the votes cast.

Louisianians found no quick surcease from their troubles. During the administration of Carpetbagger Henry Clay Warmoth, beginning in 1868, the Republicans split into two antagonistic factions, a division encouraged by shrewd Conservative-Democrats. In 1872 Warmoth worked for Democratic candidate John McEnery, who was declared the victor by the canvassing board. Supported by federal marshal Stephen B. Packard, the dissident Republicans got rid of Warmoth and placed Lieutenant Governor P. B. S. Pinchback in the governor's office for the remainder of Warmoth's term. From 1872 to 1877 the internecine party warfare continued. Two state governments were organized, one headed by conservative McEnery and the other by Republican William P. Kellogg. For a time President Grant refused to recognize either claimant. Consequently race riots developed into virtual warfare in some localities with the better-organized and better-trained white forces killing a large number of Negroes. Finally Grant sent troops to New Orleans, where General Sheridan found anarchy so widespread that he requested permission to declare lawless white Louisianians banditti and treat them as criminals. By a compromise the Kellogg administration was recognized and supported until 1877.

Even during the years of Negro majorities in the House of Representatives and a Carpetbag and a Scalawag governor, South Carolina property owners had not fared too badly. Unable to win the state, the Conservative-Democrats nevertheless contributed to the election of an able carpetbagger in 1874. Victorious Carpetbagger Daniel H. Chamberlain gave his adopted state a good administration. But by 1876 the Conservative-Democrats were hopeful of victory as they championed their erstwhile Confederate Lieutenant General Wade Hampton against Chamberlain in the gubernatorial election of 1876.

That year was crucial for the South and the nation. Eight of the former Confederate states were already Democratic. Graft and corruption of the Grant era gave Democrats confidence of victory in state and national elections. In 1876 the more realistic Democrats prophesied that the unredeemed states of Florida, Louisiana, and South Carolina would be important in the forthcoming elections. Time proved them accurate prognosticators.

REFERENCES

The literature on individual southern states is voluminous. Most established in popular conception are the interpretations of the Dunning School. Not all of the following books are the products of William A. Dunning's students, but their authors support his interpretations. James W. Fertig, *Secession and Reconstruction of Tennessee* (Chicago, 1898); James W. Garner, *Reconstruction in Mississippi* (New York, 1901); Hamilton J. Eckenrode, *The Political His-*

tory of Virginia during the Reconstruction (Baltimore, 1904); John S. Reynolds, Reconstruction in South Carolina, 1865–1877 (Columbia, 1905); Walter L. Fleming, Reconstruction in Alabama (New York, 1905); John R. Flicken, History of Reconstruction in Louisiana (to 1868) (Baltimore, 1910); Charles W. Ramsdell, Reconstruction in Texas (New York, 1910); William W. Davis, The Civil War and Reconstruction in Florida (New York, 1913); J. G. de Roulhac Hamilton, Reconstruction in North Carolina (New York, 1914); A. Mildred Thompson, Reconstruction in Georgia (New York, 1915); Ella Lonn, Reconstruction in Louisiana after 1868 (New York, 1918); Thomas S. Staples, Reconstruction in Arkansas, 1861–1874 (Little Rock, 1926); H. M. McNeely, Wade Hampton and the Negro: The Road Not Taken (Columbia, 1949); and William C. Nunn, Texas Under the Carpetbaggers (Austin, 1962). In a relative sense the studies vary: Garner's is surprisingly good, Hamilton's is biased in every chapter. General coverage in the Dunning tradition include E. Merton Coulter, The South During Reconstruction, 1865–1877 (Baton Rouge, 1947); Robert S. Henry, The Story of Reconstruction (Indianapolis, 1938); Paul H. Buck, The Road to Reunion, 1865–1890 (Boston, 1937); Nash K. Burger and John K. Bettersworth, South of Appomattox (New York, 1959); and the Reconstruction chapters in William B. Hesseltine and David L. Smiley, The South in American History (New York, 1960), a textbook on the South. Among the revisionist works are: Francis B. Simkins and Robert H. Woody, South Carolina during Reconstruction (Chapel Hill, 1932); Willie M. Caskey, Secession and Reconstruction of Louisiana (Baton Rouge, 1938); Roger W. Shugg, Origins of the Class Struggle in Louisiana (Baton Rouge, 1939); Thomas P. Alexander, Political Reconstruction in Tennessee (Nashville, 1950); Joel Williamson, After Slavery: The Negro in South Carolina During Reconstruction, 1861–1877 (Chapel Hill, 1965); and Joe M. Richardson, The Negro in the Reconstruction of Florida, 1865–1877 (Tallahassee, 1965). Additional revisionist-type books and articles will be cited after Chapter XII.

Southern lawlessness is described in Stanley F. Horn, Invisible Empire: The Story of the Ku Klux Klan, 1866–1871 (Boston, 1939), and castigated in William P. Randel, The Ku Klux Klan: A Century of Infamy (Philadelphia, 1965). Francis B. Simkins, "The Ku Klux Klan in South Carolina," Journal of Negro History, XII (1927), pp. 606–47, and Simkins and Grady McWhiney, "The Ghostly Legend of the Ku Klux Klan," Negro History Bulletin, XIV (1951), pp. 109–12, explode some Klan myths. The reader is again referred to W. E. B. DuBois, Black Reconstruction. Useful studies on special topics are: Otis A. Singletary, Negro Militia and Reconstruction (Austin, 1957); S. D. Smith, The Negro in Congress (Chapel Hill, 1940); Robert F. Durden, "The Prostrate State Revisited: James S. Pike and South Carolina Reconstruction," Journal of Negro History, XXXIX (1954), pp. 87–110; Paul L. Lewison, Race, Class, and Party: A History of Negro Suffrage and White Politics in the South (New York, 1932); David Donald, "The Scalawag in Mississippi Reconstruction," Journal of Southern History, X (1944), pp. 447–60; Thomas B. Alexander, "Persistent Whiggery in the Confederate South," ibid., XXVII (1961), pp. 305–29; Allen W. Trelease, "Who were the Scalawags?" ibid., XXIX

(1963), pp. 445–68; John R. Lynch, *The Facts of Reconstruction* (New York, 1913); and Alrutheus A. Taylor's three volumes, *The Negro in South Carolina during the Reconstruction* (Washington, 1924), *The Negro in the Reconstruction of Virginia* (Washington, 1926), and *The Negro in Tennessee, 1865–1880* (Washington, 1941). Because it was a Democratic campaign document, probably written by a white conservative, John Wallace, *Carpet-Bag Rule in Florida*, introduction by Allan Nevins (Gainesville, 1964), should be used with care.

The Grant Regime

ON COLD, cloudy March 4, 1869, the Fifth United States cavalry escorted Ulysses S. Grant down Pennsylvania Avenue to the Capitol. The petulant military hero refused to ride in a carriage with Johnson. Rather he chose the companionship of John A. Rawlins, an intimate friend of past years in Galena, Illinois, and his former chief of staff. By his side also was Schuyler Colfax, speaker of the House of Representatives and vice president-elect.

Americans expected a great administration from Grant. As a general he had demonstrated commendable selectivity in choosing his subordinates and in supporting capable ones despite unjustified criticism; notwithstanding the severe losses suffered in battles with Lee, Grant's dogged determination to finish a necessary task and his eventual success had won the hearts of most Americans. In 1869 veterans of the Army of the Potomac adored their erstwhile commander—he had ennobled them by leading them to victory over slavocracy. Other Americans, ever ready to enshrine a hero, were placing their general among the immortal leaders of the country. Even the conquered were hopeful. Grant's generous terms at Appomattox, his friendly testimony before the Joint Committee on Reconstruction, and his expressed desire for sectional harmony colored the dreams of white Southerners with visions of home rule and continued Caucasian supremacy.

The personally honest, politically naïve Grant could not meet the leadership responsibilities of his time. He entered the White House at a period in American history which called for a superb politician with a Quaker-like inner light of spirit to cope with myriad sectional, economic, and social problems. The era demanded the versatility, adaptability, and firmness of a Lincoln, but Grant possessed few of the martyred President's qualities.

Just after high noon on March 4, Chief Justice Chase, now shorn of hope for the presidency, administered the oath of office to the second West Point-trained soldier elected by the people. The short, bearded eighteenth President delivered his address of 1200 words without the force expected of a heroic commander. The President promised to execute the laws of Congress, to "exercise the constitutional privilege of interposing a veto to defeat measures which I oppose," and to demand respect for the international rights of the United States. Much of his speech related to the public debt, every dollar of which "should be paid in gold, unless otherwise expressly stipulated in the contract. Let it be understood that no repudiator of one farthing of our public debt will be trusted in public place. . . ." As an aid to paying the debt and "strengthening a credit which ought to be the best in the world," he urged "a faithful collection of revenue, a strict accountability to the Treasury for every dollar collected. . . ."

He promised to recommend policies without contravening the will of the people. And he knew of no better method of securing "the repeal of bad or obnoxious laws so effective as their stringent execution." In solving the problems of a country emerging from a rebellion, problems "which preceding Administrations had never had to deal with," he would approach them "calmly, without prejudice, hate or sectional pride, remembering that the greatest good to the greatest number is the object to be obtained." He requested settlement of the suffrage problem, a question "likely to agitate the public as long as a portion of the citizens of the nation are excluded from its privileges in any State," by ratification of the Fifteenth Amendment.

Hamilton Fish, who sat just behind the President on the ceremonial platform, was disappointed by the shortness of the inaugural address. Perhaps others shared the opinion of the man who would become secretary of state. But many persons undoubtedly welcomed the brevity. The childlike opening sentence in which the President cited his election by "Your suffrages" and his conformity with the Constitution by taking the prescribed oath of office was followed by the statement: "The responsibilities of the position I feel, but accept them without fear." Listeners casting apprehensive glances at a sky threatening precipitation must have applauded a speech filled with platitudes and puerilities for its brevity.

That evening the faithful assembled in the Treasury Building to honor their hero with an inaugural ball. Brilliant lights illuminated streets and sidewalks leading to the building. Inside, beautifully gowned ladies and immaculately dressed gentlemen danced to the pleasant rhythms of musicians. The ball might have been a social soothsayer foretelling the course of Grant's administrations. It began with orderliness and gaiety, ended in confusion and boredom. In the throng ladies lost their escorts, elaborate coiffeurs drooped, expensive dresses wrinkled, and the odor of perspiration conquered the scent of perfume. Guests sat on cold floors, their hunger pangs heightened by the smell of food on distant, unreachable tables. As late as ten o'clock the next morning almost a thousand people sought their hats and coats from harried attendants.

The irritations of disenchanted merrymakers were harbingers of more important disillusionments with the Grant administrations. The self-styled man of peace and sectional harmony found the ratification of the Fifteenth Amendment no solution to the vexing southern problem. Necessity forced him to use federal power to counteract lawlessness in the South and protect the rights of Negro citizens. Although he had no heartfelt concern for the freedmen, his acts angered white supremacists. Finally, he virtually abandoned the Negro, leaving him in the care of white overlords in all the former Confederate states except Florida, Louisiana, and South Carolina.

Grant brought to Washington none of the daring initiative characteristic of his western war campaigns. Eagerly he turned to friends for political advice only to find them divided in counsel. Without an understanding of the American system of government, politically inexperienced, often bewildered, yet forced to make decisions, he frequently chose the poorer of two possible actions or followed scheming advisers. Political leadership, he discovered, bore little resemblance to military command. As a general, he trusted those subordinates whom he liked and supported them without question against their political critics. Rarely did a lieutenant betray his commander's trust. In political life, however, Grant met a different breed of man—the selfish individual seeking to profit from political office, the promoter asking governmental support for shady schemes, the businessman demanding grants and subsidies. In politics Grant trusted those whom he liked, clung with tenacious loyalty to his friends who often betrayed him. As a result, his record in office forces a question: was Grant politically moronic or personally dishonest? With the consensus supporting his political naïveté, the historian sheds a tear for the military genius spread-eagled in the web of scheming men.

Facts do not compliment the military genius turned politician. He entered the White House with the support of a united party of Republicans weary of the strife-torn administration of Johnson, but he failed to maintain party unity. The order and discipline, decision and efficiency of his military years yielded to disorder and laxity, indecision, and inefficiency during his presidential terms. Instead of exemplifying political reform and honesty, his administrations were characterized by spoils and corruption. One by one the idealists turned away, disillusioned. Finally the man who had never liked mere politicians found them his main support in council. Yet, throughout his "nadir of national disgrace" Grant remained popular. If left to the people, who hated war but loved the hero rising from warfare, Grant might have won the presidency for an unprecedented third term.

Grant served while the United States was moving from agrarianism to industrialism. Captains of industry found the people ready to follow the laissez-faire philosophy of Adam Smith without serious question of governmental grants to corporations, the elimination of competition, and the negation of other natural laws listed by Smith as regulators of a free economy. In the process of change, farmers suffered, slum areas multiplied in cities, immigrants were exploited, and laborers found themselves virtually powerless. The American believed in Protestantism, political democracy, and material well-being. These ideals, he believed, would conquer the world and bring peace and plenty. During the Grant administrations Americans found a comforting philosophy. Confident of their destiny, they overlooked selfishness, graft, and exploitation of minorities. In the process the industrial magnate—ruthless to competitor, laborer, and consumer—developed a tremendous system of national production, and, thereby, increased the American standard of living.

The Administrative Officials

When asked to comment on the men selected by Grant for cabinet posts, Andrew Johnson dubbed them "Grant's gift enterprise Cabinet." The appellation was sufficiently descriptive to impress a reporter from the *New-York Tribune*. Some of Grant's first cabinet selections were individuals to whom he was indebted because of gifts to him and his campaign fund. A few were personal friends and others were almost unknown in political circles.

Alexander T. Stewart, the New York department-store owner with a fortune of almost 50 million dollars, was reputedly the country's third richest man. Always gentlemanly in act and appearance, he enjoyed a reputation for integrity and generosity. More than a decade before the Civil War, he had sent a ship loaded with commodities to relieve the famine-stricken Irish. This act was only one of his many philanthropies, but in 1869 newspaper reporters dwelt on his contributions to the Republican party and his check to Grant for $65,000 to pay for a mansion in Philadelphia. Although he had contributed handsomely to the house-for-Grant fund, Stewart represented many Americans in delivering the gift. Despite his good reputation and great success as a merchant, Stewart lacked the broad experience requisite for the task as secretary of the treasury. Furthermore, he was ineligible under the 1789 law, inspired by Alexander Hamilton, which barred a person engaged in trade and commerce from the treasury post. Dumbfounded by opposition to the appointment, Grant yielded to opinion and law. The Radical George S. Boutwell of Massachusetts, whose special field was finance, became secretary of the treasury.

Another millionaire merchant, Adolph E. Borie of Pennsylvania, won senate approval as secretary of the navy. He, too, had contributed generously to the house-for-Grant fund. Retired and ill, the almost-sixty-year-old

Borie never expected a reward for his gift, but he accepted the secretary-ship on a temporary basis. True to his promise, he resigned in less than five months and was replaced in July by George M. Robeson of New Jersey. According to one of his critics, the almost unknown lawyer was a first-rate judge of wines, a second-rate trout fisherman, and a third-rate lawyer. The jovial Robeson, a gallant bachelor who enlivened many a Washington so-cial event, retained his post throughout the remainder of the Grant regime.

For the war office Grant turned to his old friend John A. Rawlins. Grant's former Galena neighbor and army chief of staff was an honest man with some ability and considerable shrewdness. Unfortunately Rawlins died of consumption in September 1869, and William W. Belknap of Iowa became secretary of war. The position gave him more opportunity than any other secretary in directing the course of reconstruction and he pleased his Radical friends by working to entrench the Republican party in the southern states. Too frequently the easily led Grant followed the ad-vice of his secretary of war, thereby infuriating white Southerners while doing little to aid the Negroes. Belknap, however, retained his office until the disclosure of his corruption forced his resignation in 1876.

The three less important cabinet posts were filled with men of ability and integrity. Ebenezer R. Hoar of Massachusetts served as attorney gen-eral (a post of increasing importance after 1870) for more than a year and Jacob Dolson Cox of Ohio headed the interior department until Novem-ber 1870. The Radical John A. J. Creswell of Maryland was postmaster general for more than five years. Grant's eagerness to reward friends and relatives and the cry of liberals for civil service reform added to the trials of the postmaster. But Creswell walked through an age of political corrup-tion with dignity.

Grant's selection of a secretary of state illustrated his administrative methods. Impulsively, gratefully he offered the secretaryship to Elihu B. Washburne of Galena, who was responsible for Grant's initial command of Illinois troops and later his appointment as one of the four brigadier generals from the state. A big, ebullient man, a rough frontiersman, Wash-burne possessed neither the education nor the experience essential to direct diplomats. Washburne accepted the appointment with a condition: he would hold the place a week to give himself status as a minister to a for-eign country, the appointment he really craved. He resigned to become minister to France, a position for which he had no qualifications. At least in Paris he could do less harm than in Washington.

Before his resignation as secretary of state, reporters speculated on Washburne's successor. News leaked from the White House that James F. Wilson would be appointed. Like Boutwell, Wilson had been a member of the Johnson impeachment committee, but he was cut from a better bolt of cloth than his Radical colleague. However, Wilson had no talent for the state department job and he knew that the entertaining expected of a secretary was beyond his financial resources.

Luck smiled on Grant. His third try brought a man of exceptional ability to the office. Although the President wrote Hamilton Fish of New York on March 10, he submitted the nomination to the Senate before hearing from the New Yorker. After rejecting the offer, Fish heeded the pleas of his wife and Orville E. Babcock, the President's military secretary who was sent to New York City with the executive's request for Fish to serve at least until the adjournment of Congress.

Sixty-year-old Hamilton Fish was a cultured, traveled individual with a speaking knowledge of four languages and a broad international point of view. Family background, education, character, and graciousness opened doors to him and he possessed the means to entertain guests. A graduate of Columbia College, an experienced lawyer, a former member of the house of representatives, senate, and governor of his state, Fish had retired from politics a decade before his appointment as secretary of state to devote himself to education and philanthropy. In 1869 he was chairman of the board of trustees of his alma mater and president of the New York Historical Society. Many politicians were angered by the appointment of a man who appeared aloof from the political struggles of the party and who probably could not distinguish between a deserving Republican and an ordinary Democrat officeseeker; but his selection was applauded by intellectuals. In the years to come, Fish gave the Grant regime a veil of respectability; he handled the President with firmness and tact while at times bending to support Grant in a questionable scheme or a personal controversy to maintain his influence in fundamental concerns.

The cabinet members were neither distinguished nor unfit. On the average their ability was not high, yet among them was no prima donna demanding special handling. It was not the cabinet personnel so much as Grant's method of selecting them that made experienced politicians wince and editorial writers angry. The President offered some posts as gratuities to those who had befriended him, consulted youthful secretaries in choosing other men, submitted nominations before conferring with the nominees, and in general acted like a military commander promoting subordinates.

One member of the White House secretariat equaled or surpassed cabinet members in influence. Orville E. Babcock was a Vermonter by birth and a graduate of West Point with a reputation for distinguished service on the staffs of several army commanders. The handsome thirty-three-year-old extrovert occupied an anteroom leading to Grant's private office, greeted visitors with a flashing smile, and stood as an intermediary between the people and the President. Babcock dropped the "military" from his title to become a regular secretary, opening Grant's mail, answering letters, and settling the business of many people without allowing them to bother the President. Month after month the self-confident secretary increased his power until he won the President's complete confidence and became Grant's chief adviser. As Babcock's power increased, politicians and cabinet members who originally liked him became suspicious and even resentful of his close association with the President.

While the White House was being refurnished, Grant traveled from place to place in New England and the Middle Atlantic states. He was good copy for reporters. Americans welcomed him, applauded his plain dress and manners, identified his awkwardness at social functions as their own, and loved the squat figure dressed in a black coat with a shiny black stovepipe hat on his head. Astute observers, however, were disturbed by his associates—Ben Butler, the shoddy contractor Tom Murphy, and other men of questionable character. Even more disturbing was the President's equating gifts with patriotism and his readiness to reward givers with office. Grant's favors to the Dent family and to other relatives by blood or marriage and his appointments made without regard for merit brought shudders from friends of good government.

The Civil Service

On March 4, 1869, Edwin L. Godkin assured readers of *The Nation* that Grant would cleanse the central government of cheap politicians. Many thoughtful Americans expected the new President would bring military efficiency to the national administration. Since its appearance at the national level during the administrations of Andrew Jackson, the spoils system had grown into a giant. The Jacksonian philosophy was simple: honesty was more important than ability in filling government jobs, most of which involved routine duties; the best method of securing honest public servants was by appointing individuals who had worked for and would take pride in making the administration of their leader successful.

Though in some respects superior to the pre-Jacksonian method of selecting civil servants, the spoils system was outmoded by 1870. Federal jobholders needed more skills and abilities than in the previous generation—even the tasks of a fourth-class postmaster were more complex—and the continuance in office of a core of able men from administration to administration was essential to good government. Advocates of reform agitated with renewed vigor for a classified civil service and tests to secure qualified as well as honest men for public office.

Crusty politicians of both parties scoffed at the idea of a merit system. In power and with patronage to dispense, the Republicans were more vocal in defending the existing order than the Democrats. Special fitness as demonstrated by tests, the Republican regulars maintained, would deny many a patriot the opportunity for a job. The men who fought to save the Union, their widows or children, deserved special consideration for the sacrifices made. A merit system would benefit Copperheads and other disloyal people who had stayed at home while patriotic Republicans were fighting rebels. According to the Republican view, the country must have these loyal men in office to guarantee the fruits of victory. The politicians of both parties, who knew the value of energetic workers at election time, wished to retain the spoils system to reward the faithful and maintain political organizations.

Grant resented interference with his prerogatives. He could not silence his critics or still the voices of reformers, even if they were not molded in the grand design of ante-bellum humanitarians. In an apparent capitulation he suggested in his annual message of 1870 that legislation was needed to regularize all appointments. Although Grant specifically excluded tenure for government workers, the favorable public response to his appeal stampeded Congress into action. By adding a civil service provision to a bill ready for enactment, on March 3, 1871, Congress authorized the President "to prescribe such rules and regulations for the admission of persons in the civil service of the United States as will best promote the efficiency thereof."

Grant's response won plaudits from critics of the spoils system. Following the ideas of those who believed an investigation should lay the base for regulations, he appointed a commission, headed by George W. Curtis, to study the federal civil service. Curtis went to work at once, directed the commission in a thorough investigation, and presented the President with a severe indictment of the existing situation. The important business of government was being subordinated to the distribution of offices, the report stated, with the higher officers of government being forced to act as employment brokers. As a result, the moral tone of the country was debased and the public demoralized by displays of greed and the appointment of many unqualified men. Efficient government required efficient civil servants and the best methods of securing them were by carefully formulated rules of procedure and uniform examinations of applicants.

In cabinet meetings secretaries asked pertinent questions about appointments in their departments. Columbus Delano, who replaced Cox as secretary of the interior, requested and received exemption for his employees from competitive examinations. Fish reported several vacancies in the consular service along with nominations of men who resided a considerable distance from Washington. Since the salaries were insufficient to attract many applicants for the positions and no examining board existed, Fish won presidential approval of immediate appointments with the appointees subject to rules later adopted by the Commission. On invitation, Curtis twice appeared before the cabinet to explain his ideas. The secretaries, however, concluded his schemes impractical.

Nevertheless Grant continued a show of enthusiasm for civil service reform. In his message to Congress of April 1872, he advocated honesty and efficiency instead of political activity as the criterion for officeholding. The President had made his gestures toward reform to mend a political fence being bent by the pushing of liberal Republicans. After his re-election in 1872, he lost all of his interest in reform and Republican politicians gave a sigh of relief. A victorious Republican majority in Congress killed the civil service commission by appropriating no funds for its operation. Reform was delayed to a later decade when the assassination of a president by a disappointed officeseeker aroused the public.

Throughout the civil service fiasco Grant's actions contradicted his words. He gave little support to Jacob Cox in the latter's attempt to administer the Indian service fairly and replaced him as secretary of the interior with the pliable Columbus Delano of Ohio. After the Democrats swept New York in the elections of 1870, Grant appointed Tom Murphy collector of customs at the Port of New York. Murphy's test for retaining or appointing employees was evidence of their loyalty to New York's Senator Roscoe Conkling. The President was satisfied with the existing method of selecting federal workers. In his opinion the American civil service was the best in the world because the reliable Republicans gave the country "an educated, tried and trusted body of public servants."

Money and Taxes

As already noted, inflation was not a major issue in the 1868 campaign. After the election the hard-money faction of the Republican party proclaimed Grant's victory a mandate to Congress to redeem both the war bonds and greenbacks in gold. On March 18, 1869, in an act to strengthen the public credit Congress directed the treasury to pay bondholders "in coin or its equivalent" unless other laws expressly provided other payment. This act reinforced the policy of the secretary of the treasury and assured bondholders of gold for their bonds.

This victory of the eastern investors who held most of the bonds was bolstered by the refunding act of July 14, 1870. The wartime federal issues carried a high interest rate, too high for a reunited country with a good credit rating, and refunding the debt at lower interest was in order. By the act bondholders were given a choice of receiving payment at par or accepting new, long-term and lower-interest bonds. The act, however, guaranteed capitalists from 4 to 5 per cent and payment in coin on bonds which would not be redeemed for decades. Angered by what they considered a gift to wealthy Easterners, the western taxpayers protested the deflationary purpose of refunding and the excessive profits made by Jay Cooke in selling the bonds. Unable to dispose of the bonds without the aid of financiers, Secretary Boutwell called on Cooke, who formed an international syndicate and quickly sold all the securities allotted to him at premium prices. The entire war debt might have been refunded had the Republican inflationists kept quiet. The clash between the taxpayer of the West and the bondholder of the East forced Grant, who faced the election of 1872, to suspend funding operations. Soon after the election the panic of 1873 delayed the process until the end of Grant's second term.

Businessmen were not united on the hard versus soft money issue. During and after the war corporations sold bonds for inflated currency and they objected to repaying their creditors with "expensive dollars." The first legal tender act of February 25, 1862, made greenbacks valid for debts. In 1870 the Supreme Court ruled that this fiat money was not legal tender for a debt contracted prior to the passage of the wartime act. The *Hepburn* v. *Griswold* decision frightened railroad executives, for if applied to all bonds, the railroads and other growth industries would be forced to repay borrowed funds in deflated currency.

The inflationist faction of the Republican party had powerful allies close to the President. Ben Butler, who moved in and out of the White House at will, criticized Chief Justice Chase and the associate justices for declaring the legal tender acts unconstitutional. Railroad promoters Jay Gould and James Fisk had the ear of Grant. Certainly these and other likeminded men wished for a reversal of the decision. On the surface Grant was pressured into packing the Supreme Court in 1870 to secure reconsideration of the issue by the Court.

In reality the personnel of the Supreme Court was in process of changing before the *Hepburn* v. *Griswold* decision. On the death of James Wayne in 1867 the number of justices was reduced to eight. Congress, which had allowed President Johnson to appoint no justices, gave Grant authority to increase the Court to nine members. In an unprecedented act the Court advised the virtually paralyzed Robert C. Grier that he was no longer fit for duty. Taking advantage of a recent law allowing retirement at half pay, the enfeebled justice resigned. Prior to the date of the *Hepburn* v. *Griswold* decision, Grant nominated Attorney General Hoar and Edwin M. Stanton for the two vacancies.

The latter was quickly confirmed by the Senate, but Hoar's reputation as the ablest jurist of Massachusetts failed to save him from partisan assault.

The attorney general had refused to yield to the demands of the spoilsmen, especially in appointing circuit judges. Furthermore, the Radicals considered him pro-southern. By emphatically rejecting the nomination, the Senate underscored three points: no man with the high qualifications of Hoar should aspire to the Supreme Court in an age of political depravity, the prestige of Grant carried little weight with self-seeking senators, and the aggressiveness of the Congress extended beyond the administration of the unpopular Andrew Johnson. The death of Stanton before he could be seated left two vacancies on the Supreme Court.

Grant then nominated two railroad lawyers, William Strong of Pennsylvania and Joseph P. Bradley of New Jersey. The Senate promptly confirmed them. In 1871, two appeals on the legal tender issue were heard by the Supreme Court, and in *Knox* v. *Lee* and *Parker* v. *Davis*, the *Hepburn* v. *Griswold* decision was reversed. By a five-to-four majority the legal tender acts of 1862 and 1863 were declared constitutional, the two newly appointed justices joining forces with the three dissenting jurists of the Hepburn case.

Did Grant pack the Supreme Court? He demanded no pledge from Bradley and Strong, but their points of view on the legal tender question and their support of Congressional Reconstruction were known. Grant told Fisk that both justices were chosen for their soundness as jurists and safeness on the legal tender issue. There was an imperative need for additions to the Court in 1870 and the Senate's rejection of Hoar and the death of Stanton necessitated the nomination of more jurists. Although Grant gave due consideration to the opinions of his nominees, his primary purpose was not packing the Supreme Court.

Conservative, sound-money capitalists preferred the interchangeability of greenbacks with gold to invalidating the notes for legal debts. Approximately $450 million in greenbacks had been printed during the war. During Johnson's term a congressional mandate for reducing the amount of greenbacks in circulation aroused a storm of protest from the western debtor region of the country. When Grant entered office, $356 million in greenbacks were outstanding and their value in gold was 73 cents per dollar. The President opposed immediate resumption of specie payment, for the exchange of greenbacks for gold, dollar for dollar, would penalize debtors and depress business activity.

Grant demonstrated unusual political acumen on the legal tender and greenback questions but was less shrewd in dealing with individuals seeking personal gain by manipulating the nation's monetary policies. During the summer of 1869, Gould and Abel R. Corbin, the husband of Grant's sister, formed a combination to corner the gold market. After successful gambling ventures in gold and greenbacks as a sideline to his railroad enterprises,

Gould thought it possible to make a killing with the aid of old "lobby jobber" Corbin, who according to Jim Fisk married Grant's sister to gain influence at the White House. The plotters schemed to buy gold until they controlled the supply and squeezed short sellers, speculators who sold what they did not own with the expectation of buying later at a lower price.

The weakness of the scheme was Secretary Boutwell's practice of selling treasury gold to businessmen for foreign exchange. Gould called on Grant while the latter visited Corbin and convinced the President that a rise in the price of gold would give farmers higher prices for their products. The President ordered Boutwell to cease selling gold, told Corbin of the order, and Gould began to buy gold on the market. The price rose from 132 to 137 as he bought for himself, Corbin, and friends of Grant.

On September 13 the President began a vacation in western Pennsylvania some distance from a railroad or a telegraph line. A week later Gould brought his partner Jim Fisk into the scheme and from September 20 to 22 their purchases sent gold to 140. Fisk helped the cause by spreading rumors that Grant, Boutwell, and other officials were participating in the speculation. At this point Corbin became frightened, explained the fraud to Grant by letter, and sold gold. Forewarned, Gould also began to sell without telling Fisk, who continued to buy. Notwithstanding large sales by Gould the price of gold mounted as speculators jumped on a "sure thing" and it soared to 163. On Friday September 24 the Gold Room and stock-exchange traders were in a panic. At last realizing what was happening, Grant ordered Boutwell to sell gold and the market collapsed quickly with gold dropping to 135.

As a result of that "Black Friday" many traders were ruined. On paper Fisk was wiped out but he repudiated all his contracts and wrote Gould that "nothing is lost save honor." Neither schemer was punished for the conspiracy. By using bodyguards Gould and Fisk escaped questioning. The conspirators moved in respectable circles while laying plans for other swindles.

The public never believed that Grant and Boutwell were partners in the scheme. A congressional investigation cleared the President of everything except lack of good sense. Yet after Black Friday he accepted favors from Fisk and apparently never realized that his action in stopping the sale of gold and hiding away on vacation made the fraud possible.

Closely connected with the money problem was taxation. The Republican platform of 1868 promised a further reduction of the wartime taxes. In 1865 Congress repealed the excise tax on pig iron and coal, lowered the levies on other commodities, and reduced the revenues from excise taxes to about $45 million a year. The following year the tax on incomes of less than $1000 was abolished. By an act of July 14, 1870, practically all excise taxes were repealed except those on whiskey and tobacco. The most controversial provision of the act was the termination of the income tax in 1873. Boutwell halfheartedly opposed the repeal of a tax which was based on the best of all principles, the ability of the individual to pay.

The virtual elimination of excise taxes should have brought a drastic reduction in tariffs. A reiterated argument for high tariffs was protection for domestic manufacturers from unfair competition with foreign goods, which were not subject to levies at the place of their production. Advocates of protection admitted that whenever the excise taxes were lowered or abolished, the protective tariff should be correspondingly reduced. Manufacturers, however, forgot their comparison after the war and demanded increased levies.

Republicans were divided on the protective tariff issue. Industrialists, mostly in the East, had the support of manufacturers throughout the country. Congressmen from the South followed the leadership of protectionists in the House and Senate, disregarding the benefits of a low tariff for their raw material-producing region. In return they demanded approval of the southern Republican state governments. Western farmers, except those producing wool and flax, favored a reduction of the tariff, but western congressmen were willing to swap their votes for favorable legislation on pensions and internal improvements. Many farmers were seduced by the claim that protection gave jobs and good pay to city workers who used their income to buy farm products.

In 1867 the Wool and Woolen Act increased rates while a bill, drawn up by David A. Wells calling for moderate reductions, was rejected by Congress. Wells, who was appointed special commissioner of revenue in 1864 after his pamphlet, *Our Burden and Our Strength*, had won him national prominence as an economist, repeatedly exposed the inequities of the tariff and demonstrated its fostering of monopoly. The presence of an independent expert in office troubled high protectionists and Grant responded to their pleas by refusing to reappoint Wells. With the President, Secretary Boutwell, and a majority of the House Ways and Means Committee opposed to change, the advocates of tariff reduction were checkmated.

Continued complaints by farmers and consumers forced the administration to support a tariff bill in 1869 and 1870. The rates on tea, coffee, wines, sugar, and pig-iron and some other commodities were reduced; but the duties on a number of already highly protected articles were increased. The "indefensible exactions" of 1870 stirred reformers who won a general 10 per cent reduction in duties by an act of May 1872. This action was no more than a political maneuver. Three years later the rates of 1872 were restored by repealing the 10 per cent reduction. In tariff policy the special interests were stronger than consumers and Grant readily yielded to the more powerful.

The Election of 1872

In 1872 the Republicans sat uneasy in the saddle of national power. No realistic leader could forget the more than two generations of Democratic control prior to 1860 or the slim margin of Republican victory in three elections. In 1860 Lincoln won on a plurality of popular votes, four years later the Republican name gave way to the National Union label, and in 1868 a military hero won the presidency by little more than 300,000 votes. Following this unimpressive victory, the Democrats had meanwhile surged to primacy in many local and state contests. Congressional policies of reconstruction, one purpose of which was the creation of a solid South for the Republican party, were negated by white Southerners.

Political trends in the North frightened Republican leaders. By 1872 the rift within party ranks produced a faction determined to defeat Grant in the forthcoming election, either by preventing his renomination or forming a separate Liberal Republican organization. The Liberals won the sympathy or support of outstanding politicians, judges, lawyers, editors, and intellectuals. Lyman Trumbull, Charles Sumner, and George W. Julian gathered with former cabinet members Gideon Welles, Montgomery Blair, and Jacob D. Cox. Lincoln's great minister to England, Charles Francis Adams, brought members of his influential family into the fold. B. Gratz Brown of Missouri was representative of governors ready for reform. Chief Justice Chase and Associate Justice David Davis joined forces with poet and influential editor William Cullen Bryant. Alexander K. McClure of Pennsylvania, one of the supporters of Lincoln in 1860 and of Grant in 1868, gave his talents as a journalist and politician to the cause. Some other journalists were Horace White, whose coverage of the Lincoln-Douglas debates had won him the editorship of the *Chicago Tribune*; Theodor Tilton of New York City, editor of the *Independent*, a Congregationalist weekly; Godkin of *The Nation*; Whitelaw Reid, managing editor of Greeley's *New-York Tribune*; and, of course, the mercurial Horace Greeley.

These and other Liberal Republican leaders had no common principle. Some of them decried Grant's southern policy of using troops to support Republican governments in the South. Men opposed to a protective tariff or payment of bonds in gold associated themselves with advocates of protection or sound money. Reformers resented Grant's insincerity on civil service reform and his association with connivers. The common bond of the Liberal Republicans was opposition to Grant, a bond which simultaneously strengthened and weakened them.

As early as 1870 the liberal movement manifested itself in Missouri, where Grant relied upon John McDonald. In addition to questioning McDonald's honesty, Brown, Schurz, and other liberal-minded Republicans favored amnesty for former Confederates. By uniting with the Democratic state organization, Brown won the governorship, the Democrats secured control of the legislature, and disqualifications were removed from ex-Confederates. The Missouri senate elected Schurz to the Senate.

The success of the Liberal Republican-Democratic combination in Missouri captured the minds of reformers in other states. Southern Democrats welcomed anyone who advocated lenient treatment for white conservatives while northern Democrats envisioned a return to national supremacy by splitting the Republican party. Calls for civil service reform and political morality appealed to liberals, and minority groups sought recognition by joining in any attempt to retire Grant.

The infant labor movement contributed a footnote to the 1872 election by holding a National Labor Reform Convention at Columbus, Ohio, and nominating Associate Justice David Davis for the presidency. Although a cousin of Henry W. Davis of Wade-Davis Bill and Manifesto fame, David Davis had been a staunch Lincoln supporter. In 1862 Lincoln appointed Davis to the Supreme Court, but Davis never allowed judicial duties to hinder his political ambition. His only claim to liberalism was the *Ex parte Milligan* decision of 1867 in which he denounced the exercise of arbitrary power by the military and thereby bolstered civil liberty. Nevertheless the corpulent millionaire accepted the nomination of the National Labor Reform Convention, planning to use it as a stepping stone to leadership of the Liberal Republican-Democratic movement.

The Maryland-born associate justice of the Supreme Court spent his money freely to impress delegates to the Liberal Republican Convention who assembled at Cincinnati on May 1, 1872. The sound of music for Davis filled the air as bands marched down streets and uninhibited admirers shouted the virtues of their candidate. But in contrast to the apparently spontaneous uprising for Lincoln at Chicago in 1860, the enthusiasm for Davis seemed synthetic. On the first ballot the delegates gave a plurality of votes to Charles Francis Adams, and Davis never had a real chance to secure the nomination.

In popular opinion the coldness of the Adams's blood flowed through the veins of Charles Francis. He responded to overtures of friends with rigidly phrased letters. His record as minister to Great Britain during the war and his work to settle differences between England and the United

States needed no Madison Avenue advertising agent to pinpoint his qualifications. Despite the support of Schurz, his candidacy was opposed by Brown and Blair.

The followers of Senator Lyman Trumbull, perhaps the second best candidate of the Liberal Republicans aroused little enthusiasm for their candidate. The adroit work of Whitelaw Reid won the ultimate convention award for his newspaper boss: Horace Greeley was nominated on the fourth ballot. After emotionalism succumbed to reason, politically minded liberals urged Greeley to withdraw, but the irascible editor was transfixed by the nomination. B. Gratz Brown was selected as his running mate.

Writing a platform was more difficult for the delegates, united mainly by their opposition to Grant, than selecting candidates. The platform pledged support for the equality of all men before the law, "equal and exact justice to all, of whatever nativity, race, color, or persuasion, religious or political." It reaffirmed the results of the war and the advances made during reconstruction: the permanency of the Union, and the Thirteenth, Fourteenth, and Fifteenth amendments. But it also demanded "the immediate and absolute removal of all disabilities imposed on account of the Rebellion" and bowed to state rights by declaring that local self-government, with impartial suffrage, a better safeguard of individual rights than centralized power.

The platform's longest paragraph denounced the spoils system and called for reform. The civil service was described as a "mere instrument of partisan tyranny and personal ambition . . . an object of selfish greed . . . a scandal and reproach upon free institutions. . . ." The most pressing need of the hour was reform to make "honesty, capacity, and fidelity" the only claims to public office, free government workers from the taint of favoritism and patronage, and make their jobs posts of honor. To accomplish these purposes and to hit at Grant, the Liberal Republicans declared it imperative that no President be a candidate for re-election.

Honest but irreconcilable differences of opinion on protection and free trade forced the platform makers to leave the tariff to voters and congressmen. The Liberal Republicans reassured the bondholder by denouncing those who would repudiate any part of the public debt and by urging a speedy return to specie payment. On the other hand they objected to additional grants of land to railroads or other corporations. The one-sentence paragraph on foreign policy called for fair and equal treatment of all countries.

The platform was a short, uninspired document with several bristling sentences on civil service reform. The call for universal amnesty and the emphasis on state rights appealed to Democrats. Southern editors praised the statesmanship of the bolting Republicans, and Democratic leaders saw hope for national success in union with the Liberals. In a lackluster convention at Baltimore the Democratic party nominated Greeley from necessity. Foiled in his attempt to snare the Liberal Republican-Democratic nomination, David Davis demonstrated his lack of interest in labor by withdrawing as the Labor Reform candidate.

Regular Republicans breathed freely after their liberal brothers passed over Adams and Senator Trumbull to select Greeley. Journalist and unscrupulous politician, Thurlow Weed of New York thought no large body of men outside of a lunatic asylum would have nominated Greeley. Historian George Bancroft viewed the *Tribune* editor as the stalking horse of secessionists around whose banner would gather the rogues of New York and Brooklyn and all Catholic priests who meddled in politics. Secretary Fish believed it would be difficult to find any American of high intelligence and honesty with fewer qualifications for the presidency.

Delegates at the Republican Convention never questioned the obvious, nominating Grant without a dissenting vote. They passed over Colfax, already tainted with political corruption, to choose the "Natick Cobbler," Senator Henry Wilson, for the vice presidency. Born in New Hampshire, the one time farmer's apprentice Jeremiah Jones Colbath changed his name to Henry Wilson and apprenticed himself to a cobbler of Natick, Massachusetts. By industry and ability he prospered as a shoe manufacturer and achieved some distinction as a senator. In addition, his work on a projected three-volumed *Rise and Fall of the Slave Power* gave him status as a historian, albeit a prejudiced one, but his condemnation of Southerners endeared him to Radicals. The Republican platform praised Grant, recited the benefits enjoyed by loyal Americans under the party of the Union, and promised the continuation of everything good.

The ensuing campaign and election contributed a unique chapter to American politics. Although the national spotlight focused for a time on the Liberal Republican movement, Greeley's chance for victory depended on the votes of northern and southern Democrats. Necessity forced Democratic regulars to support a candidate identified with the Whig and Republican parties. An ardent advocate of a high protective tariff headed the tariff-for-revenue party, a weathered abolitionist appealed to former slaveholders for votes, and the country's most famous writer of anti-southern editorials led white Southerners. But Greeley was a fighter who drew crowds at hamlet and city in a vigorous campaign which left him mentally and physically exhausted.

In contrast to the disorganized Democrats, the Republicans of 1872 fused elements which would give their party strength for many decades. The capitalist-entrepreneur belatedly discovered his tremendous asset in the Republican party. Often credited with prescience, the politically un-

imaginative business leader at least realized that his countrymen were ready
to support the economic-political philosophy of laissez-faire—simultaneously ignoring high protective tariffs, other government grants to industry,
man-made monopolies, and all acts which ran counter to the classical economic principles. In the congressional elections of 1866 and the presidential contest of 1868 the business community of America was apprehensive
and searching. In 1872 the businessman took front and center on the political stage.

Immediately after the nomination of Greeley most eastern businessmen
rallied behind the Republican party. While some capitalists feared the
resurgence of southern agrarians, or a political reunion of western and
southern farmers, the entrepreneur saw greatest danger from reformers.
Manufacturer, banker, and merchant prince were not of one mind on
economic-political policy. Some demanded high protective tariffs, others
sought federal and state grants of natural resources; still others wanted
sound money, monopolies to lessen or eliminate competition, preferential
treatment in taxation, and no governmental regulation of "free enterprise."
To them the income tax on a business or citizen was indefensible (they were
satisfied with land and hidden taxes which hit the farmer and worker),
clauses protecting the public in franchise grants were unnecessary, and re-
strictions relating to the granting or using of natural resources were
detrimental to national economic progress.

Money alone did not make the Republicans dominant in 1872 or in subsequent years. Full campaign chests bolstered millions of citizens whose
organizations already leaned toward Republicanism. Liberated and enfranchised southern Negroes joined their northern brethren in voting for
the party of freedom. Veterans of the war organized into the Grand Army
of the Republic supported the party of Union, the party most likely to reward veterans with pensions. Northern and western farmers expressed their
gratitude in votes for the party that gave free soil to a free people. Skilled
labor followed the leadership of big business, and here and there some
farmers gained advantage from protective tariffs. The aura surrounding the
name of Lincoln and the successful restoration of the Union won many a
northern voter. Except for some northern cities controlled by Democratic
political machines, Republicans created a virtually rigid North for their
party in presidential election years.

The party mixed fact and fiction in its drive toward solidarity. In 1872
Republican leaders railed at the "Tammany thieves" of New York City
and Democrats in other northern cities who, according to Republicans,
were milking the taxpayer by fraud and graft. Copperheads were equated
with Democrats, Democrats with southern rebels, and all with the taint of
treason. Speakers recalled wartime atrocities, especially the mistreatment of

federal soldiers in Confederate military prisons, and emphasized the continuity of southern violence with accounts of outrages inflicted on Negroes
and loyal whites. The number of Southerners arrested on charges of Klan
activity increased as marshals and militiamen and army regulars aided the
Republican cause by frightening white conservatives.

In the North, cartoonists found Greeley an apt subject for their art. His
pumpkin-like head, his face outlined by the unkempt hair under his chin
and over his ears, his forehead enlarged by the almost bald dome of his
head, and the plain, small spectacles resting insecurely on his nose were
caricatured again and again. Thomas Nast's cartoons in *Harper's Weekly*
ridiculed Greeley. In a biting editorial William Cullen Bryant criticized
Greeley for his uncouth manners, and later chaired a meeting of Liberals
who repudiated the officeseeker.

The *Tribune* editor never wavered in his aggressiveness as he stumped
the country. He asked the people to rise above narrow party motives, to be
generous to a defeated and loyal South, and to throw corrupt politicians
out of office. While white Southerners objected to most of Greeley's past
actions, they lauded him for signing the bond to release Jefferson Davis
from prison and for the *Tribune's* spirited attacks on Congressional Reconstruction.

Southern support and the crowds drawn by Greeley frightened Republicans. Smarting from the criticism of his nepotism, his association with
connivers and acceptance of gifts from them, his liking for ease and fast
horses, and the absence of high purpose in his administration, Grant
longed to campaign. His friends and political advisers immobilized him
and prevented him from making blunders in speeches. Apprehensively they
waited for the results of the October state elections in Indiana, Ohio, and
Pennsylvania. Republicans carried Ohio and Pennsylvania impressively,
and the slim margin by which popular Democratic Thomas A. Hendricks
won the governorship of Indiana presaged a national Republican victory.

The election returns justified their confidence, for Grant carried every
northern state. His 300,000 majority of 1868 jumped to more than 750,000
with 3,596,745 men voting for him to 2,843,446 for Greeley, and the President won 286 electoral ballots to 62 for his opponent. Republican leaders
were embarrassed by the overwhelming victory. Three former Confederate
states, Georgia, Tennessee, and Texas, and the border states of Kentucky,
Maryland, and Missouri supported Greeley; all the others went for Grant.

Horace Greeley wandered back to the *Tribune* offices where understanding colleagues addressed him as "President." Filled with grief for the memory of his wife, who had died during the campaign, broken in body and
spirit, Greeley died on November 29. Despite the unpopularity of the
causes he championed—rights for women, organization by laborers, social

reform, vegetarianism, Fourierism—he was the most famous editor of his era. His timely editorials written in a clear, vigorous style gave America an anti-slavery conscience and his phrases captured the fancy of his contemporaries. Much of the credit for making freedom the second purpose of the Civil War belonged to Greeley. His conservatism encompassed little more than a protective tariff, his liberalism was virtually unbounded, and sincerity was ingrained in his character. Many who had called him a crank and ridiculed him during the election campaign shed tears. Most of his electors scattered their votes for other men when the Electoral College met in December. Three electors voted for the deceased man, but the Senate refused to count the ballots.

The Scandals

Stolid Grant accepted the impressive victory as a just political reward. To him the Liberal Republican movement had been an impertinence, not a rebuke; it had been a few voices multiplied a thousand times by reverberating echoes, possessing more sound than meaning. At the White House he accepted congratulations in an imperturbable manner. If he had nightmares, his dreams probably never involved him with graft or depression, the calamities of his second term in office.

The first notorious scandal involved Democrats instead of Republicans. New York City was controlled by Tammany Hall, a Democratic organization headed by William Marcy Tweed. This son of a chairmaker quickly demonstrated his flair for politics by acquiring influence in his ward. In 1851 he had become an alderman and the next year won a seat in the House of Representatives. "Boss" Tweed gained the headship of Tammany and control of party nominations and patronage in New York City. After the Civil War he extended his influence to the New York legislature, serving in the senate, but his power came from controlling the nation's largest city.

He and his major henchmen—the city's chamberlain, comptroller, and mayor—defrauded the taxpayers of millions of dollars. The excess of legitimate costs and profits of constructing public works were returned to Tweed; buildings were repaired, often at costs higher than the original contract, on condition that most of the take be returned; and specifications for tools and equipment were drawn to enable a co-operating firm to bid high and win the contract. Boss Tweed used much of his fraudulent gain to aid the poor, giving them coal and other supplies and brightening their drab existence with social outings. His controlled courts enabled him to dispense mercy to gain votes on election days and to guarantee decisions favorable to co-operative businessmen.

Tweed won the hearts and votes of the city's poor. His popularity defeated every attempt within Tammany to reduce his power or curb the Tweed Ring. But when the *New York Times* published evidence of wholesale graft and Thomas Nast aroused the public with his effective anti-Tweed cartoons, a citizens committee of 70 was mobilized to fight Tammany. In 1871 the committee broke the ring by electing most of its reform candidates. Although faithful followers returned Tweed to the New York Senate, most of his remaining years were spent in court, jail, and exile. Tried for felony, he first escaped punishment by a "hung" jury, was convicted in a second trial, sentenced to 12 years in prison, and won a reduction to one year by appeal to a higher court. After serving his term he was again convicted on another charge, fled the country, only to be extradited, and he finally died in prison in 1878.

Tweed symbolized the hundreds of grafting officials in local and state governments. These men who used their offices for personal gain were aided and abetted by profit-blinded businessmen. In cities controlled by Democratic and Republican organizations, a minority of businessmen cooperated with some corrupt officials. A few patrolmen and men of higher rank in police forces enabled vice-lords to operate their illegal enterprises, and "good" people supported corruption by remaining inactive. This lack of ethics existed in state and national governments, in business, and in personal conduct. The majority of Americans remained honest, but their indifference enabled the few to milk the public. Dishonesty was characteristic of the times; it was not limited to one race, one party, or one section.

The schemers and crooks of the Grant regime were not creatures of the President. Newspaper editors sent their best reporters to Washington. Weekly and monthly periodicals investigated and reported the happenings in the nation's capital. Clever artists caricatured prominent people and photographers used the medium made famous by Mathew Brady during the war to snap pictures of newsworthy politicians. Deviation from ethical conduct at local and state levels interested few citizens compared with the numbers who followed variation from idealistic norms at the national level.

During his first term Grant realized that the presidency belonged to the people. Although he received no profit from the gold manipulations of Gould and Fisk, he was severely criticized for his lack of awareness. He squirmed as congressional committees investigated the acts of his friends and political appointees. At the New York Customs House, Thomas Murphy gave George K. Leet, a minor member of Grant's wartime staff, a monopoly of the "general order" business. The general order business was the method of storing goods cleared through customs in privately owned warehouses until needed by importers. Using a letter of introduction from Grant, Leet gained part of the business. By organizing and controlling the draymen he eliminated competition and forced Murphy to grant him a monopoly. Leet then raised the storage rates to the point where his company made $260,000 a year in profits.

Among those appearing before the investigating committee were Horace Greeley and A. T. Stewart. The latter testified that he had twice protested to Grant about the monopolistic rates of Leet. In response the President urged Murphy to cancel the contract. Congressional investigators uncovered no evidence indicating participation by Grant or his close friends in Leet's enterprise or any infraction of law. Grant, however, ordered an end to the general order business. This action enabled his friends to praise him for correcting an abuse and his opponents to criticize him for tardiness in making a reform.

Irked by this congressional investigation of the executive branch, the President felt no sympathy for senators and representatives involved in the Crédit Mobilier scandal. The Crédit Mobilier was active the year before Grant took office and none of his intimate friends participated in the parasitic company. By the federal acts of 1862 and 1864, millions of dollars worth of bonds were given railroad entrepreneurs in return for their construction of rail lines and preferential rates to the government.

The larger stockholders of the Union Pacific organized a joint-stock company, the Crédit Mobilier, to build the road. These stockholders formed a dummy company which on the surface would construct the roadbed and tracks but in reality subcontract the actual work and be paid excessively in bonds and stock of the Union Pacific. In 1868 the Crédit Mobilier paid its stockholders five dividends with a total value of $341.85 on each $100 share of stock. To prevent investigation of this unjustified profit, Representative Oakes Ames suggested that he be given 160 shares of the stock for sale at $100 a share to influential members of Congress. The amount involved was not large, but ownership of a few shares of the profitable enterprise might insure the co-operation of the holder. Furthermore, congressmen without funds were allowed to pay for the $100 stock from the $341.85 dividends of 1868, thus gaining $241.85 per share without investing a cent.

During the campaign of 1872 Charles A. Dana's New York *Sun* printed a detailed but garbled account of the scheme. On December 2, 1872, Speaker James G. Blaine relinquished the chair and demanded an investigation. Luke Poland of Vermont headed a House committee which together with a similar committee of the Senate probed the affair. Vice President Colfax and Representative James A. Garfield denied owning the stock, but their lame explanations of income indicted them. Some other congressmen admitted taking advantage of the profitable offer. The House committee recommended that Ames and James Brooks, representative from New

York and a director of the Union Pacific, be expelled but the House only voted censure. Both men died within a few months; Colfax lived the last years of his life under the shadow of bribery, and Garfield was plagued by accusation for the rest of his days. Other congressmen were implicated (Bingham, Dawes, Kelley, Logan, Patterson, and Scolfield) as well as Vice President-elect Wilson. On January 30, 1873, *The Nation* declared the "total loss, one Senator; badly damaged and not serviceable to future political use, two Vice Presidents and eight Congressmen."

Congressmen and the President were subject to the public indignation aroused by the 'salary grab" act. During the last days of the Forty-Second Congress, the President's salary was raised from $25,000 to $50,000; the vice president, cabinet members, and Supreme Court justices were given $10,000 and congressmen were jumped from $5000 to $7500. A retroactive provision of the bill gave congressmen, many of whom were retiring or defeated, a gift of $5000 for their almost completed two years. Grant signed the bill, explaining to a congressman that the increase in the executive salary was necessary to prevent the need to use personal funds. Succumbing to public pressure, the Forty-Third Congress re-established the $5000 congressional salary despite the justification for higher pay for legislators.

The next scandal involved the collection of delinquent taxes. Prior to 1872 informers who reported income-tax evaders were rewarded with a portion of the taxes eventually collected. This provision was repealed by the Revenue Act of 1872, but scheming Ben Butler persuaded his colleagues to permit the Treasury Department to make as many as three contracts with private individuals by which the contractors would receive a percentage of delinquent taxes detected and collected. One of the contractors was John D. Sanborn, a Butler henchman in Massachusetts. By copying the list of delinquent taxpayers in the Boston regional office, and by sending demands to approximately 600 railroads (he secured the names of the companies from Appleton's Railway Guide), Sanborn pocketed $213,500. Early in 1874 the House Ways and Means Committee investigated the claims of Sanborn for 50 per cent of the $427,000 which he had collected. The investigation showed that Secretary of the Treasury William A. Richardson, who had replaced Boutwell in March of 1873, had made the contract with Sanborn at the suggestion of Butler. Sanborn claimed that he had spent $156,000 in looking up claims and for "expenses." Perhaps much of the money went to Butler, who used it to further his political ambition and to elect Boutwell to the Senate. Furthermore, many political observers were convinced that Richardson had aided Butler in repayment of the latter's work in obtaining the treasury post for Richardson. Despite the efforts of Butler to save him, Richardson was forced to resign and was replaced by Benjamin H. Bristow in June of 1874.

This and earlier evidences of political immorality scarcely touched the President. The next major scandals did involve him, not as a participant and beneficiary of graft, but as a defender of dishonest men. Rumors of a "Whiskey Ring" had been prevalent since the last years of Lincoln's administration. The Ring was actually formed in 1870 to raise funds for political purposes and was continued for private pelf. The organizer was John A. McDonald, a speculator, whom Grant had made supervisor of internal revenue collections for a large geographic area in the trans-Mississippi. His associates included Orville E. Babcock, the President's secretary; William Avery, the chief clerk in the Washington revenue office; John A. Joyce, a collector stationed at St. Louis; other treasury employees and collectors in regional offices; many state politicians; and William McKee, editor of the St. Louis *Democrat*. Some distillery officials were forced by threat of prosecution for technical violations of law to co-operate with the Ring while others eagerly joined in a scheme to benefit their companies through the evasion of taxes.

As long as Boutwell and the careless Richardson headed the Treasury Department, no action was taken, but Bristow was a dedicated reformer. During the late months of 1874 and the first ones of the following year, he collected evidence. George W. Fishback of the St. Louis *Democrat* helped Bristow to identify members of the Ring. (Fishback had bought the *Democrat* from McKee who continued his activities in support of the Ring with his newly acquired *Globe*.) Since Bristow knew the Treasury Department was rife with dishonest agents, he took elaborate precautions. On May 10, simultaneous raids on distillers and rectifiers in a number of cities resulted in the seizure of record books and business letters; arrests were made, grand juries returned indictments, and culprits fled the country.

The cost of operating the Ring was awesome despite the unestimated direct payoffs to petty grafters by the distillers. Perhaps two-thirds of the total take was pocketed by governmental officials; but to protect themselves and the Ring, they were forced to make large gifts to city and state Republican campaign committees. In addition there were expenses—a bill for President Grant and his entourage for a ten-day stay at the Lindell Hotel in 1874, an expensve diamond ring for Babcock, and other "worthwhile" expenditures. The distillers and rectifiers gained by giving less to the Ring than they would have paid in taxes.

According to Hamilton Fish, the President told Bristow that there was at least one honest and reliable man in St. Louis, namely McDonald, the "intimate acquaintance and confidential friend" of Babcock. "Mr. President," Bristow replied, "McDonald is the head and centre of all the frauds. He is at this very time in New York ready to take a steamer on the first indication of any effort to arrest him."

McDonald, Joyce, Avery, and others were brought to trial. Babcock's effort to save his friend and Grant's meeting with the accused and expression of sympathy for him were to no avail; McDonald was convicted, fined $5000, and sentenced to three and a half years in jail. Joyce received the same jail sentence and a fine of $2000. Grant's friends warned him that the Whiskey Ring trials were a plot against him, Babcock, and the Republican party. The President, however, forwarded one warning letter to Bristow with the notation: "*Let no guilty man escape if it can be avoided.* Be especially vigilant . . . against all who insinuate that they have high influence . . . to protect them. No personal consideration should stand in the way of performing a public duty." Newspapers picked out the "Let no guilty man escape," but Grant's actions soon contradicted his forceful words.

On December 3, 1875, Avery was convicted. In his closing argument during the trial, Prosecuting Attorney John B. Henderson made a veiled attack on the President. Grant dismissed him but appointed a distinguished Democratic attorney to represent the government in pending trials. Meanwhile Secretary of War William W. Belknap, Babcock, and other grafters worked on Grant. When William McKee was judged guilty and some of the evidence presented at the trial implicated Babcock, the President was displeased.

Nevertheless, Babcock's trial began on February 8, 1876, in St. Louis. More than a week before the opening of the trial, Attorney General Edwards Pierrepont wrote a circular letter at the request of Grant, which forbade federal attorneys from promising immunity to suspects who gave state's evidence. Babcock's attorney made profitable use of the order to cow many distillery officials who were ready to plead guilty, offer testimony, and receive suspended sentences. Thus Grant, at the instigation of Babcock, crippled the prosecution. As Allan Nevins has pointed out, "The President knew precisely what he was doing." Furthermore, in a cabinet meeting Grant declared his willingness to go to St. Louis to defend Babcock.

The cabinet members freed him from an indiscreet promise by agreeing that it would be "impossible and unseemly" for the President to testify for Babcock. The cabinet members, however, approved of Grant's giving a deposition, attested to by Chief Justice Morrison R. Waite, for the accused. This deposition was used effectually by Babcock's defense, and he was acquitted. Grant continued to befriend Babcock, but the prosecutors of the Whiskey Ring members fell on evil days. The President's coldness forced the resignation of Bristow as secretary of the treasury. Along with Bristow went Postmaster Marshall Jewell who had attempted to run the Post Office Department efficiently and had, thus, angered political henchmen.

Secretary Belknap, a supporter of Babcock, was accused of taking illegal payments in operating the War Department. Rumors of corruption in the war office were brought to a head by the New York *Herald*'s call for an investigation. A House committee found that the first Mrs. Belknap had received $6000 a year for delivering a lucrative Indian trading post to Cabel P. Marsh. After her death, Belknap married her sister, and the secretary of war received the $6000 payments from Marsh.

Forewarned of exposure, Belknap rushed to Grant early on the morning of March 2, 1876, with his resignation in hand. Surprised, confused, and thinking himself the protector of womanhood, the President accepted the resignation "with great regret." That afternoon the House impeached Belknap, but he was tried by the Senate and acquitted by a vote of 37 to 25. A number of other Indian post traders won appointment by agreeing to pay some administration official from $2000 to $10,000 a year. Orvil Grant, the President's brother, gained four posts in 1874 and gave them to men who paid him a large percentage of the profits. As much as $100,000 a year went to administration officials.

There were many other evidences of carelessness and corruption by members of Grant's administration. Secretary Robeson possessed scarcely $20,000 in assets on becoming Secretary of the Navy in 1869, but while in office deposited more than $300,000 in banks. In 1876 a House committee found him careless, extravagant, and lawless, but not corrupt in operating the naval department. Former Union general and congressman Robert C. Schenck, whom Grant sent as minister to England in 1870, taught the British how to play poker and rooked English speculators in the Emma Mine fraud. Diplomatic immunity prevented his being brought into court but he returned to Washington in disgrace. Investigation disclosed irregularities in the attorney general's office during the tenure of George H. Williams. Alexander R. ("Boss") Shepard pushed the District of Columbia into a $17 million debt for an improvement and beautification program. The President's brother-in-law allowed fictitious payrolls in operating the New Orleans Custom House.

Ulysses S. Grant was not a grafter—the total value of gifts the President accepted from admirers, or from those seeking his favor, was not large; nevertheless, he shared the blame for the corruption of his administration. His relatives possessed itchy palms and he scratched them. His negligence, impulsiveness, naïveté, and loyalty to scheming associates encouraged grafters. His "Let no guilty man escape" was changed in practice to "Let the prosecutors of the guilty beware." When conscientious public servants prosecuted members of the Whiskey Ring, the President turned on Secretary Bristow and dismissed able attorneys and revenue agents. When General George A. Custer testified to the waste and abuses in the war department's handling of Indian affairs, Grant removed the general from his command.

The Last Years of the Second Administration

Scandal made Americans realize that clay was intermixed with iron in the feet of "Galena's God." Although Grant was willing to accept the nomination for an unprecedented third term, politician and public distrusted him and his friends.

One pressing problem confronting the Forty-Third Congress was the currency. During the congressional session, inflation and deflation were debated in many legislative sessions. By the Coinage Act of February 12, 1873, later to be labeled "The Crime of 1873," Congress made the gold dollar of 25.8 grains the standard unit of monetary value, and omitted from the coinage the silver dollar of 412.5 grains. New England businessmen, academic economists, and some reformers opposed any inflation while the depression-hit western and southern farmers clamored for it. After some hesitation, eastern financial and mercantile interests advocated a sound currency; but railroad, iron, coal, and oil men demanded inflation. With the business community divided and the farmers pressing for relief, the Congress set greenback circulation at $400 million and increased national banknotes by $46 million. Grant, however, vetoed the bill, and later signed a bill which fixed the greenback circulation at $382 million.

The President's annual message of December 7, 1875, was a colorless document. He recommended a constitutional amendment which would require the states to maintain adequate elementary schools but prohibit the teaching of religion or use of public funds to aid any religious sect. After this veiled attack on Catholicism, the President urged the taxing of all church property except cemeteries and buildings used for religious services; stoppage of the importation of female Chinese laborers; and laws to wipe out polygamy. He also favored measures to give the nation a sound currency, declaring there could be no permanent prosperity without a return to specie payment. This idea was consistent with his first annual message in which he stated that one of the "evils growing out of the rebellion," and as yet unsettled, was an irredeemable currency.

Although the elections of 1874 brought victory to many inflationist-minded Democrats, the resumption of specie payments was accomplished in the Lame Duck session of the Forty-Third Congress. Senator John Sherman's bill, signed by Grant on January 14, 1875, required the secretary of the treasury to redeem in coin all legal tender notes presented, on and after

January 1, 1879, in sums not less than 50 dollars. The secretary interpreted "coin" as gold, and after 17 years of legal tender notes, the United States returned to a gold standard.

Scandal and depression were more influential in swaying voters in 1874 than deflation. In their sweep of 1872, the Republicans had won 192 House and 49 Senate seats to 92 and 19 for the Democrats; in 1874 the Republican party faced the possible loss of the House. With a majority of the former Confederate states controlled by white conservatives, crafty Republican leaders attempted to cover corruption and unemployment with a mantle of "patriotism." The glorious victory of the "Party of the Union" over the evil forces of slavocracy and copperheadism was reiterated by senators Roscoe Conkling and Oliver P. Morton. Speaker James G. Blaine detailed the suffering and dying of Union soldiers in Confederate prisons as he waved the "bloody shirt" in the hope of retaining his position in the House.

Republican strategy and tactics failed to win northern voters. Democrats gained 77 seats in the House while the Republicans lost 85. In the Forty-Fourth Congress of 1875, Michael C. Kerr of Indiana was elected speaker, the first Democrat to hold the position since James L. Orr of South Carolina in 1857–59. With only a third of the senators standing for election, the Democrats increased their number from 19 to 29. In any joint meeting of the legislature, Democrats would outnumber Republicans by 198 to 154, and some of the 16 independent members of the Senate and House leaned toward the Democratic party.

Control of the House by the Democrats stimulated an investigation of corruption by committees headed by individuals anxious to discredit the Republicans. The disclosures which followed convinced many Republicans that Grant should not be nominated in 1876.

The Republican-controlled Forty-Third Congress made a final gesture toward providing equality under the law for freedmen by the Civil Rights Act of 1875. Perhaps the motivation for the "act to protect all citizens in their civil and legal rights" was more to honor the memory of Senator Charles Sumner than to protect Negroes. As will be related, Senator Sumner suffered because of his opposition to Grant's scheme to annex Santo Domingo. Although the senator supported the Liberal Republican movement in 1872, he later returned to the party fold and was in good standing when he died in 1874.

The memorial to him provided: (1) "Full and equal enjoyment of the accommodations, advantages, facilities, and privileges of inns, public conveyances on land and water, theaters, and other places of public amusement . . . to citizens of every race and color, regardless of any previous condition of servitude"; (2) every person denying a citizen his rights, or aiding or inciting such a denial was liable for the payment of $500 to the aggrieved person and subject to a fine of from $500 to $1000 or imprisonment of 30 days to a year; (3) the United States district and circuit courts were given exclusive jurisdiction to try all individuals indicted for violation of the law. Furthermore, no qualified citizen was to be denied the right to serve on grand or petit juries because of race, color, or previous condition of servitude, and the penalty for any official denying this right to a citizen could be as much as $5000. No matter the sum involved, all cases arising under the act were reviewable by the Supreme Court. Considered, and almost included in the enactment, was the outlawing of segregated schools. Had it been enforced, the Civil Rights Act of 1875 would have prevented the establishment of a caste system in the United States.

REFERENCES

In addition to the biographies of Grant, Allan Nevins, *Hamilton Fish*, and other books already cited, Sylvanus Cadwallader, *Three Years With Grant* (New York, 1956), edited by Benjamin P. Thomas, gives a personal profile by a war correspondent friendly to Grant. James Grant Wilson, *The Life and Campaigns of Gen. U.S. Grant* (New York, 1868), was written for the 1868 campaign, and contains the Republican platform. Louis A. Coolidge, *Ulysses S. Grant* (Boston, 1917), emphasizes the positive aspects of Grant's administration, as does George S. Boutwell, *The Lawyer, The Statesman, and The Soldier* (New York, 1877). Eugene Roseboom, *A History of Presidential Elections* (New York, 1958), surveys the elections. Earle D. Ross, *The Liberal Republican Movement* (New York, 1919), and Patrick W. Riddleberger, "The Break in the Radical Ranks: Liberals vs. Stalwarts in the Election of 1872," *Journal of Negro History*, XLIV (1959), pp. 136–57, cover aspects of the 1872 election. Charles Sumner, *Republicanism vs. Grantism* (Washington, 1872), illustrates Sumner's ability to attack. W. H. Hale, *Horace Greeley* (New York, 1950), covers the Greeley campaign. David G. Loth, *Public Plunder: A History of Graft in America* (New York, 1938); Fletcher M. Green, "Origins of the Crédit Mobilier in America," *Mississippi Valley Historical Review*, XLVI (1959), pp. 238–51; Lucius E. Guese, "St. Louis and the Great Whiskey Ring," *Missouri Historical Review*, XXXVI (1942), pp. 160–83; and Clark C. Spense, "Robert C. Schenck and the Emma Mine Affair," *Ohio Historical Quarterly*, LXVIII (1959), pp. 141–60, provide interesting accounts of the scandals. Rendigs Fels, *American Business Cycles, 1865–1897* (Chapel Hill, 1959), surveys the national economy after the war. Two biographies of value are: Martin B. Duberman, *Charles Francis Adams, 1807–1886* (New York, 1960), and Norman L. Peterson, *Freedom and the Franchise: The Political Career of B. Gratz Brown* (New York, 1964).

☆ IX ☆

☆

Foreign Affairs

IN CONTRAST to its domestic failures the Johnson administration achieved notable successes in foreign affairs. The President and Secretary Seward did more to settle existing problems than to initiate policies. Major concerns near home were territorial expansion and French support of Maximilian's regime in Mexico. Demanding solution were disputes with Great Britain over the *Alabama* claims, Fenianism, fisheries, and the rights of British-born naturalized Americans. In Asia, policies with regard to Japan and China required attention.

The immediate problem was Mexico, where a British-French-Spanish venture had become the colonial enterprise of Napoleon III of France. After his troops partially conquered Mexico, a French-sponsored Mexican assembly offered the throne to Ferdinand Maximilian Joseph, brother of Emperor Franz Josef of Austria. Maximilian reached Mexico City on June 12, 1864, and succeeded in driving the forces of Benito Pablo Juarez across Mexico's northern border. But the United States refused to recognize Maximilian's government.

As Northerners tasted victory over the Confederacy, they demanded French expulsion from Mexico. Aggressive Americans denounced Seward's cautious policy. The secretary of state knew that the French public disapproved of Napoleon's Mexican adventure, but volatile Frenchmen might consider vigorous action by the United States a national affront and respond by supporting their emperor's machinations.

The press praised prominent Americans who demanded action. Among these were generals Grant, Schofield, and Sheridan; politicians Henry Winter Davis and Montgomery Blair; and cabinet members William Dennison and James Harlan. Even President Lincoln questioned the policy of his secretary of state. In the election of 1864 most congressmen who had denounced French activities in Mexico were elected senators and representatives. After the collapse of the Confederacy, General Grant gave Sheridan command of over 50,000 troops stationed near the Mexican border. Grant also secured a year's leave of absence for General John M.

Schofield. His task was to organize a volunteer army of "immigrants" from Sheridan's troops to join Mexican soldiers. Seward terminated this scheme by dangling the irresistible appointment as envoy to France before the eyes of General Schofield.

Time proved Seward's cautious policy an adroit one. Late in 1865 he expressed his concern over the continued presence of French soldiers in Mexico and told Napoleon that the United States would never recognize Maximilian's Mexican government. Reluctantly Napoleon ordered his troops to prepare for withdrawal. In response to another note from Seward, the French emperor promised in 1866 to remove his forces within 18 months. Before mid-March of the following year Maximilian ruled without the support of a French army. His decision to remain in Mexico resulted in his execution on June 19, 1867, despite the efforts of several governments to save the headstrong pawn of Napoleon.

Secretary Seward never mentioned the Monroe Doctrine in dealing with the French-Mexican situation. The doctrine, he knew, was neither needed to bolster his position nor approved by European powers. The aggressiveness of Prussia frightened Napoleon: both he and the emperor of Austria needed to protect their respective states from the Prussian powerhouse. European critics of Seward claimed that he intended to take over Mexico after removing the French, but after his victory he respected the boundaries and rights of Mexico.

Alaska and Other Territorial Expansion

The Civil War raids of the Confederate cruiser *Shenandoah* on whaling ships in the Bering and Okhotsk seas rekindled American interest in Alaska. Her experiences with British naval power during the Crimean War convinced Russia that England could take Alaska whenever she chose, but the Civil War interrupted Russian plans to sell the huge territory to the United States. After the war, Gideon Welles's desire for naval stations, Seward's expansionist tendencies, and the drain of Alaska on Russia's meager financial resources stimulated negotiation. Since the czar preferred American to European ownership of the territory, he sent Edward de Stoeckl to Washington in 1867 to sell the territory. Seward made an offer and after some bargaining, Russia and the United States agreed on $7,200,000.

Although the acquisition never really interested President Johnson, he urged Senate ratification of the treaty. The Radicals disliked Seward because of his support for the President. Their feelings and Senator Sumner's initial disapproval endangered ratification. Seward's claim that rejection of the treaty would humiliate the czar and antagonize the European country friendly to the United States during the Civil War swayed many senators. This argument influenced Sumner who was also sufficiently astute to recognize a bargain. His committee approved the treaty and the Senate ratified it on April 9, 1867.

The appropriation of funds gave the House opportunity to pass on the agreement. Both Radical hatred of Johnson and the pique of representatives because of Seward's failure to consult them resulted in debate and delay. Funds were eventually approved, but some congressmen were later accused of accepting Russian bribes in return for their votes. American forces took possession of Alaska in October 1867.

Satirical writers labeled Alaska as "Seward's Icebox" and "Seward's Folly." American officials, they claimed, knowingly bought worthless property to repay Russian friendship and to alleviate the czar's financial distress. In reality American leaders believed Alaska well worth the $7,200,000 price. Seward certainly gratified his expansionistic ambition and his twin desires to improve his country's strategic position in the Pacific and enhance the state department image. Both the American people and their congressmen sanctioned the purchase as a friendly gesture toward Russia, but the fundamental reason for their approval was the belief that Alaska was an outstanding bargain.

The twentieth-century interest of Americans in the Caribbean and the Panama Canal has recognized Seward's farsightedness in trying to acquire the Virgin Islands. A treaty with Denmark was carefully drawn: United States acquisition of St. Thomas and St. John islands would be effective only after residents approved of the transfer. The treaty was approved by the king and Rigsdag of Denmark but not by the United States Senate. Former American expansion involved contiguous (except Alaska), sparsely populated lands. Sufficient senators opposed the new type of expansion to delay American acquisition of the Virgin Islands until the twentieth century.

The secretary of state directed diplomacy successfully in the Far East, where trade instead of possession was involved. The appointment of Anson Burlingame, lawyer and former congressman, as minister to China in 1861 gave the United States "the most successful diplomat America has ever sent to Eastern lands." He prevented European countries from partitioning major segments of Asia and persuaded the Chinese to protect foreigners and their property in China. Appointed by the Chinese as their envoy to foreign countries, he negotiated the Burlingame Treaty of 1868 which established amity between China and the United States. In return for recognition of China's territorial integrity and a promise of no interference in Chinese domestic affairs, American citizens were given right of travel and residence in China, and guaranteed free exercise of religion.

China was allowed to send consuls to the United States but neither assurance of immigration nor naturalization was granted the Chinese. Burlingame died at St. Petersburg in 1870 while heading a Chinese mission seeking treaties with similar provisions from European countries.

In return for their partial acceptance of the "open door," a Far Eastern policy which antedated Seward's tenure, the secretary of state co-operated with European powers in forcing concessions from Oriental countries. The United States was party to the Convention of 1866 dictated to Japan from the deck of a British warship. When Americans on their disabled *General Sherman* mistook the friendly advance of Korean sailors and fired on them, the angry Koreans attacked the ship. Misinformed about the incident, Seward committed the United States to a joint punitive expedition against Korea. Fortunately, representatives of nations meeting at Paris abandoned plans to punish the country. In comparison with other Western nations the United States advocated liberal policies in the Far East, but even American diplomacy upheld a "Caucasian superiority" that wounded the feelings of sensitive Orientals.

The British-Irish Problem

The influx of Irish into the United States and the sympathy of these new Americans for their homeland's desire for independence from Great Britain created a number of international disputes. Organized in 1858 in the United States, the Fenian Brotherhood co-operated with the Phoenix Society of Ireland to foster independence for Ireland. Activities sponsored by these organizations amounted to little before and during the Civil War; but after the war, numbers of Irish-American veterans, some native-born and others naturalized Americans, returned to Ireland to fight the British. After many had been captured and imprisoned by the English, the United States demanded release of all political prisoners who were American citizens. Great Britain, however, relied on her doctrine of indefeasible allegiance—born a Briton, always a Briton. Yet the English released all naturalized Irish-Americans who agreed to board the first available ship bound for the United States. In 1870 Great Britain agreed that the American naturalization process conferred rights of citizenship on native-born Englishmen.

Concurrent with this dispute was another resulting from Fenian-planned invasions of Canada. Members of the organization never explained what they hoped to achieve by their aggressiveness. They played on the desire of some United States citizens who demanded the annexation of Canada and stimulated public approbation of politicians who "twisted the British lion's tail" at a safe distance. Rumors of an invasion in May 1865, interrupted

Canadian trade through the Welland Ship Canal between lakes Erie and Ontario. By the spring of 1866, Canadian officials planned to prevent a number of Fenian invasions from the United States. Johnson was denounced by American jingoists and politicians seeking votes from Irish-Americans, when on his orders General Meade prevented a Maine-based Fenian assault on Canada in April of 1866. Two raiding bands actually entered Canada: one from a site near Buffalo, New York, on June 1 and the other from St. Albans, Vermont, on June 4, 1866.

The President responded to protests from the British ambassador at Washington by issuing a proclamation on June 6, 1866. He warned all Americans of the penalties involved in aiding or participating in invasions of Canada. They were, he stated, punishable offenses for breaking American neutrality laws. Bolstered by the President, General Meade arrested Fenians and their sympathizers and deployed his troops to prevent additional raids. The Fenians, however, remained active and sent expeditions into Canada from Vermont in 1870 and Minnesota in 1871.

From a military point of view these invasions were inconsequential but their political implications impaired relations between Great Britain and the United States. Both Canadians and Englishmen were angered by the American government's slowness in halting the raids. Seward's toleration of the Fenians might be explained by his desire to add Canada to the American domain. If this were his purpose he miscalculated, for Fenian activities encouraged Canadians who sought some relationship with Great Britain that would give them autonomy while preventing annexation by the United States. At the height of the dispute, the House of Representatives approved a bill to allow warships similar to the Confederate *Alabama* to prey on commercial vessels belonging to friendly countries.

Alabama *Claims*

American reluctance to discipline the Fenian organization stemmed in part from resentment aroused by British support of the Confederacy. The Confederate cruiser *Alabama* had been owned by the South, manned by southern officers, sailors, and foreign volunteers, and directed by the Confederate naval department, but the *Alabama* and other vessels had been constructed in British shipyards. Immediately after the Civil War Seward claimed indemnity for British encouragement and aid given the Confederacy. He cited not only the loss of specific ships but also the indirect damages to the American merchant marine from the depredations of these English-built ships. The direct losses were substantial but the indirect losses could amount to so much that even the cession of Canada would not adequately compensate the injured nation for commercial losses.

Anxious to win laurels by arranging an advantageous settlement, Seward pushed American claims for indemnity. In turn prime ministers Henry John Temple, Lord Palmerston, and John Russell denied British responsibility for the depredations and rejected American requests for arbitration. In June 1866, changes in the British cabinet brought to power men who privately admitted their country's error and adopted a conciliatory attitude toward the United States.

Seward quickly sent Charles Francis Adams a list of American claims with instructions to present it to Prime Minister Edward Stanley. Although disposed to submit English-American claims and counter-claims to arbitration, Stanley delayed serious negotiation for more than a year. When Lord Stanley rejected Seward's demand that England justify her granting belligerent rights to the Confederacy back in 1861, the American secretary of state suspended negotiations. Thereafter, Adams resigned and Reverdy Johnson took his place at the Court of St. James. The new American minister concluded the Johnson-Clarendon Convention on January 14, 1869, with provisions for settling claims between Great Britain and the United States dating from 1853.

The agreement was the work of Seward. In negotiations Reverdy Johnson fumbled his assignment at times, but mostly he followed the instructions of his superior. Seward was disheartened when the Senate rejected the convention by a 54-to-1 vote. In essence the agreement provided settlement of British-American claims by arbitration. Many senators disliked giving credit to the Johnson administration for settling a major international dispute and Americans were enjoying a wave of anglophobia. In the debates on ratification of the convention, Chairman Sumner of the Senate Foreign Relations Committee demanded indemnity for the direct and indirect losses resulting from depredations of "hellhound" Confederate cruisers. In his opinion, the aid that Great Britain gave the South doubled the Civil War's duration and England was liable for half the war's costs. In lieu of paying $2,125 million, Sumner intimated that Great Britain could cede Canada to the United States.

Senate rejection of the Johnston-Clarendon Convention left the *Alabama* claims settlement to Grant and his secretary of state, Hamilton Fish. Egotistical Charles Sumner believed the inexperienced President and secretary needed his expert guidance. The appointment of John Lothrop Motley, the literary historian and friend of Sumner, as minister to Great Britain apparently enhanced Sumner's power.

Fish, however, was capable of directing foreign affairs. He thought the Johnson-Clarendon Convention allowed Great Britain to atone for her guilt without full payment for her breaches of neutrality. On the other hand he knew that insistence on a more than two-billion-dollar indemnity or the cession of Canada would either end discussion or result in war. Fish decided that successful negotiation depended on a cooling-off period with future talks in Washington instead of London. The wisdom of these decisions became apparent when under the influence of Sumner, Motley sent the secretary of state a memorandum, replete with historical errors and absurd assumptions, describing the new minister's views and giving his basis for dealing with Great Britain.

Chafing because of the slow pace of negotiation, Sumner repeatedly told the state department what should be done and derided every move of the Grant administration. On January 17, 1871, Sumner suggested that Great Britain should withdraw from the Western Hemisphere. This "hemispheric withdrawal" by Britain included relinquishing Canada and possessions in Central America, South America, and the Caribbean. In a letter of February 4, 1871, to Thurlow Weed, Fish described Sumner as "crazy, really a monomaniac; his vanity and conceit have overturned his judgment, which never was of the best." A few weeks later, he said Sumner was "vindictive and hostile . . . determined to oppose and defeat everything that the President proposes . . . crazy . . . irrational and illogical, and rants and raves. He exhibits . . . a very common incident to insanity . . . a constant apprehension of designs to inflict personal violence on him."

Fish exaggerated. Sumner was not insane, but he frequently suffered from delusions of grandeur. His decades of fighting the slavocracy and working for abolition convinced him that he was primarily responsible for preserving the Union and freeing the slaves. His territorial ambitions reflected the desire of many Northerners who longed to see Canada a part of the United States, but Sumner never made Canada or British hemispheric withdrawal absolute conditions for a settlement with Great Britain. He advanced these suggestions with the hope of obtaining desirable territory and preventing the growth of a powerful British-dominated country on the American border. If by a remote chance, England agreed to cede Canada, Sumner saw himself going into history as the statesman responsible for abolishing slavery, saving the Union, and adding immense territory to its domain. He demanded more than he expected, hoping to secure as much as possible.

However willing the "conscience of America" was to acquire Canada, that conscience prevented Sumner from supporting Grant's move to annex Santo Domingo. His spirited opposition to this presidential plan along with his other action brought the full power of the administration on Sumner's head. On March 10, 1871, the Republicans "relieved" him of his chairmanship by making Simon Cameron of Pennsylvania chairman of the Foreign Relations Committee. Motley's fall came before that of his friend as General Robert C. Schenck became minister to Great Britain.

Unshackled by these developments, Fish sped settlement of the British-American controversies. English leaders had tired of the delay; their nationals desired settlement of claims, boundary disputes, fishing rights, reciprocal trade, and the Fenian problem. Furthermore, the Franco-Prussian War and strained relations with Russia made the British ministry anxious to better relations with the United States. On January 9, 1871, Sir John Rose arrived in Washington with a proposal for a commission to discuss concerns of the two countries. The resulting Joint High Commission composed of five Americans and five Britons assembled at the conference table on February 27. Within six weeks they arrived at basic agreements and methods of settling the British-American controversies.

The commission received six topics as starting points for deliberation. The border dispute between Canada and the United States—San Juan Island boundary—was assigned the German emperor for settlement. Americans won extensive privileges to fish in Canadian waters and Canadian fishermen were allowed to sail as far south as the Delaware Bay. Equitable solutions were found for navigation of the St. Lawrence River and reciprocal trade between America and her northern neighbor was referred to a Tribunal of Arbitration. The members of this five-member tribunal were to be appointed by Great Britain's queen, the President of the United States, Italy's king, the president of the Swiss Confederation, and Brazil's emperor. The Treaty of Washington won Senate approval by a 50-to-12 vote and President Grant proclaimed it in force on July 4, 1871.

The Tribunal of Arbitration met at Geneva on December 15, 1871. Since in the treaty Great Britain had expressed a desire for an amicable settlement and regret for the escape of the *Alabama,* a considerable award to the United States seemed probable. England assumed that indirect claims—costs of pursuing Confederate cruisers, marine insurance, transfer of American ships to other countries, and prolongation of the war—were not to be considered by the arbitrators. When these claims were advanced in the poorly reasoned 480-page American Case presented to the tribunal, Prime Minister William E. Gladstone stated that the conduct of the American Government in this affair was the most disreputable he had ever known in his recollection of diplomacy. In his opinion as much as $8,000 million might be advanced for the "war prolongation claim." Members of Grant's cabinet unanimously opposed withdrawal of the indirect claims and British lawyers moved to terminate the arbitration tribunal. The attempted arbitration was on the verge of creating new animosities instead of settling old ones.

After weeks of praising the American case, editors in the United States became critical of Secretary Fish. *The Nation* placed major blame for the apparent failure on Fish, and *Harper's Weekly* joined other American periodicals in urging abandonment of the indirect claims. Fish, who had submitted the claims on principle without expecting a cent in indemnity, now worked to save the treaty. The American member of the tribunal, Charles Francis Adams, placated the British by indicating his opposition to any excessive demands of his country. On June 19, 1872, a compromise allowed the arbitrators to state "individually and collectively" that the indirect claims "do not constitute, upon the principles of international law applicable to such cases, good foundation for an award of compensation or computation of damages between nations." Secretary Fish ordered the American lawyers to accept this statement and the British counsel withdrew its motion to terminate the arbitration tribunal.

Shortly after Great Britain presented her counter-claims on June 27, the arbitrators began deliberating on awards. Their final report of September 14, 1872, gave the United States $15,500,000 in direct damages and interest for England's failure to exercise "due diligence" in preventing the escape of the *Alabama, Florida,* and *Shenandoah.* No penalties were assessed Great Britain for depredations of the *Georgia, Nashville, Sumter, Tallahassee,* and lesser known Confederate ships. England was awarded $1,929,-819 in counter-claims. Both awards were promptly paid in gold by the two countries.

Settlement of the "Alabama Claims" was the crowning achievement of Grant's administrations. Public interest centered on the claims arising from the depredations of Confederate cruisers, but other serious controversies were also resolved. The tribunal's success gave a boost to arbitration as a means of settling judicable international disputes. Also stemming from the Treaty of Washington was a British-American commission system which discussed and settled later controversies between the English-speaking countries.

Expansion and Santo Domingo

Like other peoples, Americans praise the successes of their leaders and criticize them for their failures. Historians describe the Treaty of Washington in glowing phrases: it prevented a possible British-American war; it gave arbitration international status; and it was a major step toward a world court, the League of Nations, and the United Nations. By further projection, this Anglo-American accord defeated the Kaiser in World War I and Hitler in World War II. On the other hand, Grant failed to annex Santo Domingo. Many explanations have been advanced to explain this failure. Annexation was a scheme of several corrupt Americans and a few dishonest Dominican politicians for personal profit. Grant and his cronies hoped that acquisition of the island republic would turn voter attention from domestic corruption to foreign affairs. Desire for Santo Domingo was no more than a continuation of Manifest Destiny.

Fair analysis of the annexation scheme demands enumeration of certain facts. Prior to the Civil War, many Americans longed for lands in Mexico and the Caribbean islands. Not all of these imperialists were southern slaveholders, for expansionists saw advantage to American manufacturers and traders in developing spheres of interest in Mexico, Central America, and the Caribbean. Patriotic nationals believed that control of the Gulf of Mexico and Central America was essential to their country's safety. Post-Civil War expansion was in part the lengthened shadow of ante-bellum Manifest Destiny. President Lincoln toyed with acquiring territory in Mexico and Colombia. In addition to his desire for the Virgin Islands, Secretary Seward wanted the Dominican Republic or her lands bordering on Samana Bay. Influenced by Secretary of War John A. Rawlins, President Grant hoped to add a part of Mexico and the Cuban island to the American domain.

Personal gain and national interest motivated the officials who worked to annex Santo Domingo. Grant sought no profit for himself, but his support of scheming friends demonstrated a lack of good judgment. In his study of Grant, William B. Hesseltine emphasized the profit motives of Grant's friends and explained the President's desire for Santo Domingo as a cover for domestic corruption. But Grant advocated annexation long before any breath of scandal touched his administration. In fact, throughout his first administration the President was praised for bringing honest government to Washington. There was no need to cover corruption with imperialism, as Republicans appealed to voters in 1870. Studies by other historians condemn profiteers and label the Santo Domingo fiasco the "first decisive defeat of Grant."

The Santo Domingo incident became an interesting footnote to American foreign policy. The Spanish colonial island evolved into Haiti and the Dominican Republic with the latter holding about two-thirds of the island. In 1861 the Spanish crown added the Dominican Republic to her slave-holding possessions of Cuba and Puerto Rico, but withdrew from the island during the summer of 1865. This Spanish withdrawal encouraged American expansionists who desired Cuba and Puerto Rico.

In the first month of Grant's tenure, Major General Daniel E. Sickles was offered the ministership to Mexico, but the administration turned from acquiring territory in Mexico to adding Cuba to the American domain. Sickles was sent to Spain to negotiate with Juan Prim y Prats. The Spanish prime minister seemed anxious to rid his country of Cuba, but the assassination of Prim and the death of Rawlins terminated American designs on Cuba and Puerto Rico. The Grant administration concentrated on annexing the Dominican Republic.

Attempts to obtain the republic extended over a period of more than two and one-half years. The initial effort was made during the final months of Johnson's administration. On January 12, 1869, former General Nathaniel P. Banks of Massachusetts introduced a resolution authorizing the President to extend American protection over Haiti and Santo Domingo. The House of Representatives rejected the proposal by an overwhelming majority and tabled another resolution calling for the annexation of Santo Domingo. On February 8, Senator Doolittle claimed that Cuba, Haiti, and Santo Domingo would provide homes where freedmen could achieve social equality while retaining their English language and customs. In his opinion the islands were destined to be possessions of the United States.

The second move to acquire Santo Domingo came during the first years of Grant's tenure. Buenaventura Baez, the Dominican ruler, saw profit for himself and his strife-torn land in selling the Samana Bay region to the United States as the first step in American annexation of the entire country. When Benjamin S. Hunt declined the appointment to Santo Domingo in mid-July of 1869 because of illness, Grant sent his confidential secretary, Orville E. Babcock. On the island, Babcock worked with two Massachusetts real-estate promoters, William L. Cazneau and Joseph Warren Fabens. Agents of Spofford, Tileston, and Company, then the outstanding investment firm of Wall Street, secured a monopoly for a steamship line from New York to the island along with title to land at Santa Barbara, the best port on Samana Bay. This company, the real-estate promoters, and other speculators won potential control of banking in the republic. With American ownership of Santo Domingo, these speculating businessmen would take millions of dollars from their lands and concessions.

Babcock returned to Washington on September 14 with what he and Grant referred to as a treaty. Although authorized to make a general investigation, the secretary presented an agreement whereby the United States could either buy Samana Bay for $2 million or acquire Santo Domingo in return for assuming the country's $1,500,000 debt. To seal the bargain $100,000 in cash and $50,000 worth of munitions were to be given Baez at once. Despite cabinet opposition, Grant's determination resulted in Secretary Fish's drafting a regular treaty. Babcock returned to Santo Domingo with instructions to offer the treaty of annexation to Baez along with an alternate plan for the lease of the Samana Bay region. Babcock raised the American flag over the bay and the treaty was signed by Baez and an agent of the United States.

Grant submitted it to the Senate on January 10, 1870. Eight days before he had called on Charles Sumner to discuss the annexation, and departed believing that the chairman of the Foreign Relations Committee had promised to support the treaty. Sumner, however, considered that he had agreed to do no more than consider it with care. Later a plebiscite in Santo Domingo, conducted by Baez, returned a vote of 15,169 Dominicans for and 11 against American acquisition of their country. On March 15, the senate committee presented an unfavorable report on the treaty and, in defense of his committee's stand, Sumner delivered his "Naboth's Vineyard" speech. Despite administrative pressure, including the President's corraling senators in the Capitol, the treaty was apparently doomed.

But Grant refused to admit defeat. On May 31, 1870, he sent a message to the Senate along with an addition to the treaty. The President enumerated the many advantages to be secured from acquiring Santo Domingo. It was populated by less than 120,000 people (an underestimate), its fertile land could support "10,000,000 people in luxury," European countries were anxious to control the country but the United States needed it to protect her Caribbean commerce. Santo Dominicans would produce the raw materials needed by American industrialists and buy their manufactured products. In war the United States would find the republic essential to protect national interest. The President also appealed to abolitionists: free labor in Santo Domingo would force immediate freeing of slaves in Cuba and Puerto Rico and eventually end slavery in Brazil.

Neither this message nor talks with senators won Senate approval of the treaty. On June 30, 1870, the senators divided 28 to 28 with 19 of them paired or absent. Nineteen Republicans and nine Democrats voted against the administration. Because of his opposition to annexation, Attorney General Hoar was forced to resign. The day following the Senate's adverse vote, Sumner's friend Motley was recalled as minister to Great Britain and later Sumner lost his chairmanship of the Senate Foreign Relations Committee. Had Grant accepted an amendment to eliminate eventual statehood for Santo Domingo, he would have won more Democratic support from senators representing border and southern states, but even their votes would not have been sufficient to secure ratification.

The defeat convinced neither Grant nor his friends that their cause was hopeless. In his message of December 1870, the President again stressed the ten-million-population potential of Santo Domingo. He asked congressional authorization for a commission empowered to negotiate a treaty of annexation. This request met strong opposition in both houses, but Congress did approve sending a commission to investigate the situation. This commission was specifically denied power to make any commitment for annexation.

The three-member commission appointed by Grant sailed for Santo Domingo on January 17, 1871. On it were Ben Wade of Ohio, the advocate of Negro causes who had lost his senatorship in 1868; Samuel G. Howe, an advocate of liberal principles and lifelong friend of Senator Sumner; and Andrew D. White, president of Cornell University. Frederick Douglass, who served as the commission's secretary, and saw Santo Domingo as a refuge for his race, was an admirer of Sumner. In addition, a military adviser, geologists, minerologists, and ten reporters boarded ship with the commissioners. The investigators spent five weeks in and near the island and returned to the United States 70 days after their departure.

Grant sent their report to Congress on April 5, 1871. The committee found Baez an able, intelligent, and patriotic man; Santo Domingo's fertile land possessed a tremendous agricultural potential; and Dominicans were anxious to be annexed. The commission cleared Grant of Sumner's irresponsible charge of personal gain as the President's motive for acquiring the republic. By this time, Grant realized that annexation of Santo Domingo would never receive congressional approval. He transmitted the report to justify his past advocacy of annexation and promised no further "personal solicitude upon the subject."

Smarting because of loss of his chairmanship, Senator Sumner anticipated the commission report by making a vicious attack on Grant. The senator compared the President with Pierce, Buchanan, and Johnson; he accused Grant of violating international law and castigated him for using military power to bully Haitians and interfering with the domestic concerns of Dominicans. If, according to Sumner, Grant had spent one-quarter of the "time, money, zeal, will, personal effort, and personal intercession which he has bestowed on his attempt to obtain half an island in the Caribbean [in protecting southern white and Negro Unionists] our Southern Ku Klux would have existed in name only." Instead of protecting patriotic Southerners, Sumner indicted Grant for heading a powerful and costly Ku Klux Klan in Santo Domingo. His former political magic had lost its spell, for even his Massachusetts constituents paid little attention to his animadversions.

Grant, and those who would have profited by United States possession of Santo Domingo, met defeat. Americans were not yet interested in overseas expansion. Filling the sparsely settled areas of their continental lands was a sufficient challenge for the postwar generation. With all the racial strife in the South, the Klan, and military intervention, most Americans saw no reason to saddle their nation with a country peopled mainly by Negroes. If Grant had made annexation a test of party loyalty, he might have won; but he considered and rejected this tactic. Yet from hindsight the acquisition of Santo Domingo, and eventually Haiti, could have benefitted both the islanders and Americans.

The motives for Grant's persistence have not been fully explained. Certainly he never expected any personal gain, but his gullibility and loyalty to greedy associates may explain his actions. Perhaps he was doing no more than supporting the traditional expansionism of his countrymen. The racial situation may have troubled the President so deeply that he wanted Santo Domingo as a home for some freedmen and as a lever to elevate the majority of them who would remain in the United States.

Colonization of free Negroes in Liberia or Latin America antedated the Reconstruction period. General Sickles claimed that the assassination of Lincoln prevented him from completing a presidential mission of 1864–65 to secure land in Colombia for Negro colonization. In his memoirs, Benjamin F. Butler reported conversations with Lincoln on using freedmen to dig a Panamanian canal and making estimates of the number of Negroes who could settle in Santo Domingo. Secretary Seward's interest in Caribbean land could have stemmed from a hope to give freedmen opportunity there as well as protection for his country. Frederick Douglass split with Senator Sumner on the Dominican issue because the Negro leader thought the island republic a potential home for mistreated members of his race. Douglass interviewed more than 500 Negroes from the American colony of 1824 on Samana Peninsula and found these English-speaking Methodists in favor of annexation. Commissioner Howe, also a friend of Sumner, moved to Santo Domingo and concluded that his friend had erred in opposing annexation. President Grant's scheme was supported by Hiram Revels of Mississippi and other Negro legislators.

Historian Charles C. Tansill explained Johnson's, Seward's, and Grant's desire for Santo Domingo as a continuation of Manifest Destiny. Another historian, Selden Henry, has found that Negro resettlement cannot be ignored in relation to the island republic any more than the slavery issue can be divorced from the Ostend Manifesto.

In his last message, President Grant re-examined the Santo Domingo fiasco and added a new reason for annexation. The freedmen of the South, he stated, would have found congenial homes on the island where their civil rights would have been respected and their labor desired. By migrating there, they could escape the oppression and cruelty inflicted upon them by southern whites. The President never supposed that all Negroes would leave the United States, and their migration in mass would not have been desirable, but Santo Domingo would have given them a possible escape from white domination. Since southern agriculture needed laborers, the freedmen could have secured more equitable treatment by threatening to leave for a land where they could enjoy their rights under their country's flag. A decade later, the former President, writing his memoirs and facing death, reiterated these reasons for annexing Santo Domingo.

In 1909 Andrew D. White recalled his conversations with Grant in 1871.

According to White, the President feared racial animosity in the South would reduce the Negro to peonage, and possession of Santo Domingo would give freedmen a place of refuge. Although Benjamin Butler hoped to profit from American acquisition of Santo Domingo, in his memoirs he also emphasized the President's desire to provide opportunity for freedmen in the island republic.

These statements by Grant and others may be no more than a cover for failure. If the President had been sincerely interested in aiding Negroes, he never urged Santo Domingo as a refuge for them at the time he advocated annexation. On the other hand, domestic considerations could account for his reticence. The Republican party was the emancipator of slaves and the protector of freedmen and Congressional Reconstruction was the party's method of giving Negroes civil and political rights. Armed with these rights, freedmen were called on to attain economic status from their industry and thrift.

By offering Santo Domingo as a haven to Negroes, Grant would have supplied Democrats with political ammunition. Their speakers and editors would have used the annexation scheme as an admission of Republican failure. Furthermore, the President would have divided the North and his party. Many northern humanitarians demanded first-class citizenship for Negroes, but few northern congressmen possessed the courage to guarantee it with laws enforced by police power. Along with a majority of their constituents, Republican politicians sought to prevent northward migration of Negroes by making their southern residences attractive to them. National advocacy of a haven for freedmen would have indicted northern politicians and laymen for hypocrisy.

Other Latin American problems interested Grant and his cabinet. Most prominent among them was the Cuban rebellion against Spain. In the 1860's and 1870's Cuban patriots suffered and died in attempts to attain independence. Spanish Prime Minister Prim's willingness to sell the island to its people or transfer it to the United States excited American expansionists. Because of a Peruvian protest (Peru was technically at war with Spain), fifteen gunboats built in the United States for the Spanish navy were temporarily prevented from sailing. With difficulty, Secretary Fish persuaded Grant to give neither belligerent rights nor recognition to the insurgent Cuban government. The loss of life in Cuba—perhaps as many as 150,000 patriots and Spaniards—stirred humanitarian impulses in the United States.

Early in November of 1874, Americans were shocked by the harsh treatment meted out to the crew and passengers of the USS *Virginius*. This well-known supplier of munitions to Cuban rebels was captured by the Spanish gunboat *Tornado*, and eventually Captain Joseph Fry and 52 of his crew and passengers were shot for piracy. Grant's administration prepared for war to avenge this insult to the American flag while Secretary Fish negotiated with Spanish officials for a settlement. Fish knew that the *Virginius* had been engaged in illegal acts and Spain's minister realized that the punishment had been too severe. Spain returned the *Virginius* to the United States and released her remaining crew and passengers. After impartial investigation found the ship fraudulently registered as an American vessel and Spain paid an $80,000 indemnity, the controversy was settled without recourse to war.

Grant's administration also dealt with other major disputes relating to Brazil and Venezuela. United States policies foreshadowed twentieth-century demand for headship in the Caribbean and economic penetration of other Latin-American areas, but post-Civil War Americans were not ready to support a new type of imperialism.

REFERENCES

Nevins, *Fish*, already cited, is essential to an understanding of the Grant administration's most notable achievement. Frederic Bancroft, *The Life of William H. Seward*, 2 vols. (New York, 1900), paints Seward as an outstanding statesman, and Samuel Flagg Bemis, *The American Secretaries of State and their Diplomacy* (New York, 1928), VII, 3–214, treats both Seward and Fish favorably. Dexter Perkins, A *History of the Monroe Doctrine* (Boston, 1955), pp. 107–91, and *The Monroe Doctrine, 1826–1867* (Baltimore, 1933), pp. 253–548, explains French withdrawal from Mexico. Goldwin Smith, *The Treaty of Washington, 1871* (Ithaca, 1941), covers the *Alabama* claims settlement and other agreements between Great Britain and the United States. Valuable articles are: Thomas A. Bailey, "Why the United States Purchased Alaska," *Pacific Historical Review*, III (1934), pp. 39–49; Baron Stoeckl, "Letter to Prince Gorchakov," translated and edited by Hallie M. McPherson, *ibid.*, (1934), pp. 84–87; and Donald M. Dozer, "Anti-Expansionism during the Johnson Administration," *ibid.*, XII (1943), pp. 253–75. *Old South Leaflets* (Boston, 1898), VII, pp. 137–84, has Seward's account of Alaska. Charles C. Tansill, *America and the Fight for Irish Freedom, 1866–1922* (New York, 1957), has sympathy for the Fenians. Unfortunately, Grant, *Personal Memoirs of Ulysses S. Grant*, 2 vols. (New York, 1885), mainly recalls his war experiences but defends his Santo Domingo policy in volume II, pp. 542–54. Charles C. Tansill, *The United States and Santo Domingo, 1798–1873* (Baltimore, 1938), treats Sumner more kindly than do other authors. Joseph W. Hellinger, "Charles Sumner and Santo Domingo" (typewritten thesis, University of Florida, 1960), strongly defends Sumner. Selden Henry, *Radical Republican Policy toward the Negro during Reconstruction 1862–1872* (unpublished dissertation, Yale University, 1963), emphasizes the objective of bettering the conditions of Afro-Americans by providing a haven for some of them in Santo Domingo.

☆　X　☆

☆

The People

THE South provides an almost irresistible central theme for the Reconstruction era. By ignoring many significant country-wide developments, the historian can describe and interpret the period without having his neat account disturbed. Of course he feels compelled to present presidential and congressional plans for reconstructing the former Confederate states; the conflict between the federal executive and legislative branches of government; most items relating to freedmen, the Grant regime, and foreign affairs; and the complexity of the 1876 national election. To do more would break the continuity of his story. Yet, even at the cost of unity, the economic and social changes deserve summation, for they played a signal part in America's rebirth.

Four years of war etched themselves deeply into American society. The empty chairs by family firesides, the crutches of wounded soldiers, the vacant stares of mentally disturbed veterans were constant reminders of the tragic war. With no changes other than those caused by the human ravages, life in the United States would have been profoundly altered.

But there were added ferments in society. Some of these forces were by-products of the internecine war; others stemmed from man's response to vast semi-inhabited lands; and still others from industrialization and urbanization. Sectional antagonisms, rooted in ante-bellum controversy, were sharpened by war. Neither northern nor southern whites found satisfactory methods of integrating 4 million former slaves into a free society. Millions of immigrants sought opportunity in rural and urban areas while American citizens moved from country to city or from farm to frontier. The complexity of civilization forced governments to provide new services. Philanthropists joined with states and religious societies to improve educational facilities. Evangelical ministers promised the faithful eternal salvation, and humanitarians worked to alleviate the hardships of life. These and other developments that altered the course of the nation are all a part of the Reconstruction era.

When General Beauregard fired on Fort Sumter, 34 states were in the

Union. The admission of Kansas on January 29, 1861, had extended the north-south line from Canada to the Gulf along the western boundaries of Minnesota, Iowa, Missouri, and Kansas almost 400 miles westward, but the most westerly part of Texas lay 100 miles beyond the western limit of Kansas. Between the trans-Mississippi and the states of California and Oregon were sparsely settled plains, semi-arid lands, mountains, and valleys. During the war only West Virginia and Nevada became states, but Colorado, Arizona, Dakota, Idaho, and Montana won territorial status. With the creation of the Wyoming territory in 1868, all present-day states existed or were organized as territories except Oklahoma, Alaska, and Hawaii. Nebraska and Colorado achieved statehood in 1867 and 1876 respectively. The area of these new states and territories dwarfed that of eastern commonwealths.

Not only the new "empire of the West" but also large sections of existing states, notably California and Texas, were populated during reconstruction. The course of settlement was set and the most desirable lands of the frontier were taken by miner, cattleman, farmer, and monopolist. Governmental grants to transportation companies, liberal land policies, and the subjugation of hostile Indians enabled promoter and settler to conquer the last vast frontier.

Population and Representation

From 1860 to 1880 the population increased by almost 60 per cent, rising in round numbers from 31,513,000 to 50,262,000. Most Americans lived in rural areas, 25,227,000 in 1860 and 36,026,000 in 1880; but within the two decades the urban population more than doubled (6,217,000 to 14,130,000) while the rural increased by less than 43 per cent. Although country districts added more than 10 million inhabitants to less than 8 million for the cities, the percentage of urbanites in the nation jumped from less than 20 to more than 28 per cent.

Immigration accounted for more than five million new residents. The number of immigrants rose from 91,918 in 1861 to 459,803 in 1873, declined during the depression, and again passed the 450,000 mark in 1880. In addition to the lures of freedom and opportunity, the Irish economic and political problems, the British panic of 1866, and the Prussian wars stimulated migration. Furthermore, American business and state governments sent agents to Europe to encourage migration.

Established Americans classified most of the new arrivals as desirable immigrants. In 15 of the 20 years, Germans led the migration with more than 100,000 entering in each of six years and 149,671 arriving in 1873. Only in 1870 did British arrivals surpass the 100,000 mark, but they headed the list in three of the years. The Irish led one year, reaching their maximum of 77,344 in 1873, and the Canadians in 1880 when almost 100,000 of them entered the United States. In fifth place behind Germans, English, Irish, and Canadians were Scandinavians. The number of Norwegian, Swedish, Danish, and Icelandic immigrants rose almost steadily from less than 1000 in 1861 to almost 44,000 eight years later. Although their movement continued large after 1869, it gradually declined and then jumped to more than 65,000 in 1880. In 1866 Hans Mattson began publishing *Svenska Amerikanaren* in Minnesota, and he induced thousands of Scandinavians to leave their native lands. Four years later almost 45,000 of them resided in Illinois and additional thousands made their homes in other areas of the upper Mississippi Valley. The number of immigrants from the Netherlands, Belgium, Luxembourg, Switzerland, and France surpassed 20,000 only in 1873 and averaged about 7300 yearly. Within 20 years approximately 1,500,000 Germans, 1,000,000 English, 750,000 Irish 500,000 Canadians, and 390,000 Scandinavians entered the United States.

By experience American citizens knew that these people, even the city-dwelling Irish against whom considerable prejudice remained, were acceptable, but Americans questioned the entry of other Catholics who spoke foreign languages. On Boston Common and other eastern city parks American traditions appeared in jeopardy as aliens conversed in peculiar tongues and acted in odd ways. Especially disturbing were the unskilled Italians, mostly from Naples and Sicily. Only 65,000 of them came during the war and reconstruction decades, but their appearance along with smaller numbers of other southern Europeans lifted the eyebrows of American Protestants.

Other regions of the United States received "undesirable" immigrants. Extension of the American domain to the Pacific attracted Orientals. More than 7500 Chinese arrived in 1861. The opportunities for wages, unusually high by their native standards, attracted them to mines and railroad construction companies. To the disgust of American laborers, the Chinese lived on meager rations, many of them saving money to return home to live in relative affluence. Some 175,000 of them arrived within two decades and their descendants built one of the nation's cleanest and most beautiful "towns" in the heart of San Francisco. More than 99 per cent of the Orientals entering the United States were Chinese. Less than 7500 Mexicans, an average of fewer than 370 a year, settled in the American Southwest.

Regional prejudice against these so-called undesirable immigrants supported the southern white in his discrimination against the Negro. To many Americans the Chinese were obviously inferior and the southern

European failed to measure up to the standards of the English, Scots, and northern Europeans. The Italian and Mexican were stereotyped as intellectually and physically inferior: dirty, immoral, shiftless, irresponsible, and criminally inclined; the supporters of alien economic, governmental, religious, and social ideologies. In time, fair Americans would recognize the contributions of these minorities to United States culture. The reconstruction generation, however, resented them and bequeathed their prejudice to sons and daughters.

Domestic movement as well as international migration altered the American population complex. Between 1860 and 1880 every region and state gained residents. Vermont with an addition of about 17,000 and Maine and New Hampshire each with approximately 20,000 more emphasized the slow growth of New England. The west central states of Minnesota, Iowa, Missouri, Nebraska, and Kansas and the Dakota territory almost tripled their population. The number of Nebraskans jumped fifteenfold from approximately 28,000 to 452,000 and Kansas increased from over 100,000 to almost a million. On the Pacific, California's population more than doubled. Oregon's more than tripled, and Washington territory's less than 12,-000 people increased to more than 75,000. In the South, Texas attracted almost a million new residents as the country's largest state in area more than doubled its population. Sparsely settled Florida virtually doubled by gaining 129,069 people. Settlement in the mountain region from Arizona and New Mexico to Montana and Wyoming increased the population from 174,923 to 653,119.

Internal movement and full representation of Negroes altered sectional power in the House of Representatives. Reapportionment increased the number of representatives from 241 in the 1860's to 325 in the 1880's. Mainly by the elimination of the three-fifths ratio in counting Negroes, the 11 former Confederate states jumped their representation from 61 to 85. On a percentage basis their power rose four-fifths of a point, 25.3 to 26.1 per cent of the House of Representatives. Only Virginia lost in the two decades, but her reduction from 11 to 10 representatives came from the creation of West Virginia with 4 seats in the lower house. If the West Virginia representatives were added to those of the ex-Confederate states, the total would have been 89 compared to the ante-bellum 61, and their national percentage 27.4 to 25.3.

Before the Civil War the New England and Middle Atlantic states held 87 seats in the House of Representatives, or 36.1% of the total number of seats. The Middle West and the South had 150, or 62.3% of the total. The growth of the Middle West and abolition of the Three-Fifths Compromise increased the actual and relative power of the Middle West and

REPRESENTATION *
HOUSE OF REPRESENTATIVES

	1860	% of total	1880	% of total	Change	
6 New England states	27	11.2	26	8.0	−1	−3.2
3 Middle Atlantic states	60	24.9	69	21.2	+9	−3.7
8 Middle Western states (Neb. added to 1880)	65	27.0	100	30.8	+35	+3.8
15 Former slave states (W. Va. added to 1880)	85	35.3	121	37.2	+36	+0.9
2 Pacific Coast states	4	1.6	7	2.2	+3	+0.6
Other states	0	0.0	2	.6	+2	+0.6
	241	100	325	100		
11 Former Confederate states	61	25.3	85	26.2	+24	+0.9

* This and all the following tables in this chapter are taken from U.S. Census Bureau, *Historical Statistics of the United States, Colonial Times to 1957* (Washington: Government Printing Office, 1960). Nevada (1) and Nebraska (1) added after 1860 apportionment, Idaho (1), Montana (1), North Dakota (1), South Dakota (2), Washington (1), and Wyoming (1) added after 1880 apportionment.

South, to give them 221 representatives (an increase of 71), or 68% of the total. In contrast, the New England and Middle Atlantic states gained only 8 seats and had only 29.2% of the total number of representatives.

These numerical and percentage increases have significance in contrast to the figures for the northern states. New England lost one representative (27 to 26) and her percentage declined from 11.2 to 8. The Middle Atlantic states gained nine seats in the House while their percentage was reduced from 24.9 to 21.2. The East North Central number of representatives went from 56 to 74, but on a percentage basis fell one-half of a point. Foreign and domestic migration accounted for Minnesota, Iowa, Kansas, and Nebraska going from 9 to 26 seats, a gain in representation from the 4 states which equaled two-thirds the increase of the 11 former Confederate states and surpassed them in percentage by more than 3 points with a jump from 3.7 to 8 per cent. The former slave states of Delaware, Maryland, Kentucky, and Missouri increased their representatives from 24 to 32. These relative gains by Southerners disturbed Republican politicians from the New England, Middle Atlantic, and Old Northwest regions.

Immigration and natural increase made no significant change in most vital statistics. Within 20 years the non-white population's increment was two and one-third million, but its total lagged far behind the numerical gain and slightly below the percentage of the white people. Despite the high birth rate of Negroes, the heavy infant death rate and the arrival of

REPRESENTATIVES IN HOUSE, 1860 AND 1880

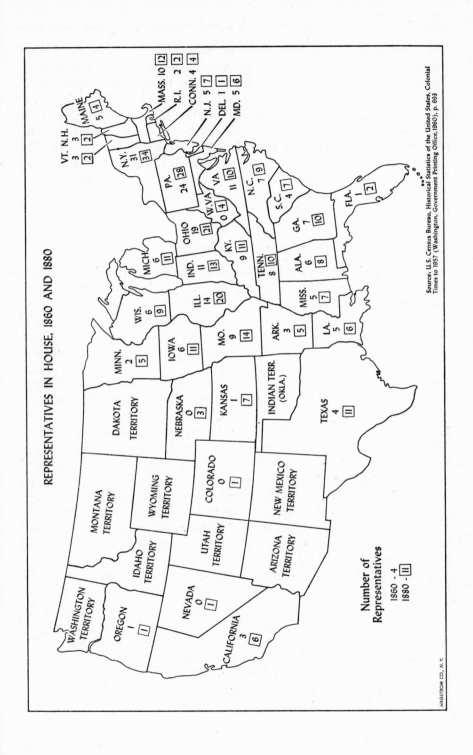

Source: U.S. Census Bureau, Historical Statistics of the United States, Colonial Times to 1957 (Washington, Government Printing Office, 1960), p. 693

Number of
Representatives

1860 - 4
1880 - [11]

HAGSTROM CO., N. Y.

Europeans reduced the percentage of non-whites living in the United States. In 1860 almost 730,000 more males than females resided in America. Although the male majority increased by more than 150,000 within two decades, the females netted a percentage advance. By 1880 almost 6,600,000 foreign-born people resided in the United States. The most notable shift was in educational achievement—compared to most other nationalities, native Americans could boast of a high literacy rate. In 1880 only 17 per cent of Americans ten years or older could not read or write. This percentage would have been lower except for the 70 per cent illiteracy of the non-whites compared to the 8.7 and 12 per cent, respectively, among native and foreign-born whites.

Western Influence

Approximately 35 per cent of America's growth in population (1860–80) was in the trans-Mississippi region. Individuals and families moved from communities lying east and west of the Mississippi River to western farms and towns. From California and Oregon people rushed to mine gold and silver in nearby mountains. The prewar patterns of migration continued, but some war and reconstruction policies affected internal movement.

Mining produced the first significant settlements in mountainous areas from California to Dakota. Gold deposits were discovered in 12 states or territories from Dakota's Black Hills to the Pacific coast. Silver mining, centered in Nevada and Colorado, was also important in Idaho, Montana, Utah, New Mexico, Arizona, California, and Washington. As many as 5000 men would respond to rumors of a strike at some distant place. Prospectors needed few tools; ore-bearing earth could be dug with a shovel and washed in pans where the heavier nuggets and particles of gold and silver sank to the bottom. These and other placer methods were supplanted by machines that crushed rock to free precious metals. As placers were worked out, vein mines went deep into the earth and the fabled prospector gave way to miners employed by corporations. Copper and lead mines were also developed.

Placer mining, however, was the prime mover in the settlement of mining towns. At first miners in the mushroom cities lived in wagons, lean-tos, tents, and caves. Restaurateurs opened cafes in wagons, cooking over open fires and using boards for dining tables; saloon keepers and gamblers enticed customers to street-side stands. Gradually wooden and masonry buildings replaced temporary housing as the town developed into a maze of short, irregular streets. With exhaustion of the ore and rumor of a strike elsewhere, the inhabitants quickly disappeared. A town might be left with one family whose head served as mayor, police chief, postmaster, and

Wells Fargo express agent. Some towns were abandoned entirely. Because of the lumber scarcity, buildings were dismantled and hauled by wagon train to the new strike, where saloons with gambling tables and floor shows were quickly established. From mining origins, some communities grew into cities—among the most important were Denver, Butte, and Boise. Every mining community had its gunmen. Tombstone, Arizona, and Deadwood, South Dakota, have the distinction of being the nation's last wild mining towns.

In western folklore, cowboys of the plains and cattle drivers share the spotlight with the gunmen of Deadwood and Tombstone. The meat industry sprang from the thousands of cattle of Spanish origin running free on the sparsely covered grasslands of the Southwest. Lean, hungry cattle produced a tasty but leathery beef that was relished by the pioneers accustomed to fat pork and greasy beans. And these roaming animals became the property of the men who hog-tied and branded them. Property lines were non-existent, fences unknown; the main concerns were grass, water, and getting the animals to a market.

Shortly after the Civil War cattle drives from Texas dwarfed all prewar treks. Abilene, Kansas, was the first "cow town." Its merchants and saloon keepers welcomed the thirsty, dust-covered cowboys with money to spend. At Abilene corrals and loading chutes lined the railroad tracks; hotels, saloons, and gambling halls bordered the unpaved street; and here and there stood general stores, houses, and the jail. Beginning with the arrival of the first cattle in the spring, the town bustled with activity. During the day buyers and sellers agreed on price, animals were prodded into cattle cars, cowboys received their pay, and drovers bought supplies for return trips. At night lamps in hotels and saloons spread patches of light on otherwise dark streets. Drinking and gambling were the principal activities, with floor shows and girls to stimulate the consumption of liquor and play at the tables. "Liquored-up" men frequently resorted to fist fights, and occasionally gunfights, western-style duels, resulted in injury or death. After several days of revelry, the cowhands headed homeward, some penniless; others, ambitious to have their own ranches, returned with wages intact.

During its lush years, 1868–71, Abilene was host to thousands of cowboys and almost 1,500,000 cattle. Then drovers herded their animals to Ellsworth, 50 miles to the west, for loading on Sante Fe railroad cars. Within a few years the terminus of the cattle drives was more than 100 miles southwest of Ellsworth at Dodge City, Kansas. By 1880 nearly 4,250,000 head of cattle had been driven to the various cow towns. Most of these animals were destined for eastern abattoirs, but many went to stock ranches to the north and northwest.

The life span of the cattle kingdom and famous trails was short. The drives, though later romanticized, were filled with hardships, but every new railroad lessened the distance between ranch and market. Grazing near railroad lines extended the cattle kingdom from the Rio Grande to the Canadian border, from the farmer's acres of the western Mississippi Valley to the foothills of the Rockies. The tremendous increase in the number and size of herds reduced the price of cattle and also caused overgrazing of the grasslands. Monopolistic practices of meat packers held down prices paid to ranchers. The arrival of sheepherders with flocks that cropped grass to its roots and left the former cattle country bare triggered fights between sheepmen and cattlemen. Small ranches became unprofitable; large capital investment was required to accumulate thousands of acres, improve the quality of the herd, and construct miles of fences.

Fencing became necessary as farmers moved into the plains. Plowmen followed the ever-lengthening railroad lines into the West. Prairie farmers had to make adjustments to a natural environment entirely different from the well-watered and forest-covered lands settled by earlier frontiersmen. In contrast the Great Plains were almost treeless. For fuel the farmer gathered buffalo dung or scooped up the droppings of cattle. In Kansas he cut and seasoned sunflower stalks for firewood. One salesman peddled the seed, claiming that an acre planted in sunflowers would produce the equivalent of 12 cords of wood, fuel supply for a year. Compressed hay and grain stalks, corn cobs, and packed grass fired specially designed stoves. The cost of bringing in lumber forced pioneers to build sod houses which withstood the elements in a dry area and furnished living quarters until the farmer could afford a lumber or masonry dwelling.

On the semi-arid plains, water was always a problem. Farmhouses were located near streams, or cisterns were used to store rainwater. Deep drilling and windmills to bring up water were not extensively used until near the end of the nineteenth century. When rains came, frequently the dry land was flooded, washing away plantings and leaving no reserve of moisture. In winter blizzards made life hazardous for man and beast; in summer dust storms choked them. Cyclones tore through croplands and carried away buildings; winters were frigid and summers unbearably hot. In *The Farmer's Last Frontier: Agriculture, 1860–1897*, Fred A. Shannon reported: "It is a common saying in Kansas that when a particularly wicked native dies he is buried in an overcoat so that he can endure the changed temperature in the afterworld. It is in the same area that the mule is alleged to have stood in a field of popcorn until the corn all popped; then looking around, he thought he was being buried in snow, and froze to death."

At times man and nature seemed to conspire against the farmer. After a dry winter, spring winds created dust storms that reduced visibility to ten feet. Following a hot, rainless summer, the smallest spark would ignite the prairie; the only recourse lay in setting backfires around the homestead, and enduring the smoke, ashes, and heat. Herds of buffalo, and later cattle, might trample the crops. Periodically locust swarmed over the fields and after stripping the wheat and corn bare, sated their prodigious appetites on household linens. Children were endangered by rattlesnakes and babies by ants. Loaded guns stood in racks, ready to ward off marauding Indians. Claim-jumpers threatened the homesteader and cattlemen denied his right to protect his crops from foraging steers. There were many lean years; yet, there were fat ones that paid for a better house, a larger barn, new furniture, and some luxuries.

The federal government stimulated western settlement by aiding railroads, offering homesteads, and confining the Indians. Congressional acts of 1862 and 1864 chartered the Union Pacific and Central Pacific companies with federal grants of rights-of-way, 20 square miles of land for each mile of track laid in territories and 10 in states, and loans in government bonds of $16,000 to $48,000 per mile according to terrain. Eventually the two companies received approximately 21 million acres of land, and in return gave the government preferential rates for hauling freight and passengers. The Union Pacific was to build westward from Omaha, the

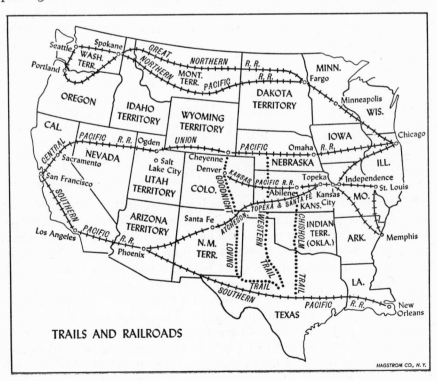

TRAILS AND RAILROADS

HAGSTROM CO., N. Y.

Central Pacific eastward from the vicinity of San Francisco with the lines meeting at a point to be determined by speed of construction.

Some work was done on both roads during the Civil War, but in 1868 the companies raced toward each other. In that year the Union Pacific laid 425 miles to the 360 of the Central Pacific. In their rivalry for grants of land and loans, the roadbed was laid with a minimum number of crossties and the lightest of rails. An interested public followed the construction, avidly reading of difficulties brought on by Indians, nature, and fights between railroad hands and stagecoach employees. On May 10, 1869, the roads met at Promontory Point (near Ogden, Utah). Gold and silver spikes were "driven" in by Leland Stanford, president of the Central Pacific, and Thomas Clark Durant, vice president and the man most responsible for the success of the Union Pacific. As locomotive engineers shook hands, corks popped from champagne bottles and the crowd toasted the joining of the Atlantic and Pacific oceans. All over the nation people, from the President to the street urchin, celebrated the momentous event.

Completion of the first transcontinental line spurred other railroad construction. Pacific coast promoters—Stanford, Collis Potter Huntington, Mark Hopkins, and Charles Crocker—bought short lines in California along with strategic ocean-front terminals. And soon the Southern Pacific, the Northern Pacific, and the Great Northern were pushing through in all sections of the West.

RAILROAD MILEAGE IN OPERATION

1860	30,626
1865	35,085
1870	52,922
1875	74,096
1880	93,262

Except for the Great Northern, railroad companies won a significant part of public lands of the West. Including about 22 million acres patented before the administration of Lincoln, the main and secondary lines gathered in more than 183 million acres from the federal government, by the intermediary action of states, and by direct grants from Texas. In addition, almost 850,000 acres came from gifts by local governments and individuals to gain stations along the routes for their towns. Failure of companies to meet contractual agreements reduced the net from land grants, but estimates of the total value of all grants range from a conservative half billion dollars to a liberal two and a half billion. Some railroads won double the amount granted the Union Pacific, or 40 square miles of land for each mile of track constructed through territories and 20 through states. Furthermore, these grants alternated from one side of the tracks to the other and promoters selected the most fertile regions for their lines. Congress also aided companies by restricting sales of public lands to allow railroads to dispose of their holdings to settlers. The average price received by railroads in 1880 was $4.76 an acre, or $2.76 more than the cost of constructing track as estimated by Northern Pacific management.

The contributions of the railroads to the development of the West outweighed the grants. Their lines opened the plains and mountains to ranchers, farmers, and miners, and tied East and West together. Without railroads, settlers could not have built homes on the plains or peopled mining towns. Thousands of construction workers brought in by the companies remained to become productive citizens. Even larger numbers of immigrants responded to railroad advertisements and agents to populate the lands of America and speed the economic growth of their adopted country. Despite high freight rates and monopolistic practices, the tonnage carried at a relatively fast rate enabled the railroads to provide less costly and more efficient service than wagons and stagecoaches. The grants from the federal government were tremendous, but the companies probably more than repaid them over the decades by carrying governmental freight and personnel at reduced rates. The first essential in developing America's great frontier was transportation, and in spite of all their malpractices the railroads supplied this need.

A second but overrated federal aid to settlement was the Homestead Act of 1862. This wartime enactment offered every adult American citizen, not engaged in rebellion, every alien who had filed citizenship papers, and every soldier with 14 or more days of duty, opportunity to claim 160 acres of unappropriated or unrestricted public land in return for a ten-dollar fee and five years of occupancy and improvements. Amendments to the act and new legislation eventually made federal land policies a mosaic difficult to delineate. The ban against Confederates was removed in 1866 but additional fees were added from time to time ranging from 8 to 24 dollars for specified lands. Except for Union veterans, applicants could homestead

FARMS, LANDS, AND VALUE

	No. of Farms	Land in Farms	Value *	Average Value per acre
1860	2,044,000	407,179,000	$7,980,000,000	$16.32
1870	2,660,000	407,723,000	9,412,000,000	18.26
1880	4,009,000	536,064,000	12,404,000,000	19.02

* Value of farmlands, buildings, equipment, and livestock

only 80 acres in areas within railroad grant regions, and husband and wife could stake out separate homesteads. In operation the Homestead and subsequent acts permitted promoters to gather in many acres but helped comparatively few settlers.

There were many reasons for this failure. Except for Michigan, Wisconsin, and four Gulf states, the public domain lay west of the Mississippi, far from the mass of industrial workers. A laborer earning $250 or less annually could not save money for land fees, transportation for his family, farm animals, basic implements, and supplies for the two or three years necessary to bring his farm into profitable production. Even the man who somehow acquired financial aid but knew nothing of farming would fail from inexperience. Without means to pay for transportation, credit to buy equipment and supplies, and agricultural skill, the city laborer could not take advantage of the Homestead Act. From 1860 to 1900 as many as 400,000 families (2 million people) may have secured and retained free land. During the same period, two and a half times that number bought farms or became agricultural tenants or workers.

After six months of residence, disillusioned homesteaders could buy their land at $1.25 an acre (twice this amount on railroad grants) and sell it. Millions of acres thus passed from homesteader to speculator. Thousands of applicants for free acres never intended to become farmers; they acquired land to turn it over to others. Sincere, hardworking homesteaders gave up after finding it impossible to earn a living on 80 to 160 acres in dry farming areas, and ranchers discovered that from 10,000 to 25,000 acres were needed for economical cattle production. Again and again the small farmer mortgaged and lost his land or sold it, and the big operator acquired an estate piecemeal. The auctioning of public lands, gifts to states and subsequent sales, Indian lands reverting to the federal government, and other practices left millions of acres which land companies and large holders could acquire. Special and general congressional acts helped promoters to acquire tremendous holdings in grazing, timber, and mining lands.

The third federal aid to Westerners was pacification of the Indians. After the War of 1812, Indian removal from east to west cleared all but a few eastern sections of the "Red Menace." In time, however, the advancing line of settlement by miner, rancher, and farmer brought the white man and Indian to armed conflict. Except for the five civilized tribes in Oklahoma, the trans-Mississippi Indians wandered over a vast region, getting their food and tepees from the buffalo or living on smaller, edible animals. The American dedicated to private ownership and fixed settlement never understood the Indian's affinity for communal lands and a nomadic way of life. Indian desire to hold extensive lands and white desire to own it brought on intermittent warfare which lasted from the first year of the Civil War until 1890. The major battles, however, were fought before 1879. After 1878 most Indian tribes had been decimated by federal forces and their remnants settled on reservations.

But the Indian tried the fire power of his adversary's guns before resigning himself to his fate. At daybreak on November 29, 1864, approximately 1000 militia under Colonel J. M. Chivington surrounded a village of 500 Cheyenne and Arapaho Indians, mostly women and children. According to one white participant, his protest against attacking peaceful Indians brought two rejoinders from Colonel Chivington: "Damn any man who sympathizes with Indians," and he "had come to kill Indians, and believed it honorable to kill Indians under any and all circumstances." Unarmed warriors, approaching with hands uplifted, were shot down; women and children, huddled together pleading for their lives, were slaughtered; and cadavers were mutilated by sexually sadistic militiamen. The Chivington Massacre cowed many Indians and rankled in the hearts of others.

The next outbreak came from the Sioux who resented federal road-building on their lands east of the Big Horn Mountains of Wyoming. Indian attacks in 1865 stopped construction of the Powder River roadway to connect the Montana mining region with the Platte River trails. The following year the Sioux wiped out an army detachment and endangered military posts. The slaughter of Indian and white aroused the ire of humanitarians. In response Congress sent a peace and study committee west in 1867 to investigate the nation's Indian policy. The commissioners reported that contact between white and Indian would inevitably result in warfare. They decided the only road to peace lay in settling the Indians on reservations. By a number of treaties, the commissioners convinced tribes to accept lands in the Indian territory (Oklahoma), and New Mexico, or the Black Hills of South Dakota and Wyoming, and northern sections of the Rocky Mountains. All Indians who remained on their former hunting grounds were declared hostile by the commissioners and subject to killing.

Treaty-making was easy compared to moving 100,000 people from their tribal homes. On the plains they roamed in search of buffalo and pitched their tepee villages near the herds. On the semiarid reservations they existed as wards of a government represented by avaricious agents. Many Indians did not understand the terms of treaties; others broke their promises by wandering back to the old hunting grounds, and still others reacted violently to the cruelty of the white man. Reports of gold in the Black Hills were confirmed by a reconnaissance expedition of General George Custer in 1874. Disregarding the rights of Indians and eluding federal forces, prospectors flowed into the Sioux lands. These acts of white aggression occurred again and again whenever Indians were discovered possessing valuable property.

In 1868 the Cheyenne, Comanche, Apache, and other Indian tribes of the southern regions took to the warpath. In November of that year General Custer, acting under orders of General Philip H. Sheridan, surrounded the Arapahoes and Cheyennes in their village of Wichita. Falling on the sleeping Indians, Custer's troops wiped out men, women, and children in a massacre accompanied by atrocities similar to those of the Chivington raid. Other tribes in the southern region were harassed or killed by General Sheridan until the survivors retreated to their reservations. Six years later the Indians rebelled once more and the Red River war did not end until 1875 after 14 bloody engagements. The southern tribes, except for a band of Apache warriors led by Geronimo, were no longer a danger.

Meanwhile to the north Sioux and Cheyenne rebelled against the restricted life on their Black Hills reservations, and wandered back to their old hunting grounds where, in the calm of morning and evening, they looked on the familiar Big Horn Mountains. Their waywardness brought federal troops in the spring of 1876, when General Alfred Howe Terry was instructed to pacify and force the Indians back to their reservations. By June his force was moving from the northeast toward the principal Sioux camp near Little Big Horn River in northern Wyoming. To scout the Indians, Terry sent a detachment under General Custer to approach the encampment from the south while the main force moved in from the north.

Custer reached position first and decided to attack on June 25. Looking "like a circus rider gone mad," the general led his men into an ambush prepared by Sitting Bull and Crazy Horse, and "Custer's Last Stand" brought death and renown to him and his 264 men. The victory won little for the Indians: General Terry drove most of them back to their reservation and chased Sitting Bull's band into Canada. In 1877 Chief Joseph led the Nez Percé in raids on Oregon settlers, and in 1890 the Sioux broke out again in the Ghost Dance wars, but massive resistance was no longer possible. By 1876 Sheridan in the south and Terry in the north had broken the Indians.

Although federal policies encouraged western settlement, individuals who believed the basic strength of the United States rested on the independent farm family were troubled by the economic trend of the Reconstruction era. While the number of farm households multiplied, city families increased at a far greater rate. Despite advertising and the lure of free homesteads, fewer American citizens settled on the land than in the cities.

Nevertheless, the West contributed much to the nation in its transition from an agrarian to an industrial economy. From mining, cattle, and farm origins, towns grew into cities. Railroads strengthened urban settlements, and the processing and shipment of ores, cattle, and crops gave employment to hundreds of city laborers. Conquest of mountain and plain was the final act of three centuries of American agrarian pioneering.

Living in semi-isolation or in small towns, the Westerner found simple community associations better than the complex governmental organizations of the populated East. Other than minimal economic and personal protection, the rugged individualist wanted no interference from government. Economically he was self-reliant and cared for young and old, the healthy and afflicted of his family. Reluctantly he accepted more social controls: regulatory laws; strong county and city governments; legislative, executive, and judicial bodies. Long after his society had grown to bewildering complexity, he denied the need for a welfare state. Yet the Westerner was an ardent nationalist. He looked to Washington for internal improvements, protection against Indian forays, and help in securing and irrigating land. He brushed aside constitutional argument whenever the exercise of federal power benefited him and relied on state rights with the hope of raiding some national resource or altering laws restricting its use.

He was resourceful and versatile, practical and wasteful, materialistic and optimistic. Worshipping the democratic ideal, he was an isolationist imbued with international arrogance. If foreigners were too backward to recognize and imitate the governmental and economic systems of the United States, the Westerner rejected them as unworthy of American concern. The last pioneers moved with ease from place to place, their eyes on the future, and their minds convinced of the inevitability of progress.

A Changing Economy

Developing the West, obtaining raw materials, and selling manufactured products kept postwar Americans busy. The vastness of continental America and a tremendous marketing area gave domestic trade priority over foreign commerce. Increasing the pace of ante-bellum development, not innovation, characterized the Reconstruction era. Despite significant ante-bellum industrial growth, the United States was agrarian in 1860. Twenty years later it still was, but the transformation of America from a country of agrarians to a nation of urbanites was well on the way.

Prior to the Civil War, the businessman was challenging the power of farmers who dominated federal, state, and local governments. During the Reconstruction era, manufacturer, merchant, and banker overwhelmed farmer, laborer, and consumer. Business-oriented judges winked at monopolistic practices that negated the natural laws of supply and demand, marginal utility, and free markets, theories so dear to classical economists. By controlling supply, limiting quantity, and eliminating competition, captains of industry multiplied their power and profit. They proclaimed their dedication to laissez-faire economic principles, but defined lassez-faire to their advantage.

The majority of Americans had little conception of the economic changes taking place. The farmer sold his crops at depressed prices without realizing that low-priced corn, cotton, tobacco, and wheat were being exported to buy capital for industrializing the United States. Accustomed to negotiating directly with the boss, the laborer was confused when owners of large companies were no longer available to him and the stockholders of corporations were unknown to him. He discovered his bargaining power gone, for wage-bargaining rested on talks between coequals.

Individualism supported the idea that a farm or store, a mine or factory, belonged exclusively to its owner and was his to operate without regulation or restraint. The average American believed himself the champion of free, private enterprise without realizing that his individualism and vote were helping a small group of men with talent and capital to win control of the major portion of the country's natural resources and productive capacity. When, in time, Americans saw that corporations and trusts had attained greater power than governments, many despaired; but a larger number battled to destroy big business, and the more intelligent recognized both the contributions of large-scale industry and the need to regulate it.

During the Reconstruction era, however, the notable achievement of American business leaders was their managerial ability. They organized enterprises to net maximum profits and set their factory production, not to the needs of society, but to their desire for the highest possible yield on investments. Yet, unwittingly, these profit-mad, power-seeking captains of industry transformed the country into a land of relative plenty. More profit was derived from mass production with a small net on each item than from a large gain on few units. Production schedules, therefore, were fixed neither at maximums nor at minimums but at the rate for which demand for a particular commodity returned the highest profit on production. This rate was high. These industrialists were ruthless: they shed no tears for competitors ruined by unfair or illegal methods, for exploited laborers, for debt-ridden farmers, or for gullible consumers. With no interest in conservation, they used the best of the nation's natural resources and littered their plant sites with the waste. Yet with all their faults, these postwar businessmen increased the productivity of America, making more and more goods for consumers, thus raising the standard of living for their countrymen.

The primary source of American industrialism stemmed from the "warehouses" stocked by the pure research of European scientists. From the sixteenth century on, the pure scientists had probed the nature of the universe and made discoveries in chemistry and physics that opened up opportunities for the applied scientists. From laboratories came essentials: the power created by water expanding into steam, the reaction of metallic ore to the application of oxygen and heat, the potential in electricity, and the pull of gravity. Americans added practicality and technology to the basic discoveries of Old World scientists.

American entrepreneurs produced the materials requisite to an industrial order. They improved European processes of manufacturing steel, used the strong, malleable metal to construct a network of railroads, developed some of petroleum's potential, preserved meat by refrigerating it, and produced consumers' goods from hundreds of practical inventions. Capitalists built factories designed for mass production which drew laborers to urban communities. Shrewd entrepreneurs discovered the "narrows" of every large industrial operation. Millions of farmers produced grain and livestock, thousands of operators pumped oil from the ground, hundreds of mine owners unearthed ores. Every raw material went through a central process to be transformed into consumers' goods: the slaughterhouse, milling plant, and refinery were the industrial narrows into which flowed raw materials and from which emerged either consumers' goods or materials that additional fabrication converted into products desired by the public. By acquiring control of these essential narrows of production, the capitalist won an entire industry. Then he set prices paid to producers of raw materials and fixed the charge for consumers' goods. By eliminating competition, he mastered the so-called natural economic laws and made a farce of laissez-faire while proclaiming adherence to its principles. He criticized government controls but demanded tariffs, grants of natural resources, and protection for his property.

Attracted by the wages paid by postwar industry, families left their acres to populate town and city. In most regions of the United States farmers hitched up their horses or mules and moved their meager possessions and many children to the urban world. Similar to piedmont Southerners other Americans found new homes on dusty or muddy streets overlooking mills whose whistles blew before dawn, calling adult and child to a ten- or twelve-hour shift. It was a hard life for people accustomed to the outdoors, but Saturday was payday—every Saturday.

Thriving industry provided many jobs at apparently fabulous wages. In reality, however, the laborers' real income in 1880 was less than that of 1860. More than offsetting the 60 per cent increase in wages was a 90 per cent jump in the cost of living. The best northern workman commanded $2.50 a day for a ten-hour stint and some 15,000 New York City women toiled for $3.50 to $4.00 per week. Eastern salesgirls stood at counters from 7:30 a.m. until 9:00 or 10:00 p.m. for six days to earn $5.00. Before the

1873 depression had run its course, wages dropped by more than 15 per cent. The average income of clerical and wage workers of 36 Massachusetts towns and cities in 1874–75 was $763, with some families receiving no more than $300 a year. The return to southern laborers varied from 30 to 40 per cent less than that of northern workmen.

Wage earners strove to counterbalance big business with big labor. Almost every employer fought these organizations which, in his opinion, contravened the basic American principle of individual negotiation between property owner and laborer. Immigrant and Negro were hired as strikebreakers with resulting riots in eastern and middle western cities. The Illinois legislature declared that any person who used threats or other forms of intimidation to prevent another person from working was guilty of a crime. Federal troops were used to break strikes called by "unpatriotic" labor leaders.

The most successful union of the Reconstruction period was the Noble and Holy Order of the Knights of Labor. Founded by a Philadelphia garment cutter, Uriah S. Stephens in 1869, it admitted members by ritual, grip, and password. The five asterisks standing for its title won it the name of the "five star union." As the influence of the Knights increased, merchant and lawyer found it profitable to join the organization. The Knights of Labor had a checkered career until the depression of 1873. Then several thousand workmen joined the organization in spite of public distrust of its secrecy and its Catholic membership. Although the union chose Terence V. Powderly, a Catholic, for president in 1879, it relaxed secrecy requirements for membership and presented a more secular image. In the 1880's the Knights attained almost 750,000 members, but it swung toward advocating public ownership of utilities, co-operative enterprise, and other "socialistic" ideas.

The Knights admitted to membership all individuals professing interest in the working class, but the immediate future belonged to the aristocrats of labor. In contrast to the "one big union," skilled carpenters, masons, or cigarmakers' unions brought together laborers with common purposes. In 1877 New York City local number 144 elected twenty-seven-year-old, English-born Samuel Gompers president. Within four years this labor genius created the Federation of Organized Trades and Labor Unions, the parent of the American Federation of Labor.

The labor movement suffered extensively in the Panic of 1873 and the subsequent years of depression. Nearly half a million workers lost their jobs when railroad construction in 1874 dropped to less than a third of its 1868–73 average. Forty per cent of the nation's steel furnaces went cold and other basic industries—mining, petroleum, and transportation—operated at minimal levels. One by one subsidiary enterprises laid off workers, for most consumers bought only necessities. Despite bountiful harvests, millions of the unemployed could not pay for bread and meat. Bread lines appeared in cities and aggressive leaders demanded public works projects, weekly food allotments for the destitute unemployed, and no eviction for nonpayment of rent. The number of Civil War "bummers" and postwar "tramps" became a horde of footloose men, some of whom turned to brigandage. Eastern and middle western communities reported thefts, fires, rapes, and murders. In 1876 hundreds of the vagrants captured a train and ran it into Beardstown, Illinois, where they fought a battle with peace officers; a gang took over and terrorized Jacksonville in the same state; and railroad management hired special guards to protect their trainmen from armed brigands.

The depression sent business enterprises into bankruptcy, but strikes triggered mainly by reduction of wages strengthened management. Employers fired and then blacklisted labor leaders, employed "scabs," and hired Pinkerton detectives to protect workers willing to accept lower wages.

In 1878, the fourth full depression year, the unemployed tramped city streets from Boston to Omaha. Striking coal miners and New England textile workers were forced to accept less than subsistence wages for a long working day. The only union success was achieved by the Brotherhood of Locomotive Engineers and allied railroad employees. Elated by their victory, trainmen responded to a 10 per cent wage reduction in 1877 by abandoning trains at isolated locations. Many of these workmen received less than $42.00 a week, a considerable portion of which went to pay for rooms and meals away from home. Non-unionized workers resorted to violence as the strike spread across the land. Governors called out militia and President Hayes bolstered the state forces with army regulars. At Cumberland, Maryland, and at Pittsburgh, the hungry unemployed marched like veterans against a hail of bullets. Destruction of railroad property and breaking into boxcars to steal provisions resulted in calling out more militia. After the armed forces had broken the strike, one cynical reporter declared that a dead laborer was the only victor among workers who demanded no more than fair wages and equitable employment.

Business also suffered during the depression. Withdrawals of funds by frantic depositors closed well-managed banks, and the price of quality stocks plummeted along with speculative ones. The sharp reduction in consumption brought a market glut with a precipitous drop in prices. Fifteen to 20 per cent reductions were common, and pig iron which had sold for $53.00 a ton in 1872 brought only $16.50 six years later. Factories closed and bankruptcies rose steadily from 5830 in 1874 to 10,478 in 1878. The twin millstones of over-extended credit and dishonest managers plunged business into deeper and deeper difficulties. Frauds, forgeries, and embezzlements convinced many Americans that brokers and bankers were a brotherhood of thieves with their headquarters on Wall Street. Few critics distinguished between avarice and errors of judgment. The average American's suspicion of the business community was not allayed by propaganda issued by manufacturers' associations or chambers of commerce, and Wall Street became the whipping boy for generations of discontented citizens. Yet, business emerged from the Reconstruction era with considerable unity of purpose, and its lobbyists swayed state legislators and national congressmen.

The financial losses of the businessmen and the meager wages of laborers found no sympathy in the farmer's eyes. Their problems seemed to him comparatively minor. Furthermore, the future apparently belonged to them while the farmer was doomed to secondary status in economic production. In 1860 more than 6,200,000 Americans gained their living from farming and 4,325,000 were engaged in non-farm activities. Twenty years later the number of Americans receiving their income from non-farm sources was over 200,000 larger than the number of gainfully employed in agriculture.

By 1880 the farmer saw the political results of his power lost. National policies favored business: sound money policies, subsidies, grants, tariffs, and other federal activities supported industrial growth even though some of these policies retarded agricultural development. More and more governors, state legislators, and judges believed that industry was the wave of the future. Financiers established credit systems to serve business while rural bankers reluctantly loaned money to farmers. The farmer was a socially desirable gambler, but nevertheless a gambler, risking his labor and capital against weather, pest, and price. Bankers preferred short-term business loans to long-term rural credits and high interest money-lenders took liens on crops instead of land. A country in the throes of industrialization taxed land relatively more than business property. A debtor nation had to secure capital for factories, machines, and transportation, and exchange of cheap raw materials for industrial equipment in international trade was the easy method of acquiring the essentials for industry. American farmers subsidized industrial advance.

Farm leaders vigorously protested the declining return on agricultural units. With peace, southern farmers sold all the cotton, tobacco, and rice they could produce at profitable prices. The domestic and foreign demand for grain, hay, and meat returned northern farmers similar profits. Waste of war and livestock depletion stimulated production, and prosperity encouraged farmers to cultivate more land and enlarge their herds. Within a few years agricultural production surpassed the demand of low-income wage earners. Resulting price reductions failed to increase consumption of inelastic products sufficiently to move the surplus. Wheat farmers received about $6 million more for 449,175,000 bushels in 1878 than for 169,703,000 units in 1866. Corn producers harvested 730,814,00 bushels in 1866 and 1,564,537,000 twelve years later and sold the larger yield for $10 million less than the smaller one. Southern tobacco growers cured 316,595,000 pounds in 1866 and sold it for $36,713,000; in 1877 their 620,770,000 pounds brought $33,521,580. The 4,352,000 bales of cotton ginned in 1870 went for 12.1 cents per pound, while the 5,074,000 of 1878 averaged only 8.16 cents a pound. The return to cotton farmers was almost $60 million less in the higher than the lower year of production. Tobacco prices declined from 11.6 cents to 5.4 cents per pound, corn from 65.7 to 31.3 cents a bushel, and wheat from $2.00 to 77.2 cents. Farmers produced more and received less for their harvests.

PRODUCTION OF MAJOR CROPS

	Corn bu.	Wheat bu.	Oats bu.	Cotton bales	Tobacco lbs.
1860	838,793,000	173,105,000	172,643,000	3,841,000	
1870	1,124,775,000	254,429,000	267,947,000	4,352,000	345,045,000
1880	1,706,673,000	502,257,000	417,942,000	6,606,000	469,395,000

Overall, however, the return from agricultural sales jumped from more than two billion to over four billion dollars from 1860 to 1880. Most of this increase came from animals sold for meat, vegetables, and fruits to supply the demand of urbanites. The traditional self-sufficiency of New England farmers continued as did the diversification of Middle Atlantic agrarians, while Southerners and Westerners specialized in staple crops. Farmers residing near cities or railroads supplying fast service to metropolitan areas found truck gardening remunerative. Before the end of reconstruction, canned tomatoes from Maryland were on grocery shelves, and preservation by canning opened new markets to fruit and vegetable growers.

One of government's major aids to farmers was education. Established in 1862, the federal Bureau of Agriculture sponsored agricultural research. Proven practice and innovation appeared in bulletins distributed to farmers and ranchers. The bureau supplied congressmen with seed to mail to their constituents. Speakers at local Grange meetings described new methods of cultivating and harvesting crops.

The other major governmental aid to farmers—homesteads—was a questionable gift. As has been mentioned, the poor could not finance the move to take advantage of the 160 acres available for fees and five years of residence provided for in the 1862 Homestead Act and its 1864 amendments.

Too frequently the speculator reaped rewards from federal largess, and changes in the basic act benefited the mine operator and lumber king more than the small farmer.

Race-sensitive politicians enacted the Homestead Act of 1866. This legislation opened over 46 million acres of public lands in Alabama, Arkansas, Florida, Louisiana, and Mississippi to settlers paying five dollars in fees for 80 acres.* Until 1867 only applicants of unquestionable loyalty received grants. Although northern veterans were eligible, the act's basic purpose was to provide land for freedmen. On August 25, 1866, a land office was opened in Florida and by 1868 more than 3000 Negroes held patents to land. This number of successful Negro applicants made white Floridians fear that their state would be dominated by freedmen. Though Florida attracted more applicants than the other four states, the land offered was poor, the cost of moving and establishing farms, notwithstanding subsistence grants by the Freedmen's Bureau, was too expensive for most Afro-Americans, and white people intimidated colored settlers. By October 1876, Negroes held 2012 homesteads containing 160,960 of the almost 20 million public acres of Florida. Three years later, only 1063 freedmen had retained their homesteads. The others had sold to whites or abandoned their land. As more and more southern states were redeemed, Bourbon leaders demanded elimination of the act. In 1876, the Senate by an overwhelming majority and the House by a small one repealed it and President Grant allowed the bill to become law without his signature.

Few southern legislatures demonstrated interest in helping the freedman become a landowner. Only South Carolina inaugurated a program with a $500,000 appropriation to buy land for resale to Afro-Americans. Most of the money went to grafters while relatively few of the 80,000 Negroes desiring homesteads acquired the inferior lands sold by the state. A Georgia project to buy 100-acre tracts for freedmen through a bond issue received little legislative support. Legislatures "dominated by irresponsible radicals and African barbarians" gave valuable franchises and lands to corporations among whose stockholders were conservative whites, but paid scant heed to the freedman's appeal for land.

The industrious Afro-American could buy a homestead by saving a part of his earnings. The Freedmen's Savings and Trust Company was chartered by congressional act on March 3, 1865, for the laudable purpose of encouraging thrift. The institution was never guaranteed by the government nor was it a responsiblity of the Freedmen's Bureau. Yet Negroes who placed their savings in its 30 branches believed the bank to be a federal agency. Bureau agents seldom challenged this false assumption

* The public lands available were: Arkansas, 9,298,012; Alabama, 6,732,058; Florida, 19,379,635; Louisiana, 6,228,102; and Mississippi, 4,760,763 acres.

about the bank headed by John W. Alvord, the Freedmen's Bureau general superintendent of education. Negroes entrusted almost $20 million to the bank. When it failed in 1874, assets totaled $3,299,000 and depositors received 62 per cent of this amount upon liquidation of the mismanaged bank.

In 1880 the Census Bureau gladdened the hearts of Americans who believed in an economy based on small independent farmers. According to bureau reports, the number of southern farms more than doubled and the acreage of each farm was halved during the Reconstruction era. Northern idealists lauded this development for it implied the end of the plantation regime, diminishing influence of the ante-bellum planter-aristocracy, and emancipating both the poor whites and propertyless Negroes. To a lesser extent, the census report indicated a national trend toward small farms operated by independent Americans.

The census reported a myth. There had been no significant increase in the number of farms: dependency instead of independence was characteristic of the farm worker. In nine former Confederate states the census bureau found 660,358 more farms in 1880 than in 1860 and an average decline from 347 to 156 in acreage. The director of the census counted 301,738 sharecroppers and other thousands of rigidly controlled tenants as independent farmers. In reality from one-third to one-half of the South's most fertile plantations had passed to absentee northern or merchant owners. The slave street lined with cabins disappeared as freedmen moved into shacks amid their sharecropped acres. Many a white man agreed to sharecrop and along with his Negro neighbor received one-half of the yield in return for his labor. Both cropper and tenant produced staple crops to satisfy the absentee landlord or to repay the sums advanced by merchants. Custom and practice combined with few urban markets, inadequate transportation, and limited storage facilities dictated increased production of money crops.

Southern agriculture underwent a triple revolution in land tenure, labor, and credit, none of which developed independence in farmers. Unable to provide themselves with corn meal and fatback during the long growing season, sharecroppers arranged open-book credit with the merchants. In addition to being charged high prices, the cropper was assessed interest of 30 or more per cent. At harvest, the landlord received his half share of the crop in return for supplying land and equipment. After settling his account with the merchant, the cropper kept whatever remained. Too frequently his share barely repaid his debt. Then the sharecropper drew anew his subsistence from the merchant in anticipation of the next harvest. Through the years his debt increased until he became captive of the landlord-merchant. In time landlord became merchant and merchant acquired land until landowner and retailer merged into one person. Despite high prices and usurious interest, the landlord-merchant seldom became wealthy. A creditor himself, he paid high interest on his stock. Often the sharecropper did not produce enough to pay his debt, and abandoned his crops or reduced its net by secretly selling a part of it.

Landlord-merchants protected themselves by securing lien laws. Legislative acts "to encourage agriculture" authorized legal pledges of crops in return for credit and provided stern enforcement. The produce lien gave the merchant first claim on the harvest. Since the latter's main concern was immediate income, he paid little heed to soil conservation and demanded concentration on one salable product which continued the ante-bellum southern system of soil depletion and staple crop production.

Although problems of sharecropping and dependent tenancy were most acute in the South, they were severe in the nation's other agricultural regions. By 1880 the country was saddled with almost 600,000 southern cropper-tenants and more than a million northern tenants. Tenancy embraced all races and colors. Tenant and owner-operator bought in a high-priced market and sold in a low one. As expenses exceeded income, farm debt multiplied until the word farmer almost became a synonym for debtor.

Education

Whatever their means of earning a living or their economic philosophy, a majority of Americans were interested in educating youth. Perhaps Horace Mann and the public school system had made ante-bellum Americans the most generally educated people on earth. A majority of children attended schools in the North; a few states and a number of cities in the poorer and more sparsely settled South supported good public educational programs. The southern elite employed tutors, enrolled their children in some 3000 private academies, and gave collegiate education to a larger percentage of white Southerners than northern parents did for their youth. The ignorance of 4 million slaves, about 200,000 of whom could read and write, lowered the national average of literacy. North Carolinians boasted of opening the first state university and Virginians claimed that they gave secular, state-supported education the push which resulted in 21 universities operating in 20 states by 1860. Religious denominations supported colleges located in urban communities and on rural hilltops. There were also non-sectarian private institutions of higher learning, and Wesleyan in Georgia and Mount Holyoke in Massachusetts claimed the honor of being the first colleges for women.

At best pedagogy was archaic. The most invigorating development stemmed from Mann's liberalism which, as late as 1865, was opposed by hidebound pedagogues and social conservatives. Dwelling on the past and blind support of slavery characterized southern academies and colleges. But few professors at northern institutions attempted to stimulate the mental processes of students. Other than at Virginia and Michigan, youths enrolled in prescribed courses in ancient classics, ethics, and rhetoric; occasionally a professor performed elementary scientific experiments before his class; and the study of modern languages or English literature were either unavailable or conducted by intellectually blind instructors. Despite their limitations, northern educational institutions offered their secondary and collegiate students more freedom of inquiry than did southern ones. After 1865 Northerners claimed that a public school system and collegiate training in the ante-bellum South that emphasized content of speeches instead of form would have prevented secession and war.

The Civil War checked educational development as restoration of the Union took precedence over training youth. Empty benches in lower school classrooms and vacant seats in college halls reflected the need for laborers and soldiers. In the South the faculty and student body of some institutions had enrolled almost en masse for Confederate service. As students attained college age they volunteered or had been drafted. Funds earmarked for educational use had been diverted to war.

There was a marked contrast between northern and southern response to peacetime educational needs. Proud of their institutions, Northerners not only spent their relatively ample funds freely on schools but also financed missionary teachers in the South. The main support of many ante-bellum southern institutions, the literary funds, had been depleted or wiped out by investment in Confederate securities. Few southern planters could afford tutors or tuition. During Presidential Reconstruction, state legislators feared to tax their struggling constituents. Economic survival seemed more important than token support for the educational needs of white and Negro children.

Reports of the freedman's burning desire for education, of grandparents not fearing death if they could only read the Bible, and of parents sending their scrubbed children to every available school warmed the hearts of politician and philanthropist. In addition to building schools, Oliver O. Howard's Freedmen's Bureau agents converted abandoned plantation houses and former slave markets into classrooms. Northern publishers shipped more than 200,000 old textbooks into the South. Philanthropist George Peabody earmarked a portion of his more than $8 million in gifts for communities that would provide matching funds to construct and operate schools. Approximately 5000 northern teachers moved into the South.

Personal deficiencies and southern white attitudes accounted for the failures of these well-intentioned Northerners. Many "schoolmarms" descended on the South to educate the children of a race held back by the lash, and to demonstrate Christian love to benighted white natives. These women, some with no valid claim to intellectuality, were considered by white Southerners as representative of the best human intelligence of the North. Northerners who went south, considering themselves missionaries to the heathen, expected and were prepared to bear ostracism and persecution. They experienced both: doors of white homes closed in their faces. Forced to secure room and board with Negro families, the whites interpreted this necessity as an attack on southern racial customs. A few former southern aristocrats believed that education would make the freedman a better workman. The majority of Southerners opposed any education for Negroes unless freedmen paid for it by a head tax or monthly fee, and practically any payment discouraged impoverished former slaves. According to prevailing white opinion, a literate Negro would be less honest, less concerned with morality, and a poorer workman than an unlettered freedman. Galling, also, would be the "uppishness" of Negroes flaunting their accomplishment before illiterate whites.

Rumors of the instruction given students strengthened white opposition to Negro education. Colored children sang "John Brown's Body," listened to laudatory biographical sketches of abolitionists, and drank in criticism of Confederates. Lee was a prejudiced traitor, Sherman made a glorious march to the sea, and Lincoln was murdered by a Confederate agent. Rumor-mongers spread these and other tales and fearful whites believed them. They had heard some northern teachers advocate equality and fraternity and "knew" they indoctrinated students with pernicious social doctrines. They lumped together the stupid and bright Yankee teacher, and many able northern men and women who made contributions to southern education were ostracized and vilified.

Although initiated by federal agents and altruistic Northerners, Negro education was the work of southern states. Without exception constitution-makers operating under the aegis of Congressional Reconstruction inserted public school provisions in state constitutions. An educated citizenry was an essential ingredient of republican government, every child should have educational opportunity, and the taxpayer had a duty to provide schools. These were the noblest designs of southern Republican regimes. Elaborate and costly educational programs of some legislators brought nightmares to white property owners. Diversion of appropriated funds from schools to avaricious hands saddened idealists. Yet, the number and percentage of white and Negro children enrolled and attending public schools steadily increased. The educational year lengthened to 100 or more days. Students sat on benches, some beginning classes passed one primer or speller from hand to hand, and teachers received their major material rewards from rooms and meals provided by parents; but the rate of illiteracy gradually declined. By 1880, 86 per cent of white Texans over ten years of age could at least read and write, and 28 per cent of Tennessee's Negroes were literate. At worst, 32 per cent of white North Carolinians and 82 per cent of colored Georgians existed in an educational void. Even when the beloved redeemers saved southern civilization from "African barbarity" and reduced school appropriations, the ire of their constituents eventually forced more liberal support for public schools. To a limited extent the Negro child on his bench at an inferior, segregated school shared this largess, and his descendants benefited from educational foundations laid during Congressional Reconstruction.

The southern public school system was established with few interracial classrooms. Provisions in the Louisiana and South Carolina constitutions opened schools to all children regardless of race or color. The constitutions of other former Confederate states either ignored integration or provided for two school systems. Idealists denounced separate schools as undemocratic and astute Negroes knew that separation meant inferior schools, but the racial prejudice and economic power of the whites prevailed.

The 1880 census reflected national educational progress. Almost 10 million American youths were enrolled in public schools. This number included more than 65 per cent of the 5- to 17-age brackets, and their school year averaged 130 days. High schools enrolled 110,000 students, almost 24,000 of whom graduated. Every school, north or south, felt the weight of sectionalism, local politics, and religious orthodoxy. The bias of northern teachers was reinforced by textbooks which emphasized propaganda more than reason. The southern-owned University Publishing Company of New York City advertised for manuscripts that would be "unsectional, unpartisan, and unpolitical . . . prepared by the most Eminent Southern Scholars and entirely acceptable to Southern Teachers and Parents." The company's textbooks, written from "an unbiased Southern point of view," appealed to legislatures of redeemed states and were widely adopted by school boards. Eager male applicants attempted to forestall ministerial opposition by promising to teach the "flat or round systems [that the world is flat or round] according to the wishes of the school trustees." The freedom of teachers was restricted by watchful matrons, ever ready to condemn any deviation from community norms.

A constituency dispersed over a large geographical area gave the college professor more latitude. Different opinions within states or religious orders allowed instructors to question the established order and delve into new fields of learning. The integration phobia closed the University of North Carolina and transformed South Carolina College (renamed the University of South Carolina in 1865) into a Negro institution. When only one student enrolled at Alabama in 1865, the fire-gutted institution was closed and reorganized in 1871 by a redeemer legislature. Other southern universities fared well under Republican legislatures. Arkansans created a state university in 1871 and the following year Alabamians established the forerunner of Auburn University. The University of Kentucky appeared in 1865 and Mississippi opened a state agricultural and mechanical college in 1878.

The Morrill land-grant act with federal gifts of 30,000 acres per congressman benefited existing state universities and created new ones. Between 1865 and 1874 the universities of Kansas, Illinois, West Virginia, California, Nebraska, Oregon, Ohio State, and Nevada opened their doors. Complying with the act, new and old land-grant universities established "agricultural and mechanical colleges" to meet the popular demand for practical education. Born in the South, the secular state university attained maturity in the Middle West, where taxpayer support raised that type of institution to national prominence.

Continuity and innovation characterized higher educational development. Vassar, Wellesley, Smith, and Radcliffe created new halls of learning for women; religious orders continued to found colleges; teachers were trained at state institutions, and Akron University and Hunter College headed the list of new municipal facilities. Demand for scientific education established Massachusetts Institute of Technology in 1861, special colleges at Harvard and Yale, and the Missouri School of Mines. Howard University at Washington and Hampton Institute in Virginia headed the parade of Negro colleges, among which were Lincoln University of Jefferson City, Missouri, Wilberforce in Ohio, Morgan State at Baltimore, Fisk at Nashville, Talladega in Alabama, and Atlanta University. Some of these institutions that later catered to Negroes opened with white students. Five white girls and two white boys were the student body during the first year of Howard's existence, and Hampton Institute was conceived as a means of giving poor whites training in mechanical arts. Its first graduate to win fame, however, was Booker T. Washington. Berea in Kentucky enrolled white and Negro until a twentieth-century state legislature prohibited interracial colleges. In the South, Bennett at Greensboro, North Carolina, accepted only Negro women, and a number of southern states established Negro coeducational institutions.

New curricula overshadowed the establishment of additional institutions. Discovery of natural law gave science a support unknown during ante-bellum years. Even the most conservative institutions offered courses in biology, chemistry, and physics, and provided laboratory equipment to test established phenomena as well as to investigate the unknown. Enlarged and enriched universities became not only the conservators of cultural heritages but also added to mankind's knowledge. In this scientific awakening, students studied history and political economy, learned French and German, and read the many literary works of English authors as well as sampling the poems and novels of American writers. While Negro students at Fisk translated Latin, others at Hampton Institute studied manual arts. Practical education, scientific and technological training, and inquiry into history and political economy became respectable on the college campus; humanists lingered fondly on the Greek and Latin classics, but admitted that modern languages and English and American literature deserved attention.

Even college administrators who required students to verse themselves in classical and biblical studies allowed some leeway in course selection. The elective system of Thomas Jefferson's University of Virginia was strengthened by Michigan's policies. President Charles W. Eliot extended it at Harvard where by 1875 seniors had only one prescribed course and juniors only three.

The resources of state and privately supported institutions enabled them to provide graduate education for some of the almost 13,000 graduates of 1880. In 1871 Yale concentrated all nonprofessional advanced study in a separate school and a year later Harvard required three years of graduate work for the Ph.D. or Sc.D. degree. Youthful Americans, among them Herbert Baxter Adams and Andrew D. White, studied at German universities. Backed by Ezra Cornell, White organized Cornell University and as its first president (1868–85) he allowed undergraduates choice of courses and emphasized graduate education. In 1876 Johns Hopkins University became the first American institution to devote itself primarily to research and graduate work. Northern and southern-born scholars, trained in the seminars of Adams at Hopkins, went forth to direct advanced students in history and political science at other institutions. Universities added graduate schools to their established colleges as they sought to achieve high standing in the American educational system. In 1870 one male student won a doctorate. Ten years later, almost 900 students received the master's degree and 54 doctoral degrees were awarded to 51 men and 3 women.

Religion

Thousands of churches and millions of communicants made the United States a church-supporting country. In 1870 almost 73,000 congregations owned nearly as many religious buildings, with the Methodists leading both in number of churches and of members. The Baptists held second place, trailed by Presbyterians with Catholics fourth, their number increasing rapidly. Gentlemanly, socially prominent individuals attended their smaller but influential Episcopal churches. Methodists and Baptists were proportionately more numerous in the South.

American religious leaders ranged from highly educated men to illiterates. Catholic and Episcopal organizations demanded a trained priesthood and Presbyterians tried to provide their churches with educated ministers. Neither a majority of Baptists nor of Methodists preferred the semiliterate preacher to the literate one, but members of both denominations believed "the calling" essential to the ministry. Many an unlettered minister regaled his congregation with the story of his being struck blind by the Holy Ghost and seeing, on recovering his sight, "G.P.C." blazened across the sky. After enduring his sermons, the dubious communicant concluded that the minister had misinterpreted the heavenly message; instead of "Go Preach Christ," the G.P.C. was evidently a command to "Go Pick Cotton." Although other sects chided Methodists and Baptists for the educational deficiencies of their clergy, members of those faiths headed all denominations in establishing and supporting colleges.

Ante-bellum controversy and the war left an almost indelible stain on American religion. A decade and a half before secession, Baptists and Methodists had separated and Presbyterians had split over slavery. Episcopalians fared better, their wartime division was healed in 1865, at least in organization; and American Catholics retained their hierarchal unity. Northern Methodism allied itself with the Radical Republicans who demanded hanging of traitors, confiscation of rebel property, and Negro suffrage. "Instead of giving the rebels place and power again," a New Hampshire Methodist minister wanted them "to be taken by the nape of the neck and held over hell until they squalled like cats." Southern clerics responded in kind. A Presbyterian divine told his congregation, "I do not forgive. I try not to forgive." An Alabamian described the "reverend black-guards" sent into the South as "liars" and "malignant slanderers." A Georgian damned northern preachers who had "the Devil in their hearts" and were "missionaries of wrath, stirring up strife, kindling hate . . . [dressed] in clerical robes spotted with sin and dripping with crime, their Bible 'a league with hell,' their text the enmity of man with man, and the gospel of lust as their creed. . . ." These antagonisms prevented regional agreements among Protestants other than minimal ones on the ownership of church property.

Ideology and morality widened the breach between northern and southern Protestants. A tradition of Unitarian and Transcendental liberalism prepared many Northerners for scientific challenges to literal acceptance of the Bible. The idea of a million-or-more-year-old earth spinning in a universe controlled by natural laws, comparative study of religions, and critical analysis of biblical literature stimulated open skepticism. John Fiske and Edward L. Youmans explained the Darwinian theory and its refinements by Herbert Spencer in magazine article and college lecture. President White of Cornell answered critics who demanded banning "atheistic-evolutionaries" from college campuses with his "Battlefields of Science" speech at Cooper Union. Throughout the ages, he declared, the bigoted religious conservative had attempted to stem the advance of knowledge. Henry Ward Beecher accepted evolution and boldly presented it to his congregation.

Southerners rejected any "ism" or scientific theory not consistent with their literal interpretation of the Holy Writ. Defeated and impoverished, they raised the faith of their fathers as a shield against dreadful change. As they glorified the past, it seemed as though they were trusting a tribal god who was pitting his chosen people against the onslaughts of Yankee liberals enrolled in the devil's legions. Southerners calvinized Jehovah, the stern master of everything; they knew that he had dictated eternal truths to Jewish scribes, but accused the Jews of crucifying Christ; and they unconsciously employed religion as a factor in polarizing their region. Literate and semiliterate "parsons" dictated morals: their commands to observe the Sabbath, shun dancing and gambling, and refuse whiskey became the guiding principles of proper conduct. Cockfight and school-board meeting, horse race and revival were opened with a prayer of thanks and a plea for godly blessing. Ministers who understood human frailty advised sinners "to go and sin no more," but preacher and parishioner demanded public tribute to God. Southerners who enjoyed play, song, and drink compromised by being hedonists in practice and puritans in principle.

Regional differences appeared in church buildings and religious services. Affluent northern urbanites erected imposing edifices with stained glass windows. Most southern agrarians worshipped in dilapidated frame buildings. The Northern urban church was on its way to becoming a religious club for middle-class Americans. Such ministers as Beecher and Phillips Brooks used their oratorical powers to support their faith in man's essential righteousness and their theology adapted to modern life appealed to the religious. Piety was a major force among religious Northerners, a gentle and rational piety. Religious Southerners were more apt to display their faith in routine tributes to God.

Few rural Northerners or Southerners worshipped in buildings comparable to those of their urban cousins. Surreys and wagons brought families to the churchyards. Worshippers sat on hard wooden benches and focused their eyes on handmade pulpits bearing large bibles. The preacher lined the hymns and voices responded with more gusto than melody to "Nearer My God to Thee," "Rock of Ages," and "Jesus, Lover of My Soul." After reading from the scripture, the minister announced a text which often had little relation to his sermon. Although lacking theological training, his mind was a reservoir of experiences accumulated by observation and study. Varying the pitch and volume of his voice, he admonished his audience with devout sincerity, and with tender understanding of their trials, he advocated patience and promised eternal bliss. He lashed the hardened sinners and called them to repent. Few sinners could resist—one by one they moved down the aisle to kneel at the altar where before God they admitted their errors and promised exemplary behavior.

At revivals and camp meetings, communal pressure brought hardened and youthful sinners to the mourner's bench. As the preacher exhorted, lay brothers encouraged the hesitant to declare themselves for Christ. Young men exchanged glances to bolster their resistance and young women compressed their lips in stubborn defiance, but eventually they walked down the aisle to shed tears of release at the altar. Evangelists who pitched their tents in towns or rented halls in cities specialized in mass conversion. Eloquent, dogmatic Dwight L. Moody and Ira D. Sankey, a gifted tenor, conducted revivals in almost every American and some European cities. So effective was their 1876 campaign at the Hippodrome that New York theaters suffered reduced patronage for a year. Revivals convinced many citizens to demand enforcement of existing blue laws and passage of additional ones, and stimulated the activities of northern and southern prohibitionists.

The southern Negro enjoyed attending churches controlled by his race. Abolition ended the ante-bellum arrangement whereby slaves sat in balconies or other designated sections of churches, or filled an entire building to hear messages of white ministers or Negro preachers supervised by the dominant race. The emancipated Negro wanted a religious freedom which could be obtained only by establishing his own religious organizations. The formality of Catholic and Episcopal services appealed to few Negroes; most of them desired to sing, underline the preacher's phrases with comments, and express themselves in other ways. They flocked to the Baptist and Methodist churches. Some of their meetings or revivals lasted almost until dawn as emotion swept worshippers into frenzied outbursts. The Negro church developed leaders—ministers, deacons, and Sunday school teachers. Some leaders betrayed their trusts by yielding to white pressure, but every experience in leadership stored experience for that day when the Negro would boldly demand human dignity for himself. To a considerable degree, the Negro of the Reconstruction era imitated his white brother by wearing his religion on his sleeve and proclaiming more than observing high principles.

With all its deficiencies religion was a mighty force in America. Religious impulse supported the Young Men's and Young Women's Christian associations. Never resorting to aggressive tactics, these Christian organizations provided wholesome living quarters, educational opportunity, and recreational facilities for native and immigrant in the unfriendly city. Churches supported colleges and trained student as well as teacher in Sunday schools. Men and women identified with church-affiliated bodies worked to alleviate hardship. Religion motivated philanthropists to establish libraries and endow educational institutions. Though often more discredited in breach than honored in practice, religious ideals bettered the life of many Americans and directed them into worthy activities.

Attitudes and Ideas

Religion comforted the troubled and encouraged optimistic Americans. Rid of the evil of slavery and elated by the restoration of the Union, affluent Northerners foresaw a rosy future. Their material well-being convinced them of the values inherent in a democratic materialistic society. The benefits of free enterprise, representative government, and Protestant Christianity were so obvious they believed that the American system would conquer the world.

Yet diversity in thought characterized reconstruction society. Here and there among northern optimists lived pessimists who feared an influx of freedmen or deplored the number of Catholic immigrants entering their Protestant country. Some Northerners questioned a military victory over the "lords of the lash"; this resulted in increased representation of the vanquished in the House of Representatives and reduced the political power of the victor. Many immigrants realized their dreams in America, but others buried their hopes on unproductive farms or in crowded tenements. Successful manufacturers, bankers, and merchants displayed their wealth by erecting pretentious houses and giving lavish parties, while the poor existed in agrarian hovels or urban slums and ate at tables bearing the meager necessities of life. The contrast between wealth and poverty troubled intellectuals who advanced utopian schemes to create a society of economic plenty.

Relatively few Southerners, white or Negro, shared the optimism of their northern brothers. Fifteen years after Appomattox, visitors reported the South crushed, wretched, and still licking its wounds. The heart of Charleston remained scarred by wartime fires and fire-blackened ruins marred Columbia's landscape. Although New Orleans was shipping more cotton and sugar than ever before, the city's old buildings needed restoration and little new construction was in progress. Mobile appeared to be a city of the past; Galveston's population was declining; and Savannah, Wil-

mington, and New Bern were struggling to hold the *status quo*. In the late
1870's Memphis and Vicksburg were blighted by yellow fever. Except for
Richmond, Atlanta, and Nashville, the cities lying between the Potomac
River and the Rio Grande were either withering away or barely holding
their own.

Throughout the rural-dominated Southland, visitors found evidence of
poverty. Roads were sandy ruts or muddy mires, some rivers but few creeks
were bridged, many abandoned plantation houses were falling into ruins,
and the poor of both races existed in dilapidated hovels. One observer reported that both the dress and manner of living reflected their poverty.
Even large landowners, he declared, wore coarse clothing and the fare was
less than that of ordinary mechanics of the North. Lines of migrants
passed through southern towns en route to Texas, their wagons containing
few possessions and a brood of scrawny children. Lean fathers carrying
rifles and lank mothers holding baskets of food herded ten or more offspring into railroad coaches. Whatever frontier conditions might be, they
believed they could not be worse than the ones from which they were
escaping.

Northern visitors found difficulty in reconciling southern poverty with
the national faith in opportunity and progress. They attributed the destitu-
tion of Negroes to race, but more difficult to explain was the poverty of the
English, Scots, and Irish. Most northern observers concluded that these
members of the "superior race" were the victims of a slave economy or the
residue of a frontier riffraff. Many Southerners discovered and reiterated
the causes for their lag amid national progress—the devastation of Yankee
armies and inequities of alien-imposed reconstruction gave them an alibi
which they passed on to their sons. These deterrents and not laziness, the
white conservative claimed, were responsible for southern economic conditions.

Some pessimistic white Southerners found solace in an idealistic never-
never land of ante-bellum years. Others, unable to defend past actions on
so crass a motive as the perpetuation of slavery, advanced altruistic reasons
for secession and war. In their opinion brute force and unconstitutional
acts had conquered right, and they turned to force and irresponsible
citizenship to maintain white supremacy. Though defeated on the battlefield, they worshipped their generals and embraced semi-militarism to prepare their sons for future exigencies.

To force they added a peculiar spiritualism. Instead of blaming their
God for deserting his favored people, they lashed themselves for failing to
worship Him with complete faith. Millions of Southerners who professed
obedience to God's every command shifted without qualm from Christian
idealism to worldly practicality. Although proclaiming the brotherhood of

man under an omnipotent deity, they saw no sin in making decisions on the basis of "white blood," or, in court, returning verdicts with appropriate regard for race.

Southern Negroes were more bewildered than their white neighbors. Former slaves exercised their independence in various ways, moving from place to place, joining secret organizations, attending political rallies, voting, holding office, serving in the militia, or meeting for worship in their own churches. The ruling class laughed at some of the freedmen's methods of demonstrating status. According to one story, a Negro girl knocked at the front door of a white home. "Tell the *woman* of the house," she said, "that a colored *lady* is willing to work." Some Negroes who first conceived of emancipation as synonymous with the absence of work had to adjust to the responsibilities of free men. From the beginning of their freedom, however, most Negroes sought work at fair wages.

Despite a background of servitude which had denied him education and other training for freedom, the Negro yearned for several things. In the first place, he thought of himself as an American. Few freedmen knew that some members of their race had left Pensacola, Florida, to settle in Mexico in the 1850's or of the prewar colonization in Santo Domingo. President Lincoln supported the chimerical scheme of ante-bellum idealists to settle Negroes in Africa, Mexico, Central America, or the Caribbean islands. Ben Butler advocated the colonization of 150,000 freedmen, and Grant claimed in his 1876 message and in his memoirs that one reason for the attempted annexation of Santo Domingo was to secure land for Negroes. But freedmen rejected these colonization schemes. The United States was their home; they felt themselves entitled to American citizenship.

Suggestions for relocating Negroes within the United States received less support than attempts to colonize them. The idea of converting some Deep South states into Negro commonwealths appealed to many Northerners. At best, the Negro could enjoy a society under his control and economic opportunity free of white overlords. At worst, transforming South Carolina, Georgia, Florida, Alabama, Mississippi, or Louisiana into Negro states would be retribution levied on the leaders of rebellion. The Northerner who proclaimed his love for the Negro and feared a mass movement of freedmen into the North, thought the creation of a Negro-dominated region within the South an admirable solution. Undoubtedly many Negroes wished to move to areas lying north of the Mason-Dixon Line; but without financial aid, they were tied to their accustomed locales.

Realistic Negroes wanted farms near their homes. The lands offered by homestead acts were beyond their reach. Few Republican-dominated southern states even made gestures toward supplying land for Negroes. Left to their own resources, industrious and thrifty freedmen bought land, but most Negroes achieved no economic status higher than that of day laborers or sharecroppers.

Education was another desire of the Negro. Schools established by the Freedmen's Bureau or other federal agencies gave him some hope. The number of dedicated but often untactful whites who traveled southward supplied a basic instructional staff. Northern philanthropists granted funds for schools. Grateful as he was for these supplementary aids, the Negro knew that educational opportunity depended on local and state governments. Constitutions of the reborn southern states had provisions for public school systems, but only a few states provided integrated schools, and in practice segregation was the rule. The appeal for educational opportunity in any form silenced the objection of militant Negroes to separate but unequal facilities, for most Negro parents were more interested in elementary education for their children than in breaking racial barriers.

A final request of Negroes was first-class United States citizenship. No more than a handful of representatives and senators in Congress supported this desire of a submerged minority for equal status. Northerners gave the Negro freedom, reluctantly granted him the franchise, and seriously questioned his demand for equality. Before passage of the Civil Rights Act of 1875 and even afterwards, the political situation in the South made the act meaningless. Republican legislatures of southern states provided Negroes with more rights than did Congress. The only equality promised, the only commitment deferred to freedmen came from a hopelessly outnumbered band of Northerners and an even smaller number of Southerners. During the Civil War and Reconstruction eras, equality never secured the backing given union and freedom. Not until far into the twentieth century, when the Negro had power to demand his rights, did equality become a potent movement. Yet the nineteenth-century gifts of freedom, citizenship, and suffrage—although two were later revoked in practice and freedom was severely restricted—were major steps toward a better democracy in the United States.

The Negro's survival depended on adjusting himself to conditions imposed by southern whites. He eked out his bread as sharecropper or tenant farmer. As the urban white took over more skilled jobs, the Negro was reduced to domestic service and unskilled labor. The fortunate few secured land or engaged in business catering to their racial brothers. Economically, socially, and politically the Negro became the lower caste. As long as he confined himself to a status determined by his "biological inferiority," he was seldom bothered. In fact the obeisant Uncle Tom won many gifts in food and clothing from the "master race." Whenever the "good nigger" strayed because of weakness of the flesh or burdens of caste, his white protector bailed him out of minor legal difficulties.

Just as his ancestors had mitigated slavery with beautiful melodies while awaiting deliverance, the caste-bound freedman sought relief from his plight in singing and dancing. The sympathetic white who thought good Negroes were childlike adults happy with their lot never knew what was in the Negro's heart and mind. Before and after 1865, affection marked thousands of interracial economic and social associations, but deep within the hearts of supposedly happy Negroes discontent festered. More than security, more than largess, he wanted to be treated with human dignity.

Reconstruction was a tragic era in American society. The tragedy did not lie in victorious Northerners and militant Negroes trampling on white Southerners. Neither did the tragedy rest on the poverty of southern whites nor the hardships of immigrants—their children, at least, experienced no insurmountable barriers of prejudice which denied them opportunity or prevented their assimilation into American life. The Negro was the tragic figure of the Reconstruction era. Although freed by the war, with the completion of southern-style reconstruction, the Negro's pigmentation limited his means of livelihood and denied him first-class citizenship. In the South where most Negroes lived, the lawful and extra-legal acts of white people restricted or denied the freedman economic opportunity, political activity, and social equality. The secondary tragedy of the era was the baleful effects of the caste system on white Southerners. Even the poorest comforted himself with racial superiority over Negroes, but his prejudice retarded the South and the methods he used to degrade Negroes rebounded on him.

REFERENCES

Convenient summaries of America's growth are in U.S. Bureau of the Census, *Historical Statistics of the United States, Colonial Times to 1957* (Washington, 1960). The *Histories of the American Frontier Series*, edited by Ray A. Billington, will provide brief accounts of westward expansion. Pertinent volumes in process or published are: *The Frontier of the Far Southwest, 1850–1890; The Expulsion of the Red Men, 1865–1890; The Transportation Frontier, 1865–1890; The Frontier of the Cattlemen, 1865–1890; The Advance of the Farmer's Frontier, 1865–1890;* and *Mining Frontiers of the Far West, 1848–1880.* Fred A. Shannon, *The Farmer's Last Frontier: Agriculture, 1860–1897* (New York, 1961), is a quality study, as is Edward C. Kirkland, *Industry Comes of Age: Business, Labor, and Public Policy, 1860–1897* (New York, 1961). Muriel S. Wolfe, *The Bonanza Trail* (Bloomington, 1955), follows the shifting scenes of mining. Railroads are the theme of *They Built the West* (New York, 1934) by Glen C. Quiett. E. W. Howe, *The Story of a Country Town* (New York, 1947), describes the development of a Kansas town. Agriculture and ranching are presented in Everett Dick, *The Sod-House Frontier: 1854–1890* (New

York, 1938); Ernest S. Osgood, *The Day of the Cattlemen* (Minneapolis, 1954); and Carl C. Rister, *Southern Plainsmen* (Norman, 1938). A classic is Walter Prescott Webb, *The Great Plains: A Study in Institutions and Environment* (Boston, 1931). Roy M. Robins, *Our Landed Heritage: The Public Domain* (Princeton, 1942), has the standard account of public lands. Useful articles are: Horace M. Bond, "Social and Economic Forces in Alabama Reconstruction," *Journal of Negro History*, XXIII (1938), pp. 290–348; Paul W. Gates, "Federal Land Policy in the South, 1866–1888," *Journal of Southern History*, VI (1940), pp. 303–30; Oscar Zeichner, "The Transition from Slave to Free Agricultural Labor in the Southern States," *Agricultural History*, XIII (1939), pp. 22–33; Jacqueline P. Bull, "The General Merchant in the Economic History of the New South," *Journal of Southern History*, XVIII (1952), pp. 37–59; Elsie M. Lewis, "The Political Mind of the Negro, 1865–1900," *ibid.*, XXI (1955), pp. 189–220; William W. Sweet, "Methodist Church Influence in Southern Politics," *Mississippi Valley Historical Review*, I (1915), pp. 546–60; Robert H. Woody, "The Labor and Immigration Problem of South Carolina During Reconstruction," *ibid.*, XVIII (1932), pp. 195–212; and LaWanda Cox, "The Promise of Land for the Freedman," *ibid.*, XLV (1958), pp. 413–40. Negro education is described by William T. Alderson, Jr., "The Freedmen's Bureau and Negro Education in Virginia," *North Carolina Historical Review*, XXIX (1952), pp. 64–90, and Martin Abbott, "The Freedmen's Bureau and Negro Education in South Carolina," *South Carolina Historical Magazine*, LVII (1956), pp. 65–81. Henry L. Swint, *The Northern Teacher in the South, 1862–1870* (Nashville, 1941), is a critical study. The personal experiences of a northern schoolteacher are told by Cornelia Hancock, *South After Gettysburg*, edited by Henrietta Jaquette (New York, 1956). Oscar Handlin, *The Uprooted* (Boston, 1951), describes the difficulties of immigrants; and Blake McKelvey, *The Urbanization of America, 1860–1915* (New Brunswick, 1963), follows the national move into cities. Ralph Morrow, *Northern Methodist and Reconstruction* (East Lansing, 1956), considers religious support for the Radicals.

The Disputed Election

DEMOCRATS anticipated the presidential election of 1876. Their victory in 1874 apparently foretold a successful sweep: retention of the House, winning the presidency, and possible control of the Senate. They had reason for optimism. The worst scandals of the Grant regime had been uncovered by House committees and these evidences of corruption should turn many voters to the Democratic party. Since 1874 additional southern states had been "redeemed" by white conservatives and a solidly Democratic South was a distinct possibility. Evidence also pointed to northern indifference to the seemingly eternal southern problem; only the extremely skeptical feared the re-enslavement of the Negroes. Many Northerners believed that sectional peace and national prosperity could be achieved by allowing southern whites to control southern governments. Wartime animosities were subsiding, recollections of peace Democrats and Copperheads were becoming dim, rebellion was in the past, the Union was safe.

Civil service, honest government, and other reforms were more important than maintaining Republican governments in the South or protecting the rights of Negroes. In the opinion of editor Godkin, the reduction of political graft was the paramount issue, greater than the suffrage or reconstruction itself. Following his bow toward a civil service merit system, Grant and his aides relied on the spoils system in making most appointments. Inefficient or conniving civil servants harassed businessmen, especially importers. By law a false declaration of imported goods made the entire importation, not merely the tax involved, subject to seizure, with half its value assigned to the collector of the New York Customs House for his fee and the legal expense entailed in making the collection. By adroit use of spies and informers and by playing on the desire of importers to escape duties, clever customs-house inspectors collected large fees from mercantile houses. One tremendous haul was made by collector Chester A. Arthur, Senator Conkling's spoilsman. Phelps, Dodge & Company paid almost $275,000 to save $1,750,000-worth of goods on which a tax error of a few thousand dollars had been made. In addition to sharing his fee with inspectors of the Customs House, Arthur paid $50,000 to Conkling and Ben Butler for their legal work.

Many businessmen found corrupt government costly at a time when their fears of an anti-business, political combination of Southerners and Westerners were subsiding. In fact leaders of the agrarian South gave evidence of becoming ardent supporters of industrialization. Former secessionists found the reason for the Confederacy's defeat in the South's inadequate railroads, manufacturing, and banking facilities. Representatives from the southern region clamored for internal improvements, financed with federal aid, and gave state lands and encouraging legislation to corporations. Agents from the South sought capital in northern financial centers for railroads and cotton mills. Every indicator foretold southern support for a governmental climate favorable to business.

The abundant natural resources of the South attracted the interest of northern capitalists. There was coal, iron ore, limestone, timber, and land to produce the basic raw materials of cotton, sugar, and tobacco. Cotton mills, iron foundries, tobacco factories, and sugar refineries could be developed with sufficient capital and able management. Furthermore, the millions of Southerners would furnish an ample labor supply and a tremendous market for the manufactured goods. Domestic tranquility was essential to exploitation of profitable industries and markets. Never enthusiastic about the political and humanistic phases of Congressional Reconstruction, businessmen now yearned for the demise of southern Republican governments. White conservative control of local and state affairs seemed the best hope for order and a government favorable to business.

Northern public opinion was also veering toward sympathy for the white Southerner. Fewer editorials condemned or criticized the South, more editors urged their readers to forgive and forget, to stop fighting rebellion, and to strive for sectional harmony. Magazines with national circulation printed the reminiscences of Confederates, and these personal accounts pictured sincere individuals fighting for honor and ideals, instead of killing Northerners to perpetuate slavery. The American's concern for the underdog asserted itself. Extreme Radical politicians of former days grew tired of reading reports about the mistreatment of Negroes and Unionists in the South and criticized the Scalawag and Carpetbag politicos. Even Grant grew weary of the repeated calls by southern Republicans for federal intervention to protect and uphold their regimes.

Many Northerners, however, resisted the propaganda of harmony. They recalled the personal sacrifices of war, the vacant chairs around the family table. Their emotions could still be aroused by politicians who waved the bloody shirt. For them the living symbol of the triumph of freedom and union over slavery and division was President Grant. However much the intellectuals criticized the executive, he remained a popular hero. Millions of northern voters would have cast their ballots for him had he been selected by his party for a third term in 1876, but a House Resolution of December 1875 had stated that a violation of the traditional two terms for one man "would be unwise, and fraught with perils." This declaration which was passed by a vote of 234 to 18, and was therefore supported by a majority of Republican representatives, nipped the bud from the third-term flower. Despite this action by their representatives, relatively few northern Republicans repudiated the military hero or their party.

Democratic strength lay in northern cities, the border states, and southern states controlled by white conservatives. But this combination could not produce the electoral votes to win a presidential contest. Victory hinged on weaning individuals from Republican ranks to give the Democratic candidate key northern states. It behooved the Democrats to soft-pedal foreign affairs, the most successful adventure of Grant's administration, and concentrate instead on reform and relief for farmers and laborers. The party needed a candidate whose public honesty would contrast with the corruption of Republican officials.

The Southern Political Situation

White conservative victories in Alabama and Arkansas in 1874 assured the Democrats of seven former Confederate states. As has been related, Mississippi conservatives redeemed their state in 1875–76, and the election of a Florida Democrat to the United States Senate in 1875 indicated that the state's four electoral votes would be Democratic. This situation left only South Carolina with seven and Louisiana with eight electoral votes to be contested by the parties. In a close election, the fifteen votes could determine the winner.

Republicans did not consider Florida lost to them. Since 1872 the divided Republicans had achieved unity under an able Carpetbag governor, Marcellus L. Stearns. Although he had won the gubernatorial nomination in 1872, the Negro convention delegates hooted him into declining and he accepted second place on a ticket headed by Ossian B. Hart, the first native-born Floridian to win the governorship. Hart was an ill man and after his death, Stearns not only won the support of Negro voters but also placed the state on a sound fiscal basis. Costs of government were reduced, some reduction was made in the small public debt, and more appropriations made for schools. In 1876 Stearns won the Republican nomination with ease. To oppose him the Democrats (the name of "conservative" had been gradually dropped) selected George Franklin Drew, a native of New Hampshire who settled in Florida before the war. Although a former

Unionist, he was never active in politics and by tending to various business enterprises had accumulated sufficient wealth to be known as "Millionaire Drew."

The plan of Florida Democrats was similar to that of Democratic organizations in other unredeemed states. Negro voters would be intimidated by threats of violence; by organized rifle clubs whose members used Negro dummies for target practice; shadowing Republicans on city streets; and shooting guns at nights near the dwellings of politically active Negro and white Republicans. Voting Republicans were threatened with eviction from farm cabins and the loss of industrial jobs. Many merchants and professional people announced their intention to charge registered, voting Negroes higher prices for goods and services. The Florida Democratic platform contained no white-supremacy plank, but every campaign action implied unity of all white voters to maintain political, economic, and social dominance over Negroes.

If need be, the Democrats would resort to trickery and extra-legal methods. In an age without uniform ballots, party workers marked and gave ballots to illiterate Negroes. Smooth-talking, apparently sincere agents of the Democratic party convinced some that their Republican ballots were really marked for Democratic candidates, thereby substituting a Democratic ballot for the Republican one. In counties with white population majorities and two Democratic precinct inspectors to one for the Republicans, the Democrats planned on repeated voting. Already redeemed Georgians were to enter some northern counties of Florida to vote for Democrats. Wherever Republicans had a majority of precinct inspectors, the Democratic worker was to encourage irregularities and later demand that the precinct vote be thrown out because of illegal voting.

The Republicans were far from helpless. They possessed a tremendous advantage in controlling the canvassing boards, and the whispered comment of dishonest politicians was "It don't matter how the people vote as long as we count the ballots." Republicans encouraged wavering party members and met threat with threat. Negroes were promised jobs, school children recited carefully prepared catechisms to influence their fathers, the freedman's fear of re-enslavement was played upon, and marked ballots were distributed. In predominantly Negro counties, Republican bosses organized gangs to move from precinct to precinct for repeated voting. White Democrats were threatened with bodily injury, a threat which was occasionally carried out.

Far worse than in Florida was the political situation in South Carolina. After years of corrupt Republican governors, Daniel H. Chamberlain gave the state a reform administration. This native of Massachusetts who had been educated at Harvard and Yale won the respect of low-country Democrats and they favored him as a coalition candidate. Up-country Democrats with their burning passion for white supremacy would have no dealing with a Carpetbag Republican; nor would they support a Negro-backed candidate. In consequence the Democrats nominated Wade Hampton, a planter and former Confederate general, to oppose Chamberlain. Shrewd Carolina Democrats hid their white-supremacy purpose by expressing their determination to protect the freedman. They organized Negro Democratic clubs, supported some colored officeseekers, and declared their whole-hearted approval of the three postwar amendments.

The overwhelming majority of Negroes, however, foretold Democratic defeat; without effective intimidation of Republican voters, Chamberlain would be victorious. The apparent hopelessness of their cause was the main reason why low-country Democrats advocated coalition with an honest Republican, but the Carolina white supremacists gave fainthearted conservatives a lesson by demonstrating the effectiveness of intimidation. Using the "shot-gun system," Edgefield Plan, rifle clubs, or Hampton's Red Shirts, the whites displayed arms to "protect themselves" from "radical tyranny" and marched or rode in military formation in an impressive show of strength. Some Republican meetings were broken up by the Red Shirts and others by planting hecklers in the audience. Negro houses and crops were burned. Threats of death and actual beatings forced many Negro Republicans to forswear political activity and then, in turn, deny that they had been threatened. Again and again the Democrats promised to protect Negro rights but demanded that he vote for Hampton or not vote at all.

Wary of northern opinion, the white people attempted a campaign of "force without violence." The Negro State Militia at Hamburg paraded on July 4 in a counter-demonstration of military power. Some of the Negroes were arrested on charges of blocking traffic. When their trials were postponed, hundreds of armed white men infiltrated the small South Carolina town. A former Confederate general ordered the Negro militiamen to apologize and give up their arms. Their "insubordinate refusal" triggered the Hamburg Riot in which an undetermined number of Negroes were shot, five of whom were murdered after laying down their arms. More than two months later from 15 to 150 Negroes were killed in the Ellenton Riot.

President Grant correctly described the Hamburg killings as "cruel, bloodthirsty, wanton, unprovoked, and uncalled for," but he hedged in response to Governor Chamberlain's request for federal troops. The continuation of disorders forced action by the President who, on October 17, proclaimed a state of insurrection in certain South Carolina counties and ordered all persons implicated to disperse within three days. Even independent northern newspaper editors praised the President for an action necessitated by the behavior of both factions in Carolina. In Columbia, the headquarters of the federal forces, the white supremacists curtailed their activities, but mocked the presidential order by reorganizing their company as "the Hampton and Tilden Musical Club" with musicians accomplished at playing twelve four-pounder "flutes."

The presidential order and troops stilled what may have developed into statewide racial warfare. In most counties, however, the Red Shirts continued to ride; at their meetings Republicans were branded as liars, thieves, and rascals; and Negro voters were frightened into subservience.

In Louisiana mutually antagonistic and dishonest Republicans faced aroused Democrats. Shortly after winning the governorship in 1868, Illinois Carpetbagger Henry C. Warmoth broke with the Custom House Ring, the gang of grafters with lines leading to the White House. Preferring cooperation with white conservatives to making terms with the Ring, Warmoth supported the Conservative-Democrat, John McEnery, in 1872 against William P. Kellogg. The weight of evidence supports McEnery's claim to victory by a comfortable majority, but federal marshal Stephen B. Packard, aided by a corrupt federal judge and the army of occupation, secured the governorship for Kellogg and the impeachment of Warmoth. For the remainder of Warmoth's forty-three-day term, Lieutenant Governor Pinckney B. S. Pinchback, a former Negro officer in the army, served as governor. Kellogg and McEnery set up rival governments backed by rival Republican and Democratic legislatures. As a consequence, civil war raged in some Louisiana communities. In 1873 almost sixty Negroes and two whites were killed at Colfax, and in the following year riots at Coushatta and New Orleans took many lives. Victory in the 1874 election was claimed by both sides and powerful White Leagues sprang up throughout the state to aid the conservatives.

After deliberating, Grant supported the Kellogg government and gave General Sheridan extraordinary powers as military commander. Unable to control the white organizations, Sheridan requested authority to brand their members bandits and inflict summary punishment upon them. The harsh implications of this request brought on a congressional investigation. William A. Wheeler of the investigating committee arranged a compromise whereby Kellogg was to be left undisturbed in the governorship until the expiration of his term in 1877 and the Democrats were given control of the state house of representatives.

In 1876 the Democrats ran Francis Riddin T. Nicholls against Republican Packard. Force without violence were the watchwords of the Democrats and the Louisiana campaign was fairly peaceful. The crusade for white supremacy possessed an excellent symbol in Nicholls, who had lost an eye, arm, and leg in Confederate service.

The National Campaign

Tainted with corruption and battered by the elections of 1874, the Republicans assembled in convention at Cincinnati on June 14, 1876. A majority of the delegates represented northern political machines and southern Republican organizations. These spoilsmen had no interest in selecting a liberal independent for candidate. Richard H. Dana headed the reform faction which nominated former Secretary of the Treasury Benjamin H. Bristow. Grant might have done his party a service by insisting on Hamilton Fish but the President did nothing and Fish inspired few spoilsmen or reformers. Roscoe Conkling possessed little support other than that of his large New York delegation. In addition to his Indiana machine, Olvier P. Morton controlled a considerable number of southern delegates. Simon Cameron was ready to shift his powerful Pennsylvania delegation to the political candidate who would make him the best offer. The favorite, however, was James G. Blaine of Maine who was nominated by the noted orator and professed atheist Robert Ingersoll. He described Blaine as a "plumed knight" who had thrown "his shivering lance full and fair against the brazen forehead of every traitor to his country."

Speaker of the House from 1869 to 1875, Blaine had endeared himself to western Republicans by adroitly waving the bloody shirt. To counter rumors of graft involving leading Republican politicans, he had temporarily relinquished his speakership to move for a thorough investigation but was later accused of being a grafter. In the spring of 1876 a Democratic House investigating committee charged him with using his position as speaker to obtain a liberal land grant for the Fort Smith and Little Rock Railroad and making personal profit from the deal. Blaine denied the accusation and denounced the investigation as a plot of former Copperheads and rebels. James Mulligan brought incriminating letters written by Blaine to Warren Fisher, Jr., a promoter from Boston. By outwitting the rather stupid Mulligan, the speaker obtained the "Mulligan Letters." His refusal either to return the letters or to allow the investigating committee to see them hurt Blaine's reputation. One day in the House he read carefully selected passages from the letters, pausing after each quotation to make dramatic explanations of his written words. His effective presentation pictured a patriotic, devoted father working to provide for his family and being persecuted by traitors and grafting politicians. Publication of the excerpts in the *Congressional Record* was sufficiently damaging to make Blaine unacceptable to reformers. A second handicap to his nomination was the determined opposition of the spoilsmen led by Conkling.

Nevertheless, Blaine's 285 votes on the first ballot placed him within

striking distance of the nomination. Five additional roll calls were inde-
cisive: the political machines of Cameron, Conkling, and Morton continued to hold firm against Blaine, and the reform delegates refused to vote
for a man associated with dishonest deals and the champion of continued
Congressional Reconstruction of the South. The stalemate convinced the
politicians and the reformers of the impossibility of securing the nomination for one of their respective favorites. On the first ballot Rutherford B.
Hayes, a former Union general and reform governor of Ohio, had received
61 votes. In subsequent balloting, the Ohio delegation held firm for him
and he picked up some other support. His record of party regularity commended him to politicians and his public honesty endeared him to liberals.
On the seventh ballot, spoilsman and reformer joined forces to give Hayes
the nomination by a vote of 384 to Blaine's 351. Whatever his opponents'
opinion of him, Blaine was a loyal Republican; on his demand, the delegates cast a unanimous ballot for Hayes. William A. Wheeler of New
York, author of the Wheeler Compromise for Louisiana, won second place
on the ticket.

Optimistic Democrats convened at St. Louis on July 2. Convivial
delegates explained the nomination of Hayes: the Republicans discovered
one honest man in their party and selected him. A campaign keyed to honesty and reform appealed to the delegates. Passing over former leader
Horatio Seymour and Winfield S. Hancock, hero of the Battle of Gettysburg, the Democrats needed only two roll calls to nominate Samuel J.
Tilden. A somewhat colorless corporation lawyer considered safe by big
business, Tilden's action in destroying the notorious Tweed Ring had won
him the governorship of New York in 1874. He further enhanced his reputation for reform by giving the state an honest administration and by
breaking up the corrupt Canal Ring. Although not enthusiastic about the
former Tammany official, southern delegates pointed to Tilden's disapproval of the Civil War and his sympathy for the defeated South. To
placate western demands for inflation and counter the hard-money policies
of Tilden, the Democrats selected Thomas A. Hendricks of Indiana, a
leader of the inflationist wing, for the vice presidency.

Both party platforms attested to the political dominance of big business.
The Republicans promised redemption of all greenbacks and the resumption of specie payments while the Democrats pledged full payment of the
national debt in specie. The latter's meaningless provision on the tariff indicated no legislative fight against the Republican guarantee of a high tariff
for the protection of American labor. The Republicans thanked Grant for
his great service in war and peace and assured the nation that the Negro
would be protected by strict enforcement of the reconstruction amendments. Coupled with promises of reform and honesty were Democratic

denunciations of the graft and corruption of national and southern state Republican regimes.

In his letter accepting the nomination, Hayes warmly espoused reform of the civil service, promised Southerners the right to govern themselves without federal interference, and declared himself opposed to more than one term in office. All these statements hit so directly at Grant that Hayes felt compelled to explain their purpose as an attempt to unite all factions of the party, not to criticize the President. Nevertheless, the solid backing of Hayes by Grant's critics and independent editors disturbed the chief executive. The speeches of Carl Schurz contained sharp denunciations of "Grantism"; the liberal press extolled Hayes as the antithesis of Grant; former Secretary Bristow joined others in demanding honesty in public office; and on November 2, *The Nation* commended the Republicans for breaking with "the peculiar system of administration called Grantism. . . ." In vain the Republican National Committee attempted to tone down the criticism of some speakers and Grant's *National Republican* denounced anti-Grant utterances, but the voices of conscientious Republicans were not stilled. Though harboring resentment, Grant remained faithful to the party. He hit at his detractors by dismissing the reformers placed in the treasury department by Bristow and in public warmly supported the candidacy of Hayes. In the close election of 1876 his silence might have given victory to Tilden.

The Republican campaign was unique. In New York Alonzo B. Cornell rebuked the Union League for its "imprudence" in passing resolutions calling for the election of honest public servants and worked industriously to elect a reformer. Although disliking Hayes, the spoilsmen or stalwart Republicans swung behind him. To maintain their rank in the Republican party, Blaine, Boutwell, Cameron, and Morton took the stump for Hayes. Even the reluctant Conkling recovered sufficiently from imaginary ills to make speeches for the Republican candidate. Belatedly, these machine stalwarts realized that victory in November would almost obliterate past misdeeds and give them influence with the new administration.

News of the identification and retention of Boss Tweed in Spain gave Republicans hope of puncturing the reformist balloon of Tilden. Informed men knew that the New York governor had co-operated with Tammany Hall until public opinion turned against the organization. Then Tilden made his reputation as a reformer by amassing evidence against Tweed. The extradition of Tweed might result in his casting aspersions on the white knight of the Democratic party, but Tweed was not sent to the United States until after the November elections.

Blaine took the stump to reiterate his condemnation of Copperheads and rebels. Waving the bloody shirt anew, he told veterans to "vote as they shot." The election of Tilden, he stated, would restore Southerners to political power and win the peace for those who had mistreated patriots. His speeches and those who repeated his messages persuaded many wavering Republicans to overlook the corruption of the Grant regime and vote for the party of Unionism.

Democrats countered by advocating national harmony and dwelling on the failure of Congressional Reconstruction in the South. They emphasized the American heritage of local self-government, detailed the graft of Carpetbagger and Scalawag in the South, and proclaimed the loyalty of chastised Southerners. Unfortunately for the Democratic cause, riots in the South, especially the killing of Negroes in South Carolina, made many Northerners fear that southern whites were determined to keep the freedmen in subjection. Some Republican newspaper editors found their readers still responsive to reports of southern outrages, but the columns devoted to the South were fewer than in prior campaigns. Democrats concentrated on comparing the honesty of their candidates to the grafters of the Grant regime. Republicans lauded the record of Hayes and reiterated their party's contributions to the country. Long before the voting, advocates of both parties resorted to mud-slinging and vile accusations; however, neither Hayes nor Tilden participated in dirty political activities.

On election night, November 7, *New-York Tribune* editors studied the returns for direction in composing a morning headline proclaiming the election of Tilden. But the *Tribune*'s city rival, and ardent Republican organ, hedged in its first edition and suggested victory for Hayes in the second. The story of a *Times* editor persuading Zack Chandler to issue a victory statement has been told again and again. In reality the chairman of the Republican National Committee needed no urging. On November 5, Governor Kellogg of Louisiana had written Chandler about the Democratic intimidation of Negro voters. In a close election with the slightest possibility for Republican success, the party command was prepared to claim fraud and contest all questionable returns.

Complete returns gave Tilden 4,284,020 popular votes to 4,036,572 for Hayes, a majority of almost 250,000 votes. Even counting the 81,737 ballots for Greenback candidate Peter Cooper and the 9522 of Green Clay Smith, the prohibition nominee, Tilden amassed 155,189 more votes than the total of his opponents. Republicans admitted his majority of votes but raised two questions: how many voters were kept away from the polls by intimidation and how many illegally cast votes had been counted? But they wasted little time in needless debate, for electoral, not popular, votes determined the winner. Of the 369 total electoral college votes, Hayes was in undisputed possession of 165 and Tilden of 184. By obtaining all the 20 in dispute, Hayes would win the presidency by the margin of a single vote.

In reality 166 Republican electors had won clear-cut victories. Oregon's three Hayes electors received approximately 1000 more votes than their Democratic opponents. But one successful Oregon elector was a postmaster and, therefore, constitutionally disqualified from serving in the Electoral College. The state's Democratic governor appointed a Democrat to replace the ineligible Republican elector, and two sets of returns were sent in from Oregon: one with three votes for Hayes and the other with two for him and one for Tilden. No Republican and few Democrats considered the obviously Republican vote of Oregon a legitimate point for argument. The key states were Florida with four electoral votes, Louisiana with eight, and South Carolina with seven. Had these states been "redeemed" prior to the 1876 election, as had the eight other former Confederate commonwealths which gave overwhelming majorities to Tilden, there would have been no contested election. The Democrats of Florida, Louisiana, and South Carolina used tactics similar to their sister states to hold down the Negro vote and obtain the maximum vote from white supremacists. The only difference was Republican power to count and certify the election returns.

Immediately after the returns, "visiting statesmen" of both parties entrained for Florida, Louisiana, and South Carolina to see that an "honest" count was made. In Florida irregularities had occurred in only 14 precincts. The Republican canvassing board threw out returns from a few precincts where intimidation was obvious or the recorded vote totaled more than the number of registrants. As a result, the official Republican return gave four electoral votes to Hayes and certified Marcellus Stearns as governor. Without question the Democrats had secured majorities in both houses of the state legislature. The Democrats demanded a recount of the votes. Despite the Republican claim that the canvassing board's existence terminated with its original work, a Republican state supreme court ordered a recanvass. The second tabulation gave Democratic candidate George F. Drew a small majority of the votes.

Governor Stearns made a rash promise to his supporters. Under no circumstances would he surrender his office to Drew. As inauguration day approached and the armed white Conservatives outnumbered the combined Negro and white armed backers of Stearns, the governor's determination to retain his office weakened. On January 7, 1877, in the "peaceful surroundings" of white-manned guns pointing from buildings near the capitol, Drew took the oath of office and Florida joined the other redeemed former Confederate states. Nevertheless, returns of the state's four electoral votes had been forwarded to the United States Senate, one set for Hayes, and the other for Tilden.

In South Carolina stuffing of ballot boxes resulted in considerably more

THE DISPUTED ELECTION OF 1876

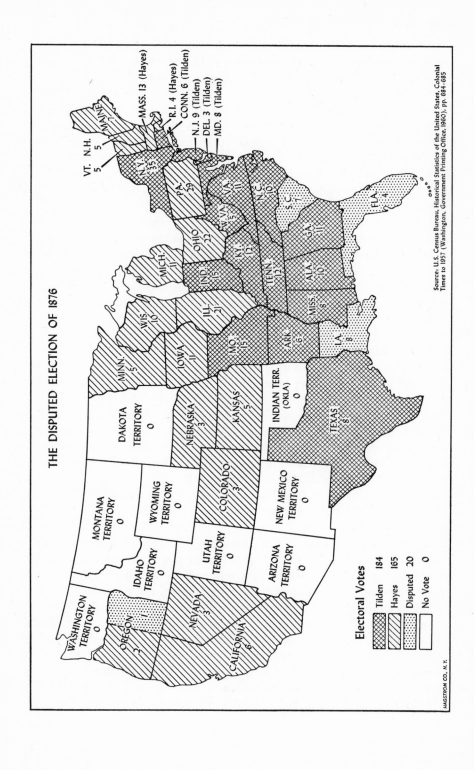

VT. N.H. MASS. 13 (Hayes)
5   5   R.I. 4 (Hayes)
        CONN. 6 (Tilden)
        N.J. 9 (Tilden)
        DEL. 3 (Tilden)
        MD. 8 (Tilden)

Electoral Votes

	Tilden	184
	Hayes	165
	Disputed	20
	No Vote	0

Source: U.S. Census Bureau, Historical Statistics of the United States, Colonial
Times to 1957 (Washington, Government Printing Office, 1960), pp. 684–685

HAGSTROM CO., N.Y.

votes than the number of registrants in many precincts. On the face of the returns, Wade Hampton, a Democratic house and senate, and Tilden electors were all victorious. The Republican canvassing board, however, certified the election of Hayes electors. Both Hampton and Chamberlain were inaugurated as the state's governor with legislatures supporting each of the contenders, and federal forces protecting the Republican claimant. Like Florida, South Carolina sent two sets of electoral returns to the Senate.

The Democratic electors of Louisiana had majorities ranging from a low of 6000 to a high of 9000 votes. Basing their decision on the illegal activities of the White Leagues, other intimidation of voters, the thousands of fraudulent votes, and the preponderance of Negro registrants in counties which returned Democratic majorities, the state canvassing board threw out returns and certified the eight Hayes electors.

The actual results of the 1876 elections in the three states will never be known. If the people had enjoyed free exercise of the franchise in Florida, Louisiana, and South Carolina and honest counting of the returns, the Hayes electors and the Republican governors would have been elected. Acceptance of the returns without question would have given victory to the Tilden electors and the Democratic governors. By eliminating the illegal ballots and assuming that intimidation by Democrats and Republicans was an offsetting factor, the Republicans would have won in Louisiana and South Carolina and the Democrats in Florida. The last possibility would have given Tilden 4 of the 19 votes in question and elected him by an electoral vote of 188 to 181 for Hayes. Certainly the electoral votes of the three states did not belong to Hayes while a majority of the other votes went to the Democratic gubernatorial candidates. Without doubt every possible influence was brought to bear on Republican canvassing boards and direct or implied offers of jobs were given board members. The "visiting Democratic statesmen" were equally willing to bribe members of the boards. The fundamental difference between the representatives of the parties lay in the fact that Republicans had more money and more jobs to offer. The Republican canvassing board members who supported the party line were later rewarded with federal jobs.

The Compromises of 1877

The ultimate decision in the unique election was left to the Congress. The Constitution outlined no means of determining valid electoral returns from a state. The Constitution provided in Clause 2, Section 1 of Article II that: "The President of the Senate shall, in the Presence of the Senate and House of Representatives, open all Certificates, and the Votes shall then be counted." If no candidate had a majority of the electoral votes, "then from the five highest [changed to three highest by the Twelfth Amendment] on the List the said House shall" elect a President with the delegation of each state having one vote. This provision of the Constitution had been resorted to in 1824 when John Quincy Adams won the presidency by a state-by-state vote in the House. Three years before, in the sectional controversy over Missouri, the president of the Senate had declared James Monroe re-elected by a vote of 231, if the Missouri electoral votes were counted, and by 229 if they were disregarded. The overwhelming electoral vote for Monroe made this equivocal decision meaningless. During the Civil War and the first years of the Reconstruction era, votes from a few southern states were not recorded. In 1872 the Senate refused to count three votes cast by electors to honor the memory of Horace Greeley.

In none of these instances had there been a question of choosing between two sets of returns from a state. One possible solution for this problem was joint action by the Senate and House. After the Civil War, Congress had passed the twenty-second joint rule which gave each legislative chamber the right to reject any disputed electoral votes. Had this rule been in force, the House would have thrown out the Republican returns from Florida, Louisiana, and South Carolina, and declared that neither candidate had a majority of the electoral votes. This action would have thrown the decision to the House resulting in the election of Tilden, but the rule had been withdrawn by the Senate. In consequence there was no statutory or constitutional provision for determining the valid return between two sets of electoral votes from a state. The moot question was whether the Senate could investigate a state election or go behind the official return to determine the accurate report. On their face, the Republican electoral votes in question had the stamp of approval by legal boards. Southerners found themselves in a dilemma. To advocate congressional rejection of a state's action contravened southern ideas of state rights, but the acceptance of official returns would give victory to Hayes.

Action awaited convening the final session of the Forty-Fourth Congress in December 1876. Meanwhile, rumors of armed resistance to a declaration for Hayes and of potential civil war in Louisiana and South Carolina worried the Grant administration. Discussion at the first cabinet meeting following the November elections centered on precautionary action to prevent violence and rioting. According to Secretary Fish, former Confederate cavalryman John S. Mosby had been forced to flee from arrest by Virginia officials because he had prevented a Democrat from assaulting a Negro at the polls. Mosby, who coined the "Solid South" phrase and was considered a renegade by Virginia conservatives, thought "the language of the Democrats now was more desperate and more threatening and violent than that of Southern men on the election of Lincoln in 1860." He reported talk of assassination with Grant the first target.

Republican victory and southern defeat, the twin desires of Zack Chandler, could be attained by federal interference in Florida, Louisiana, and South Carolina. Supporting him were Secretary of the Navy Robeson, James D. Cameron, the heir apparent to his father's Pennsylvania political machine and secretary of war, and the portly Attorney General Alfonso Taft. Letters from William Eaton Chandler, who was in Florida directing Republican tactics in the South, emphasized the necessity for federal action. In South Carolina rifle companies planned to march on Columbia to insure the inauguration of Wade Hampton and the installation of a Democratic legislature. To prevent violence, the President directed Cameron to support Governor Chamberlain and the secretary of war ordered federal troops concentrated at Columbia.

The army occupied the state house. On November 28, rival delegations from Edgefield and Laurens counties arrived. The military officers admitted the Republican legislators and the party proceeded to organize a legislature with a quorum but not a majority of the elected assemblymen, whereupon the Democrats gathered at Assembly Hall to organize and elect their house speaker and clerk. Governor Chamberlain requested federal aid to disperse the Democratic contenders. In Washington, Hamilton Fish objected in cabinet meeting to the use of federal troops for any purpose other than to prevent violence. Despite pressure and appeal, Grant decided to let the Republicans and Democrats in South Carolina "worry it out" in a grim deadlock. The presence of the army, however, prevented the Hampton adherents from taking control of the state government.

Grant consulted his cabinet before putting the final touches on an annual message to be sent to Congress convening amidst the rumors of possible civil war. The President feared the baneful effects of a return for Hayes from a Louisiana canvassing board, the reputation of whose members would deprive it of any claim to fairness. Secretary Fish advised using cautious phrases while the anti-southern cabinet members urged vigorous condemnation of the discrimination against Negro voters in the three southern states. Prior to the cabinet discussion Grant had promised Abram S. Hewitt, Democratic national chairman, that federal troops would not be used to give victory to Hayes electors or Republican claimants to governorships in the South. The only justification for exercising military power, the President told Hewitt, was to preserve order. In his annual message, Grant refrained from condemning anyone and suggested no more than congressional action to prevent irregularities in counting future electoral returns.

His decision bore the mark of statesmanship. The presence of army regulars in Louisiana and South Carolina prevented bloodshed and left solution of a political situation to compromise.

When Congress convened in December, astute Republicans discerned a difference between the attitude of northern and southern Democrats. The main purpose of the former was the inauguration of Tilden. Hewitt warned that stealing the election would bring to arms Democratic veterans in the northern states. Hewitt viewed the contemporary scene and feared civil war, and historian Paul L. Haworth, appraising the crisis with perspective, concluded that more Americans dreaded bloodshed in 1877 than in 1861. Southern Democrats, however, longed more for state rule by white conservatives and financial aid to develop their region than occupancy of the White House by Tilden.

Writing to Hayes on December 12, James A. Garfield suggested that overtures be made immediately to former Whigs within the southern Democratic organizations. Even before the date of Garfield's letter, unsuccessful attempts to get southern leaders in conference with Hayes had stimulated analysis of the Democratic party in the South. In the two decades since the demise of the Whigs as a national party, most Northerners had either forgotten or had never known that the South was historically a two-party region. Strongholds of both the Federalist and Whig parties had existed in the southern states, and prior to 1856 division of political power between Democrats and Whigs had been almost equal. After the disintegration of the Whig party, hundreds of thousands of Southerners who could not bring themselves to unite with an old political enemy cast votes for American or Constitutional Union party candidates.

Regional patriotism during the Civil War had united most white Southerners in what would have been a temporary union had it not been for Congressional Reconstruction. The white supremacy issue had produced a crazy-quilt organization in the South. At first these champions of the master white race found "conservative" the most satisfactory name to describe a party organization composed of former secessionists and unionists, former Democrats and Whigs, and even repentant Carpetbaggers and Scalawags. Eventually these men with diverse political philosophies and without a common denominator, other than a determination to maintain white supremacy, accepted the Democratic label for their party. In later years, historians called them "Bourbons," an inaccurate label; "Redeemers," to designate their success in overthrowing Republican state governments; and "New Departure Democrats," a name which implied continuity and change.

But no historian has coined a title to describe accurately southern political organizations called "Conservative-Democrats" or "Business-Democrats." The party was composed of whites formerly associated with many parties and for a time it also included some Negroes. It favored big business while appealing to farmers for votes, it demanded federal aid in one sentence and in another proclaimed its adherence to state rights; it allowed the Negro to vote as long as it controlled and used his vote for the white man's purposes. The ideal front man of the new order had roots in the Old South, a record of service in the Confederate army or government, and a penchant for accusing Northerners of impoverishing the South. His craving for the material well-being made him jump when businessmen, who often remained behind the political scene, pulled strings. In the process these southern Democrats imitated and surpassed the dishonesty of former Republican regimes in counting election returns and obtaining personal gain from public office. They eagerly voted valuable franchises or natural resources to promoters and corporations and refrained from saddling "free enterprise" with restrictive regulations.

In the political power structure the businessman was dominant, but the politician had to have votes to place him in a position to further the interests of business. Essential, therefore, was some means to satisfy the mass of white southern voters. While government jobs and federal financing of internal improvements, railroads and industry, interested influential people, home rule for the South had virtually a universal appeal to white Southerners. By using the disputed election controversy to end the remaining Republican governments in the South and to obtain firm promises of the withdrawal of federal troops, the southern politician could endear himself to the mass of voters. The attitude of Hayes encouraged both southern and northern compromises. During the campaign he had not waved the bloody shirt and afterwards he expressed confidence in the fair play of white Southerners. His statements almost paraphrased those of southern conservatives; namely, the Negro deserved justice and the enjoyment of citizenship but he could best secure these by trusting the honorable and influential southern whites. By offering no more than token opposition to his claim, Southerners would place Hayes in their debt. Gratitude would bolster his intention to end federal interference with state and local governments in the South. Southern advocates of home rule and northern supporters of Hayes quickly saw that this compromise was basic to peaceful solution of the election controversy.

This interpretation reaffirms old explanations and de-emphasizes the revisionist ideas of C. Vann Woodward. Many factors minimize the importance of the home rule-troop removal compromise; Hayes's sympathy for the South was well-known; with their control of the House, Democrats could have cut off appropriations for an army used in part to intimidate conservative whites; and two months before the inauguration of Hayes,

Florida Democrats won over their Republican opponents. Therefore, by supporting Hayes the southern politicians won nothing; home rule and troop removal were theirs without compromise.

These statements, however, stand on certain hypotheses and ignore some political realities. Although white Floridians inaugurated their governor, the presence of a small occupational force was a constant danger to politicians who had to rely on intimidation of Negro voters to win future elections. While Hayes was sympathetic toward white Southerners, his attitude did not guarantee removal of troops. Like Presidents before him, he would be subject to pressures from politicians who still demanded federal protection of Negroes. Definite assurance was a necessity to southern politicians who yearned for credit. Placing a Southerner in the cabinet, building a levee along the Mississippi River, or getting a railroad in the Southwest would win plaudits from relatively few people compared with the near universal appeal of home rule and troop removal.

The argument that the House could force Hayes to remove troops cannot withstand careful examination. Among its assumptions are virtual unity of House Democrats, indefinite withholding of all army appropriations for a purpose not considered essential by a majority of northern congressmen, and the inability of the President to command loyalty of unpaid troops. The house inserted a clause in the pending appropriations bill prohibiting the use of federal funds to pay salaries of the forces of occupation, the Senate deleted the provision, and the House then refused to provide any money for the army. This lack of action did not disband the army or remove troops from the South. A continued stalemate might have resulted in overwhelming Republican or Democratic victory in the elections of 1878, but one must keep in mind that corruption and depression of the Grant regime did not prevent the Republicans from gaining 31 House seats in the 1876 election which left the Democrats with a majority of only 13. On the other hand, the same election reduced the Republican majority in the Senate to three. The appeal of the bloody shirt to Northerners cannot be ignored. Southerners needed assurance of troop removal and home rule by white Democrats.

This home rule-troop removal was considered essential by leaders of both parties before Congress authorized a commission to settle the election controversy. The well-known Wormley House bargain confirmed old ideas instead of producing new ones. By the bargain, representatives of Hayes— James A. Garfield, John Sherman, Stanley Matthews, and Charles Foster —promised Henry Watterson, Benjamin Harvey Hill, John B. Gordon, Lucius Q. C. Lamar, and other Southerners that Hayes would remove federal troops from the South in return for southern acceptance of Hayes. Although the Republican contender was not a direct party to the bargain, the Southerners had confidence in his spokesmen. Watterson, editor of the influential Louisville *Courier-Journal*, who had on January 8, 1877, called for 100,000 Democrats to march on Washington to ensure the inauguration of Tilden, now advised Southerners to accept Hayes. Southern politicians had their great desire, the removal of federal troops and state and local rule by white people with a promise of non-intervention by the central government.

During this period of accommodation, the anti-southern cabinet cabal continued to work on Grant. On January 2 and 7, the President reported applications from Governor Kellogg of Louisiana for troops. Despite the objections of Secretary Cameron, Grant refused to act until clear evidence of violence in the southern states forced action to keep the peace. He hoped that Hayes would be his successor but considered untenable the Republican claim that the power to count electoral returns resided with the president of the Senate.

The President conferred with the representatives to persuade them to establish an electoral commission. The bill for this purpose proposed a 15-member commission to review conflicting returns from all states and to determine "the true and lawful electoral vote" of each state. After the bill passed the House on January 26, Grant expressed his delight with the sizeable majority vote it had received. Senate Republicans, however, objected to what was considered a Democratic victory. Defection from the party by Senator Conkling and other spoilsmen who did not approve of the reformist utterances of Hayes sped the bill through the Senate. In signing the bill on January 29, the President sent Congress a well-written state paper in which he praised the legislators and called for "peace and quiet and harmony between all parties and all sections."

The Electoral Commission Act ordered the appointment of 15 men, 5 each from the Senate, House, and Supreme Court. Three Republicans from the Senate and Three Democrats from the House, plus two others selected from the minor parties of each legislative body, would give both parties equal congressional representation on the committee. Two Democratic and two Republican justices chosen from the Supreme Court were to elect a fifth man from the judicial branch. It was understood that he would be Justice David Davis, an independent; but a combination of Democratic and Greenback senators in Illinois made him a United States senator. The justice with ambitions for the presidency removed himself from a tight situation. The only other justices on the Court were Republican and dissatisfied, but already committed Democrats found it impolitic to reject the selection of Justice Joseph P. Bradley. The contemplated eight-to-seven advantage of the Democrats was reversed in favor of the Republicans.

In accordance with another provision of the Electoral Commission Act, the national legislature met in joint session on February 1, 1877, to count the electoral votes. As expected, no objection was voiced to returns until, in alphabetical order, Florida's three sets of electoral votes were opened. Then congressmen referred the controversy to the commission. A majority of the Democrats maintained that the commissioners had the authority and obligation to investigate the facts and declare the correct return on the bases of its "best legal title" and "moral right." Their party's contention placed southern congressmen in a dilemma. They disliked the idea of the national government going behind or investigating the act of a state—it reminded them of federal interference in the South. For Southerners, the controversy could best be settled by accepting the returns signed by state canvassing boards. This solution would give Hayes the 19 votes of Florida, Louisiana, and South Carolina, but award the presidency to Tilden by allowing him the one Oregon vote and at the same time deny that a federal agency had the right to question the legal act of a state. The Republicans argued that the commission was not empowered to receive any evidence which went behind the official canvassing board returns as certified by a governor. If, for instance, after hearing the evidence relating to Florida, the commissioners found that the Hayes returns of the board, signed by Governor Stearns, complied with the state election laws, they must accept it. Republican and southern ideas diverged with regard to Oregon, where according to the former, the governor acted illegally by naming a Democrat to replace a duly elected but disqualified Republican elector.

The decision of the commission on the Florida return was crucial. The composition of the commission and the partisanship of fourteen of its members were well-known.* Certainly the congressional representatives would follow the policies of their respective parties, and few people thought that Justices Clifford, Field, Miller, or Strong would rise above partisan feeling. Any hope for judicial fairness rested on Joseph P. Bradley. Selection by his four colleagues placed an obligation which must have weighed heavily on him. According to the reminiscences of Democratic campaign chairman Abram S. Hewitt, a close friend of Bradley visited the justice the evening of February 8 and read the judge's decision to count the Democratic return from Florida. The next day, however, Bradley joined the seven other Republicans in voting to accept the Hayes return from Florida.

Based on evidence inadmissible in court, this statement of Hewitt was later used to charge Bradley with succumbing to political pressure. According to the accusation, the justice changed his opinion sometime during the

---

* The commission members were Senate Republicans Edmunds, Frelinghuysen, and Morton; Democrats Bayard and Thurman; House Democrats Abbott, Hunton, and Payne; Republicans Garfield and Hoar; Republican Justices Bradley, Miller, and Strong; Democrats Clifford and Field.

period from midnight to sunrise on February 9. Implied in the charge was an assumption that Thomas A. Scott, president of both the Pennsylvania and the Texas Pacific railroads, had in some way gotten to Bradley. Critics of the justice pointed out a decision of his which favored the Texas Pacific Railroad and claimed that Bradley was Scott's puppet. The charge has neither been proven nor disproven. The weight of evidence, however, indicates that Bradley simply followed his Republican fellows by deciding to render a decision for the Hayes electors of Florida.

That state was the best hope of the Democrats. After the commissioners refused to go behind the returns and by a seven-to-eight vote on February 9 counted Florida in the Republican column, the Republicans anticipated other favorable decisions. By the identical eight-to-seven vote, the Electoral Commission declared the contested returns from Louisiana, South Carolina, and Oregon belonged to Hayes. These decisions, however, did not assure the inauguration of the Republican candidate. The commission concluded its proceedings on February 23, but official counting of the electoral votes by the joint session remained to be done.

With inauguration day less than two weeks away, some Democrats advocated a filibuster to delay or prevent a legal count of the electoral votes. Delay beyond March 4 would at least deny Hayes a legal claim to the presidency; it might arouse slumbering Tilden or develop other possibilities which could benefit the Democrats. But most party leaders had no stomach for this maneuver. Confident of victory, they had agreed to the Electoral Commission and had been caught by the election of David Davis to the Senate. To repudiate the commission's work by a filibuster would arouse the indignation of fair-minded Americans and damage the Democratic party. Although a filibuster would not have prevented the eventual inauguration of Hayes, its nuisance value gave southern Democrats opportunity for sectional gain and forced northern Republicans to make concessions.

To further the home rule-troop removal arrangement, Republicans, even some who had advocated federal support for Packard's government in Louisiana and Chamberlain's in South Carolina, now urged Grant to do nothing. Secretary Fish underscored the policy of inaction by suggesting that interference might embarrass and possibly jeopardize the administration of Hayes. Settlement of the Louisiana and South Carolina controversies, the President told his cabinet, would be left to Hayes. Furthermore, Grant answered an appeal of Packard by declaring that public opinion was opposed to maintaining a government in Louisiana by force and during his remaining days in office he would neither aid nor recognize either of the rival Louisiana governments. Thus by masterly inactivity Grant encouraged the basis of the 1877 compromises.

Southerners used the threat of filibuster to clinch other concessions from Hayes's adherents. Similar to the home rule-troop removal arrangement, other demands had been mulled over long before the Electoral Commission completed its work. Many former Whigs and Unionists in the southern Democratic party disliked the Jacksonian principles of their colleagues. These business Democrats had little in common with ante-bellum farmers; they wanted railroads, manufacturing plants, banks, and internal improvements. Their economic and political philosophies allied them with the former Whigs in the northern wing of the Republican party. Fearing the leveling influence from the excessive democracy of the South's numerous farmers, these businessmen wanted governments controlled by the few and catering to "responsible" property-owners.

The anachronistic political alignments of northern and southern businessmen in the South were obvious. As Professor Woodward has pointed out, the Republican party "of abolitionist radicalism had now become the party of vested interests and big business; the old Whig element was on top, its program had been enacted, and its leader was Rutherford B. Hayes, an ex-Whig and a staunch conservative. Yet in the South the party still appealed for the votes of a propertyless electorate of manumitted slaves with a platform of radical equalitarianism." In the North, former Whigs had wrested control of the Republican party from former Free-Soilers and liberals; in the South, former Whigs had joined with business Democrats to gain ascendency within the Democratic party.

This situation presented a unique opportunity for compromise. In return for acquiescence to Hayes's claim to the presidency, the Southerners demanded appointment of a former southern Whig to the cabinet and a change in Republican attitude toward the South. Instead of relying on the almost propertyless Negro, the party should encourage a lily-white organization which businessmen could support without being condemned by white supremacists. Southerners also indicated their willingness to defect from the Democratic fold, to elect James A. Garfield speaker of the Forty-Fifth Congress, and give the Hayes administration control of both houses.

This arrangement satisfied the political wing of the southern Democratic party, but left the economic realists knocking for recognition. The ruling class of Southerners found themselves strapped after the Civil War. Individually and regionally they needed capital to develop their region's resources and to reward enterprising business leaders. To alleviate his financial distress, the ambitious Southerner demanded federal aid for local projects. There were levees to be raised along the banks of the Mississippi River, streams to be widened and deepened, harbors to be dredged and protected from silting by jetties, and many other local projects to bring employment to laborers and profit to contractors. But Southerners who demanded pork-barrel appropriations for their region found Republicans, whose states and districts had benefited from federal aid, now economy-minded. Federal expenditures, the Republicans claimed, should be curtailed to give businessmen confidence and restore prosperity.

But Southerners desperate for capital and internal improvements demanded their proportional share of federal grants and favorable legislation. One cherished project was completion of the Texas and Pacific Railroad. Backed by northern and southern entrepreneurs, this enterprise was designed to build a southern route to the Pacific Coast, one which would compete with the transcontinental monopoly enjoyed by the Union Pacific and Central Pacific roads. Thomas A. Scott, who had advanced from a station agent on the Pennsylvania Railroad in 1850 to the company's general superintendent in 1858 and vice president two years later, was rewarded for his efficiency in moving troops during the Civil War by appointment as a colonel of volunteers and as the assistant secretary of war in charge of governmental transportation. In 1871 he became president of the politically potent Union Pacific, but resigned a year later to head the Texas and Pacific project. His election to the presidency of the Pennsylvania in 1874 gave him control of the country's most prestigious railroad along with control of the Texas and Pacific enterprise.

The high hopes of Scott for a southern transcontinental railroad were slashed by the 1873 panic. He found European speculators cool toward his bonds and the Granger movement in the United States was detrimental to obtaining federal subsidies to bail him out of his financial difficulties. In conjunction with the knowledgeable lobbyist and construction engineer Grenville M. Dodge, Scott appealed to southern politicians for support.

They could point to claims of about 16 million acres of land granted by the territories of Arizona and New Mexico and the state of California. Subsidiaries of the Texas and Pacific also had land grants from Texas in addition to an appropriation of $6 million in bonds, enactments which the legislature had passed over the veto of the state's Republican governor. To win votes in Congress for a bill to aid their enterprise, Scott and Dodge projected four eastern, or Mississippi River, termini for their railroad. Lines to New Orleans, Vicksburg, Memphis, and a connection to a railroad already serving St. Louis were designed to give landlocked cities of eight states and three territories escape from isolation. Although the proposed branch lines would have more trackage than the trunk line and were economically unsound, their inclusion in the bill would garner votes from interested congressmen. In addition, eastern steel fabricators would envision tremendous sales and southern politicians representing states and districts lying east of the Mississippi would see regional advantages in the new transcontinental railroad.

The two promoters secured press and political endorsement of their project. Forty-two of the most influential newspapers from Virginia to Texas gave them editorial and news support. Even the National Grange admitted the railroad would benefit farmers. Southern chambers of commerce and former Confederate officials, including Jefferson Davis, approved of the southern route to the Pacific. To Southerners, the bill promised the realization of ante-bellum plans to tie the Southwest and the Pacific Coast to the South. The new business Democrats of the South thought federal aid to a southern railroad no more than regional justice to match grants made to northern enterprise.

The opposition to a subsidy by northern Democrats and Republicans was formidable. This situation offered the supporters of Hayes an opportunity to win additional southern congressmen by promising them Republican help in passing the Texas and Pacific bill. As Professor Woodward has lucidly explained, three almost simultaneous developments convinced friends of Hayes that compromise was essential to their candidate's inauguration. In the first place, some Republican congressmen toyed with the idea of abandoning Hayes; secondly, Democratic politicians called for a massive march on Washington in support of Tilden; and finally, the rivalry between the Central Pacific's Collis P. Huntington and Scott for control of and federal subsidy for a southern transcontinental line had been settled to mutual advantage in a conference on December 24, 1876. Following this meeting, Dodge co-ordinated the lobbies of other railroad promoters with those of Huntington and Scott.

On January 24, 1877, L. Q. C. Lamar, chairman of the House Committee on Pacific Railroads, reported the Texas and Pacific bill with a strong endorsement. The proposed legislation asked governmental guarantee of the interest on 50-year, 5-per cent bonds to finance the construction of 1187 miles of main and 1378 miles of branch lines at costs ranging from $30,000 to $40,000 per mile. The yearly interest to be guaranteed by the federal government was $4,473,500. Furthermore, the security offered the government for this pledge was inadequate and the potential profits to promoters and stockholders were tremendous. Northern Democratic and independent publications characterized the bill as a revival of the Crédit Mobilier. The vitriolic attacks made by supporters of Tilden underscored the cleavage between northern Democrats and the business Democrats of the South. These attacks reminded southern Democrats of instances where the Republican-dominated Senate had approved appropriations for southern projects—levees along the Mississippi, reclamation of flooded lands, harbor improvements, and other federal grants—that were killed by committees of the House-controlled Democrats.

The rumor that Justice Bradley had reversed his decision on the Florida electoral vote during the night of February 8 aroused the ire of northern Democrats. In caucuses on February 17 and 19, they demanded united party action on a filibuster to prevent completion of the electoral vote count, but Southerners refused to support their northern party members. In vain Speaker Samuel J. Randall warned southern representatives of the perfidy of Republicans. His prediction that Hayes would keep Republican regimes in southern states by military force failed to convince congressmen to vote for united Democratic action. Failure of the Southerners to support them and fear of adverse public opinion in their own region forced northern Democrats to abandon the filibuster. With Southerners voting almost as a unit, the Democratic caucuses favored completion of the electoral count. The inauguration of Hayes now appeared assured. But an intemperate editorial in the *Ohio State Journal,* a paper edited by a close friend of the Republican candidate, which waved the bloody shirt with vigor and made a vituperative attack on the Democrats of Louisiana, frightened Southerners. Despite Republican repudiation of the untimely editorial, some Southerners demanded and received renewal of the essential home rule-troop removal guarantee in the Wormley House Conference. After obtaining this essential guarantee, southern congressmen offered no real objection to completing the electoral tabulation and the joint session declared Hayes the victor by a vote of 185 to 184.

The overall compromise of 1877 was a series of compromises whereby three groups of Southerners were appeased. The politicos gained promises of more representation in national office along with hope for national party support of a lily-white Republican organization in the South, businessmen won pledges of federal help for internal improvements and capital to develop their region's natural resources, and white Southerners received assurances of home rule and troop removal. Undoubtedly all of these contributed to the settlement of 1877, but assignment of pre-eminent importance to any of them awaits the day when some investigator can determine with accuracy the effect of each idea on the vote of individual southern congressmen. Until that day, the home rule-troop removal compromise remains the essential ingredient of the compromise of 1877, for it was the *sine qua non* of all southern participants in the peaceful solution of a crisis fraught with danger. The compromise ranks in importance with those of 1787, 1820, and 1850. In Latin-American countries such a close contest would have brought civil conflict. Had it not been for fresh memories of the Civil War, the only instance wherein United States citizens rejected compromise, the disputed election may have set brother against brother.

The fact of the compromise belongs to history. The religiously inclined Hayes disliked being officially inaugurated on Sunday, March 4. In a private ceremony at the White House on the evening of that day, Chief Justice Waite administered the oath of office. The following day the new President was inaugurated in the traditional public ceremony in an atmos-phere of quiet and peace. That evening Mrs. Grant presided over her last dinner in the White House. Then she and her husband went to the home of Secretary Fish where they relaxed for a time. The days of the Grant regime were over.

REFERENCES

The Dunning School writers, Davis on Florida, Lonn on Louisiana, and Rey-nolds on South Carolina, already cited, depict conditions in those states and describe the elections. Simkins and Woody, *South Carolina during Reconstruc-tion*, and Caskey, *Secession and Restoration in Louisiana*, also cited; and Henry C. Warmoth, *War, Politics, and Reconstruction: Stormy Days in Louisiana* (New York, 1930); Garnie W. McGinty, *Louisiana Redeemed: The Over-throw of Carpetbag Rule, 1876–1880* (New Orleans, 1941); and Alfred B. Williams, *Hampton and His Red Shirts: South Carolina's Deliverance in 1876* (Charleston, 1935), present good background and election material. Paul L. Haworth, *The Hayes-Tilden Disputed Election* (Indianapolis, 1927), should be used with C. Vann Woodward, *Reunion and Reaction* (Boston, 1951). Pri-mary sources include such government documents as *Electoral Count of 1877* (Washington, 1877), and *House Miscellaneous Documents*, produced by the 44th Congress, 2nd session, and 45th Congress on Florida, Louisiana, and South Carolina. Allan Nevins, *Selected Writings of Abram S. Hewitt* (New York, 1937), favors the Democrats but also goes into Bradley's decision. A. M. Gibson, *A Political Crime* (New York, 1885), condemns the Republicans. Magazines printed articles by participants or contemporary commentators: Mil-ton H. Northrup, "A Grave Crisis in American History," *Century*, LXII (1901), pp. 923–34, was written by the secretary of a congressional committee; G. F. Edmunds, "Another View of the Hayes-Tilden Contest," *ibid.*, LXXXVI (1913), pp. 192–201, is pro-Republican; and H. W. Watterson, "The Hayes-Tilden Contest for the Presidency," *ibid.*, LXXXVI (1913), pp. 3–20, is pro-Democratic. Harry Barnard, *Rutherford B. Hayes and His America* (Indianapo-lis, 1964), and Alexander C. Flick, *Tilden, Samuel Jones: A Study in Political Sagacity* (New York, 1963), are excellent studies. Leon Burr Richardson, *Wil-liam E. Chandler, Republican* (New York, 1940), is sympathetic in describing Chandler's role in the election. E. W. Stroughton, "The Electoral Conspiracy Bubble Exploded," *North American Review*, XXV (1877) points out the posi-tive accomplishments of Carpetbag governments and C. L. Sanders, "The Pres-ident Who Hurt Negroes Most," *Ebony*, XIX (1964), pp. 110–12, indicts the compromise of 1877.

☆ XII ☆
☆

The Completion of Reconstruction

THE INAUGURATION of Hayes ended weeks of promises and brought months of fulfillment. Recalling the prediction of Speaker Randall, Southerners waited for the President to honor the pledges of his friends. Hayes's first cabinet post went to John Sherman of Ohio, but on March 12 one Southerner was among the other six appointees. For postmaster general the President chose David M. Key of Tennessee, former Whig and Confederate army officer, who was finishing the senatorial term of Andrew Johnson. The appointment brought sharp criticism from some Republicans who denounced the selection of a former rebel, but it was lauded by Southerners.

The President also honored another pledge. On April 10 he ordered federal troops from the capitol of South Carolina. Wade Hampton was left in possession of the executive office and Democrats controlled the legislature. Removal of troops stationed in Louisiana on April 24 gave white Southerners headship in every former Confederate state.

In time white solidarity brought practically all Caucasians into the Democratic fold, assuring the party successive political victories. The contradictory Republican policies of welcoming and rebuffing Negroes confused Negro voters, but were less responsible for making the colored man politically inarticulate than Democratic policies of controlling the freedman and eventually denying him the franchise. As a result of eliminating the Negro, the southern Republican party became the organization of political self-seekers. Thus party hacks made a show of activity during presidential campaigns, granted the Democrats victory in state and local elections, and found advantage in a limited Republican membership in the South. As long as the Grand Old Party won national elections, the southern members found personal prestige and economic advantage in distributing federal jobs. Failure of the party to develop a meaningful organization in the South worried few southern businessmen, for they won control of a Democratic party dedicated to their interests.

The other pledges and promises of the 1877 compromise fell by the wayside. In his inaugural address Hayes recommended internal improvements for the South and favored a bill to promote the railroad. Letters from southern business Democrats convinced the President that Republicans could achieve stature in no less than eight former Confederate states. In September, with Governor Hampton, Hayes visited and spoke in the Southeast. In Atlanta he advised Negroes that their rights would be safer and their advancement greater under governments controlled by southern whites than by federal wardship. Leading southern politicians carried the story of a new South to the Northeast. It was a tale of reconciliation, support for business, and unity.

But Congress broke the accord. Reneging on their promise to elect Garfield speaker, southern congressmen helped re-elect Samuel J. Randall and organize the House for the Democrats. These congressmen also frightened a powerful Republican faction by flooding Congress with internal improvement bills. If the cost of sectional alliance was national bankruptcy, northern congressmen decided to forego conciliation. President Hayes widened the breach by casting doubt on the Texas and Pacific project and warning his countrymen against Crédit Mobilier-type operations. The southern compromisers of 1877 received neither federal subsidy for the transcontinental railroad nor significant appropriations for internal improvements.

Other actions sped the breakdown of the eastern-southern alliance. Huntington, having split with Scott, began building a railroad along the southern route without federal aid. Eventually the South got the transcontinental line but by a slower process than would have been possible with governmental largess. Then the southern business Democrat found himself temporarily unable to deliver the congressional votes necessary to give eastern capitalists their desired legislation. After attaining home rule, depression-hit southern farmers turned from "redeemers" to politicians who promised to alleviate economic distress.

Within southern legislatures politicians frightened eastern bankers by repudiating or scaling down state debts. A popular argument for repudiation was the fraud and corruption of southern Republican regimes. Since most of the money received from bond issues went to grafters, the repudiators denied a state's obligation to honor contracts. However, once repudiation gained momentum, bonds of Democratic and Republican governments, as well as pre-reconstruction issues, were scaled down or repudiated. From the point of view of practicality, necessity forced impoverished states to ease overly burdensome debts.

Repudiation sent eastern financiers into a frenzy. Obviously, "responsible" businessmen could not depend on "irresponsible" perpetrators of such acts. Once friendly northern editors and politicians rediscovered a South peopled by rebels unprepared for the enlightened civilization of the North. In response to this criticism Southerners recalled ante-bellum arguments for southern-western unity—the common interests of agrarians, the natural transportation routes of rivers flowing from west to south, and ethnic similarities. In the 1878 elections southern Democrats allied themselves with Westerners to defy the cherished economic interests of eastern businessmen. The Republican party won nothing in southern states courted by a conciliatory President. The "Solid South" became a political reality. Nationally, the Democrats lost four seats in the House while gaining three in the Senate, but the Republicans lost ten places in the lower and three in the upper house. The 14 independents elected to the House, however, usually voted with the Democrats which gave that party valid claim to victory in 1878.

The southern-western marriage terminated in divorce. Realizing their mistake, northern conservatives abandoned economic argument and returned to moral principle. By rejecting conciliation and waving the bloody shirt, party leaders successfully wooed Westerners, who had always responded to indicting Southerners for defending slavery, instigating civil war, and mistreating prisoners of war. This political strategy of big business left Southerners one of two choices—isolation or union with northern economic royalists. In many "I-told-you-so" speeches and editorials, southern compromisers of 1877 declared the only route to economic survival lay in following eastern businessmen.

Southerners in 1880 lined up behind a national Democratic platform which businessmen found acceptable. The elections of that year brought victory to the Republican presidential nominee and most of the Republican candidates for the House. In the following presidential elections the southern business Democrat made his region a stronghold for economic principles acceptable to big business. As C. Vann Woodward described the situation: "It took a lot of hallowing and heading off by the conservative leaders to keep the mass of Southerners herded [into the conservative fold, for] agrarian mavericks were eternally taking off [from the corral gates, but] New-South propagandists . . . by frequent resort to repressive or demagogic device [kept] the South fairly faithful to the Eastern alignment—until the advent of the Populists." The southern partner of the eastern-southern alliance were Democrats, not Republicans, but the results were the same—two national parties supporting big businessmen in their demand for political headship in a country moving from an agrarian to an industrial economy.

Reconstruction, Southern Style

No interpretation of American history is more inaccurate than the idea which sees the end of the Reconstruction era in the removal of federal troops from Louisiana and South Carolina. The presidential, congressional, and conservative-white phases of reconstruction have been studied and re-studied by biased and impartial historians. These investigators have accepted the 1877 date as the termination of reconstruction and have labeled the subsequent decades as the era of the New South. In reality, some undeterminable day during the years from 1868 to 1877 marks the beginning of the fourth and final phase of reconstruction—that phase which ended in Southerners' winning a portion of the peace. Pinpointing the exact date is impossible, for southern-style reconstruction began in the 11 states at different times.

The central theme was state and local rule by white men. The fundamental issue in the South was neither allowing a controlled Negro vote nor disfranchising the Negro. The fourth phase of reconstruction was primarily a movement to place the Negro in an inferior position—politically, economically, and socially. It substituted a caste system for slavery. In the process of accomplishing this end, white Southerners successfully negated the Fourteenth and Fifteenth amendments. Those Negroes who broke, or were accused of breaking, state and local laws found themselves sentenced by venal judges to months and years of servitude. Blinded by racial bias, judges and courts authorized peonage, instituting a modified form of slavery for a minority of Negroes despite the Thirteenth Amendment.

Most impoverished Southerners had no part in exploiting the Negro. They arose early to till their acres and remained in the fields until twilight. The men, helped by their wives and children, eked out a living from worn-out land. Their food was common, their clothes threadbare, and their enjoyments few; but they existed, hoping for a better day without exploiting their more destitute Negro neighbors. There were some, however, who rang the work-bell at dawn, cracked the whip, and juggled accounts to give themselves a maximum return and their Negro laborers a minimal wage. Other Southerners obtained contracts for Negro convicts, and either worked or leased them for profit.

The common principle of all these whites—sharecropper, tenant, small farmer, honest planter, exploiter of the Negro, banker, industrialist—was white supremacy. To them, government and laws, police officers and courts were tools to guarantee white domination. If need be, on the pretext of protecting southern womanhood, lower-class whites, supported by the silence of their affluent white compatriots, resorted to beatings or lynchings to keep the Negro in his place. White owners of property used their economic power to regulate the Negro laborer.

The caste system was not established quickly or with ease. For a decade or more after a southern state was redeemed, Negro citizens continued to vote and to win seats in the state legislature. As described, during the Reconstruction era the freedmen worshipped in their own churches, and in most states their children attended segregated schools, but national laws allowed colored citizens the unsegregated use of railroads, restaurants, and hotels. This social contact between Negro and white was well-known in the ante-bellum South; but in that bygone age, the Negro always shared white society as servants of the master class. In the new order, the freedman sat in a railroad coach or ate at a restaurant as an equal. Social equality in public places galled the southern white and reminded him of Congressional Reconstruction.

The first step toward segregation was absolute political control of state and local governments. For more than a decade whites controlled many Negro voters by cash payment and economic or physical intimidation. Monetary or economic rewards were the tools of the upper class whose members privately but not publicly condemned force as a method of control. Realistic conservatives feared any activity that would arouse Northerners, but they also refrained from breaking white unity by denouncing those of their race who resorted to beatings and lynchings.

The business Democrat preferred legal devices to force in negating majority rule. They created "safe" election districts by slicing Negro-dominated areas and joining each piece to predominately white areas. This old device of gerrymandering had been refined by Republican regimes in the South. The Democrats also adapted the Republican method of controlling counties with conservative white or Negro majorities. In Florida the Republicans had given the governor power to appoint every county official except constables. This scheme enabled the Republicans to select Republican sheriffs, tax collectors, judges, and commissioners for counties peopled by white conservatives or prevent election of Negro officeholders in counties populated mainly by freedmen. The appointive powers of the governor remained virtually unchanged in the state's constitution of 1885, and by amending the document, local self-government was given to white-dominated counties. North Carolina Redeemers gave their legislators power to appoint justices of the peace who selected county commissioners. This strategy assured offices for white officials in Negro counties of eastern Carolina and for business Democrats in the Republican counties of the western part of the state. The conservative governor of Louisiana was empowered to appoint a police jury for the state's parishes which levied local taxes, enacted local laws, and selected school board members, judges, registrars, and other parish officials. Since registrars determined qualifications of registrants, they could discriminate between those individuals who did or did not meet "legal requirements." By these and other methods both Negro and rural white "radicals" were controlled.

Additional electoral devices enabled conservative county and state political rings to maintain their pre-eminence in local and state politics. By requiring male citizens to register months before elections and present certificates to precinct officials, the conservative denied the vote to white and Negro who were slow in registering or lost their certificates. Virginia disfranchised residents convicted of petty larceny, thus eliminating many Negro voters. The South Carolina multiple-ballot box law invalidated any ballot not deposited in the proper box. The so-called secret or Australian system identified party affiliation of candidates neither by name nor symbol, and gave the voter little time to mark the ballot. The semiliterate and illiterate voter was completely confused by these tactics. Since the precincts were manned by Democrats, the illiterate white received direction while the Negro was left in confusion or misled.

If all else failed, fraud produced the desired results. Repeated voting, tissue ballots, substitution of false ballot boxes, and other illegal acts were instruments of the white conservative. He changed polling places without advance notification and located voting booths at maximum distances from Negro voters. By congregating at polling places and voting leisurely, white men kept Negroes from casting ballots. Improperly folded or torn ballots (and officials could easily mar "undesirable" ballots) were thrown out as illegal under whole-ballot laws. Like the Republicans, Democratic canvassing board members changed results when tabulating and certifying returns.

White liberals repeatedly protested the manipulated elections. In 1890 one Mississippian accused his white compatriots of stuffing ballot boxes, perjuring themselves, and winning elections by fraud and violence. There had not been a reasonably honest election in the state, he said, since the ousting of the Republicans in 1875. A Virginian described the elections in his state as a farce, and decried a situation which replaced "Negro government" with white government resting on fraud and chicanery. This critic ignored the fact that Negroes had never controlled Virginia or any other southern state. Conscientious men did see the moral degradation associated with political fraud. The business Democrat did not strive to disfranchise Negroes. On the contrary, he frequently controlled Negro voters to block the desires of a white majority.

For more than a decade southern politicians feared Supreme Court or northern objection to their laws and practices which restricted the Negro voter. If constitutional and statutory provisions which on the surface treated all citizens equally could be enacted, they might satisfy Supreme Court justices more interested in upholding property than human rights, and also salve the consciences of northern idealists. These measures, however, must be phrased with care to disfranchise the Negro indirectly. In the "Second Mississippi Plan" the Mississippi Constitutional Convention of 1890 found a solution.

By 1890 the problem was not white supremacy—that was assured in the South. Repeatedly the common man protested against his under-representation compared with over-representation of the land-rich whites of the Black Belt counties peopled mainly by disfranchised or white-dominated Negroes. The situation in Mississippi was similar to that in other southern states. The political argument was not over the disfranchisement of Negroes but a contest between white "haves" and "have nots."

In this struggle the Negro became a pawn. His elimination as a political factor was essential to compromise between the white factions. There was also a danger from outside the South. In 1890 Henry Cabot Lodge of Massachusetts introduced his "Force Bill" in the House. One of its provisions authorized federal supervisors to pass on the qualifications of voters. Southerners knew that action by racially unbiased officials would multiply the number of Negro registrants, thereby endangering white control of many southern counties and a few states. If unappeased, the desire for political equality might force poor whites to support federal intervention. As Woodward has pointed out, the fundamental question was not the preservation of white supremacy but determination of *"which whites* should be supreme." Any compromise depended on the willingness of delegates from counties with thousands of voteless Negroes giving up some power and delegates from white counties forsaking the principle of manhood suffrage. But southern politicians assured white men that some arrangement would be made to prevent their being disfranchised. Tortured by conscience, some Southerners requested that records of constitutional debates never be published.

The 1890 Mississippi Convention disqualified most Negroes by requiring literacy and property tests, denying political rights to men convicted of minor criminal offenses, and making long residence requirements in county and precinct a prerequisite to registration. The Mississippians also adopted a poll-tax requirement. Strict enforcement of the vitally important literacy test would have eliminated approximately a third of the state's white adult males. An "understanding clause," however, permitted registrars to enroll anyone who could give a reasonable interpretation of a section of the state constitution read to him. This power enabled registrars to base the correctness of the interpretation on the color of the applicant's skin, thereby guaranteeing whites the franchise and disqualifying Negroes.

Later southern constitutional conventions adopted and refined the Second Mississippi Plan. Members of these conventions shrugged off criticism of the understanding clause as disgraceful, fraudulent, sham, and makeshift. Benjamin Tillman of South Carolina brought laughter from his colleagues by denying any fraud or illegality in the clause, though admitting that it did allow some partiality and discrimination by registrars. In Virginia, Carter Glass declared discrimination the major purpose of his state's convention. Late in the 1890's the Louisiana convention rejected the understanding clause by inventing a "grandfather clause" which exempted all males entitled to vote on January 1, 1867, their sons and grandsons, from meeting the literacy or property tests for registration. Grandfather clauses adopted by other states varied in language but their intent was the same. The understanding and grandfather clauses gave white citizens exemptions for periods ranging from 2 to 15 years. Then white and Negro would supposedly be on an equal basis. In 1916 the Supreme Court found the grandfather clauses of Maryland and Oklahoma unconstitutional. Long before that decision, the clauses had accomplished their purpose.

Southern states enacted no uniform code to limit Negro voting. The only law common to all was the poll tax. In Florida, it reduced the Negro voter to an ineffectual minority. In contrast to most other devices, the tax was considered permanent, and it probably did more to check Negro voting than any other law. In operation, however, it also kept thousands of whites from casting ballots in state, congressional, and presidential elections. Eight southern states used literacy and property tests to screen out "undesirable" registrants. Here and there, in no set pattern, other devices were utilized to discriminate against Negro citizens. During the last decade of the nineteenth and the first of the twentieth centuries, the number of southern voters decreased markedly, the relative Negro decline being many times that of white.

The Democratic white primary has been given undeserved credit for eliminating the Negro. Years before the primary system of the late nineteenth and early twentieth centuries, law and custom had reduced Negroes to an ineffectual political minority. The Democratic white primary stabilized an established situation. It exempted white men from the poll tax and other requirements, enabled them to select a party candidate whose victory on election day was certain, kept Negroes, however high their qualifications, from participating in a political organization masquerading as a private white club.

The key men who maintained white political supremacy were the registrars. By a simple refusal to register a Negro, they kept him from enrolling and voting. Local and state police powers backed the registrar regardless of his discrimination. The only recourse of the Negro was in the courts, and expense of this action gave most aggressive Negroes no choice. The few who could afford the cost of appeals wasted their money, for state courts ignored evidence and confirmed the decisions of registrars. Furthermore, the "uppity" Negro ran afoul of whites who used economic or physical powers to convince him that subservience was the best policy. Thus the Negro remained politically inarticulate until organizations with financial resources appealed to the Supreme Court. Even then decisions favorable to Negroes were not forthcoming until justices gave more weight to evidence than to prejudice. In most southern areas where Negroes voted, they did so because conscientious registrars allowed them to register. At times acute political rivalry between white factions in cities and towns gave Negro property-owners opportunity to participate in local elections. As a general rule, only the "good nigger," the Uncle Tom, enjoyed the franchise.

White solidarity became the watchword of southern politics. Laborer and banker, farmer and industrialist, poor and rich found unity in the color of their skin. This combination of different economic interests and common race produced the Solid South. In election after election Democrats won local and state offices, party faithful went to the House and Senate, and Democratic electors cast state votes for presidential candidates.

After the dominant party incorporated the "best" Populist ideas in its platform, southern local and state elections were decided by the personality of the officeseeker. A candidate avoided fundamental issues by listing church service, displaying wife and children, and depending on civic, religious, and family virtues to win voters. Whenever divisive principles arose, southern candidates buried them beneath an avalanche of shibboleths: the Lost Cause, the "Negro governments of reconstruction," southern patriotism, gray-haired mothers, and pure white women saved from spoliation. Introducing one's blonde, blue-eyed daughter at campaign rallies and asking, "Do you want a nigger to marry or have her?" erased all differences of principle. In 1916 the successful candidate for the governorship of Florida told white voters that they had three friends in an unfriendly world: Christ, a Sears-Roebuck catalogue, and the candidate.

Political supremacy, however, did not completely satisfy the white supremacist. To guarantee political control, he demanded that Negroes be kept in economic and social bondage. The independent or "uppity" Negro must be made to realize his subordinate place in society. White ownership of land and other property eased the task. Negro sharecroppers worked the land and depended on landlords or crossroad merchants for housing and supplies. When the propertyless Negro found himself in legal difficulty, his patron was his landowner or merchant. Thus the old system of slavery yielded to a new one in which the Negro enjoyed a measure of personal freedom but depended on the white man for a meager existence. In cities and towns the Negro male was powerless as the whites took his jobs as skilled artisan and relegated him to menial, dirty occupations. Negro wives supplemented their husbands' income by domestic service. Color of skin affected wages, and the cord of wood or railroad crosstie cut by the Negro commanded a smaller return than the same product made by white labor.

In social affairs, color was the distinguishing mark of superiority and inferiority. No white gentleman neglected to open doors for his ladies or to show them deference in public, but the most degraded white male ignored the Negro lady's claim to respect. In stores Negro customers hung back until all whites were served. In sex relations the white male had access to females of both races; but the Negro male suffered the humiliation of sharing his women with immoral white men. The lot of Negro women was more precarious than that of their men. Taken by force or persuaded by promises, Negro girls found themselves at the mercy of white seducers. The legal protection afforded white mothers of illegitimate children did not cover Negroes. Any "un-American" Negro girl who appealed to law endangered herself and her unborn child, and bore the wrath of both races. Without the protection of the ante-bellum system of slavery, she fended for herself or granted favors for money. Many a white father assumed responsibility for his child. Too frequently, however, males involved in illicit and interracial affairs were almost as destitute as their partners.

Although the caste system was mainly the creature of folkways and mores, laws and court decisions gave legality to many customs and practices. Long before the 1890's, segregation was firmly established in the South. Separation of the races in religious services came from Reconstruction; integrated schools of the Republican era were abolished by the Redeemers; eventually laws placed walls between Negro and white in public accommodations; and racially mixed marriages were prohibited. A Tennessee law of 1875 allowed railroads and other businesses serving the public to select their clientele. After its overthrow by a federal court in 1880, the legislature segregated first-class passengers but kept second-class coaches integrated. In 1887, Florida passed the South's first "Jim Crow" law.

Between 1881 and 1887 a Supreme Court decision and rebellion by southern whites against domination by business laid foundations for Jim Crow laws. In declaring the Civil Rights Act of 1875 unconstitutional, Justice Bradley found no federal authority in the Fourteenth Amendment to protect social rights of individuals. As to the Thirteenth Amendment, the justice asked in 1883: "Can the act of a mere individual, the owner of an inn, the public conveyance, or place of amusement, refusing the accommodation, be justly regarded as imposing any badge of slavery or servitude upon the applicant, or only as inflicting an ordinary civil injury, properly cognizable by the laws of the State, and presumably subject to redress by those laws until the contrary appears?" After a man emerged from slavery, "there must be some stage in the progress of his elevation when he takes the rank of a mere citizen, and ceases to be the special favorite of the laws, and when his rights as a citizen, or a man, are to be protected in the ordinary modes by which other men's rights are protected."

The Court found no vindication for the Civil Rights Act in either the Thirteenth or Fourteenth amendments. A vigorous dissenting opinion by Kentucky-born John M. Harlan went for naught: the Negro was no longer the ward of the nation, he must look to his state government for protection, and Congress was limited to "corrective legislation . . . for counteracting the effect of state laws, or state action, prohibited by the Fourteenth Amendment." The decision ended federal enforcement of guarantees of the reconstruction amendments. While Justice Bradley believed the Negro was no longer entitled "to be the special favorite of the laws," federal withdrawal allowed state governments to enforce practices which limited his citizenship rights. State and local governments denied the Negro civil and social rights, disfranchised him, and condoned peonage.

No longer fearful of the Supreme Court, Florida required separate accommodations on trains. A year later Mississippi enacted a similar law, and before the end of 1891 Texas, Louisiana, Alabama, Arkansas, Kentucky, and Georgia followed suit. Mississippi legislators separated the races in railroad stations while Georgia did the same in streetcars. Segregated transportation facilities were probably the South's most typical Jim Crow law. Eventually, however, state and local enactments, and frequently custom—backed by a white police force and a white court—segregated the Negro in churches, schools, hospitals, prisons, insane asylums, parks, theaters, hotels, restaurants, barbershops, courtrooms, at drinking fountains, in rest rooms, on town and courthouse square benches, in cemeteries, newspaper columns and marriage, in fact everywhere. "When completed," as Woodward has written, "the new codes of White Supremacy were vastly more complex than the ante-bellum slave codes or the Black Codes of 1865–1866, and, if anything, they were stronger and more rigidly enforced."

The caste system produced some paradoxes. Costs of running separate streetcars for Negro and white, and later, motor busses, allowed transportation companies to seat the "inferior" race in the rear. Separate elevators were installed in the first southern skyscrapers, but impatient Southerners pushed into the almost vacant uplifts reserved for Negroes, and segregation in elevators was quickly abandoned without serious protest. Air transport companies later seated Negro and white side by side. White men gave Negro entrepreneurs almost exclusive control of burying their own dead and Negro beauticians monopolized that business. For many decades white owners of barbershops employed Negroes to cut hair, but in time white workers elevated barbering to a profession and took it over. The respectful Uncle Tom found the white man friendly, helpful, and generous, but the independent Negro ran afoul of custom and law, often paying for his non-conformity by servitude. Doctors and dentists opened separate entrances and provided two waiting rooms and business enterprises maintained distinct facilities for whites and Negroes.

Closely related to Jim Crow laws was the political rise of the white masses. In Florida, where discontented whites frightened conservative Democrats by almost winning the 1884 gubernatorial contest, the state led in segregating railroad coaches and enacting a poll tax. In other southern states agrarian discontent was associated with or followed by discriminatory laws. Competition between white and Negro laborers for subsistence wages stimulated the former's demand for some mark of distinction. He found it in a caste system which gave all whites superiority over Negroes. Few business Democrats favored legal discrimination: they preferred to leave the Negro alone, use his labor for profit, and guide him at election time. Realistic Negroes identified the white social class behind Jim Crow legislation. Since their jobs and hope for protection stemmed from the upper-income whites, Negroes supported conservatives by choice. In a few states a combination of Populist and Negro voters temporarily checked the movement toward legal segregation. In the end, however, rebellion against business Democrat domination of the party relegated the Negro to a second-class citizenship.

In no sphere was the paternalistic image of the Redeemer as the protector of freedmen more tarnished than in treatment of Negro lawbreakers. Emancipation shifted the penal burden from master to community. Under the old system, theft had been a means whereby the slave improved his standard of living. Many free Negroes justified their light-fingered activities on the ground that their contribution to plantation and farm gave them valid claim to property. A larger number of freedmen stole to satisfy personal desires or to feed and clothe their families. Their past servitude had developed no clear definition of right and wrong.

Southern agriculture made theft easy and detection difficult. A bag of cotton picked at night could be exchanged at the crossroad store, operated by a white man willing to suborn dishonesty to support his family; chickens, hogs, melons, and vegetables disappeared with hardly a trace. Impoverished whites had reason for demanding protection against theft. Mississippi legislators responded with the "pig law" which made stealing of property valued at ten dollars or more grand larceny and subjected offenders to as much as five-years imprisonment on conviction. Other southern legislators enacted drastic punishments for stealing cotton, melons, animals, and other products. Major thefts, assault, rape, and murder brought additional culprits into the courts, and neither local nor state jails could house all the convicts.

The economy-minded business Democrats refused to build new prisons.

Prior to the Civil War, Louisiana had leased convicts. This tax-saving device was adopted by federal occupation forces and subsequent Republican regimes. By enlarging the convict-lease system, the Redeemers made it profitable to governments and businessmen. Contractors paid a specified annual sum per prisoner in exchange for the convict's labor. The contractor supposedly furnished prisoners with food, clothing, and housing, but the food was inadequate and often inedible, clothing and bedding vermin-ridden, and housing not fit for humans. Perfunctory inspection of living and working conditions allowed bosses to evade regulations. The annual death rate ran to about 10 per cent, and in specific years up to 16 per cent in Mississippi and 25 per cent in Arkansas. Where subleasing by contractors was allowed, the loss of convicts was worst of all. The "penitentiary ring," which included state prison wardens, local government officials, prominent politicians, and leading industrialists, became the dictator of prison policies.

Among those hiring convicts were mining companies, turpentine producers, railroad-construction contractors, and planters. Usual procedure assigned prisoners a specified daily task and failure to produce resulted in inhuman beatings. Turpentine workers of Florida were shackled together, leg and waist, and forced to trot from tree to tree in collecting resin. In some mining camps, men worked during the four seasons without shoes or sufficient clothing to protect them from cold or heat. Recalcitrant convicts were thrown into pits, given a diet of bread and water, and lashed with bull whips. At times men and women were chained together at night. Goaded beyond human endurance, some prisoners cut their tendons or broke their legs with sledge hammers. A modern southern historian concluded that the only parallel to the convict-lease system was "the persecutions of the Middle Ages or in the prison camps of Nazi Germany."

But the system made fortunes for contractors and profits for stockholders and planters. On a salary of $2000 a year, Alabama's state warden, John H. Bankhead, became wealthy by dealing in convicts. Senator Joseph E. Brown, one of Georgia's Redeemers, had a 20-year contract for a minimum of "three hundred able-bodied, long-term" prisoners to work his coal mine. He paid the state about eight cents a day for each convict. Contractors in Florida bid the annual payment per prisoner to $151.50. One of the leading Redeemers of Tennessee and general counsel of the Tennessee Coal, Iron and Railroad Company, leased about 1300 prisoners for less than $80 a year per man.

In some states, county convicts outnumbered state prisoners. Smaller unit leases, avarice of local officials, and needs of planters brought the worst treatment to Negro convicts. The remarkable increase in the number of Negroes arrested by sheriffs and sentenced by judges during periods when the labor needs of local employers were greatest, suggests conviction of many on trumped-up charges. Both Negro and white prisoners were leased, but the number of the former was larger and treatment more harsh.

Closely akin to the convict-lease system was another method of securing a controlled labor supply. In return for paying a Negro's fine, the planter or some other entrepreneur gained his labor for a time sufficient to repay fine with interest. This involved no lease; it was an agreement between two individuals whereby one avoided prison and the other got a laborer. Arresting officer and local judge were not officially involved since there were no legal papers drawn in these personal agreements; but the desire of police and judge for strict enforcement of laws frequently coincided with the demand for workers. A prisoner who failed to keep his promise was quickly arrested on some charge. The number of people involved and the profit potential attracted middlemen who paid fines and "sold" their "contracts," a strong indication of collusion between agents and officials.

A larger number of controlled laborers came from indebted Negroes. Until he paid his obligation, or was bought by another employer, the laborer was virtual property. White men kept the account books, and a callous employer never allowed the most frugal worker to become debt-free. Negroes who ran away found themselves at the mercy of the white power structure. Although the peon enjoyed some freedoms not possessed by his slave ancestors, he received less in food, clothing, housing, and medical care. Security of the ante-bellum years vanished: lessors of convicts worked them for maximum return, death was often better than freedom for worn-out men. Whenever returns from a laborer failed to equal advances, the employer evicted his debt-ridden work hand.

Beneficiaries of the convict-lease, fine-payment, and peonage systems constituted a small minority of the southern population. Most white bookkeepers kept honest accounts, worked under economic handicaps similar to those of their Negro neighbors, and relied on hope of heavenly reward. Many Southerners denounced the worst features of the caste system. Damaging evidence in official reports, and selfless efforts of white reformers (Julia Tutwiler of Alabama, for instance) mitigated the treatment of convicts. While hundreds of whites made a Roman holiday of a lynching, other hundreds bowed their heads in shame and in time they found courage to speak out against white barbarians. Perceptive whites realized that the caste system seared consciences and weakened the moral fiber of the dominant race. In their anguish and helplessness, they salved mental wounds by taking care of their faithful Negroes: paying fines, giving food and clothing, and ignoring irresponsibility and shoddy work.

These people, however, failed to discover the heart of the problem. They ignored man's yearning for dignity; they gave more importance to heredity than to environment; and they closed their eyes to their responsibility for continued racial indignities. Instead of recognizing that ignorance and economic survival forced thousands of Negroes into Uncle Tomism, the white man accepted subservience as a characteristic of race. He saw no relationship between educational facilities, economic opportunities, and social recognition, and the failures of the race. With few personal exceptions, white Southerners justified the caste system on the theory of racial inferiority. Protests of enlightened Southerners went unheeded. A majority of Northerners not only allowed southern ideas to win the racial part of the peace, but paid the compliment of adopting the same racism in the North.

Northern Acceptance of Southern Reconstruction

The truism that times change is underscored by the nation's advocacy of rights for freedmen for a decade and then abandoning the former slaves, leaving them to the "tender mercy" of southern whites. Equality under law was a belated objective of the Civil War. Its embryonic appearance during the conflict never gave it the same standing as the ideas of union and freedom. After these aims had been achieved through military victory and the Thirteenth Amendment, equality became the cardinal objective of some northern intellectuals and politicians. The Civil Rights Act of 1866, the Fourteenth and Fifteenth amendments, and the Civil Rights Act of 1875 reflected real humanitarian concern for the Negro.

These idealists were too optimistic. They predicted a meteoric rise for a subjugated race but almost ignored the freedman's need for land or some means of making a living. National laws and officials attempted to secure fair treatment and just wages for the Negro. The federal government used its power to check obvious violence; its agents sought to guarantee a degree of equality and recognize man's desire for dignity, and it joined with northern philanthropic organizations in providing limited educational opportunity for an unlettered people. More important than any of these was the idealist's belief that the Negro would demonstrate initiative and attain success by individual effort in a free American society.

The history of the colonies was largely the success story of white colonists who rose from poverty to relative plenty. After becoming free, many indentured servants attained affluence, political prominence, or intellectual distinction by hard work, frugality, and study. Freedom, therefore, gave the former slave opportunity to emulate the white colonists of the seventeenth and eighteenth centuries. Some idealists extended Charles Darwin's thesis of the survival of the fittest in nature to human society and predicted unrealistic achievements by freedmen.

Although the economic situation after the Civil War differed from that of colonial days, millions of acres of public land awaited stockraiser and plowman. The wartime Homestead Act made these lands available to enterprising Negroes. But free homesteads in the West offered no real opportunity for the poverty-stricken family to acquire land. Even in the five southern states where the federal government owned land, the propertyless Negro family could not avail itself of the opportunity offered by the special Homestead Act of 1866. Government payment of transportation and subsistence for a brief period were insufficient to give the most industrious freedman a chance for economic independence.

Federal action voiding provisions in black codes which prohibited Negroes from acquiring rural or town property benefited few freedmen. They did not have the financial resources to acquire land or houses. Only the footloose, or the foolhardy, wandered to distant places to stake out homesteads on federal lands. Most who attempted it failed. With few exceptions the freedmen were dependent on sharecropping, tenancy, and domestic service.

Idealistic Northerners believed that their gift of freedom should have enabled the freedman to prove himself. After a decade or more, however, the mass of southern Negroes remained virtually propertyless. This failure disillusioned many northern humanitarians; in recoil they turned Social Darwinism against the Negro. In the survival-of-the-fittest test, the freedmen had failed. So northern intellectuals turned away from the Negro to other causes.

A larger number of Northerners tired of the "eternal" Negro problem. For decades before the Civil War and for more than ten years following that conflict, slavery and the protection of freedmen made newspaper headlines and provided politicians their topic on the hustings. If the Negro could be forgotten, the commonplace enjoyments of courtship, marriage, family, and work would be heightened. The obvious solution was to leave the freedman to Southerners. Northerners escaped by retreating to hallowed catchwords—union and emancipation—and let the "South govern the South."

This theme was reiterated in newspaper story and magazine article. Quick to sense the desires of readers, editors and writers produced articles sympathetic to white Southerners. The time for vengeance had passed; the day of understanding and appreciation had arrived. Former anti-southern journalists shifted their bias. After the compromises of 1877, Godkin's *Nation* declared the Negro could never be worked into a government respected by better-class Americans; on April 7, 1877, the *New-York Tribune* condemned the freedman who had been given "ample opportunity" to demonstrate his latent talents but proved himself a member of an "idle, ignorant and vicious" race. One after another of the pro-Negro newspapers barbed the freedman in editorials until few journals remained to defend the southern minority.

In the 1880's almost every issue of a national magazine contained articles on the South. These articles portrayed a moonlit, magnolia-scented Southland. Spanish moss, romantic orange blossoms, mysterious swamps, and other wonders of nature vied for attention with plantation houses and quaint city buildings. Authors recounted historical lore from the colonial era to battlefields of the Civil War. Northern writers found only two classes of whites: former plantation aristocrats and their descendants, and the poor. The latter were ignored; but the ideas, acts, and economic situation of the upper class were reported in detail. The Negro was portrayed as a childlike adult, slow, quaint, strange in speech, enjoying a happy-go-lucky utopia from white benevolence. Few writers probed beneath the surface to uncover poverty, cruelty, or the struggle for survival. Their public demanded a romantic view of the South and authors complied.

Both northern and southern authors thus created an atmosphere conducive to the caste system. Albion W. Tourgée, a native of Ohio, was educated at the University of Rochester. Wounded twice as a Union soldier he spent some time as a prisoner of war in a southern camp. During his tenure (1868–74) as judge on a North Carolina superior court, he was denounced as a Carpetbagger.

After 1875, however, white Southerners looked on him as a champion. His first novel *Toinette* appeared in 1874, written under the pen name of Henry Churton, and dealt with miscegenation. It was not great literature, but a good story written with spirit and filled with murders, secret rooms, and ghosts. The plot portrayed a mulatto who murdered her white master because economic necessity forced him to sell her and their daughter. The almost white Toinette became the mistress of another master and proved her love by nursing him back to health from a serious wound. He eventually denounced her because of her Negro blood. In a sad and tragic story Tourgée claimed that slavery was not the inhumane institution most Northerners believed it to be.

More famous than *Toinette* was *A Fool's Errand* (more than 200,000 copies sold after 1879) by, as Tourgée subtitled it, one of the fools. The first novel to deal with the Reconstruction era, it described the treatment of Unionists in the South; the shootings, stabbings, drownings, hangings, and intimidation of Negroes by the Ku Klux Klan. Tourgée did not condemn white Southerners for this barbarism but blamed Congressional Reconstruction for inciting lawlessness. He found that fundamental differences between the civilizations of North and South were not erased by Union victory. Secondly, he believed it necessary to return control of the South to the prewar ruling class. Finally, he explained away white violence;

it was not directed against the individual Negro or white Republican, but against governments that contravened the best in southern civilization.

A few southern writers applied some of Tourgée's themes to southern historical lore. Encouraged by the *Southern Literary Messenger*'s publication of his poems and stories, John E. Cooke of Virginia gave up a legal practice for a literary career. After serving in the Confederate army, he divided his time between farming and writing. *Surry of Eagle's Nest* (1866) was his best account of combat experiences. In it and later novels his romantic plots treated sympathetically the warrior fighting for home and fireside. He idolized and idealized the chivalric Southerner.

Another Virginian, Thomas Nelson Page, was a youth of twelve at war's end. The Negro's "ole marster" and "ole missis" which appeared in his stories, published in 1884 by the *Atlantic Monthly*, came from imagination. In *Marse Chan* and other stories he made the Negro a simple, lovable child who adored his white master and enjoyed working for him. The slave Sam recalled the good old times of slavery: "Niggers did' hed nothin' 't all to do—jes' had to 'ten' to feedin' an' cleanin' de hosses an' doin' what de marster tell 'em to do an' when dey wuz sick, dey had things sont 'em out de house, an' de same doctor come to see 'em whar 'ten' to de white folks when dey wuz po'ly, an' all. Dyar warn' no trouble nor nuttin'!"

Besides building myths of an idyllic prewar South, Page promoted reconciliation by romance between northern officers and southern beauties. His rosy picture of ante-bellum society became drab under direct light, but his appealing plots and recording of Negro dialect gave him status in literary circles.

The only Southerner to surpass Page in the use of Negro dialect was Joel Chandler Harris. A native of Eatonton, Georgia, he began a career in journalism at thirteen as a printer on *The Countryman*, a weekly published on the plantation of Joseph A. Turner. Harris listened avidly to tales told by the plantation slaves, particularly those of "Old Harbert" and "Uncle George Terrel." Throughout adulthood Chandler depended on these sources. Harris began a 24-year association with the Atlanta *Constitution* in 1876. His first stories were published in that newspaper and in 1880 *Uncle Remus: His Songs and His Sayings* originated a series of books which continued almost to Harris's death in 1908. Harris told entertaining stories narrated by kindly Uncle Remus to a white boy, stories of humanized animals with the ideals and baseness of men. Harris employed a device already used by others, but he developed an absorbing tale from its raw folk version with surpassing artistry. His creativeness encompassed more than the Uncle Remus tales; he also penned short stories about mountaineers, poor whites, southern aristocrats, and former slaves who retained personal devotion for their masters. Harris did much to placate northern hostility toward the South.

Few men have won more fame with less originality than Henry W. Grady of Athens, Georgia. Fifteen and fatherless when the war ended, after various ventures in journalism, he joined the Atlanta *Constitution* and in 1880 bought one-fourth of the newspaper with money loaned him by Cyrus W. Field, promoter of the Atlantic cable. In editorials and speeches Grady became the voice of a reformed South. Frequently lifting ideas and paraphrasing sections from prewar southern advocates of industry, he proclaimed that the South's future lay in obtaining capital to develop its industry and diversify its agriculture. On December 21, 1886, he began a speech to the New England Society of New York stating "There was a South of slavery and secession—that South is dead. There is a South of union and freedom—that South, thank God, is living, breathing, growing every hour." He became the "Spokesman for the New South," a section favorable to industry, one allied with and having common purposes with the North. To Grady the South was a region in which the white man ruled but cared for the childlike Negro—a region of people proud of their past but looking to the future.

Francis Hopkins Smith of Baltimore, engineer, painter, and novelist, portrayed a mint julep-drinking, hospitable Southerner in *Colonel Carter of Cartersville* (1891). The simple-hearted colonel was chivalrous, charming, and eloquent, but without an understanding of the commercial world. When overwhelmed by profiteering merchants of New York City, he challenged them to duels. The discovery of rich veins of coal on his lands saved him from bankruptcy, and he joined his profit-motivated fellows in the reconciliation brought about by affluence.

Few southern writers resisted these romantic myths. The most prominent one who did was George W. Cable of New Orleans. At sixteen, his belief in slavery and white supremacy forced him into the Confederate army. He returned to New Orleans as a paroled prisoner with no love for the Union, but in time concluded that the southern war had been fought to perpetuate an indefensible institution. His observations convinced him that the "masterly inactivity" of conservative white citizens during the Reconstruction era harmed the South; they should have supported the best Republican proposals and demanded fair treatment of freedmen. Cable's ideas of racial inferiority were shaken by the dignity displayed by Negro teachers and the educational advancement of children at an integrated school. In 1875 he was denounced for advocating integrated schools.

Cable attained his creative peak in *The Grandissimos* (1880) and *Madam Delphine* (1881). In the first and better novel, he depicted racial intermixture with candor and skill. At times brilliant, at times tedious, he was always humane and spirited in the story which began with American acquisition of Louisiana. He found comic and tragic incidents in the usually ignored and embarrassing subject of miscegenation. Proud Creoles of New Orleans claimed his historical interpretations faulty and resented his portrayal of their ancestors as illiterate. Worst of all, they resented implications of Negro blood in white veins.

In *The Silent South* (1885) he raised some pertinent questions. Why did Northerners demand the liberation of slaves and then do so little to lift the freedmen from his former economic status? Why did Southerners fight for state rights and then forget their principle on being forced back into the Union? Northerners, he claimed, would not have fought just to abolish slavery—their vital concern was preservation of the Union and they had no real interest in uplifting the Negro. Southerners, he stated, used state rights as a pretext to fight for slavery; once they found it possible to put the freedman into economic and social subservience, they lost interest in constitutional rights.

Americans preferred trite romances and folk tales to Cable's serious writings. Cooke romanticized the revolutionary South, Page did the same for the ante-bellum era, and they joined other writers to ennoble Confederate soldiers and make Negroes a race of happy children. They gave Southerners escape from military defeat and poverty. They urged Northerners to shed animosities and accept formerly rebellious Southerners as the bulwark of unionism. And Northerners, having destroyed slavery but distressed by slums and poverty amid mansions and affluence, also found escape in a glamorized Old South, peopled by genteel whites living in rural tranquility and looking after their carefree slaves. By accepting this never-never Southland, many Northerners salved consciences troubled by the postwar vituperation heaped on white Southerners.

The northern businessman welcomed all contributions toward sectional peace and stability. Neither the amoral profiteer pictured by his detractors nor the humanitarian described by his advocates, he exerted powerful economic influences which affected political and social beliefs. He wasted no energy in finding reasons for the lawlessness of Republican regimes in the South or the tranquility under conservative governments. He knew that the former condition interfered with trade and profit and the latter promoted them. After his fear of an agrarian, anti-business union of Westerner and Southerner had been erased by the favoritism given free and unregulated enterprise by southern political leaders, the northern businessman wholeheartedly supported the conservative establishments in the South. He applauded Grady's claim that the economic salvation of his section lay in co-operation and emulation of northern businessmen. The plight of the Negro may have given some northern manufacturers and merchants moments of uneasiness, but these were consumed by the pleasant prospect of profits. "Let the South govern the South" evoked admiration from northern businessmen no longer fearful of southern roadblocks on the industrial highway.

Northern Democrats also forgot southern Negroes, for the party's existence depended on the whites in the South. Political machines in northern cities could not keep the party going without aid from the former Confederate states. Segregation appealed to border-state voters, and many residents of the Middle West traced their origins to the South Atlantic region and were almost as racially bigoted as Southerners. Supporting the caste system endangered no Democratic congressman in northern urban districts, for migration of Negroes to industrial cities was a future phenomenon. Northern Negroes were neither numerous nor politically potent. Since their vote went to the party of emancipation, northern Democrats could ignore them. Northern Republicans actually had more in common with the propertied southern white than with the Negro fieldhand. As a result the Republicans gave lip service to equality and joined Democrats in sanctioning the caste system.

Racial tensions in the North strengthened the bias of white workers. Hysterical whites in northern cities assaulted Negroes and destroyed their property to show the race freed by Lincoln their place in American society. According to John H. Franklin, the rioting in the North "was as vicious and almost as prevalent as in the South," as competition for jobs and employment of Negroes as strikebreakers infuriated whites. Although lynching was known as a southern barbarism, it also occurred in the North. While labor leaders advocated equal rights in employment, they allowed unions to exclude Negroes. Laws limited Negroes to certain areas of cities and towns; schools were segregated by statute or by grouping pupils by residence; white churches turned away colored worshippers, and Negroes learned by experience to stay away from certain hotels, restaurants, theaters, and other businesses. As in the South, the relative poverty and ignorance of the Negro set him apart. Northerners, however, could not use the high Negro population percentages as an excuse for caste. Gradually the federal government adopted southern practices in employment and social policies. The caste system was never as firmly rooted in the North as in the South, but the Negro became a second-class citizen in most northern communities.

In a series of decisions the Supreme Court moved irregularly but steadfastly toward legal justification of the caste system. The primary question in the Slaughter-House cases of 1873 was a monoply given by Louisiana to a slaughtering company in New Orleans. The justices found a "recognized and established" distinction between citizenship of the United States and citizenship of a state. The clause in the Fourteenth Amendment that said "No State shall make or enforce any law which shall abridge the privileges or immunities of citizens of the United States" prohibited state discrimination against citizens of the United States, but citizens of states were dependent on their states for protection of their citizenship. This decision closed federal courts to Negroes seeking redress against state laws which infringed upon their civil rights. Two years later in *Minor v. Happersett* the Court ruled "that the Constitution of the United States does not confer the right of suffrage upon any one . . ." and, therefore, women were not enfranchised by the Fourteenth Amendment. If this decision had stood, it would have opened many ways for states to disfranchise Negroes. However, in *ex parte Yarbrough* (1884) the Court denied a writ of *habeas corpus* to persons imprisoned for conspiracy to keep a Negro from voting for a congressional condidate. The judges declared that their state in *Minor v. Happersett* had been taken out of context by defense attorneys and that the federal government had the power and obligation to prevent control of national elections "by violence and by corruption." In *Strauder v. West Virginia* (1880) the Court ruled that states which denied jury service to Negroes violated the Fourteenth Amendment.

These victories for Negroes were dwarfed by other decisions adverse to them. In *United States v. Cruikshank* (1876) and *United States v. Harris* (1882), the Court voided sections of the Ku Klux Klan acts on the ground that the reconstruction amendments gave the federal government authority to proceed against states but not individuals. The only obligation of the United States, according to the Court, was to see that states did not deny rights to individuals; the central government was not empowered to protect individual against individual. As has been described, the Civil Rights cases of 1883 declared unconstitutional the Civil Rights Act of 1875. In his penetrating dissenting opinion, Justice Harlan believed that Congress could enact laws to protect people "against the deprivation, *because of their race*, of any civil rights. . . . It is perfectly well known," he continued, "that the great danger to the equal enjoyment by citizens of their rights, as citizens, was to be apprehended not altogether from unfriendly state legislation, but from hostile action by corporations and individuals in the States."

The Court moved toward making the Fourteenth Amendment a protecter of corporate enterprise instead of the Negro. In essence, the Court applied the "privileges and immunities" and the "due process of law" clauses of the amendment to corporate persons to protect them from the regulatory legislation of state legislatures and, to a considerable extent, from similar laws of the Congress. Justices concerned with protecting property rights and dividing authority between state and central governments rendered decisions which prohibited both governments from limiting the freedom of corporations. In the process the Court severely restricted the federal government's trusteeship of the Negro, placing him instead under state codes, state police power, and state courts.

The twisting and turnings of the Supreme Court were resolved in *Plessy* v. *Ferguson* (1896). The case originated when Plessy, who was seven-eighths white, bought a railroad ticket for transportation between two Louisiana cities. He was ordered from the white coach and after refusing, was arrested and convicted under an 1890 law which directed railroads to provide "separate but equal accommodations for the white and colored races." Plessy appealed on the grounds that the Louisiana law violated the Thirteenth and Fourteenth amendments. In its majority opinion, the Court conceded that the Fourteenth Amendment "was undoubtedly to enforce the absolute equality of the two races before the law, but in the nature of things it could not have been intended to abolish distinctions based upon color, or to enforce social, as distinguished from political equality or a commingling of the two races upon terms unsatisfactory to either." According to the Court, the appeal resolved itself into the questioning of reasonable regulation and fair exercise of police power by a state to uphold "established usages, customs and traditions of the people . . . [for] preservation of the public peace and good order," but the provisions of the Louisiana law were no more "unreasonable, or more obnoxious to the Fourteenth Amendment than the acts of Congress requiring separate schools for colored children in the District of Columbia, the constitutionality of which does not seem to have been questioned, or the corresponding acts of state legislatures."

Furthermore, a majority of the judges considered "the underlying fallacy of the plaintiff's argument to consist in the assumption that enforced separation of the two races stamps the colored race with a badge of inferiority." Any stigma of inferiority, therefore, arose not from the provisions of the law but from its interpretation by the Negro. Social prejudices could not be overcome by legislation, the justices concluded; the enjoyment of equal rights did not depend on enforced commingling of the races, and laws could not "eradicate racial instincts or abolish distinctions based on physical differences. . . . If the civil and political rights of both races be equal, one cannot be inferior to the other civilly or politically. If one race be inferior to the other socially, the Constitution of the United States cannot put them upon the same plane. . . ."

The Court's argument was accepted as truth for half a century by a majority of white Americans. Consistent with his opinion in the Civil Rights cases of 1883, Justice Harlan attacked the reasoning of his associates. He admitted that the white race was dominant "in prestige, in achievements, in education, in wealth, and in power" in the United States.

> But in view of the Constitution, in the eye of law, there is in this country no superior, dominant ruling class of citizens. There is no caste here. Our Constitution is color-blind, and neither knows nor tolerates classes among citizens. In respect to civil rights, all citizens are equal before the law. The humblest is the peer of the most powerful. The law regards man as man, and takes no account of his surroundings or of his color when his civil rights as guaranteed by the supreme law of the land are involved. It is, therefore, to be regretted that this high tribunal, the final expositor of the fundamental law of the land, has reached the conclusion that it is competent for a state to regulate the enjoyment by citizens of their civil rights solely upon the basis of race. . . .

In Harlan's opinion the arbitrary separation of citizens on the basis of race did place a badge of servitude on the one with inferior accomplishments. Furthermore, this indictment was inconsistent with "civil freedom and equality before the law established by the Constitution" and could "not be justified upon any legal grounds." Whatever evils might arise from the commingling of the two races, he thought they would "be infinitely less than those that will surely come from state legislation regulating the enjoyment of civil rights upon the basis of race." He found it impossible to reconcile the boasted freedoms of Americans with laws which, "practically, puts the brand of servitude and degradation upon a large class of our fellow citizens, our equals before the law. This thin disguise of 'equal' accommodations for passengers in railroad coaches will not mislead any one," he concluded, "nor atone for the wrong this day done."

With all his insight, Justice Harlan was a poor prophet. The "thin disguise" did mislead many. Under its philosophy, state, local, and national governments authorized and required different treatment of the races —economically, educationally, politically, and socially—with the "separate" being observed and the "equal" being ignored.

Despite the indifference of parties and presidents some efforts were made to aid and protect Negroes. On December 4, 1883, Senator Henry W. Blair introduced a federal education bill which authorized appropriations ranging from $15 million the first year to $1 million for the tenth and final year. Because these sums were to be divided among the states on the basis of illiteracy, it was estimated that $11 million of the first year's $15 million would go to the southern states. Segregated schools were permitted but the money was to be used for Negro and white children without discrimination. The $11 million federal grant was more than the total educational expenditures of the southern states in 1880. The Blair bill was debated from 1883 to 1890. Southern senators who voted against it or abstained from casting ballots were motivated as much by their ideas of state rights as by their fears of an educated Negro citizenry. In 1884, 13 southern senators voted for it, 5 cast ballots against it, and the others evaded the issue by being absent at roll call. Two years later 15 southern senators voted for the bill, and in 1888, 14 of them favored a revised version. The Blair bills passed the Senate but not the House.

Some congressmen were still reformers but realistic Republicans objected to a representation from the South out of proportion to the number of the region's citizens allowed the franchise. In June 1890, Representative Henry Cabot Lodge of Massachusetts introduced a bill to give federal supervisors power to control voter registration, determine the qualifications of voters, and pass on the legality of federal and state canvassers of an election. Confronted by the most serious threat to white domination of national elections since 1876, Southerners promptly dubbed Lodge's proposal the "Force Bill." Their opposition did not prevent its passage by the House. In January of the following year, the Senate quieted southern fears by rejecting it. Republicans representing silver-producing and inflationary constituents who wanted southern senatorial votes joined their colleagues to defeat the bill. Although the 1892 Republican platform promised "every citizen, be he rich or poor, native or foreign born, white or black" the right to vote, the party virtually abandoned the Negro. The Democratic platform of the same year denounced any federal supervision of elections.

Meanwhile southern states proceeded to put the stamp of inferiority upon the Negro by law, words, and violence. In 1892 the number of lynchings amounted to 235, and between 1882 and 1900 more than 3000 persons were murdered by mobs. In addition to boasting of taking rights from freedmen, southern demagogues regaled audiences with imaginary situations illustrating the incapacities of Negroes. In 1898 John Williams of Mississippi said, "You could ship-wreck 10,000 illiterate white Americans on a desert island, and in three weeks they would have a fairly good government, conceived and administered upon fairly democratic lines. You could ship-wreck 10,000 negroes, every one of whom was a graduate of Harvard University, and in less than three years, they would have retrograded governmentally; half of the men would have been killed, and the other half would have two wives apiece." This slander against the Negro pleased his white constituents. Nor did Williams's racism harm him with his northern Democratic colleagues: in 1903 he became his party's leader in the House.

Senator Ben Tillman of South Carolina profited politically and economically from his diatribes against the Negro. South Carolinians, he admitted, had used illegal means to disfranchise the freedmen: "We stuffed ballot boxes. We shot [Negroes]. We are not ashamed of it." He received applause from Chautauqua audiences by saying that Negroes were "akin to the monkey"; they came from an "ignorant and debased and debauched race." Perhaps unconsciously imitating William Lloyd Garrison, Tillman consigned the Constitution of the United States to hell, if that document interfered with lynching rapists. Tillman blasted the Constitution to justify discrimination, Garrison to demand human dignity.

All over the South the means to mold public opinion belonged to those who condemned the Negro. Southern planters claimed that the freed Negro was less efficient than the slave; southern governors told reporters that the Negro was gradually becoming less productive. Newspapers reported criminal acts of Negroes but not their religious, social, and educational activities. Vilifiers possessed many voices, the defenders of the race few.

Works of racist authors found favor in North and South. Detractors of the Negroid race won temporary recognition from their books, titles of which often indicated the thesis: Charles Carroll for *Negro a Beast* (1900), William P. Calhoun for *Caucasian and the Negro in the United States* (1902), William B. Smith for *Color Line: A Brief in Behalf of the Unborn* (1905), and Robert W. Shufeldt for *Negro, a Menace to American Civilization* (1907). Three of these books were published by northern firms and one by a Missouri publisher.

Thomas Dixon, however, won more than fleeting fame with a pseudo historical trilogy of hate. Born at Shelby, North Carolina, he became a Baptist minister in 1886 and three years later accepted an appointment at a church in New York City, where he remained for ten years. A militant Southerner and racial bigot, he expressed his views in three novels: *The Leopard's Spot: A Romance of the White Man's Burden—1865–1900* (1902), *The Clansman: An Historical Romance of the Ku Klux Klan* (1905), and *The Traitor: A Story of the Fall of the Invisible Empire* (1907). Broadway audiences applauded *The Clansman* in stage version, and ten years later David W. Griffith used it to produce the first notable full-length American movie, *The Birth of a Nation*. Three generations of theatergoers eventually watched the film portray Negro bestiality and white gentility. Millions of Northerners accepted this version as the correct interpretation of the Reconstruction period.

At home and abroad the Negro was dominated by the white race. European imperialism awoke and surpassed its former vigor. Africa was partitioned, parts of Asia were grabbed, and almost every other underdeveloped area of the world became the possession or economic dependency of some country. The "white man's burden" thesis justified territorial acquisitions and economic gains, and extended white supremacy.

The Spanish-American War drew the United States reluctantly into the new imperialism. In contrast to former territorial additions, the nation acquired noncontiguous, overseas lands, densely populated by alien races. In a series of decisions known as the "Insular Cases," the Supreme Court decreed that guarantees of the Constitution did not follow the American flag. At the same time the federal government was spending millions of dollars to subdue the Philippine insurrectionists. Then Ben Tillman accused Henry Cabot Lodge, almost the sole senator still advocating some protection for southern Negroes, of shedding crocodile tears for "black babies" of the South while voting funds to kill the "brown babies" of the Philippine Islands.

The United States accepted the southern ideas of racial superiority. After the passage of almost a century, white Southerners again enjoyed the pleasant midstream waters of Caucasian history.

The caste system of the United States was accepted by a Negro leader, Booker T. Washington. His mother was a mulatto slave and his father a white man. After emancipation, Washington labored in salt and coal mines of West Virginia until he entered and worked his way through Hampton Institute. After teaching and additional study, he was selected in 1881 to organize a school for Negroes in Alabama. At Tuskegee Institute he made famous an institution for Negro industrial training. Ability as a speaker and a pleasing personality gave him access to white audiences and association with males and females of the white society. Personal success perhaps convinced Washington that Southerners would ignore skin color and recognize individual accomplishments.

A speech in 1895 to a racially mixed audience in the Atlanta Cotton States and International Exposition won him national acclaim. "I was born in the South," he said, "and I understand thoroughly the prejudices, the customs, the traditions of the South [and love the region]." He advocated many policies: agitation of Negroes for social equality was folly; northern intervention in southern affairs was misdirected humanitarianism; reforms in the Southland should come from white Southerners; and Negroes were more interested in industrial education and economic opportunity than in casting ballots or serving in state legislatures. Rewards would come to Negroes, he said, if they proved themselves worthy by "severe and constant struggle" to deserve recognition.

Washington urged members of his race to forge ahead in agriculture, mechanics, commerce, domestic service, and the professions. He warned them not to forget in the great leap from slavery to freedom that manual labor was still their main source of livelihood: "No race can prosper till it learns that there is as much dignity in tilling a field as in writing a poem. It is at the bottom of life we must begin, and not at the top." He asked white people not to rely on aliens with their strange language and habits, but on the 8 million Negroes, a people who had proven their loyalty in peace and war.

Washington's willingness to yield political and civil rights and his promotion of a type of education most likely to keep the Negro economically and socially subordinate to the white endeared him to southern leaders. By overlooking mistreatment, by emphasizing the best past performances of whites and relying on them to treat the Negro fairly, and by advising his people to labor, elevate themselves, and be law-abiding, he won the hearts of southern whites. His ideas meshed well with Social Darwinism; Negroes would demonstrate their fitness for leadership or become mudsill laborers. But whites ignored the ultimate goal of his program—eventual integration of Negroes into American society.

After more than half a century it is difficult to evaluate Washington. He won fame and power unparalleled in the history of his race. Federal authorities and heads of philanthropic agencies turned to him for approval of Negro applicants for jobs and welfare projects. At times so dictatorial that few Negro individuals or newspapers dared to criticize him, his word could dash hopes and wreck projects; but his recommendations secured economic opportunity for thousands and won millions of dollars for educational and other projects of his people. He appeared at a critical time—the Negro was being disfranchised, hounded, shorn of civil rights, almost abandoned by Northerners, and hated by southern extremists. By accepting caste, perhaps the Negro lost nothing he had not already lost or was in the process of losing. Washington's "Atlanta Compromise" eased racial tension and gave the Negro time to build a base for a fight for his rights as an American.

But Washington riveted the iron mask of caste on his people. He neither originated the caste system nor conceived of it as a permanent arrangement. His greatest failure was his optimistic appraisal of his white countrymen. Most southern and many northern whites had no intention of granting first-class citizenship to any Negro, however successful he was in demonstrating his right to equal status. For these people the color of one's skin classified him.

For almost half a century following the Civil War, equality under law was the subject of debate and experiment. Former secessionists and Confederates relegated freedmen to a status similar to that occupied by the free Negro in the ante-bellum South. Northerners gave the Negro a taste of political and civil equality, but did little to aid him economically. Despite their confusing verbiage, the principle objections of conservative white Southerners to Congressional Reconstruction were enfranchisement of the Negro and federal protection of the freedman. No knowledgeable southern white believed that the "bottom rail had been placed on top"; at the high-water mark of Congressional Reconstruction, Negroes remained economically, politically, and socially subordinate to the white man. Absolute white supremacy motivated the southern drive for a racial settlement. By the early twentieth century, white Southerners won complete victory and the Negro was relegated to a status more rigorous in many respects than that of the slave or black codes.

The caste system extended Negro servitude into the twentieth century. Always a land of freedom and opportunity for white immigrants, even indentured servants and poverty-stricken peasants, America offered these wonderful gifts to comparatively few Negroes. Whatever their ambition or ability, they were held in check by slavery, restrictive custom and law, and the caste system. In February 1900, George H. White, the last Negro congressman of the Reconstruction era, replied to southern demagogues: "It is easy for these gentlemen to taunt us with our inferiority. It is rather hard to be accused of shiftlessness and idleness when the accuser closes the avenue of labor and industrial pursuits to us. It is hardly fair to accuse us of ignorance when it was a crime under the former order of things to learn enough about letters to even read the Word of God."

Completion of the Reconstruction era brought victory to the southern white, a victory which made the United States Constitution color-conscious. Southern-born Justice Harlan's idea of a "color-blind" Constitution remained a goal for the future.

REFERENCES

The best overall view of the South is C. Vann Woodward, *Origins of the New South, 1877–1913* (Baton Rouge, 1951). The same author traces the caste system in *The Strange Career of Jim Crow* (New York, reprint edition, 1966). Joel R. Williamson, *After Slavery: The Negro in the South During Reconstruction* (Chapel Hill, 1965), exposes many myths and finds that segregation began just after the Civil War, but Charles E. Wynes, *Race Relations in Virginia, 1870–1902* (Charlottesville, 1961), believes that the color line became rigid after 1890. Vernon L. Wharton's *The Negro in Mississippi, 1865–1890* (Chapel Hill, 1947) is a model study. Other valuable studies of Afro-Americans in southern states are: George B. Tindall, *South Carolina Negroes, 1877–1900* (Columbia, 1952); and Frenise A. Logan, *The Negro in North Carolina, 1876–1894* (Chapel Hill, 1964). Negro thought is analyzed in: Rayford W. Logan, *The Negro in American Life and Thought: The Nadir, 1877–1901* (New York, 1954); Earlie Endris Thorpe, *The Mind of the Negro: An Intellectual History of Afro-Americans* (Baton Rouge, 1961); and August Meier, *Negro Thought in America, 1880–1915* (Ann Arbor, 1963). The Negro and politics are described by Vincent P. DeSantis, *Republicans Face the Southern Question: The New Departure Years, 1877–1897* (Baltimore, 1959); Stanley P. Hirshson, *Farewell to Bloody Shirt: Northern Republicans and the Southern Negro, 1877–1893* (Bloomington, 1962); Luther P. Jackson, *Negro*

Officeholders in Virginia, 1865–1895 (Norfolk, 1945); Helen Gray Edmonds, *The Negro and Fusion Politics in North Carolina, 1894–1901* (Chapel Hill, 1951); and Jack B. Scroggs, *The Republican Party in Georgia* (Athens, 1964). Good biographies of Washington are: Basil Mathews, *Booker T. Washington: Educator and Racial Interpreter* (Cambridge, 1948); and Samuel R. Spencer, *Booker T. Washington and the Negro's Place in American Life* (Boston, 1955). Otto H. Olsen evaluates a reconstruction novelist and politician in *Carpetbagger's Crusade: The Life of Albion Winegar Tourgée* (Baltimore, 1965). Despite the title, Edmund Wilson covers the writings of the Reconstruction period in *Patriotic Gore: Studies in the Literature of American Civil War* (New York, 1962). Arlin Turner has an outstanding book in *George W. Cable: A Biography* (Durham, 1955). Wilbur J. Cash, *The Mind of the South* (New York, 1941), is a penetrating study. The best general account of Afro-Americans is *From Slavery to Freedom* (New York, 1947) by John Hope Franklin. Two recent and selective articles on southern historiography are Paul W. Gaston, "The 'New South,'" and George B. Tindall, "Southern Negroes Since Reconstruction: Dissolving the Static Image," in Link and Patrick (eds.), *Writing Southern History* (Baton Rouge, 1965).

GENERAL HISTORIOGRAPHY AND BIBLIOGRAPHY

In comparison with the Civil War, Reconstruction has attracted few writers. Nevertheless, the total historical literature on the period is impressive, too large to be described completely except in a reference volume. This summary provides a guideline. Even with the "References" at the end of each chapter, only partial bibliographical coverage is presented. This general account lists and comments on articles and books which cover the Reconstruction era, or more than one phase of it. Some books herein presented are also referred to in chapter references, designed primarily for special studies.

Similar to other periods of American history, the Reconstruction period has been interpreted and reinterpreted. The partisan school defended or condemned the North or the South. Its authors relied on emotion and prejudice more than reason and fact. With few exceptions, Northerners praised their people and condemned Southerners, and southern writers did the reverse. Trained historians turned to primary sources but still failed to overcome sectional bias. Members of the Dunning School at Columbia University searched successfully for sources and used them effectively to produce studies of the individual southern states. These southern-born historians concentrated on politics and were generally pro-southern. Some of them so ardently defended white Southerners that their books are examples of distortion; others were surprisingly fair in their work. Later in the twentieth century, revisionism became popular. Revisionist covers many interpretations; in a sense the Dunning scholars were revisionists. Revisionists rehabilitated President Johnson and then other revisionists turned on him. The motives and acts of Radicals, moderate Republicans, and Democrats, individually and collectively, have been assessed and reassessed. For decades the Afro-American was either condemned or ignored. Then he too was rehabilitated as his role in reconstruction was frequently analyzed. Responding to variations in communist thought, Marxian writers have reflected their philosophies in studying the postwar era. No interpretation is entirely abandoned; all of them partially appear in many modern works, and bias cannot be completely eliminated even by the most conscientious authors.

An excellent starting point for students are articles on reconstruction historiography. The most recent one is Vernon L. Wharton, "Reconstruction," in *Writing Southern History*, edited by A. S. Link and R. W. Patrick (Baton Rouge, 1965), pp. 295–315. Another excellent essay is Bernard Weisberger, "The Dark and Bloody Ground of Reconstruction Historiography," *Journal of*

Southern History, XXV (1959), pp. 427–47. An early and influential article is Howard K. Beale, "On Rewriting Reconstruction History," *American Historical Review*, XLV (1940), pp. 807–27. Still useful are: John Hope Franklin, "Whither Reconstruction Historiography?" *Journal of Negro Education*, XVII (1948), pp. 446–61; Francis B. Simkins, "New Viewpoints on Southern Reconstruction," *Journal of Southern History*, V (1939), pp. 49–61; Alrutheus A. Taylor, "Historians of Reconstruction," *Journal of Negro History*, XXIII (1938), pp. 16–34; and T. Harry Williams, "An Analysis of Some Reconstruction Attitudes," *Journal of Southern History*, XII (1946), pp. 469–86.

Recent general histories take issue with the older ones. Brief, readable, and revisionist are John Hope Franklin, *Reconstruction after the Civil War* (Chicago, 1961), and Kenneth M. Stampp, *The Era of Reconstruction* (New York, 1965). The second and smaller part of James G. Randall and David Donald, *The Civil War and Reconstruction* (Boston, 1961), provides a carefully written modern text and a quality bibliography. The grandfathers of the anti-radical, often pro-southern, and anti-freedman writings are James Ford Rhodes, in Vols. V–VII of *History of the United States from the Compromise of 1850* . . . , 7 vols. (New York, 1893–1906), and William A. Dunning, *Reconstruction, Political and Economic, 1865–1867* (New York, 1907). Following their interpretations were Walter L. Fleming (a Southerner), *The Sequel of Appomattox*, and Claude G. Bowers (a Midwesterner), *The Tragic Era* (Boston, 1929). E. Merton Coulter, *The Story of Reconstruction, 1865–1877* (Baton Rouge, 1947), concentrates on the South and emphasizes social and economic history. In political affairs, he is an ardent member of the Dunning School. The sprightly accounts of two southern newspapermen, George F. Milton, *The Age of Hate, Andrew Johnson and the Radicals* (New York, 1930), and Hodding Carter, *The Angry Scar* (New York, 1959), demonstrate a change from pro-southern and anti-Negro to more liberal points of view. Although not a Marxian when writing *Black Reconstruction* (New York, 1935), W. E. B. DuBois interpreted the reconstructing process in the South as a proletarian movement. Even though he used almost the same sources as Dunning School historians, he made an important contribution by emphasizing Negro achievements. Henderson H. Donald, *The Negro Freedman* (New York, 1952), introduces a subject which should be investigated in depth. A Marxist interpretation is *Reconstruction: The Battle for Democracy, 1865–1876* (New York, 1937) by James S. Allen.

Source collections, government documents, and periodicals are essential in evaluating various interpretations. Edward McPherson's *The Political History of the United States of America during the Period of Reconstruction* (Washington, 1875) is a selection of political documents, but Walter L. Fleming's two volumes, *Documentary History of Reconstruction* (Cleveland, 1906–1907), cover most phases of the period. *The Reconstruction: A Documentary History of the South after the War* (New York, 1963), edited by James P. Shenton, has carefully selected, pertinent sources. The *Congressional Globe* and the *Congressional Record* contain a storehouse of political, social, and economic information. House and Senate documents are mines of information on conditions in the South, public opinion, and political investigations. Benjamin B. Kendrick has edited a most useful document, *The Journal of the Joint Committee of Fifteen on Reconstruction* (New York, 1914). Microfilms of the *New York Times* are accessible, and hours spent in the files of northern and southern newspapers will be both interesting and rewarding experiences. Politicians and statesmen bequeathed memoirs to Americana.

The number of biographies overemphasizes the biographical approach to the era. President Johnson was rehabilitated by Robert W. Winston in *Andrew Johnson: Plebeian and Patriot* (New York, 1928) and eulogized by Lloyd P. Stryker in *Andrew Johnson: A Study in Courage* (New York, 1929). Milton Lomask continued to admire the reconstruction President in *Andrew Johnson: President on Trial* (New York, 1960), but Eric L. McKitrick, *Andrew Johnson and Reconstruction* (Chicago, 1960), severely criticized the President for an intransigence which drove moderate Republicans into supporting the Radicals. McKitrick's work is not limited to Johnson, and neither are John H. and La-Wanda Cox, *Politics, Principle, and Prejudice, 1865–1866* (New York, 1963), and W. R. Brock, *An American Crisis: Congress and Reconstruction, 1865–1867* (New York, 1963). The American authors and the English Brock charge Johnson with political ineptness in his relations with congressmen and Northerners.

Recent biographies of northern leaders clarify their motives and actions. Fawn M. Brodie, *Thaddeus Stevens: Scourge of the South* (New York, 1959), provides new insight into Stevens's private life and stresses psychological motivation instead of political ambition. Charles A. Jellison, *Fessenden of Maine: Civil War Senator* (New York, 1961), has a well-documented study of the influential moderate Republican. Indispensable is *Stanton: Life and Times of Lincoln's Secretary of War* (New York, 1962) by Benjamin P. Thomas and Harold M. Hyman. Hans L. Trefousse, *Benjamin Franklin Wade: Radical Republican from Ohio* (New York, 1963), credits Wade with courage and principle. Richard S. West, Jr., *Lincoln's Scapegoat General: A Life of B. F. Butler, 1818–1893* (New York, 1964), admires the "independent idealist" in a well-researched biography. *Sword and Olive Branch: Oliver Otis Howard* (New York, 1964) by John A. Carpenter depicts Howard as an extravagant but honest head of the Freedmen's Bureau and emphasizes his contributions to Negro education. Mark M. Krug, *Lyman Trumbull: Conservative Radical* (New York, 1965), is the best study of the senator. The scholarly nature of David Donald's *Charles Sumner and the Coming of the Civil War* (New York, 1960) makes one yearn for his second volume.

Many other biographies deserve consideration. Ralph Korngold stresses the high principles of the Radicals and in particular those of Stevens in *Thaddeus Stevens: A Being Darkly Wise and Rudely Great* (New York, 1955), and is a contrast to Richard N. Current's *Old Thad Stevens, A Story of Ambition* (Madison, 1942). William B. Hesseltine concentrates on Grant's presidential years in *Ulysses S. Grant, Politician* (New York, 1935). *Meet General Grant* (New York, 1928) by W. E. Woodward presents a lucid view of Grant's life in an interesting style. Allan Nevins, *Hamilton Fish, The Inner History of the*

Grant Administration (New York, 1937), is essential for studying the Grant regime and foreign affairs. Carl Schurz, *Charles Sumner* (Urbana, 1951), edited by A. R. Hogue, contains material of value.

The books by McKitrick, John and LaWanda Cox, and Brock, cited above, are provocative studies of politics. David Donald analyzes congressional voting in *The Politics of Reconstruction, 1863–1867* (Baton Rouge, 1965). The Beardian economic thesis as developed by Howard K. Beale in *The Critical Year: A Study of Andrew Johnson and Reconstruction* (New York, 1930), Matthew Josephson in *The Politicos* (New York, 1938), and Louis M. Hacker in *The Triumph of American Capitalism* (New York, 1940) should be checked by using Robert P. Sharkey's *Money, Class and Party: An Economic Study of Civil War and Reconstruction* (Baltimore, 1959) and Irwin Unger's *The Greenback Era: A Social and Political History of American Finance, 1865– 1879* (Princeton, 1964).

Excellent interpretation is found in Carl N. Degler's *Out of Our Past: The Forces that Shaped Modern America* (New York, 1959). *The Road to Reunion, 1865–1890* (Boston, 1937) by Paul H. Buck is the standard account of northern acceptance of southern ideas on race. The ideas relating to reconstruction in C. Vann Woodward, *The Burden of Southern History* (Baton Rouge, 1960), and Charles G. Sellers, Jr., *The Southerner as American* (Chapel Hill, 1960), are worthy of consideration.

INDEX